D0341779

Sudden Genius?

Sudden Genius?

The Gradual Path to Creative Breakthroughs

ANDREW ROBINSON

OXFORD
UNIVERSITY PRESS

OXFORD
UNIVERSITY PRESS

Great Clarendon Street, Oxford OX2 6DP

Oxford University Press is a department of the University of Oxford.
It furthers the University's objective of excellence in research, scholarship,
and education by publishing worldwide in

Oxford New York

Auckland Cape Town Dar es Salaam Hong Kong Karachi
Kuala Lumpur Madrid Melbourne Mexico City Nairobi
New Delhi Shanghai Taipei Toronto

With offices in

Argentina Austria Brazil Chile Czech Republic France Greece
Guatemala Hungary Italy Japan Poland Portugal Singapore
South Korea Switzerland Thailand Turkey Ukraine Vietnam

Oxford is a registered trade mark of Oxford University Press
in the UK and in certain other countries

Published in the United States
by Oxford University Press Inc., New York

British Library Cataloguing in Publication Data
Data available

Library of Congress Cataloging in Publication Data
Library of Congress Control Number: 2010930304

Typeset by SPI Publisher Services, Pondicherry, India
Printed in Great Britain
on acid-free paper by
Clays Ltd., St Ives plc

ISBN 978–0–19–956995–3

1 3 5 7 9 10 8 6 4 2

For Dipli

CONTENTS

PART I
INGREDIENTS OF CREATIVITY

PART II
TEN BREAKTHROUGHS IN ART AND SCIENCE

PART III
PATTERNS OF GENIUS

LIST OF ILLUSTRATIONS

PLATE SECTION

ILLUSTRATIONS IN THE TEXT

PREFACE

Meetings with Remarkable Creators

One of the most admired scientists of the last century, Linus Pauling, was once asked by a student: 'Dr Pauling, how do you have so many good ideas?' This was back in the 1930s, two or three decades before Pauling would win two Nobel Prizes, one for chemistry, the other for peace. Pauling thought for a moment and replied: 'Well, David, I have a lot of ideas and throw away the bad ones.'

True enough for Pauling, no doubt. But of course his disarming answer begs more questions. Where do ideas come from? Why do some people have many more of them than others? How do you distinguish the good ideas from the bad? Most intriguing of all, perhaps, why do the best ideas sometimes strike the mind with suddenness, apparently in a flash? These questions are the subject of this book, which tries to understand exceptional creativity—'genius'—in both scientists and artists by following the trail that led ten individuals from childhood to the achievement of a famous creative breakthrough as an adult, in archaeology, architecture, art, biology, chemistry, cinema, music, literature, photography, and physics. They are: Leonardo da Vinci (*The Last Supper*, 1498); Christopher Wren (St Paul's Cathedral, 1711); Wolfgang Amadeus Mozart (*The Marriage of Figaro*, 1786); Jean-François Champollion (decipherment of Egyptian hieroglyphs, 1822); Charles Darwin (evolution by natural selection, 1859); Marie Curie (discovery of radium, 1898); Albert Einstein (special relativity, 1905); Virginia Woolf (*Mrs Dalloway*, 1925); Henri Cartier-Bresson (*The Decisive Moment*, 1952); and Satyajit Ray (*Pather Panchali*, 1955).

Creativity is protean: it takes many forms. It is also amorphous: the forms are not easily defined. Hence the fact that 'creative' is today so ubiquitous an adjective—among artists and scientists, but also among stage performers, sports celebrities, politicians, business leaders, advertising executives, and even lawyers and accountants. A dubious new phrase, the 'creative industries', has gained currency. The word's overuse provokes justifiable scepticism. Let me therefore explain, quite briefly, my personal involvement with the study of creativity.

How the creative process works in both science and art has long interested me professionally. During two decades of research and writing as an author and biographer, academic, journalist, and literary editor based in London (at *The Times Higher Education Supplement*), I have come to know personally a variety of exceptionally creative individuals from different cultures. They range from Nobel Prize-winning scientists like the physicists Philip W. Anderson and Subrahmanyan Chandrasekhar to artists such as Cartier-Bresson, the film director Lindsay Anderson, and the writers Arthur C. Clarke and V. S. Naipaul.

Each of these people is considered a star in his particular domain, be it physics, photography, cinema, or literature. Domain specialization has been the norm among the highly creative over the centuries—as in the case of, say, Curie and Darwin, Mozart and Woolf. Yet, a significant minority of exceptional creators have worked in more than one domain, epitomized by Leonardo da Vinci and, more recently, Lewis Carroll, the writer of *Alice's Adventures in Wonderland*, who was also a photographer and professional mathematician. Clarke, for example, as well as being the writer of *2001: A Space Odyssey*, was a noteworthy scientific thinker (he conceived the communications satellite in 1945); Lindsay Anderson, as well as being the director of the film *If...*, was a leading theatre director and literary critic; Cartier-Bresson, as well as being the photographer of *The Decisive Moment*, exhibited and published a considerable body of drawings and paintings. Such 'doubly gifted' versatility is, it seems, a potentially revealing and somewhat under appreciated facet of exceptional creativity.

By far the most versatile creator I have known was Satyajit Ray, the Indian film-maker who was the subject of my first biography, *Satyajit Ray: The Inner Eye*. After training as a painter and graphic designer, Ray directed more than 30 features beginning with the Apu Trilogy in the 1950s, at least ten of which are generally regarded as classics; they won him an Oscar for lifetime achievement before his death in 1992. For these films Ray wrote the screenplays solo, cast every actor personally, designed his own sets and costumes, operated the camera, edited each frame, composed his own music (including some extremely popular songs), and even drew his own posters. In addition, he was a successful book and magazine illustrator, and a bestselling novelist in Bengali. Naipaul compared Ray's artistic level with Shakespeare's; Gérard Depardieu (who produced a Ray film) with Mozart's. Another very versatile artist in film, the Japanese director Akira Kurosawa, was moved to say: 'Not to have seen the cinema of Ray means existing in the world without seeing the sun or the moon.'

Ray once volunteered to me the following concise reflection on creativity in general. 'This whole business of creation, of the ideas that come in a flash, cannot be explained by science. It cannot. I don't know what can explain it but I know that the best ideas come at moments when you're not even thinking of it. It's a very private thing really.'

Ray's remark stayed with me as I wrote four more biographies of other versatile individuals. One was again in the arts, a biography of Asia's first Nobel laureate, *Rabindranath Tagore: The Myriad-Minded Man*, describing a poet and novelist who was also an adored song composer and a remarkable painter. Another was in the sciences, *Einstein: A Hundred Years of Relativity*, published in 2005, the centenary of Einstein's 'miraculous year' of scientific breakthroughs. My last two biographies were of lesser known but brilliant English figures who crossed the art/science divide in making their breakthroughs.

The Man Who Deciphered Linear B told the story of the mid-twentieth-century decipherment of Europe's earliest readable writing—Linear B, a script of the Minoan civilization of Crete—by Michael Ventris. He was a brilliant polyglot who is revered by archaeologists and codebreakers alike. Yet Ventris's professional training lay in architecture, not linguistics or archaeology. The BBC television programme based on this book was appropriately entitled *A Very English Genius*.

The Last Man Who Knew Everything narrated the life and work of Thomas Young, an eighteenth-century child prodigy in languages and an adult polymath. Best known as a physicist for his experimental proof of the wave theory of light in 1801, which Einstein compared in importance to Isaac Newton's optical experiments, Young also deciphered the Rosetta Stone. Yet, he trained and practised professionally as a London hospital physician, not as a physicist or Egyptologist. 'Young probably had a wider range of creative learning than any other Englishman in history', according to a Science Museum exhibition arranged for his birth bicentenary in 1973.

In both cases—Ventris and Young—their decipherment breakthroughs depended on their knowledge of disparate domains, which their scholarly rivals did not have. Their best ideas arose from their versatility. As an architect, Ventris had trained himself to marshal and analyse large bodies of information and visual data. He did the same with the 3500-year-old Linear B clay tablets from Crete. After long and intensive scrutiny and several false starts, involving some bad ideas that had to be discarded, Ventris at last recognized order in the disorder of the ancient signs in 1952. Then, he made an inspired guess about the language spoken by the Minoan scribes—pre-Homeric Greek—which demonstrably corresponded with the patterns in the signs. Young, as a physicist and physician, applied comparable analytical powers to the Rosetta Stone and various Egyptian hieroglyphic inscriptions. His breakthrough came around 1815, again after intensive study and some mistakes, when Young guessed how one of the oval hieroglyphic cartouches in the Rosetta Stone spelt the name of the Egyptian king, Ptolemy, in phonetic symbols like an alphabet. Suddenly, sounds could be associated with particular hieroglyphs, and the language of the pharaohs began to speak. Young's pioneering work triggered the decipherment of the entire Egyptian hieroglyphic system by Jean-François Champollion in 1822–24.

With all of my biographical subjects—Ray, Tagore, Einstein, Ventris, and Young—I became fascinated by the breadth, as well as the depth, of the knowledge feeding their creativity. Despite the diversity of their professional backgrounds, spanning cinema, languages and literature, archaeology, architecture, physics, and medicine, I began to see that their breakthroughs had key elements in common. While I agree with Ray that the most creative ideas appear to come unexpectedly out of nowhere, I am convinced they are not as unpredictable as they seem, and that science can shed light on the act of creation. Detailed study of breakthroughs, and the lives of those who make them, will never be able to explain Ray's 'very private' mystery of exceptional creativity in full. Probably, we would be disappointed if it could. But as this book will show, it can reveal much about the sources, ingredients, and patterns of genius.

ACKNOWLEDGEMENTS

I n late 2006, just after leaving a long-time job as literary editor of *The Times Higher Education Supplement* to become a full-time writer, I was chatting to Sara Abdulla, my first editor at *Nature*. By chance, she mentioned the wide-ranging research grants given by the John Templeton Foundation.

This book has been made possible by the Foundation, which awarded me a research grant in 2007–09 with the freedom to study more or less any aspect of exceptional creativity that caught my fancy. I particularly wish to thank present and former Templeton staff members Megan Buek, Charles Harper Jr, Mary Ann Meyers, and Christopher Stawski for their personal interest in the project; and also Paul Davies.

Philip W. Anderson (Princeton University); Brian Fagan (University of California at Santa Barbara); Winston Fletcher (The Royal Institution); Chris McManus (University College London); and Tom Palaima (University of Texas at Austin) generously supported the project, as did Sir Michael Holroyd and Sir David Weatherall. Taken together, their various disciplines cover physics, archaeology and anthropology, business and management, psychology, classics and linguistics, literature and biography, and biochemistry and medicine: testimony to the all-embracing nature of creativity and creative breakthroughs.

Gordon Johnson, historian of modern India—which first brought the two of us in contact—and president of Wolfson College, Cambridge, where I was a visiting fellow during the period of research and writing, stalwartly backed my project from the start, for which I am grateful. Wolfson College and the staff of Cambridge in America, who administered the Templeton Foundation grant, also deserve thanks.

At Oxford University Press, my editor Latha Menon, who shares my interest in both art and science, has been receptive and imaginative throughout. I am pleased to be part of her diverse and impressive list of books aimed at the non-specialist reader. I would also like to thank Emma Marchant and Deborah Protheroe, the book's picture researcher, and Claire Thompson.

Lastly, I owe a lifelong debt to the exceptionally creative artists and scientists—some of them mentioned in my preface—who have been so exciting to know in person over the past two or three decades. Without their examples, and their enduring works, I would certainly not have had the urge, or the temerity, to attempt this study of artistic and scientific genius. To quote the cautionary words of that irresistible songwriter and mathematician Tom Lehrer: 'It is a sobering thought that by the time Mozart was my age, he had been dead for two years.'

INTRODUCTION

The Science and Art of Breakthroughs

Having drunk a pint of beer at luncheon . . . I would go out for a walk of two or three hours. As I went along, thinking of nothing in particular, only looking at things around me and following the progress of the seasons, there would flow into my mind, with sudden and unaccountable emotion, sometimes a line or two of verse, sometimes a whole stanza at once, accompanied, not preceded, by a vague notion of the poem which they were destined to form part of. Then there would usually be a lull of an hour or so, then perhaps the spring would bubble up again.

A. E. Housman, *The Name and Nature of Poetry*, 1933

Some of the world's great creative breakthroughs are reputed to have begun with a 'eureka experience' of sudden insight. Archimedes, archetypically, while taking his bath two millennia ago, is said to have perceived the principles of displacement and flotation, jumped out of the tub, and run naked through the streets with a cry of 'Eureka!'—Greek for (roughly speaking) 'I've got it!' Johannes Gutenberg, casually watching a wine press during the grape harvest in the fifteenth century, supposedly got the idea for the printing press. Isaac Newton, seeing an apple fall from a tree in the seventeenth century, apparently visualized the law of gravitational attraction. Samuel Taylor Coleridge, while reading a passage in a book about the 'Khan Kubla' in the eighteenth century, fell into an opium-induced sleep, and when he awoke, immediately produced the poem 'Kubla Khan: Or, A Vision in a Dream'. Dmitri Mendeleev, too, experienced a dream while pondering chemistry in the nineteenth century, and when he awoke, wrote down the periodic table of the elements. Alexander Fleming, while culturing *Staphylococcus* bacteria in a Petri dish in the early twentieth century, quite by accident spotted the presence of a bacteria-killing mould, *Penicillium*, which became the source of the first antibiotic drug penicillin.

Closer in time, Henri Cartier-Bresson, chancing in Paris upon a photograph of African boys running, taken by the sports photographer Martin Munkácsi, decided to take up photography in earnest in 1932. 'I suddenly understood that photography can fix eternity in a moment. It is the only photo that influenced me', he wrote. 'I felt it like a kick up the backside: go on, have a go!' Satyajit Ray, at a screening of the recently released Italian film *Bicycle Thieves* in London in 1950, immediately grasped how he would make his first film *Pather Panchali* back in India. 'It just gored me', he wrote. James Watson, while playing with cardboard models of biomolecules in Cambridge in 1953, suddenly saw how the two halves of the structure of DNA fitted together, and solved the biomolecular mechanism of heredity. 'My morale skyrocketed', wrote Watson in *The Double Helix*.

The further back in history we go, the slimmer is the evidence for these eureka experiences. There is nothing at all in the case of Archimedes, except hearsay; only one rather doubtful letter from Gutenberg; and no written statement about the apple from Newton, only remarks made to others in old age. Yet, such anecdotes cannot be discounted as simply false, because there are numerous reliable accounts of flashes of inspiration by both scientists and artists, such as the 'sudden and unaccountable emotion' mentioned above by the poet and classical scholar A. E. Housman. Moreover, they chime with our personal experience: we all know that good ideas can spring unheralded from casual conversations, chance associations, leaps of imagination, and irrational inputs such as dreams.

On the other hand, eureka experiences are by no means the whole story. A great idea may have seemed to have come 'out of the blue', but in every such experience the mind seems to have prepared itself by long study. The individual concerned was deeply immersed in thinking about the problem that he or she eventually solved. Fleming, for example, had been working in the bacteriology department of a London hospital for some two decades before he made his breakthrough with *Penicillium* mould in 1928. During the First World War, he had become interested in finding antibiotics to treat sepsis in the wounds of servicemen. After the war, he began an active programme of research; in 1922 he discovered the antibiotic enzyme lysozyme in nasal mucus, tears, and saliva. Fleming's discovery of penicillin is a classic example of Louis Pasteur's dictum: 'Where observation is concerned, chance favours only the prepared mind.'

Let us zoom in on another well-known, much-discussed, scientific eureka experience: the discovery of the hexagonal ring structure of the six carbon atoms in the benzene molecule by the German chemist August Kekulé in the 1860s. This was a crucial step in the foundation of organic chemistry (to which Linus Pauling added in the 1930s by explaining the stability of the ring structure in terms of quantum theory). It offers an excellent illustration of the real complexity of breakthroughs.

In 1890, a quarter of a century after the event, Kekulé recollected what happened in a public speech. A first flash of inspiration occurred some time in 1855 while he was riding on top of a London omnibus in a 'reverie' on a summer's evening after talking chemistry with a friend. Before the conductor at last cried out 'Clapham Road', Kekulé had visualized a dance of atoms, large and small, forming pairs, threesomes, and combinations up to a valency of four, making chains of atoms. But the breakthrough came about seven years later while dozing in front of a fire, he said:

> During my residence in Ghent, in Belgium, I lived in an elegant bachelor apartment on the main street. However, my study was situated along a narrow alley and had no light during the day. For a chemist who spends his day in the laboratory this was not a disadvantage. [One evening] I was sitting there, working on my textbook, but it was not going well; my thoughts were on other matters. I turned my chair towards the fireplace and sank into half-sleep. Again the atoms fluttered before my eyes. This time smaller groups remained modestly in the background. My mental eye, sharpened by repeated visions of a similar kind, now distinguished larger forms in a variety of combinations. Long chains, often combined in a denser fashion; everything in motion, twisting and turning like snakes. But look, what was that?! One of the snakes had seized its own tail, and the figure whirled mockingly before my eyes. I awoke in a flash, and this time, too, I spent the rest of the night working out the consequences of the hypothesis.

Kekulé concluded: 'Gentlemen, let us learn to dream, and perhaps then we will find the truth... but let us also beware not to publish our dreams until they have been examined by the wakened mind.'

It is a compelling picture. Perhaps too compelling to be strictly true. Indeed, some historians of chemistry have doubted if any such daydream occurred. However, there is evidence that Kekulé told the story to family and friends many times during his life before finally publishing it in 1890: this is what his son testified; and in 1886, a well-known spoof inspired by the dream snakes seizing their own tails was published, which suggests that the story had already circulated widely. Furthermore, Kekulé was known for his caution as a chemist, unlike some of his contemporaries, so it is not likely that he would publicize a bizarre dream if it were not basically true. Assuming it did happen, how much weight can be placed on it as describing a eureka experience?

In 1858, well before the breakthrough, Kekulé had published a paper setting out his structural theory of how four-valent carbon atoms become linked to form open-chain ('aliphatic') molecules, followed by the first volume of his textbook in 1859–61; but during this time he made no published mention of the structure of closed-chain ('aromatic') molecules, such as benzene, bar one very cryptic reference that shows he was thinking about the problem. The dream appears to have taken place early in 1862, or at least before Kekulé got married in June of that year (since he refers in his speech to his bachelor apartment). He did not actually publish his closed-chain ring structure of benzene until 1865–66, some three years after the dream.

This period, the late 1850s and early 1860s, was one of spectacular growth in the coal-tar dye industry and also the petroleum industry. Knowledge of organic chemistry expanded rapidly in chemical laboratories, and some of the newly discovered aromatic compounds were clearly similar to benzene (which was discovered in compressed oil–gas by Michael Faraday in 1825). But what was lacking was a concomitant theory of chemical structure into which the new knowledge could be fitted. Several chemists other than Kekulé were trying to work out the molecular structure of benzene. Josef Loschmidt, for instance, proposed three alternative benzene formulae in 1861, none involving a ring structure; however, Loschmidt chose to symbolize benzene with a large circle to indicate that it was still structurally indeterminate. Archibald Couper hypothesized ring structures in 1858 for two different organic compounds, but neither of them was benzene. Kekulé was not at all convinced by their work, yet revealed little about his reasons, either in print or in correspondence. It appears that he deliberately kept his thoughts on the subject to himself, while remaining fully abreast of competing ideas. Presumably, though, the speculations of Loschmidt, Couper, and other chemists were among the many ideas jostling in Kekulé's mind as he attempted to write a further volume of his organic chemistry textbook and, one evening in 1862, fell into a doze by the fire.

His delay in publishing his theory was partly for personal reasons. His wife died in childbirth in 1863, leaving him with an infant son and a feeling of depression and lack of purpose. But he was also waiting for experimental evidence of the existence of novel compounds predictable on the basis of a ring structure for benzene. This appeared only in 1864, in the work of two chemists who synthesized ethyl- and amyl-phenyl, benzene-related compounds with structures and properties Kekulé expected on the basis of his as-yet-unpublished theory. These new experimental results pushed him into action and triggered the publication of his theory in January 1865.

Confusingly, his breakthrough paper began by claiming that his theory was 'fully formed' in 1858—that is, long before the dream in his apartment in Ghent—moreover, the paper failed to emphasize either the benzene ring structure or its potential derivative structures. Nevertheless, the benzene ring was undeniably stated. The more Kekulé now thought about it, the more his theory of aromatics seemed elegant: 'an inexhaustible treasure-trove', as he told a chemist friend in April 1865. Within months, he and his students, working in the laboratory, were able to report the synthesis of further novel compounds (polybromo- and polyiodobenzenes) explained by the ring structure of the benzene nucleus. In 1866, he published three-dimensional perspective drawings of benzene. The ring was quickly accepted in principle by almost all organic chemists, because its theoretical predictions received such extensive experimental confirmation.

Kekulé's celebrated dream was therefore part of a continuous period of enquiry into the structure of benzene over more than five years up to 1865, not an isolated insight. It was not truly the eureka experience he implied (he did not use the actual word eureka)—emotionally important though the dream clearly was to Kekulé. Most probably, he started contemplating a ring structure in the late 1850s well before his dream; persuaded his 'wakened mind' of its existence from 1862 onwards; but felt insufficiently confident to go public until after the publication of experimental support by others in 1864. 'Contrary to most accounts, and to the implication of the dream anecdote told out of context, it is now clear that the benzene theory did not fall into Kekulé's half-awake mind fully formed—or even partially formed', writes the historian of science Alan J. Rocke after exhaustive consideration of the historical evidence. 'It was at most the ring concept that arrived by this semi-conscious or unconscious process, a concept which . . . was not without precedent. The theory itself was developed only slowly, one might even say painfully, over the course of several years, before its first codification in 1866.'

Such gradual evolution turns out to be typical of creative breakthroughs, when their histories are examined in detail. They may or may not involve a recognizable eureka experience, but they are always preceded by a long period of thought and labour, and always followed by intensive scrutiny and development. Here are three more examples—the first of them from the ancient world, the other two from the late twentieth century.

The invention of writing, which I have studied in several of my books, might be said to be the ur-breakthrough, since there would be no history, no science, and no literature (other than oral traditions) without it. How did so momentous an invention occur? 'Proto-writing'—that is, signs capable of expressing a limited range of meaning but not the full range of spoken language—seems to have existed during the last ice age, in the form of enigmatic cave drawings, petroglyphs, and notched bones, perhaps 20,000 years old. (Modern examples of 'proto-writing' include international transportation symbols at airports, mathematical symbols, and musical staff notation.) 'Full writing'—that is, a sign system able to express any and all thought—most likely started some five millennia ago in the expanding cities of Mesopotamia, in the form of pictographic and other symbols that fairly quickly evolved into wedge-shaped cuneiform marks inscribed in clay tablets. The Egyptian hieroglyphs appeared very soon after the earliest cuneiform, around 3000 BC, perhaps under the influence of neighbouring Mesopotamia, although this link is unproven.

The breakthrough that transformed proto-writing into full writing was the *rebus*. The word comes from a Latin word meaning 'by things'. Rebuses permit spoken words to be written in terms of their constituent parts—vowels, consonants, syllables, and so on—that cannot be depicted pictographically. With the rebus principle, the sounds of a language can be made visible in a systematic way, and its abstract concepts symbolized. Rebus writing is familiar today from puzzle–picture writing, and also to some extent from electronic text messaging. Lewis Carroll liked to write puzzle–picture letters to child friends. One of them has little pictures of a deer as a rebus for 'dear', an eye for 'I', and a hand for 'and'. Other English examples of rebuses would be a picture of a bee with a picture of a tray standing for 'betray', or a picture of a bee with a figure 4 representing 'before'. In Egyptian hieroglyphs, which are full of rebuses, the 'sun' pictogram, ⊙, pronounced r(a) or r(e), stands for the sun god Ra and is the first symbol in the hieroglyphic spelling of the pharaoh known to us as Ramesses the Great.

How was the rebus conceived? Some scholars believe it resulted from a conscious search by an unknown Sumerian in Uruk (biblical Erech), circa 3300 BC—the place and date of the earliest clay tablets that apparently record full writing. Others posit invention by a group, presumably of clever administrators and merchants. Still others think it was an accidental discovery, not an invention. Many regard it as the result of lengthy evolution from proto-writing, not a flash of inspiration. These are all reasonable hypotheses, given the severely limited evidence, and we shall probably never know which of them is actually correct. Even in the modern period, the contributions of individual inventors, corporate research and development, and the *Zeitgeist*, to technological breakthroughs, have often been unclear and controversial.

What is certain, from the archaeological evidence, is that proto-writing existed long before full writing; and that cuneiform took centuries to develop the capacity to record advanced thought such as poetry. The world's oldest surviving literature, in Sumerian cuneiform, dates from about 2600 BC, 'though because the script did not yet express language fully, these early tablets remain extremely difficult to read', writes a translator, Andrew George. In other words, there must once, in the late fourth millennium, have been a breakthrough into rebus writing—yet to modern eyes writing appears to have been a gradual development during the third millennium, without any eureka moment.

Moving forward five millennia, the World Wide Web launched in 1990–91 took about ten years to invent, beginning with an experimental web-like computer programme, known as Enquire, written by Tim Berners-Lee in 1980 as a sort of 'intranet' for physicists working at CERN, the European Laboratory for Particle Physics. In 1999, Berners-Lee recalled: 'The Web resulted from many influences on my mind, half-formed thoughts, disparate conversations, and seemingly disconnected experiments.' The discovery of fractal geometry required a similar length of time, beginning with the primitive computers available in 1963–64. Benoit Mandelbrot, the IBM mathematician who coined the term fractal in 1975, commented in 2001: 'the application of the fractal concept to nature was a very gradual development; I did not realize immediately the full meaning of the landscape images and was to understand its full impact only later'.

Both Berners-Lee and Mandelbrot deliberately eschew the word eureka. 'Journalists have always asked me what the crucial idea was, or what the singular event was, that allowed the Web to exist one day when it hadn't the day before. They are frustrated when I tell them there was no "eureka" moment', says Berners-Lee. 'The moment when we generated the first landscape figures was no key "eureka!" moment, no dramatic revelation prompting me to say, "I have found a key to the universe"', says Mandelbrot.

Even so, the majority of breakthroughs do involve an identifiable, pivotal episode of revelation, whether one calls it a eureka experience or not. (Another term might be 'epiphany', which is favoured by the Nobel Prize-winning physicist Leon Lederman.) As we shall see, at least five of the breakthroughs investigated in Part II—those of Champollion, Curie, Darwin, Einstein, and Ray—involved a eureka experience; and a good case can be made for Cartier-Bresson, Mozart, and Woolf. With the remaining two individuals, Leonardo and Wren, the evidence is unclear, given the lack of information about much of their lives several hundred years ago, especially Leonardo's life (in which not even the dates of his starting and finishing *The Last Supper* are securely known). What is absolutely clear in all ten cases is the long lead-up needed for the breakthroughs, and the effort required, following the revelation, to explore and substantiate the achievement.

Part I of the book, 'Ingredients of creativity', introduces the scientific study of creativity, covering talent, genius, intelligence, memory, dreams, the unconscious, savant syndrome, synaesthesia, and mental illness—beginning with the psychologist Francis Galton in the 1860s, and discussing the theories and experiments of some current thinkers, not only in psychology but also in psychiatry, neuroscience, and sociology. Part II, 'Ten breakthroughs', tells the stories of five breakthroughs by artists and five by scientists, who have been chosen for the significance of their achievements and the diversity of their domains. Part III, 'Patterns of genius', tackles three basic questions: What do highly creative people who achieve breakthroughs have in common? Do breakthroughs in science and art follow patterns? Do they always involve imaginative leaps and even 'genius'?

In 1869, Galton, who was Darwin's first cousin, published *Hereditary Genius: An Inquiry into its Laws and Consequences*, a seminal survey of eminent people. He defined eminence by criteria such as the length and quality of a person's biographical entry in major reference publications. Galton endeavoured to show genius as running in families, but in the event he demonstrated that it is talent, rather than genius, that seems to be hereditary (especially among English judges). A genius has yet to beget another genius.

Genius, creativity, and talent overlap each other (see Chapter 1), if we choose to define talent as the possession of a particular, innate gift, say for playing the violin or doing mathematics, which must be trained to reach a very high level of proficiency. Genius clearly requires both creativity and talent—an uncreative or talentless genius is an oxymoron—but the relationship between creativity and talent is not so clear. Is it possible to be creative without being talented? Perhaps this is true of the polymath Thomas Young referred to in the preface. Exceptional though he was by ordinary standards, it would be difficult to maintain that Young scaled the very peak of proficiency in any of the numerous domains in which he studied—physics, physiology, medicine, Egyptology, linguistics, and others (including life insurance)—and yet he made original contributions to many of them because his mind was creative. Can someone be talented without being creative? Surely this is true of those child prodigies who 'burn out' as adults, and also of many adult musical performers who are technically astounding, but lack the imagination to move an audience with their undoubted talent. As the advertising expert Winston Fletcher remarks in his *Tantrums and Talent: How to Get the Best from Creative People*: 'Just as the creative world is crowded with people who have ideas but no talent, it is also crowded with people who have talent but no ideas.'

During the first half of the twentieth century, psychologists concentrated on intelligence (Chapter 2) rather than creativity, by developing intelligence tests and the controversial concept of intelligence quotient (IQ). The best-known investigations—of gifted children as they grew up in the 1920s–50s— were conducted by the Stanford University psychologist Lewis Terman, inventor of the Stanford-Binet IQ test still widely used in the United States. Terman initially assumed that IQ measured both intelligence and creativity, but his test results forced him to change his assumption. Individuals with very high IQs are generally not highly creative; highly creative people, while always intelligent, do not generally have very high IQs. Above an IQ of about 120, there is no correlation between IQ and exceptional creativity. Terman's IQ tests of young people (known as 'Termites') selected no future Nobel laureates or Pulitzer Prize-winners, and indeed rejected two youths who later won Nobel Prizes in physics.

Around 1950, come the cold war, the United States was felt to be in danger of lagging behind the Soviet Union in scientific creativity. The president of the American Psychological Association, Joy Guilford, challenged American researchers to pay more attention to creativity. The field expanded dramatically. Creativity tests and insight problems mushroomed, designed to measure 'divergent' (or 'lateral') thinking—as opposed to the 'convergent' (logical) thinking measured by IQ tests—and led to bestsellers like Edward de Bono's *Lateral Thinking: A Textbook of Creativity*, first published in 1970. Some of these tests, for instance, the well-known 'nine dots problem', have produced undeniably fascinating results in controlled settings. However, creativity tests have been much more heavily criticized by psychologists than intelligence tests. They ignore the many factors that cannot be quantified in a laboratory, such as the fact that creative ideas often arrive at unexpected moments during idleness, not while concentrating on a problem against a test deadline. Today, it is generally recognized that whatever ability creativity tests may be measuring, this has little to do with real-life creativity and breakthroughs.

The creative role of unconscious processing (Chapter 3) was recognized long before the work of Sigmund Freud, perhaps as early as the beginning of the eighteenth century. 'Our clear concepts are like islands which arise above the ocean of obscure ones', wrote the philosopher Gottfried Wilhelm Leibniz at this time. '[Yet] it is not easy to conceive that a thing can think and not be conscious that it thinks.' Manifestations of the unconscious include the existence of memory, the tip-of-the-tongue phenomenon, the power of hypnosis, and the fact that we react instinctively to other people with like or dislike, without being able to give a conscious reason (though we may later discover the reason on reflection). It is obvious that unconscious processing plays a part in thinking and creativity, but it is not at all obvious how it collaborates with conscious processing. Einstein, for example, located the source of our sense of 'wonder' at some experience in the conflict between the experience and a world of unconscious concepts that is fixed in us as a result of earlier experiences. He regarded thinking as being 'in a certain sense a continuous flight from "wonder"'. At its most intense, such wonder can produce flashes of insight.

Dreams, giving access to unconscious processing, may or may not have led to celebrated examples of breakthroughs. Coleridge claimed that most of 'Kubla Khan' had come to him while dreaming, until his flow of inspiration was terminated by a 'person from Porlock' who called him away on business. However, scholarly study of Coleridge's poem and his manuscripts has shown the poet's claim to be a pleasant fiction. There are various early drafts of 'Kubla Khan', which contain versions of the insight story that describe the experience in very different ways; and the poem contains influences and even phrases from other writers. In science, we already know there is reason to doubt the centrality of Kekulé's dream to his discovery of the benzene ring. And yet, a dream in 1920 by the Nobel Prize-winning neuroscientist Otto Loewi does appear to have led directly to an experiment that proved the chemical nature of the transmission of nerve impulses.

From the 1990s, the advent of brain scanning with functional magnetic resonance imaging (fMRI) has enabled neuroscientists to advance their understanding of how the brain operates. Although fMRI is far from being able to examine creative thinking directly, it can be used to investigate phenomena such as savant syndrome, autism, and synaesthesia (Chapter 4), as experienced by the mathematical and linguistic savant Daniel Tammet and described in his book *Born on a Blue Day*. The title comes from the fact that Tammet was born on a Wednesday and the date is blue in his mind, because 'Wednesdays are always blue, like the number nine or the sound of loud voices arguing'. Among the highly creative, the writer Vladimir Nabokov and the physicist Richard Feynman were both synaesthetes. From an early age, when Feynman saw mathematical equations, their letters were coloured. Neither writer nor physicist claimed that synaesthesia was important to their creative work. However their personal testimony, and that of other outstanding synaesthetes like the composer Olivier Messiaen and the painter Vincent van Gogh, has helped to turn synaesthesia from a little-regarded mental illness into a substantial academic field.

Brain scans show activity in the colour vision centre of the brain when a blindfolded synaesthete hears words, no activity with a non-synaesthete under the same conditions. But as yet the causes of synaesthesia, and its evolutionary purpose, are poorly understood. Indeed, no consensus exists about whether it is an abnormal or a normal brain function. Even its prevalence is unknown: proposed numbers range from 1 in 20 people to 1 in 20,000 people. However it is clear that synaesthesia occupies a spectrum. Tests of students at a fine arts academy found a gradual distribution of synaesthesia scores ranging from 0 to 100 per cent. Understanding synaesthesia is probably one of the keys to unlocking the creative process that produces breakthroughs.

Understanding psychosis (Chapter 5) may be another. Ever since the Romantic Movement of the nineteenth century, epitomized by the poet Lord Byron, creativity and mental illness have been associated in the public mind. Freud was not much interested in the connection, or in psychosis, but later in the twentieth century the study and measurement of psychoticism (the tendency towards psychosis) was taken up by many psychologists and psychiatrists, most recently Nancy Andreasen, Kay Redfield Jamison, and Daniel Nettle. Nettle's book, *Strong Imagination: Madness, Creativity and Human Nature*, takes its title from William Shakespeare's phrase for psychoticism in *A Midsummer Night's Dream*, in which Shakespeare also writes that 'the lunatic, the lover, and the poet/ Are of imagination all compact.' Nettle compiles an amazingly long list of artistic creators with mental illness, such as George Frederick Handel, Van Gogh, Alfred Tennyson, and, of course, Virginia Woolf. Scientists are comparatively less prone, though mental illness certainly affected one of the greatest, Newton. Nettle concludes that: 'most of the canon of Western culture was produced by people with a touch of madness'.

Does mental illness in some way assist creativity, or is it an unwanted by-product of being creative? The early twentieth-century poet Rainer Maria Rilke famously said: 'If my demons leave me, I am afraid my angels may take flight as well.' A current poet Tony Harrison says of his lifelong periods of depression: 'Now, darkness is a familiar friend...I'm afraid it's a co-producer of my creative work.' However, many creative people, including those who suffer from mental illness, deny any idea of such co-productivity. The scientific jury is still out. For example, a study of the manic-depressive poet Emily Dickinson suggests that better poems emerged from her manic periods. But a year-by-year analysis of Robert Schumann's musical output and mental state shows that while he certainly produced more compositions in his manic years, they were not of higher quality (judged by today's Schumann catalogue) than those composed during his depressed years.

Part III of the book looks for significant resemblances and differences between breakthroughs, drawing upon the ten described in detail in Part II and comparable breakthroughs, such as Michael Ventris's decipherment of Linear B, and Alfred Russel Wallace's discovery of evolution by natural selection. What is the part played in breakthroughs by genes, family upbringing, and formal education? What is the relationship between scientific and artistic breakthroughs? Is there such a thing as a creative personality? Why does reputation as a genius fluctuate over a long period? Finally, are there any factors common to all breakthroughs that might hint at a plausible theory of exceptional creativity?

In all cultures, there are families where talent appears to be inherited: the Bach family in Germany; the Darwins in Britain; the Tagores in India, for instance. But exceptional creativity, 'genius', does not run in families (Chapter 16). Giorgio Vasari illustrated this in his sixteenth-century *Lives* of the leading Renaissance artists: most, including Leonardo and Michelangelo, came from non-creative origins. Galton proved it, if unintentionally, in his *Hereditary Genius*. An interesting modern example is that of Cartier-Bresson and Ray (who fervently admired each other's work). Neither had a genius in the family. Both, however, had a second string to their bows: Cartier-Bresson as a painter, Ray as an illustrator. These secondary talents may have been partly inherited, since Cartier-Bresson's painter uncle won the Prix de Rome, while Ray's father and grandfather were greatly admired illustrators; moreover all three forebears died before they could influence the growing Cartier-Bresson or Ray in person. Of course, it is difficult to disentangle genetic from environmental factors in talented families, as discussed by the psychiatrist Andreasen. In an admittedly small sample of writers at the Iowa Writers' Workshop, she found evidence for genetic transmission of creativity in the fact that the writers' near relatives were creative not only in literary fields but also in art, music, dance, mathematics, and science.

It seems intuitively obvious that parental support should develop creative potential in children. In fact, the evidence is conflicting. Darwin had to disobey his doctor father's wish that he become a doctor or a clergyman—yet his *Beagle* voyage would have been impossible without generous paternal financing. Mozart owed his childhood success to his violinist father's formidable tutelage—yet he was compelled to break with his father in his mid-twenties before he could compose his greatest works. One study of 400 eminent people of the twentieth century found that 85 per cent had come from highly troubled homes: 89 per cent of the novelists and playwrights, 83 per cent of the poets, 70 per cent of the artists, and 56 per cent of the scientists. Moreover, a disproportionate number of creative achievers lose one or both parents in childhood. Examples include Coleridge, Newton, and Orson Welles. Among the ten individuals in Part II, six of them—Champollion, Curie, Darwin, Ray, Woolf, and probably Wren—lost a parent before the age of 18, and Leonardo grew up away from his natural mother.

With scientists, formal education at school and university tends to be accepted and welcomed, while with artists it is often resisted and even rejected (Chapter 17). This distinction is by and large true of the individuals in Part II. Among the scientists, Champollion was an excellent student in

Paris and was appointed a university teacher at the age of only 18. Curie was a star pupil at school in Poland and later at university in Paris. Wren excelled at Oxford University and quickly became a fellow of All Souls College. Darwin, it is true, disliked his schooling and his early medical education at Edinburgh University, but he flourished at Cambridge University. Even Einstein, though he certainly disliked his conventional German school, was actually a good student and enjoyed studying at a more enlightened Swiss school; only afterwards, as a college student at the Zurich Polytechnic, did he fail to shine. Among the artists, by contrast, Leonardo and Mozart never attended a school, but were taught entirely 'on the job'. Woolf, too, was educated at home in London, with the run of her father's enormous library. Cartier-Bresson was a mediocre student at school in Paris, who failed the baccalaureate three times and never went to university. Ray, though he attended school and college in Calcutta and did quite well, felt he learned there little of use to his artistic work; after graduating, he abandoned art school half way, and took a job as a commercial artist. Extensive evidence shows that there is no correlation between early formal education and later artistic creativity.

This difference between the scientists and the artists is perhaps not too surprising, given the collaborative and consensual structure of science, unlike the arts. What unites the two groups is typically the existence of a mentor who fosters an early enthusiasm, provides an example, and nudges a creative person in a particular direction. This person may or may not be part of a formal education system. In Darwin's case, it was the botanist, geologist, and clergyman John Stevens Henslow at Cambridge, who proposed his protégé for the *Beagle* voyage. In Ray's, it was the film director Jean Renoir, who visited Bengal at a lucky moment for Ray. In Champollion's, it was his stalwart elder brother who paid for his education and encouraged him at every stage. Of the ten individuals in Part II, only Einstein had no obvious mentor before his breakthrough of 1905; in fact the young Einstein had no personal contact at all with the leading physicists of the time (though plenty of interaction with younger scientists).

The musically minded Einstein is reported to have said of Mozart, his favourite composer along with J. S. Bach: 'Mozart's music is so pure and beautiful that I see it as a reflection of the inner beauty of the universe.' The similarities between scientific and artistic creativity (Chapter 18) have been of interest to many eminent scientists, such as Subrahmanyan

Chandrasekhar and Peter Medawar. Darwin, on the other hand, lamented in his autobiography that with age he had lost all the delight he once took from classic poetry, plays, and music. Something similar happened to the literature-loving Curie, partly because of the tragic accident that killed her husband when she was only 39; in fact, Einstein was privately very critical of Curie for her lack of aesthetic response. As for the five artists in Part II, with the obvious exception of the scientifically minded Leonardo, three of them—Cartier-Bresson, Mozart, and Woolf—were indifferent, or even hostile, to science. Only Ray, who wrote and illustrated science–fantasy novels *à la* Conan Doyle, showed an interest; he included scientific references in many of his films. Indeed, judging from most interviews with artists, very few of them are interested in science, although this attitude may now be gradually changing. It is a rare artist who would say, as V. S. Naipaul said: 'It is my great regret that I didn't do science at [university]. I think I would probably have been a better man if I had studied science profoundly.'

Many psychologists have made attempts to compare scientific and artistic insights, for example, Arthur Koestler in *The Act of Creation* (a book condemned by Medawar for its ignorance of real scientific research) and David Perkins in *The Eureka Effect*. Among the more revealing is Robert Weisberg's comparison of the discovery of the structure of DNA in 1953 with the painting of Pablo Picasso's *Guernica* in 1937. Weisberg reconstructs both of these creative acts as a process of step-by-step problem solving without any recourse to inexplicable creative leaps, using the evidence recorded by the discoverers and by the artist in notebooks, sketchbooks, letters, memoirs, and interviews. James Watson's memoir *The Double Helix* is a key source, along with the series of preliminary sketches of compositions and characters for *Guernica* made by Picasso and thoughtfully dated by him in sequence.

The ten individuals in Part II differ vastly in personality (Chapter 19), it perhaps hardly needs to be said. Einstein flourished in the limelight, Curie tended to shrivel in it; Ray hardly ever lost his temper, Cartier-Bresson was only too easily provoked; Leonardo's curiosity spread itself in many domains, Wren's focused on one—to take just three examples. Is it futile to look for any common personality traits among the highly creative? Psychologists who study personality have looked for traits they can measure and correlate as factors, on the basis that personality is in some sense a fixed entity, stable throughout our lives and generalizable to all contexts. One currently favoured model has five factors: extraversion, neuroticism, conscientiousness, agreeableness, and openness. But this approach is particularly difficult to sustain when applied to highly creative people, especially as openness—the trait most closely correlated with exceptional creativity—is the least well defined of the five factors.

Exceptionally creative people often show a chameleon-like propensity to change their personality depending on context. Thus Einstein, in the years prior to his breakthrough in 1905, was part of a small club of friends, ironically nicknamed the Olympia Academy, dedicated to discussing books and ideas while enjoying food, drink, smoking, music, scatological humour, and practical jokes. This gregarious, sensual personality was utterly at odds with that of the lone theoretical physicist who during the same period worked late into the night on his highly abstract papers. Woolf, judging from her *Diary*, clearly relished, and required, literary, social, and sexual gossip—sometimes snobbish—with like-minded individuals, such as Lytton Strachey and at Bloomsbury Group parties. At the same time, she painfully struggled alone over months and years to write her novels and maintain her equilibrium in the face of incipient mental breakdowns. Ray displayed a forceful, outgoing, enthusiastic personality while directing his films on set, yet at home he was a modest, private, aloof figure used to working alone for long stretches. Even Darwin, despite secluding himself and working fanatically hard at Down House from his mid-thirties onwards, was earlier an adventurous, gallivanting explorer with a passion for shooting, horses, and dogs. The only obvious trait in common between the personalities of the highly creative seems to be strong self-discipline. If creativity researchers have proved anything about 'a' creative personality, it is that beneath a huge variety of external behaviours, often unconventional, all highly creative people preserve a steely, autonomous determination.

The idiosyncrasies of the lives of the highly creative exert a considerable influence on posthumous reputation for genius (Chapter 20), beginning with Archimedes's apocryphal bath-time escapade. Newton's fanatical solitude, Mozart's penchant for scatological jokes and absurdly premature death, Darwin's love of earthworms, Van Gogh's cutting off his ear, Einstein's unkempt hair and lack of socks, Woolf's struggle with mental illness and her final suicide, are well-known examples of distorting factors in scientific and artistic reputation. Although apparently irrelevant to the significance of breakthroughs, such personal details subtly alter our perceptions of who is a genius and who is not. Hence the point of Tom Lehrer's wonderfully deadpan remark quoted earlier: 'It is a sobering thought that by the time Mozart was my age, he had been dead for two years.'

The reason for this is our doubt about whether 'genius' is something inherent in an individual, or a status bestowed by others. According to the influential domain/field/person model of the psychologist Mihaly Csikszentmihalyi, the creativity of a person in a particular domain, such as mathematics or literature, is by definition bestowed by the community or field of experts. A genius is only a genius if others say so. This implies that if a genius falls far enough in reputation, he or she is no longer a genius—and vice versa.

'Once you're dead, you're made for life', said a witty Jimi Hendrix. However, reputation is not so simple. The music of J. S. Bach was largely ignored in the half-century and more following his death in 1750, yet nowadays Bach generally tops surveys of musical geniuses. Various rankings of classical composers by professional musicians and musicologists in surveys conducted at different points during the twentieth century show that there is no dramatic discontinuity in ranking—no quantum leap in reputation—that allows a highly talented composer to be reliably distinguishable from a 'genius'. In science, Darwin, Einstein, and Curie may be equally famous geniuses to the general public, but the ideas of the first two are still at the forefront of science, whereas Curie's theory of radioactivity is far from it, even though she won two Nobel Prizes a century ago. Is Curie therefore still a genius like Darwin and Einstein? Like scientific and artistic reputation, genius is a concept perpetually in flux.

Among all the patterns observable in exceptional creativity, perhaps the most intriguing is the so-called ten-year rule of breakthroughs (Chapter 21). First identified by John Hayes in 1989 and soon endorsed by several other psychologists, it states that a person must persevere with learning and practising a craft or discipline for about ten years before he or she can make a breakthrough. Remarkably few breakthroughs have been achieved in less than this time.

The initial scientific evidence for the ten-year rule came from studies in the 1960s and 1970s of chess players, who take ten years and more to become masters of the game. Then it was found to apply to athletes such as Olympic swimmers, and performers such as concert pianists. Subsequent studies of scientists and mathematicians, composers, painters, and poets— living and deceased—further supported the rule. No rule of human psychology has the universal validity and precision of the laws of physics and chemistry, and this one certainly has some noteworthy exceptions. Yet there are a sufficient number of breakthroughs by scientists and artists that obey the ten-year rule to make it worth investigating seriously.

In the sciences, Einstein is a good example. His first insight into the basis of special relativity occurred around 1895, and his theory was created and published in 1905. So is Darwin, whose theory of natural selection, although not published until 1859, was conceived in 1838, ten years after Darwin immersed himself in science at Cambridge in 1828. Wren's design for St Paul's Cathedral, the so-called Great Model of 1673–74, was constructed ten years after his first architectural commission in 1663. Michael Faraday demonstrated the electromagnetic principles of the motor and the dynamo in 1821, a decade after he began studying science in 1810. Kekulé's theory of the benzene ring was published in 1865, about ten years after his first dream of his structural theory on a London omnibus. Pauling's quantum-mechanical theory of the chemical bond was published in 1931, ten years after he started to study the problem at university in 1920–21. Tim Berners-Lee invented the World Wide Web in 1990, ten years after his first web-like computer programme. It is not difficult to multiply examples.

The arts frequently show the rule in operation, too. Percy Bysshe Shelley's creative explosion of 1819–20 (The Mask of Anarchy, Prometheus Unbound, etc.), occurred ten years after he wrote and published his first poetry and fiction in 1809–10. Ernest Hemingway's The Sun Also Rises was written in 1925–26, ten years after he began publishing fiction and journalism in his school magazine. Picasso's Les Demoiselles d'Avignon was painted in 1907, a decade after he began training as an artist in Barcelona in 1896. Toulouse-Lautrec's At the Moulin Rouge was painted in 1892, ten years after he entered the atelier of his first art teacher in 1882. Ray's first film in the Apu Trilogy, Pather Panchali, was completed in 1955, a decade after he created woodcuts to illustrate an edition of the original novel in 1944 and began writing scenarios. Igor Stravinsky's The Rite of Spring was composed in 1912, ten years after he began his apprenticeship to Nikolai Rimsky-Korsakov in 1902. Even The Beatles seem to obey the rule: they composed Sergeant Pepper's Lonely Hearts Club Band in 1967, ten years after John Lennon started playing with Paul McCartney in 1957.

The last chapter discusses in some detail examples of the ten-year rule taken from Part II, some counter-examples, such as Newton's discovery of gravity after a mere four or five years of study, and some apparent counter-examples, such as Van Gogh's first breakthrough with Sunflowers, barely eight years after he took up painting. If the rule does have general validity, what could be the cause? At first sight, it seems unlikely that breakthroughs should follow any rule at all, if they involve a large element of chance. Plainly, however, they also involve knowledge, training, and practice, which is why there has never yet been an instance of a teenage breakthrough—not even by Newton or Mozart. Perhaps the ten-year rule will offer us a clue to the underlying processes in exceptional creativity.

PART I

INGREDIENTS OF CREATIVITY

CHAPTER 1

GENIUS AND TALENT

Reality or Myth?

The word 'genius' is often used in a misleading manner. Too frequently it is applied as if it were a categorical label. This application assumes that a person either has genius or none at all, without admission of gradations between. Hence, Einstein was a scientific genius, whereas Marcel Grossmann, his onetime college classmate and sometime collaborator [on general relativity], was not. This dichotomous usage overlooks the fact that an underlying continuous dimension connects Einstein and Grossmann.

Dean Keith Simonton, *Creativity in Science*, 2004

The only person to have won the Nobel Prize in physics twice was John Bardeen—the first time for co-inventing the transistor in 1947, the second for his theory of superconductivity proposed with two other physicists in 1957. The first breakthrough changed the course of the twentieth century by giving birth to the semiconductor industry and computer chips, while the second may eventually change the course of the twenty-first century through superconducting devices with low power dissipation, high operational speed, and extreme sensitivity, such as magnetically levitated passenger trains. The biography of Bardeen by Lillian Hoddeson and Vicki Daitch is entitled *True Genius*.

Bardeen, however, was no Einstein or Richard Feynman: two charismatic physicists who were seldom out of the headlines. The biography of Feynman by James Gleick, entitled simply *Genius*, has just one passing reference to Bardeen, despite the fact that Feynman also worked in the field of superconductivity. Bardeen operated at the opposite pole from the stereotype of genius approximated by Einstein and Feynman. He was precocious (in mathematics) as a student, but not original; he showed no signs of

eccentricity, let alone abnormality; he was not self-taught, but had extensive formal training; he did not work alone, but collaborated extensively; he
did not report any eureka-like experiences; and he was not skilled in verbal
communication, which is why he seldom spoke to the press. Apart from
quietly doing physics in the office, Bardeen's idea of a good time was a
Sunday picnic with the family or a game of golf. 'Utterly unassuming in his
personal life, Bardeen was uninterested in appearing anything but ordinary', write his biographers. Hence the fact that hardly anyone outside of
solid-state physics has heard of him—unlike Bardeen's colleague in the
invention of the transistor, fellow Nobel laureate, and personal antithesis,
William Shockley. The aggressive and paranoid Shockley, besides being the
founding father of Silicon Valley, was a eugenicist who donated to a Nobel
Prize sperm bank and became so notorious for widely promoting his belief
in a link between race and intelligence that he ended his life as a pariah
among scientists. His biography by Joel Shurkin has an appropriate title:
Broken Genius: The Rise and Fall of William Shockley, Creator of the Electronic Age.

What does it mean to call Einstein, Feynman, Bardeen, and Shockley all
physics 'geniuses'? Not a lot, say some psychologists, who try to avoid using
the word in their research, and prefer instead 'exceptionally creative'. But
'genius'—with us since ancient Greece and Rome—cannot be put back in
the bottle so easily by scientists. Francis Galton tried to avoid using the
term in the text of his best-known study, yet nevertheless entitled the
book *Hereditary Genius: An Inquiry into Its Laws and Consequences.* To understand
creative breakthroughs, it is necessary to consider how to define and
estimate genius, even if we then try to use the word cautiously.

Galton, who coined the phrase 'nature versus nurture', was a fanatical
measurer of the human body and behaviour. He was, for example, a pioneer
in the use of fingerprints for identification. In one of his prolific variety of
scientific papers, 'The measurement of fidget', published in *Nature* in 1885,
Galton even observed that a large audience at a lecture fidgets around once
a minute on average, about half as often when gripped by the speaker's
words, and that the fidget of an engaged listener is briefer than the fidget of
a bored listener.

In addition, Galton was a highly intelligent member of the Darwin
family; his maternal grandfather, Erasmus Darwin, was the paternal grandfather of Charles Darwin. It was the publication of his first cousin's book
about natural selection, *On the Origin of Species,* in 1859, which persuaded
Galton that high intelligence must be inherited. By ranking the abilities of

past and present 'men of eminence'—mainly but not exclusively English-men—and searching for the occurrence of eminence in families, Galton hoped to prove his thesis, as set out in the opening words of his introductory chapter:

> I propose to show in this book that a man's natural abilities are derived by inheritance, under exactly the same limitations as are the form and physical features of the whole organic world. Consequently, as it is easy, notwithstanding those limitations, to obtain by careful selection a permanent breed of dogs or horses gifted with peculiar powers of running, or of doing anything else, so it would be quite practicable to produce a highly gifted race of men by judicious marriages during several consecutive generations.

Not surprisingly, Galton was a keen eugenicist.

To obtain his data on eminence, Galton made the reasonable but problematic assumption that high reputation is an accurate indicator of high ability. He then analysed the records of achievements and honours set out in three printed sources: a leading contemporary biographical handbook, *Men of the Time*; the obituary of the year 1868 published in *The Times* newspaper; and obituaries published in England going back into the past. If he were working today, he would no doubt have analysed lists of Nobel Prize winners, too. On this basis, Galton arbitrarily defined an 'eminent' person as someone who had achieved a position attained by only 250 persons in each million, that is 1 person in every 4000. (He argued for this number poetically, since 4000 is perhaps the number of stars visible to the naked eye on the most brilliant of starlit nights—'yet we feel it to be an extraordinary distinction to a star to be accounted as the brightest in the sky'.) An 'illustrious' person—much rarer than an eminent one—was one in a million, even one in many millions. 'They are men whom the whole intelligent part of the nation mourns when they die; who have, or deserve to have, a public funeral; and who rank in future ages as historical characters.' Significantly, Galton left a 'genius' undefined.

The bulk of *Hereditary Genius* consists of Galton's attempt to fit his identified 'illustrious' and 'eminent' persons into families. Beginning with a chapter on 'The judges of England between 1660 and 1865', he moves through chapters on, for example, 'Literary men', 'Men of science', 'Musicians', 'Divines', and 'Senior classics of Cambridge', and concludes with 'Oarsmen' and 'Wrestlers of the North Country'. Clearly, for Galton (as for all subsequent researchers), the concept of genius was meaningful only when applied to a domain, such as a genius for music or a genius for rowing.

In comparing his results obtained for different domains, Galton claimed that they supported, but did not prove, his hereditarian thesis. 'The general result is, that exactly one-half of the illustrious men have one or more eminent relations.' The highest proportion of the illustrious with an eminent family, 0.8, he found among senior judges (24 out of 30 lord chancellors) and men of science (65 out of 83), the lowest, 0.2–0.3, among divines (33 out of 196) and musicians (26 out of 100), with an overall average for all domains of 0.5. However, Galton admitted that his personal bias could easily have influenced his choice of illustrious and eminent individuals. Among the men of science, he was undoubtedly disturbed enough by Newton's patent lack of intellectual ancestry or descendants to add a lengthy and unconvincing note that attempted to find signs of eminence in Newton's family. The intriguing lack of eminence in Thomas Young's family (apart from a physician great-uncle) was simply ignored, despite the fact that Galton is known to have researched Young as an 'illustrious' candidate. Most surprisingly, some highly reputed English scientists, including the mathematician George Boole; the chemist John Dalton; the physicist Michael Faraday; the astronomer Edmund Halley; the naturalist John Ray; and the architect Christopher Wren, are not even mentioned in the book. Faraday, the most celebrated scientist of the Victorian era, is a particularly revealing omission, since, as the son of a humble blacksmith, he and his family could lend no weight to the book's thesis.

Despite Galton's finding of high inherited ability in scientists, a standard biographical study of great mathematicians, Men of Mathematics by the mathematician Eric Temple Bell, first published in 1937, shows just how little inherited mathematical ability is, at the highest level of achievement. Some great mathematicians came from lowly backgrounds. Newton was the son of a yeoman farmer; Carl Friedrich Gauss, who is omitted by Galton, the son of a gardener; Pierre-Simon Laplace, also omitted by Galton, the son of a parish official and cider merchant. Others came from professional backgrounds. Leonhard Euler, included by Galton, was the son of a pastor; Blaise Pascal, omitted by Galton, the son of a civil servant who forbade his son to look at mathematics books. Gottfried Wilhelm Leibniz, the inventor of the calculus independently of Newton, was the son of a professor of philosophy, whose father was a professor of jurisprudence and whose brother was a renowned jurisconsult, as noted by Galton. There is no hint of any mathematical ability in these six families, with the doubtful exception of Euler's father. In fact, of the 28 mathematicians of all time described by Bell, beginning with Zeno in the fifth century BC, where ancestral information is available, it shows that there is hardly a trace of mathematical achievement to be found in any of the fathers and close relatives.

Fascinating though Galton's eminent families are, they decidedly do not demonstrate the inheritance of genius. For there is a basic flaw in his analysis: Galton's criteria for genius (which of course he never defines) are not strict enough, allowing in too many high achievers whose distinction may be considerable but is far from enduringly original. *Hereditary Genius* is, so to speak, closer to the Queen's honours list than the Nobel Prize. As the psychologist Hans Eysenck observes, with a touch of exaggeration, in his own book *Genius: A Natural History of Creativity*, 'Galton in his book dealt with reasonably eminent people, but in spite of the title of his book there was hardly any genius among them.' When Galton speaks of the heritability of 'a man's natural abilities' in his thesis, what he really seems to mean is the heritability of talent, rather than genius. As most psychologists now agree, the evidence for inherited talent running in families is considerable, if controversial, while the evidence for inherited genius is slight or non-existent.

Distinguishing talent from genius is inevitably fraught with difficulty, since neither term has a widely agreed definition or method of measurement. Leaving aside heritability for the moment, the most obvious question to ask is whether talent and genius form a continuum, or are separated by a discontinuity? Put another way, the question becomes: should we speak of greater and lesser geniuses—instead of simply genius? Physicists generally feel that Einstein is a greater genius than, say, Feynman, Bardeen, or Shockley. Musicians tend to feel the same about Mozart, as compared with his contemporary (and fervent admirer) Joseph Haydn.

Rankings of composers throw some light on this issue. During the twentieth century, various rankings were compiled by psychologists, based on asking orchestral players and musicologists to rate lists of composers in order of significance, and also on tabulating the frequency of performance of a composer's work. In 1933, the members of four American orchestras (the New York Philharmonic, and the Boston, Minneapolis, and Philadelphia Symphony Orchestras) were given a list of 17 names of the best-known classical composers, plus the names of two modern popular composers to create a reference point. All four orchestras ranked Ludwig van Beethoven top at number one and the two modern popular composers

(Edward MacDowell and Victor Herbert) bottom at numbers 18 and 19. They also all ranked J. S. Bach, Johannes Brahms, Mozart, Richard Wagner, and Franz Schubert high, and ranked Edvard Grieg, César Franck, Giuseppe Verdi, and Igor Stravinsky low. On average, Brahms was at number two, Mozart at three, Wagner at four, Bach at five, and Schubert at six. (Amazingly, Handel was excluded from the list.) A similar survey, but this time of 100 composers, answered by members of the American Musicological Society in 1969, produced similar rankings to the 1933 survey, though now with Bach at number one, Beethoven at two, and Mozart still at three (and Handel now at six). Around the same time, 1968, a third survey—this time of performance frequencies—showed Mozart as the most performed composer, followed by Beethoven, then Bach, Wagner, Brahms, and Schubert, in that order. So there are some grounds for thinking that 'Taste is lawful', in the words of the 1969 survey.

But what is perhaps more interesting is the fuller result of the 1933 survey. When each musician was asked to compare each of the 19 composers with each of the rest and indicate his preference, and their rankings were then suitably scaled and plotted on a graph of falling preference against increasing rank numbers 1–19, the line of the graph was seen to fall gradually from Beethoven to Grieg (before dropping precipitately down to MacDowell and Herbert). The drop in performance frequencies of the 100 composers in the 1968 survey was also gradual, from Mozart at number one to Giuseppe Tartini at number 100, without any obvious breaks. An abrupt drop in performance frequency would seem to indicate a discontinuity between genius and talent—but this was not observed. 'It does seem that we must accept the view that genius is just the top of the iceberg, continuous with lesser talents and not qualitatively differentiated, as it might appear if we compare the most exalted with those of little talent, omitting all those in between', writes Eysenck.

If talent is a necessary component of genius—necessary, co-extensive, but not sufficient—of what does talent consist? Inherited ability? Passion? Determination? Capacity for hard practice? Responsiveness to coaching? A combination of all of these? Before tackling this, let us hear the views of four people with very different kinds of talent.

The tennis coach Robert Lansdorp has trained three former number one players, Pete Sampras, Tracy Austin, and Lindsay Davenport. But Lansdorp says he is no 'talent scout': 'It's not about recognizing talent, whatever the hell that is. I've never tried to go out and find someone who's talented.

First you work on fundamentals, and pretty soon you find out where things are going.' The painter and art teacher Françoise Gilot, best known as the companion of Picasso, recalls a question put to her by some of her students: 'How can anyone know if he or she is a potentially original artist?' Her answer: 'I can tell you that it's very simple. How many hours can you remain alone during a day, a week, a month, a year, a lifetime? If you can remain alone almost all of the time you can be a painter.' The piano virtuoso Vladimir Horowitz, who was still performing in his eighties, remarked: 'If I skip practice for one day, I notice. If I skip practice for two days, my wife notices. If I skip for three days, the world notices.' Lastly, the psychologist R. Ochse, in his excellent book *Before the Gates of Excellence: The Determinants of Creative Genius*, reminds us that: 'no talent is a free gift waiting to be unwrapped'.

The relationship between inherited ability and long practice is the most contentious aspect of talent. It is very difficult to disentangle genetic from environmental influences. There are seven parent–child pairs of Nobel laureates in science, for example. Four are in physics: J. J. Thomson (1906) and George Thomson (1937); William and Lawrence Bragg (1915); Niels Bohr (1922) and Aage Bohr (1975); Manne Siegbahn (1924) and Kai Siegbahn (1981). The other three are in chemistry and physiology or medicine: Marie Curie (1911) and Irène Joliot-Curie (1935); Arthur Kornberg (1959) and Roger Kornberg (2006); and Hans von Euler-Chelpin (1929) and Ulf von Euler (1970). But it is impossible to determine how much of the success of the child was genetically determined. In addition to having shared genes, the Braggs literally worked together (hence their joint prize); Aage Bohr worked for decades at his father's Institute of Theoretical Physics; while Joliot-Curie was intensively trained by her mother in her laboratory from early on. The fact that there are no parent–child pairs among Nobel laureates in literature (admittedly a much smaller number of individuals than in science), where training is largely solitary, is at least suggestive that training may be more important to success than inherited talent.

Mozart, famously, is a compelling instance of the difficulty. He was the son of a considerable musician: the violinist, music teacher, and composer, Leopold Mozart. He also had musical relatives on his mother's side of the family. So he surely inherited some musical ability. But at the same time, he underwent a unique course of training at the hands of his father, a hard driver and an inspired teacher, who controlled Wolfgang's life for over two decades. However, there is a way of separating the effect of the Mozart family genes from the family training, which is not normally available. Wolfgang's elder sister Maria Anna, known as Nannerl—four and a half years older than him—who naturally shared half of his genes, was also a talented piano player as a child. She too was exposed to the intensive training of Leopold, side by side with her brother. As soon as the children were ready, Leopold took them on a tour of the courts and major cities of Europe in 1763–66, where together they became celebrities. Yet, Nannerl did not go on to compose, unlike her brother. Why not?

The obvious explanation will not do. Women in the eighteenth century were permitted to excel in music, if not in many other fields. And there is no plausible reason why the hugely ambitious Leopold would have chosen to hold Nannerl back during her teenage years in the 1760s, long before the premature death of her mother (after which Nannerl had to act as a companion to her demanding father). Contemporary examples of young female performers include: the blind Austrian piano virtuoso Maria Theresia von Paradis, who toured through Germany, France, and England, and who also composed concertos and operas that were successfully staged; the violin virtuoso Regina Strinasacchi, who toured extensively in her teens; and Nancy Storace, the soprano who sang leading roles in Italian opera by the age of 16. Mozart composed works for Von Paradis and Strinasacchi, while Storace took the role of Susanna in the premiere of his opera *The Marriage of Figaro*.

'I suggest the explanation for Nannerl Mozart's lack of progression beyond performance is that she lacked the capacity for creating original music', writes the psychologist Andrew Steptoe, who has written a major study of Mozart's operas. Steptoe thinks:

> It is extremely unlikely that Wolfgang Mozart's genius was a simple product of his training. Seldom has there been such a clear case of a creative individual and a close relative living in the same family and undergoing similar dedicated training in a particular domain of activity. There is a strong case for supposing that the differences between the capacities of the two people who emerged were the product of their personal biological endowments. On the other hand, it is indisputable that without the intense nurturance provided by Leopold, Wolfgang's creativity would not have blossomed.

Mozart's musical ability was transparently obvious to his father (and sister) in childhood, as has been the case with many successful musicians and some composers. This fact has lent credence to the common view—predominant among music educators—that talent is essentially innate: you are born with it and cannot acquire it, though you can (and must) hone it, if you want to make a profession out of it. Thus, people often say that someone they know plays an instrument well because she has innate talent. How do they know she has talent? It's obvious—because she plays so well!

Nonetheless, hundreds of studies by psychologists, conducted over decades, have failed to provide unimpeachable evidence for the existence of innate talent. Although there is certainly evidence of a genetic contribution to intelligence, as we shall see in the next chapter on IQ, the correlations between general intelligence and various specific abilities—such as playing a musical instrument well—are small. No genes 'for' domain-specific talents have yet been located, although the search continues; any resolution is almost certain to involve a complex interaction between many genes and the environment, as well as requiring a long time to discover. Furthermore, the indisputable and astonishing improvement in performance standards observed during the past century, in sports, chess, music, and some other fields, has happened much too fast to be explained by genetic changes, which would require thousands of years. Rather than genes, psychologists' study of talent suggests the importance of the other factors mentioned above: passion; determination; practice; and coaching.

In one study, young students at a music school were divided into two groups based on the evaluation of their ability by teachers—that is, the teachers' perception of the student's talent. The division was done secretly, so as not to bias the students' future performance. After several years, the highest performance ratings were achieved by those students who had practised the most in the intervening period, irrespective of which 'talent' group their teachers had earlier allotted them to. 'This suggests that practice is the cause of achievement, not merely something correlated with it', writes the musician and neuroscientist Daniel Levitin in *This is Your Brain on Music*.

In another study, by the music psychologist Gary McPherson, children were asked a simple question before they started their first music lesson: 'How long do you think you will play your new instrument?' The options were: through this year; through primary school; through high school; or throughout life. On the basis of their answers, McPherson categorized the children (again in secret) into three groups: showing short-term commitment; medium-term commitment; and long-term commitment. He then measured the amount of practice by each child per week and came up with three more categories: low (20 minutes per week); medium (45 minutes per week); and high (90 minutes per week). When he plotted the children's actual performance on a graph, the differences between the three groups were astonishing. Not only did the long-term committed perform better with a low level of practice than the short-term committed with a high level of practice (presumably forced by their parents!)—the long-term committed performed 400 per cent better than the short-term committed when they, too, adopted a high level of practice. 'We instinctively think of each new student as a blank slate, but the ideas they bring to that first lesson are probably far more important than anything a teacher can do, or any amount of practice,' in McPherson's view. 'At some point very early on they had a crystallizing experience that brings the idea to the fore, that says, *I am a musician.*'

Recent neuroscientific research offers clear evidence for the physiological effects of determined practice. The brain is plastic, and it alters through practice. One of the best-known studies, published in 2000 by Eleanor Maguire and colleagues, used functional magnetic resonance imaging (fMRI) to examine the hippocampus of London taxi drivers. The hippocampus is a site in the brain where memories are consolidated. Cabbies in London, unlike most cabbies, are required to spend two years memorizing the map of the city (the so-called 'Knowledge') in order to pass a stiff test, so that they can obtain an official licence. The fMRI scans showed the hippocampus to be activated when a taxi driver was asked to imagine his route to reach a particular destination. Practising their spatial memory assiduously had measurably increased the size of the drivers' hippocampi relative to the hippocampi of a control group. Moreover, the increase in size correlated with the number of years the driver had spent on the job.

Other studies have looked at musicians. Reading staff notation in a musical score while playing an instrument, and simultaneously coordinating one's playing with fellow musicians of various kinds and a conductor, all in different locations, evidently requires the development of special aural and visual/spatial skills. When practised for many years, this must affect a musician's brain. A technique known as morphometric magnetic resonance imaging (mMRI)—capable of measuring brain anatomy rather than the changes in blood flow indicated by fMRI—was applied by Vanessa Sluming and colleagues to 26 experienced male musicians from symphony orchestras and to a control group. The results, published in 2002, showed that the musicians had significantly more grey matter than the control group in Broca's area of the cerebral cortex. This was explicable on the basis that Broca's area is associated with language processing, and the reading of music involves language skills. However, the scans did not show the expected enlargement of the musicians' right parietal lobe, which is associated with the type of visual/spatial skill useful in an orchestra, even though a separate (non-mMRI) test, the Judgement of Line Orientation, showed that the skill was in fact highly developed in the musicians compared to the control group.

A second musical study, published in 2005, used yet another MRI technique known as diffusion tensor imaging (DTI), sensitive to changes in white rather than grey matter, to investigate the brains of professional pianists. Its main author, Fredrik Ullén, is a piano virtuoso as well as a neuroscientist, interested in the effect of musical practice on white matter. Myelin, the white fatty substance that sheaths the conducting axons (thread-like nerve fibres) of the adult brain like plastic insulation around a wire, was found by Ullén to grow gradually thicker with practice, increasing the strength of the DTI signal. The more a pianist practised over time, the thicker was the myelin, the less leaky and more efficient the axons, and the better the communication system of the brain's synapses and neurons. 'Certainly white matter is key to types of learning that require prolonged practice and repetition, as well as extensive integration among greatly separated regions of the cerebral cortex. Children whose brains are still myelinating widely find it much easier to acquire new skills than their grandparents do', thinks the neuroscientist R. Douglas Fields, who directs the Laboratory of Developmental Neurobiology at the National Institutes of Health in the United States. 'You built the brain you have today by interacting with the environment while you were growing up and your neural connections were still myelinating. You can adapt those abilities in many ways, but neither you nor I will become a world-class pianist, chess player, or tennis pro unless we began our training when we were children.'

So practice can, it seems, do much to perfect the brain for specific tasks, such as playing the piano, chess, or tennis. But of course the brain initially forms and develops under the direction of an individual's genome, like every other part of the body, uninfluenced by conscious decisions. Which brings us back to the knotty problem of the genetic or innate element in talent.

Since this has, as yet, no solution, the best that can be offered is probably the analysis of two psychologists and a musicologist, Michael Howe,

John Sloboda, and Jane Davidson, who together surveyed the entire scientific literature on talent. In 1998, they published a much-discussed paper entitled 'Innate talents: reality or myth?' in the journal *Behavioral and Brain Sciences*. Near the beginning, intending to provoke, they set out five properties commonly believed to be true of talent, which we have discussed in this chapter:

> (1) It originates in genetically transmitted structures and hence is at least partly innate. (2) Its full effects may not be evident at an early stage, but there will be some advance indications, allowing trained people to identify the presence of talent before exceptional levels of mature performance have been demonstrated. (3) These early indications of talent provide the basis for predicting who is likely to excel. (4) Only a minority are talented, for if all children were, then there would be no way to predict or explain differential success. Finally (5), talents are relatively domain-specific.

Having reviewed all the available evidence, Howe, Sloboda, and Davidson conclude that assumptions two, three, and five are unproven. As for one, they cautiously agree that: 'individual differences in some special abilities may indeed have partly genetic origins'. As for assumption four, 'there do exist some attributes that are possessed by only a minority of individuals. In this very restricted sense, talent may be said to exist.' Overall, however, they claim that 'there may be little or no basis for innate giftedness', and that the prevalence of the idea in education produces the undesirable effect of discriminating against able children who might otherwise become 'talented' adults. Some fellow psychologists agree with them, but others accept all five assumptions.

Genius is even more problematic than talent—its definition and measurement still embroiled in the arguments that dogged Galton's *Hereditary Genius* well over a century ago (though thankfully now free of his obsessions with eugenics and race). It would be absurd to deny the existence of genius, faced by the achievements of, say, a Darwin or a Leonardo, an Einstein or a Mozart. But it would be equally absurd to insist that genius has nothing at all to do with 'mere talent', as witness a physicist like Bardeen, the double Nobel laureate who did not think of himself as a genius. Although genius is never inherited or passed on, it seems, like talent, to be partly genetic in origin in many cases, as with Leopold and Wolfgang Mozart, or Erasmus and Charles Darwin. Unlike talent, though, genius is the result of a unique configuration of parental genes and personal circumstances. Since a genius never transmits the full complement of his or her genes—only a half-helping—to offspring, whose personal circumstances inevitably differ from those of the parent genius, this configuration never repeats itself in the offspring. Thus, it is not surprising that genius does not run in families, but that talent sometimes does.

CHAPTER 2

INTELLIGENCE
IS NOT ENOUGH

[Lewis] Terman devised a method of quantifying and measuring verbal, mathematical, and logical skills, but his tests could not measure those elusive gifts of talent and imagination. Intellectual skills and artistic creativity are surely not mutually exclusive, but one does not necessarily go with the other.... Paul Gauguin, existing in abject poverty in the South Pacific, selling his paintings to survive, living with native women while his wife and daughter scraped by in Europe, would have been at the bottom of [Terman's] C list. Terman had no illusions about that; he admitted this shortcoming.

Joel N. Shurkin, *Terman's Kids*, 1992

It would be intriguing to know the intelligence quotients of a large sample of past and present geniuses when they were still unknown, in their teens. Would the IQ of the brilliant student Curie be far higher than the IQ of the dull student Darwin? Would the speculative Einstein have an IQ ahead of Curie's? Would the polymathic Leonardo da Vinci have a low or a high IQ? What about the prodigious but narrowly focused Mozart? And the highly articulate but wholly unscientific Virginia Woolf?

Unfortunately, there is not much quantitative information available on the intelligence of exceptionally creative people, for fairly obvious reasons. In the first place, intelligence testing began only in the first decade of the twentieth century, with the psychologist Alfred Binet's testing for mental retardation in French primary schools. It did not become widespread until the 1920s, in North America. So there are effectively no numerical data for anyone born before the twentieth century. Second, its use in all cultures has been controversial, and far from universal, even in the country where it is most common, the United States. Moreover, the results of different intelligence tests taken during different periods, especially if they were devised in different cultures, are tricky to compare with each other. Third, tests are generally carried out in youth, but since that is before exceptional creativity reveals itself, educational psychologists will not always spot the potential of a future genius and administer a test. Finally, one suspects that very few of those recognized as a genius would be willing to sit a standard intelligence test. Although widely used in education, business, government, and the armed services, intelligence tests do not have a high reputation, not least among many psychologists. No one puts their IQ in their curriculum vitae, nor does it appear in biographical reference books, even supposing a reliable figure is known.

Nevertheless, scattered information offers some suggestive hints about IQ and genius. Consider the IQs of three American Nobel laureates in physics. In 1965, the year he won his Nobel Prize, Richard Feynman gave a talk at his former high school in New York and told the students that when he took an IQ test at school, he scored 125. A 'merely respectable' figure (notes his biographer), somewhat below the level of about 130 generally considered to indicate 'giftedness'. William Shockley was tested twice at school in the 1920s and failed to reach the IQ of 135 required to join Lewis Terman's pioneering survey of gifted children, started in 1921 at Stanford University. (Shockley's wife later declined his suggestion that their daughter be intelligence tested.) Luis Alvarez, too, was rejected by Terman—which meant that Terman's programme lost a further opportunity to 'discover' a future Nobel laureate.

The much older Einstein was of course never tested as a youngster. But when he visited the US in 1921, he was informally subjected to a question set by the inventor Thomas Edison, an advocate of intelligence testing for his prospective employees. Some journalists asked Einstein: 'What is the speed of sound?' He confessed he did not know, and replied patiently that there was no need to carry this information in his head, as he could look it up in a book. Next day, the inevitable headline was: 'EINSTEIN SEES BOSTON; FAILS EDISON TEST'.

Data on the intelligence of the exceptionally creative must therefore be derived from historical information, culled from printed sources such as biographies, and contemporary documents. The most substantial study is the one conducted by Terman's doctoral student Catharine Cox, published as an 850-page book by Stanford University Press under the title *The Early Mental Traits of Three Hundred Geniuses*, as long ago as 1926. It covers not only the sciences and the arts, but also many other walks of life with a marked intellectual element.

Today, opinions of the worth of Cox's study vary wildly. Certain psychologists, beginning with Terman, have been strong supporters. The *American Journal of Psychology*, in an obituary of Cox published in 1986, praised 'Dr Cox's meticulous attention to reliability of measurement and validity of evidence [that] has made the study a model of historical and biographical research'. Robert Albert wrote in 1983 that although the study is 'a half century old it remains one of the most fertile pieces of research on the subject [of genius]. Unmatched in the range and depth of their analyses, Cox's results foreshadow many later findings'. Hans Eysenck called it in 1995 'the only proper study of the field', a 'classic work...cited more frequently perhaps than any other book on genius'. But the Harvard University biologist and palaeontologist Stephen Jay Gould, in the 1996 edition of his polemic against intelligence testing, *The Mismeasure of Man*, was contemptuous; Gould regarded Cox's study as 'a primary curiosity within a literature already studded with absurdity'. And Joel Shurkin, a Pulitzer Prize-winning science writer, in *Terman's Kids: The Groundbreaking Study of How the Gifted Grow Up*, published in 1992, called the study 'one of the silliest experiments in the colourful history of social science'. On the whole, unless one is a psychologist of a certain stripe, it is hard not to agree with these latter two judgements, while accepting that Cox's study, for all its debilitating flaws, still does tell us something worthwhile about intelligence and genius.

Its original inspiration was the work of Francis Galton: in the first place his 1869 *Hereditary Genius*, second, his attempts at mental testing conducted in the 1880s on volunteers at his so-called Anthropometric Laboratory. In effect, Terman and Cox decided to take Galton's classification method for remarkable individuals (discussed in Chapter 1) a stage further and give numbers to his 'eminent' and 'illustrious' rankings—so as to create what Gould terms 'fossil IQs'. By comparing the reported achievements of past geniuses at various ages, such as first reading and first mathematical performance, with the normal record of achievement of the developing child, Cox and her colleagues tried to calculate the mental age for each achievement of a historical genius, and hence his or her IQ.

Terman began the process with a paper in 1917 in which he calculated the IQ of Galton himself. The first volume of a four-volume biography of Galton by Karl Pearson had appeared in 1914, soon after Galton's death at the age of 89 in 1911, giving Terman ample information about the childhood and youth of his subject, up to his marriage in 1853.

He was particularly struck by a letter written by the child Francis on 15 February 1827, the day before his fifth birthday. It was addressed to his sister Adèle, then aged about 17, who had been his devoted teacher from his earliest childhood:

> My dear Adèle,
>
> I am four years old and I can read any English book. I can say all the Latin Substantives and Adjectives and active verbs besides 52 lines of Latin poetry. I can cast up any sum in addition and can multiply by 2, 3, 4, 5, 6, 7, 8, [9], 10, [11].
> I can also say the pence table. I read French a little and I know the Clock.
>
> FRANCIS GALTON
Febuary-15-1827

'The only misspelling is in the date', wrote Terman. 'The numbers 9 and 11 are bracketed above, because little Francis, evidently feeling that he had claimed too much, had scratched out one of these numbers with a knife and pasted some paper over the other!'

Other relevant information from Pearson's book included the following. At the age of twelve months, Francis knew his capital letters, and six months later his alphabet; aged two and a half, he could read a little book, *Cobwebs to Catch Flies*; before he was three, he could sign his name. In his fourth year, according to his mother, he wrote and spelt correctly, without assistance, a simple letter to an uncle (reproduced by Pearson). That his reading was more than merely mechanical was shown when he was five: a school friend asked Francis's advice on what he should write in a letter to his mother about his father, who was apparently in danger of being shot over some political affair, and Francis immediately quoted Sir Walter Scott's lines: 'And if I live to be a man,/ My Father's death revenged shall be.' At the age of six, he was thoroughly familiar with Homer's *Iliad* and *Odyssey*; was reading Shakespeare's works for pleasure; and was able to repeat a page by heart after reading it twice over. At seven, he was collecting insects, shells, and minerals, then classifying and studying them in a more than childish way—a strong hint of his adult preoccupations. Later, aged thirteen, he created a series of drawings of a passenger-carrying flying machine with large flapping wings powered by some kind of steam engine, which he called 'Francis Galton's Aerostatic Project'.

Reading at the age of three—compared with the normal age of six—is equivalent to an IQ of six divided by three then multiplied by 100 (the average, or base, IQ, by definition), which gives an IQ of 200. The normal age for classification and analysis of a collection is twelve or thirteen, which implies an IQ of around 180, given that Galton was classifying and analysing insects and minerals aged seven. After comparing all of Galton's precocious behaviours with the normal mental ages for such behaviour, Terman concluded that he could estimate 'with considerable assurance' a minimum IQ for Galton that would account for the facts in Pearson's biography. 'This was unquestionably in the neighbourhood of 200, a figure not equalled by more than one child in 50,000 of the generality'.

Cox, following a methodology basically similar to Terman's, and under his supervision, faced more constraints. Few of her chosen individuals had lives as completely documented as Galton's. (Strangely, Galton was not included in the study, presumably on the grounds that he was not a bona fide genius.) So little could Cox discover about Shakespeare's life that he had to be excluded. Living individuals were deliberately excluded, so there is no Curie or Einstein, no George Bernard Shaw or William Butler Yeats in the study, for instance. In addition, Cox chose to eliminate those born before 1450, along with all aristocrats, and anyone else whose achievements could not be attributed to them without dispute. All this was understandable. But some of the other omissions were hard to defend: among the scientists, no Jean-François Champollion, Carl Gauss, Robert Hooke, August Kekulé, Charles Lyell, James Clerk Maxwell, Dimitri Mendeleev, Louis Pasteur, or Christopher Wren; among the artists no Gian Lorenzo Bernini, Johannes Brahms, Paul Cézanne, Anton Chekhov, Francisco de Goya, Franz Schubert, Percy Bysshe Shelley, Leo Tolstoy, or Oscar Wilde. The Cox/Terman list is an idiosyncratic choice of geniuses, to put it politely, even when we allow for the fluctuation of reputation between the 1920s and now. (The genius of all these omitted individuals was accepted in the mid-1920s.)

The nearly 300 subjects who remain break down into the following groups: 39 scientists (including Newton); 13 visual artists (including Leonardo); 11 composers (including Mozart); 22 philosophers (including Immanuel Kant); 95 men of letters (including Byron); 27 soldiers (including Oliver Cromwell); 43 statesmen (including Abraham Lincoln); 9 revolutionary statesmen (including Robespierre); and 23 religious leaders (including Martin Luther).

Having combed biographies and other documentary sources for data, Cox ended up with dossiers totalling 6000 pages of typed material. These she and her co-workers used to rate both intelligence and personality characteristics, and make comparisons between the various groups.

Two intelligence ratings per individual were calculated: an A1 IQ for the period up to the age of 17, and an A2 IQ for the period between 17 and 26 years old. The A1 IQ was based on the subject's mastery of universal tasks, such as speaking, reading, and writing, and on school performance, plus evidence of distinctive childhood achievements of the kind reported in Pearson's biography of Galton. The A2 IQ relied chiefly on the subject's academic record and early professional career. The personality profiles were created mainly by rating each subject with respect to 67 traits, using a seven-point scale.

Five co-workers, including Terman, carried out the IQ rating by independently reading the dossiers and assigning a score for each individual. But when Cox compared their five sets of scores, she found that only three of the assessors agreed substantially; the other two awarded an IQ either well above, or well below, the IQ of the first three. Arguing that these consistently high and low scores would have cancelled each other out, she controversially decided to omit them altogether and depend entirely on three, rather than five, ratings. According to her final IQ averages for each group, the soldiers had the lowest IQs (A1 IQ 115/A2 IQ 125), the philosophers the highest IQs (147/156). Visual artists and scientists fell in between, with visual artists (IQ 122/135) lower than scientists (IQ 135/152). On this basis, all but the soldiers would rank as 'gifted' (with an A2 IQ above 130). Darwin was rated at IQ 135/140, Leonardo at IQ 135/150, Michelangelo at IQ 145/160, Mozart at IQ 150/155, and Newton at IQ 130/170. The highest rating was given to John Stuart Mill at IQ 190/170.

Even the most sympathetic critics today stress that not too much weight should be placed on the individual IQs and the group averages. 'There is no question that the Cox study was carefully and conscientiously done, and is of great importance for every student of the subject', writes Eysenck. 'Yet it is imperative to resist the temptation to take the actual figures too seriously'. As he neutrally comments: 'the more data are available, the higher is the IQ estimate'. This is why, for every group, and for most individuals, the A2 IQ is higher than the A1 IQ: fully 40 points higher for Newton, whose childhood is obscure. Inevitably, there is more information available about the later than about the earlier period of a genius's life.

Gould (whose book is quietly ignored by Eysenck) castigates the whole study for precisely the above weakness:

> Two basic results of Cox's study immediately arouse our strong suspicion that her IQ scores reflect the historical accidents of surviving records, rather than the true accomplishments of her geniuses. First, IQ is not supposed to

alter in a definite direction during a person's life. Yet average A1 IQ is 135 in her study, and average A2 IQ is a substantially higher 145. When we scrutinize her dossiers..., the reason is readily apparent, and a clear artefact of her method. She has more information on her subjects as young adults than as children... Second, Cox published disturbingly low A1 IQ figures for some formidable characters, including Cervantes and Copernicus, both at 105. Her dossiers show the reason: little or nothing is known about their childhood, providing no data for addition to the base figure of 100. Cox established seven levels of reliability for her figures. The seventh, believe it or not, is 'guess, based on no data'.

Faraday, too, was awarded an A1 IQ of 105 (derived from two ratings of 110 and one of 100), by virtue of slim reports about his 'faithfulness' as an errand boy and that he was a 'great questioner' when young, set against the otherwise silent background of his humble parentage and limited formal education. But this low rating for Faraday's early years jumps to an A2 IQ of 150 for his young adult years, simply because much more information is available after his employment, aged 21, at the Royal Institution by Humphry Davy. Cox openly admits the incompleteness of the data on Faraday, and many others—such as Napoleon Bonaparte's great general Jean-André Masséna (A1 IQ a mere 100, as opposed to 135 for Napoleon himself)—but this admission does nothing to increase confidence in the validity of her IQ ratings as a whole. One must assume that she omitted Shakespeare mainly because her method would have forced her to award the Bard a below-average IQ (less than 100)—thus exposing the overall weakness of the study.

There is no answering this fundamental criticism of Cox's study. She herself was aware of it: 'It appears that all of the IQ ratings are probably too low... and that the *true* IQ for the group... is distinctly above the estimated ratings of this study, since the estimated ratings are dependent upon data whose unreliability introduces a constant reduction of the estimated IQ from its true value'. Cox attempted to 'correct' the scores obtained from her three co-workers by adjusting them upwards to take account of missing information for certain individuals. Her correction pushed the average A1 IQ for all groups up from 135 to 152, and the average A2 IQ up from 145 to 166. But she offered no convincing rationale for these higher figures, which look more like the results of a 'fudge factor': a somewhat desperate strategy to correlate high IQ with exceptional creativity, than a scientific argument.

The truth is that insufficient information exists to allot IQs to historical geniuses. It is certainly not accurate to claim of Cox's study, in the words of the *American Journal of Psychology*, that: 'The net result was a clear demonstration that whatever other factors may have entered into the achievement of eminence, high IQ was undubitably present for those whose careers lay in statesmanship, literature, philosophy, the fine arts, and sciences—though not in the military realm'. If, for the sake of argument, we take 'high IQ' to be any IQ above about 135 (the threshold chosen by Terman in his Stanford study), then Cox's study shows that roughly as many of her geniuses fell below this figure in the period up to age 17 as rose above it, since her average (uncorrected) A1 IQ is 135. And even this conclusion assumes that her IQ ratings are reliable and her individuals well chosen—neither of which assumption is really warranted.

A more accurate statement would be that the net result of Cox's formidable assemblage of data and its analysis is that we know that almost all geniuses, other than military ones, have an IQ well above average (100)—but that to have an IQ well above average is no guarantee of genius. While this result is not too surprising, it does give the lie to the most common expectation about geniuses: that they must by definition be extremely intelligent. After all, Richard Feynman is generally considered an almost archetypal modern scientific genius, not just in the US but wherever in the world physics is studied. Yet Feynman, as already mentioned—along with Shockley and Alvarez—had an IQ well above average, but not especially high (10 points short of 135, Cox's A1 IQ average). By contrast Galton, Terman's favourite psychologist, was reckoned by him to have had a truly astonishing IQ (200). However, neither Cox and Terman, nor Galton's fellow Victorians, nor late twentieth-century psychologists, rated Galton a genius.

If a high score on an intelligence test is a poor predictor of genius, a high score on a creativity test is even less reliable at predicting exceptional creativity.

Creativity tests of the kind devised by psychologists since the 1950s, mainly in the United States, aim to test divergent or lateral thinking, as opposed to the convergent or logical thinking of intelligence tests. There are always many 'correct' answers to an item in a divergent thinking test, not just the single right answer to be deduced by logical methods usually expected in a convergent thinking test. Instead of posing a problem and asking the subject to converge on one answer—by selecting the correct word, number, or drawing from a set of multiple-choice solutions, the prototypical divergent thinking test requests, say: as many uses as possible for a paper clip, a range of titles for a story, or an unspecified number of plausible interpretations of an abstract line drawing. In other words, the tests search for the ability to show originality and imagination, as determined, of course, by the testers. An individual is judged to be 'creative', psychometrically speaking, if he or she can consistently produce a spectrum of divergent responses to a request, of which a proportion are markedly different from the responses of other individuals. But not *too* different, otherwise they are not recognizable as answers to the request. Creativity tests are reminiscent of the mathematician Tom Lehrer's ironic comment on 1960s New Math teaching and learning: 'The important thing is to understand what you're doing—rather than to get the right answer'.

Three or four decades of creativity testing—frequently with student volunteers at colleges and universities—revealed several conclusions of note. Encouragingly, the tests are reliable. That is, if someone takes the same divergent thinking test twice, he or she will generally have a similar score; and the score will correlate significantly with his or her score on other divergent thinking tests. This is also true of convergent thinking tests. Less encouragingly, at least for creativity testers, measures of convergent and divergent thinking do not correlate well. To be more precise, below an IQ of about 120, there is some correlation, but above 120 there is little or no correlation: a person with a high IQ may or may not test as creative. Least encouragingly of all, there is no correlation between high scorers on divergent thinking tests and their creativity in real life—in distinct contrast with the track record of convergent thinking tests in predicting scholastic achievement at school and university and careers in many professional occupations, such as government, the police, and the armed forces.

This last conclusion is what turned Howard Gardner, a leading educational psychologist and long-standing creativity researcher, off creativity tests. Their lack of validity is, in Gardner's view, 'devastating for the enterprise of measuring creativity using paper-and-pencil tests', he wrote in the 1990s. 'High scores on a creativity test do not signal that one is necessarily creative in one's actual vocation or avocation, nor is there convincing evidence that individuals deemed creative by their discipline or culture necessarily exhibit the kinds of divergent-thinking skills that are the hallmark of creativity tests'. Given the artificial conditions of tests, compared to the complexity of the real world in which creativity must flourish, their failure was really to be expected.

But the chief difficulty in linking intelligence with creativity and genius is more theoretical than experimental. Psychologists may be able to measure intelligence, but ever since Galton's day, they have been unable to agree on even an approximate definition.

Back in 1921—as Terman was launching his study of gifted children, Cox was beginning her research on historical geniuses, and IQ tests were about to take hold of American schools—the *Journal of Educational Psychology* published a symposium, 'Intelligence and its measurement', in which 14 experts were invited to define their conceptions of intelligence. Five of them did not address the issue directly in their replies. Of the other nine answers, Terman's stood out from the rest. He said intelligence was 'the ability to carry on abstract thinking': a surprisingly narrow definition from someone interested in linking intelligence with genius. A second psychologist favoured 'the capacity for knowledge, and knowledge possessed': a definition that would probably have pleased Edison (though not Einstein). The other seven answers perhaps had more in common. They were as follows: (a) the power of good responses from the point of view of truth or fact; (b) having learned or ability to learn to adjust oneself to the environment; (c) the ability to adapt oneself adequately to relatively new situations in life; (d) the capacity to learn or to profit by experience; (e) the capacity to acquire capacity; (f) the capacity to inhibit an instinctive adjustment in the light of imaginally experienced trial and error, and the volitional capacity to realize the modified instinctive adjustment into overt behaviour to the advantage of the individual as a social animal; (g) a biological mechanism by which the effects of a complexity of stimuli are brought together and given a somewhat unified effect in behaviour. Varied as these nine definitions were, all of them involved the capacity to learn from experience, and adaptation to one's environment. None, though, mentioned any connection between intelligence and creativity. With the possible exception of Terman's idea of abstract thinking, the experts' emphasis was firmly on intelligence as something reactive, rather than creative.

Almost a century later, the diversity of views about intelligence persists. 'Innumerable tests are available for measuring intelligence, yet no one is quite certain of what intelligence is, or even of just what it is that the available tests are measuring', wrote Robert Sternberg, a leading researcher in the field, in 1987. Another well-known researcher, James Flynn, admits this, too. But his own beguiling book, *What is Intelligence?*, published in 2007, does not clarify the confusion very much. Flynn compares the debate over the nature of intelligence to the old debate in physics about the nature of light, settled (sort of) by the advent of quantum theory and the concept of wave-particle duality. 'Much time was wasted before it was realized that light could act like a wave in certain of its manifestations and like a stream of particles in other manifestations. We have to realize that intelligence can act like a highly correlated set of abilities on one level and like a set of functionally independent abilities on other levels', says Flynn. These levels are: the brain's neural clusters, individual differences in performance, and society. This sounds promising, but then Flynn adds, honestly if not too helpfully: 'We are a long way from integrating what is known on these three levels into one body of theory'.

His research does offer some clues, though. It cannot tell us anything directly about exceptional creativity, but it sheds new light on the slippery concept of IQ, and why it caused Cox so much trouble in her study. It may also explain why Feynman's IQ, measured around 1930, was rather lower than we might have expected for so brilliant an intellect.

In the mid-1980s, Flynn discovered an astonishing and subversive fact about mean IQ figures, which was soon widely accepted and later dubbed the 'Flynn effect' by other psychologists. In the post-war decades, mean IQ had trended steadily upwards, not just in one or two countries but in all developed countries where sufficient IQ data were available, including the United States, Britain, Belgium, The Netherlands, Norway, Israel, and Argentina. Over the second half of the century, some two generations, mean IQ had grown by almost 20 points in the United States and Europe. Other, less reliable, data suggested that the growth went back to 1900, and that the mean IQ in 1900, scored against current norms, would have been somewhere between 50 and 70—in other words, mentally retarded.

The picture is further complicated by the fact that the rise is not equally spread among the various components of intelligence tests that are aver-aged together to give a single IQ: the changes in different abilities do not correlate well. Essentially, without going into details, young people have got much smarter on tests that measure the ability to compare and classify concepts, whether in words or pictures, but they have shown almost no improvement in their vocabulary, general knowledge, and arithmetical ability. Between 1947 and 2002, Americans gained 24 points on tests for the first skill, four points on vocabulary tests, and just two points on general knowledge and arithmetic tests.

All this was wholly unexpected, because IQ tests are normalized by testing an age cohort at regular intervals, in order that the mean IQ will remain the same from generation to generation. Without such normalization, some individuals will receive obsolete tests and be compared not with their contemporaries but with a previous generation. The puzzling rise in mean IQ suggests that, in Flynn's words: 'Either the children of today [are] far brighter than their parents or, at least in some circumstances, IQ tests [are] not good measures of intelligence'.

His tantalizing discovery has generated a lot of discussion, and there is, as yet, no consensus on the reason for the rise in mean IQ. Obviously, more and more children went on from school to college and university in the twentieth century, which must have some relevance to IQ. Also evident is that each new generation acquires skills, such as computing, that challenge the intelligence of their parents. Undoubtedly, too, there has been a continuing rise in the amount of information available to the average person, which may have affected abilities that form part of intelligence. 'The ability to improve working memory through training might well be the key to understanding the entire Flynn effect', speculates the neuroscientist Torkel Klingberg in *The Overflowing Brain*. Flynn himself puts the rise in IQ mainly down to what he calls increasing adoption of 'scientific spectacles', which allow us to compare and classify concepts easily. 'During the twentieth century, people invested their intelligence in the solution of new cognitive problems. Formal education played a proximate causal role but a full appreciation of causes involves grasping the total impact of the industrial revolution'.

To express the issue raised by Flynn another way, it appears that Feynman's school-tested IQ (circa 1930) might have been more like 150–55, rather than 125, were he to have been tested today. As for the geniuses in Cox's study, such as Shakespeare and Faraday, who belong to the period before 1900, their 'fossil IQs' would seem to have required correction for rather more than just her lack of information about their early years. The debate about the relationship between high intelligence and exceptional creativity continues to churn.

CHAPTER 3

STRANGERS TO OURSELVES

There are theologians like St. Thomas Aquinas, mystics like Jacob Brehme, physicians like Paracelsus, astronomers like Kepler, writers and poets like Dante, Cervantes, Shakespeare, and Montaigne; by all of these the importance of the unconscious was taken for granted.

H. J. Eysenck, *Genius: The Natural History of Creativity*, 1995

Without our unconscious mind—those complex mental activities that proceed without our awareness—we would find it difficult to survive. Mundane, automatic, acts like walking along, riding a bicycle, or driving a car, would require conscious decisions about, say, whether to put our left or right foot forward first. Even the swallowing of food would need to be consciously monitored to avoid choking, as would the very act of breathing to avoid suffocation—when asleep, as well as when awake. Those unfortunates who suffer from the very rare disorder known as congenital central hypoventilation syndrome, as a result of which they lack autonomic control of their breathing, are at risk of respiratory arrest during sleep. The syndrome is also known as 'Undine's curse' after a water fairy, Undine, who discovered her mortal lover, a knight, in the act of adultery. At the time she had married him, he had sworn he would be faithful to her with his every waking breath. Now Undine cursed him such that when he fell asleep, he would forget to breathe; eventually he became exhausted, nodded off, and thereby suffocated to death.

We would also have almost no memory without our unconscious mind, since memories must subsist there, given that in the present moment we are aware of only a tiny fraction of all that we know and require conscious acts of mental recollection to access our unconscious store of knowledge. Most likely we would not be able to dream, either, as dreaming seems to be intimately linked to memory. And probably creativity would desert us, too, if the theory that new ideas are created out of the combination of unconscious with conscious ideas is true, as is widely accepted. It is the undetected and seemingly unexpected intervention of unconscious processing that is believed to be responsible for 'this whole business of creation', the familiar but enigmatic sensation expressed in the preface by Satyajit Ray: that 'the best ideas come at moments when you're not even thinking of it'. The unconscious mind, though it constantly influences us, makes us strangers to ourselves, since we can never observe its elusive workings in detail except by inference—in our dreams or via Freud's well-known slips of the tongue.

Freud is often credited with the discovery of the unconscious mind, around the period when he published *The Interpretation of Dreams* in 1899. But in fact the concept long predated Freud, rather as the concept of evolution predated Darwin's thinking in the decades leading up to *On the Origin of Species*. In 1868, when Freud was only a boy, Eduard von Hartmann published a three-volume *Philosophy of the Unconscious: Speculative Results according to the Inductive Method of Physical Science*, in German. Although the book was neither good philosophy nor good science, it went through nine editions and was soon translated into French and English, and was widely reviewed, such was the currency of the concept of the unconscious in the mid-nineteenth century. Von Hartmann discussed 26 aspects of unconscious mental activity in man, as well as the origins of thought about the unconscious, which date back to the time of René Descartes in the seventeenth century. Indeed, 'the idea of unconscious mental processes was, in many of its aspects, conceivable around 1700, topical around 1800, and became effective around 1900, thanks to the imaginative efforts of a large number of individuals of varied interests in many lands', writes Lancelot Law Whyte in *The Unconscious before Freud*.

Descartes's distinction between mind and matter, in his *Discourse* of 1637, and his definition of mind as awareness, provoked the discovery of the unconscious mind in Europe. For if Descartes's dualism was to be accepted, then mind would have to involve more than awareness. On its own, awareness could not explain the many aspects of mental activity mentioned above that evidently continue without awareness.

Thus, in the second half of the seventeenth century, Newton, not wanting to be bothered to give a mathematical proof of an assertion, was content to state that: 'It is plain to me by the fountain I draw it from.' A. A. Cooper, the third earl of Shaftesbury, observed: 'One would think, there was nothing easier for us, than to know our own minds...But our thoughts have generally such an obscure implicit language, that it is the hardest thing in the world to make them speak out distinctly.' And according to Leibniz, ordinary perceptions emerged from countless smaller perceptions of which we cannot be aware, because they lie below a quantitative threshold. (One might compare our ordinary perception of the macroscopic structure of a physical object, which is made up of atoms invisible to the naked eye.) Leibniz also considered that these small, 'unconscious' perceptions constitute a wider field than those of which we are aware.

By about 1700, says Whyte, a tentative concept of the unconscious mind had come into existence, incorporating habitual activities, memory, perception, ideas, sleep, dreams, insight, the threshold of consciousness, and the birth of myth. Still to come were: 'the link with instinct, will, and the emotions; the frequency of dissociation, conflict, and distortion; the connection with pathology, techniques for investigation, and the application to therapy'. These were introduced between 1700 and the time of Freud: by the Romantics, such as Byron and Coleridge, who sought in the unconscious a link with universal powers; by writers and philosophers, such as Arthur Schopenhauer, who were influenced by non-dualistic Eastern traditions of a pervasive unity between mind and matter; by biologists, such as Darwin, who supplied an evolutionary explanation for unconscious motives; and by psychologists, such as William James, who looked for a continuity underlying transient moments of awareness through his theory of a 'stream of consciousness'.

One of those influenced by the concept of the unconscious at this time was the mathematician Henri Poincaré, whose work between about 1880 and his premature death in 1912 established him as one of the great mathematicians of any age. Originally trained as a mining engineer, he also distinguished himself in branches of science other than mathematics. Poincaré received the unique honour of being elected a member of the French Academy of Sciences in all five of its different disciplines, as well as a member of its fellow Academy in the arts for his literary flair as a writer on science and philosophy. Poincaré's *Science and Hypothesis* stimulated the young Einstein while he was pondering his 1905 theory of special relativity. Later, Poincaré recommended Einstein for a professorship as 'one of the most original minds I have known', adding that: 'As he searches in all directions, one must...expect the majority of the paths on which he embarks will be dead ends.' But it is for his seminal remarks on his own creative process, published in French in 1908 and in English shortly after his death in a collection of his writings known as *The Foundations of Science*, that Poincaré is regarded as a key source by psychologists of creativity.

'Other mathematicians have recorded the role of the unconscious in their creative work, but Poincaré's complete confidence in the power of his unconscious mind seems unparalleled', write the psychiatrist Michael Fitzgerald and the mathematician Ioan James in their study, *The Mind of the Mathematician*. They quote the striking description of Poincaré's individual style of thinking written by his philosopher nephew:

> It was often observed that Henri Poincaré kept his thoughts to himself. Unlike certain other scientists, he did not believe that oral communication, the verbal exchange of ideas, could favour discovery ... my uncle regarded mathematical discovery as an idea which entirely excluded the possibility of collaboration. The intuition, by which discoveries are made, is a direct communion, without possible intermediaries, with the spirit and the truth ... He thought in the street as he went to the Sorbonne, while he was attending some scientific meeting or while he was taking one of his habitual grand walks after lunch. He thought in his antechamber or in the hall of meetings at the institute, while he walked with little steps, his physiognomy tense, shaking a bunch of keys. He thought at the dinner table at family get-togethers, even in the sitting room, interrupting himself; often brusquely in the midst of a conversation.

To understand Poincaré's own illuminating account of his mathematical thinking in the early 1880s, it is necessary to quote him at some length. Although he uses occasional technical expressions, he himself regards them as unimportant to the non-mathematical reader, and notes, without exaggeration, that one can understand the circumstances of his discoveries without understanding anything about the theorems. He writes:

> For fifteen days I strove to prove that there could not be any functions like those I have since called Fuchsian functions. I was then very ignorant; every day I seated myself at my work-table, stayed an hour or two, tried a great number of combinations, and reached no results. One evening, contrary to my custom, I drank black coffee and could not sleep. Ideas rose in crowds; I felt them collide until pairs interlocked, so to speak, making a stable combination. By the next morning I had established the existence of a class of Fuchsian functions, those which come from the hyper-geometric series; I had only to write out the results, which took but a few hours ...

Next, Poincaré describes three mathematical breakthroughs:

> Just at this time I left Caen, where I was then living, to go on a geological excursion under the auspices of the school of mines. The changes of travel

made me forget my mathematical work. Having reached Coutances, we entered an omnibus to go some place or other. At the moment when I put my foot on the step the idea came to me, without anything in my former thoughts seeming to have paved the way for it, that the transformations I had used to define the Fuchsian functions were identical with those of non-Euclidean geometry. I did not verify the idea; I should not have had time, as upon taking my seat in the omnibus, I went on with a conversation already commenced, but I felt a perfect certainty. On my return to Caen, for conscience's sake I verified the result at my leisure.

Then I turned my attention to the study of some arithmetical questions apparently without much success and without a suspicion of any connection with my preceding researches. Disgusted with my failure, I went to spend a few days at the seaside, and thought of something else. One morning, walking on the bluff, the idea came to me, with just the same characteristics of brevity, suddenness, and immediate certainty, that the arithmetical transformations of indeterminate ternary quadratic forms were identical with those of non-Euclidean geometry.

Returned to Caen, I meditated on this result and deduced the consequences...that...there existed Fuchsian functions other than those from the hyper-geometric series, the ones I then knew. Naturally I set myself to form these functions. I made a systematic attack upon them and carried all the outworks, one after another. There was one, however, that still held out, whose fall would involve that of the whole place. But all my efforts only served at first the better to show me the difficulty, which indeed was something. All this work was perfectly conscious.

Thereupon I left for Mont-Valérien, where I was to go through my military service; so I was very differently occupied. One day, going along the street, the solution of the difficulty which had stopped me suddenly appeared to me. I did not try to go deep into it immediately, and only after my service did I again take up the question. I had all the elements and had only to arrange them and put them together. So I wrote out my final memoir at a single stroke and without difficulty.

Reflecting on the above three flashes of insight, Poincaré explicitly introduces the role of unconscious processing:

Most striking at first is this appearance of sudden illumination, a manifest sign of long, unconscious prior work. The role of this unconscious work in mathematical invention appears to me incontestable...Often when one works at a hard question, nothing good is accomplished at the first attack. Then one takes a rest, longer or shorter, and sits down anew to the work. During the first half-hour, as before, nothing is found, and then all of a sudden the decisive idea presents itself to the mind. It might be said that the conscious work has been more fruitful because it has been interrupted and the rest has given back to the mind its force and freshness. But it is more probable that this rest has been filled out with unconscious work and that the result of this work has afterwards revealed itself to the geometer just as in the cases I have cited.

What exactly persuaded Poincaré that unconscious processing had solved these problems, rather than his conscious attack on them? First and foremost was the unforgettable impression of 'suddenness': the solutions popped into awareness out 'of the blue', as opposed to being gradually derived, step by conscious step. In support of this, he says he was not consciously thinking about mathematics during any of the three breakthroughs; and he implies that nothing in his physical surroundings—climbing onto an omnibus, walking on the cliffs above the sea, crossing the street in military uniform—could have provided any stimulus. Second, there was his 'immediate certainty': the conviction that the solution was correct, without his having to verify it. Of course, he could have been wrong—strong conviction is certainly no guarantee of a scientist's correctness—and so verification was necessary; but so strong was the conviction that he felt no urgency about verification. Third, there was the fact that the solutions appeared only after a conscious 'systematic attack' had failed. In no case did they arise by sheer accident: instead, the more ideas Poincaré generated, the better was his chance of producing a solution. This made sense to him, on the basis of his mental experience of having a rush of ideas after drinking black coffee (though in that instance, it is worth noting, he does not claim any role for unconscious processing).

Poincaré was persuaded, but should we be? His sleepless vision of colliding ideas interlocking to form a stable combination is reminiscent of the chemist August Kekulé's sleepy reverie of dancing chains of atoms forming rings, discussed in the introduction. We know that Kekulé's account of his discovery of the benzene ring, however honest, is seriously incomplete, because the idea of the ring was already in his mind long before he dozed. Poincaré in 1908, like Kekulé in 1890, was recalling events a quarter of a century after they occurred. Maybe he, too, forgot some preparatory steps in his thinking and misremembered his precise circumstances.

One significant clue that this may have been so comes from his nephew's description of Poincaré. As he says, wherever his uncle happened to be—at a scientific meeting, taking a walk, crossing the street, sitting at the dinner table—he was always thinking. If this was true of the older family man, it seems yet more likely to be the case for the bachelor Poincaré in his twenties. Invited by a mathematician friend, who excitedly demonstrated a new theorem to him before dinner, the young Poincaré ate his meal in silence like an automaton, then after dinner proved the theorem wrong on the spot. Very probably, he thought regularly about mathematics, however irrelevant his setting: whether on a geological excursion, holidaying by the seaside, or on military service. No doubt his focus on such occasions was less intense than when he was concentrating at his worktable, but his mind surely still played with concepts and equations. When looking back more than two decades, he may easily have failed to recall all of the ideas that were consciously preying on his mind around the time of his 'sudden illuminations'.

A second clue comes from Poincaré's own doubt about whether the resting and refreshing of his mind, or the letting of the unconscious have its way during the period of rest, was the more responsible for his successes. He thinks the latter explanation 'more probable'—implicating unconscious processing—but he offers no evidence for this assertion.

Given Poincaré's unquestioned stature in mathematics and science, however, most psychologists have taken his self-reports at face value, and have been highly influenced by them in studying creativity outside of mathematics. Examples include Graham Wallas in *The Art of Thought* (1926), Arthur Koestler in *The Act of Creation* (1964), and Dean Keith Simonton in *Origins of Genius* (1999), all of whom accept Poincaré's intuition that creativity emerges from the combination of unconscious and conscious ideas.

Wallas, drawing on the writings of Poincaré, Hermann von Helmholtz, and other highly creative individuals, postulated a four-stage creative process. Wallas's model consists of preparation, incubation, illumination, and verification. Preparation is a conscious activity, involving the thinker's immersion in the problem and attempts at solutions. If the attempts fail, the problem is put aside. Incubation then occurs, as the unconscious mind continues to work on the problem, while the conscious mind is otherwise occupied. In due course a combination of an unconscious idea with a conscious one produces the experience of sudden illumination. In other words, the egg hatches, giving birth to a new idea. Finally, this idea must be tested for its validity by a process of verification.

Neat as it is, the Wallas model does not survive laboratory testing. Studies of it are tricky to design. For example, the experimenter cannot expose a subject to a problem, and then compel the subject only to incubate the problem rather than to think consciously about a solution; neither can the presence of unconscious processing be detected except by conscious means. The favoured approach has been to ask a group of artists and a control group of non-artists to create a picture in response to a poem. Working sketches, diaries, and observation of the two groups show that they do not tackle the task in the same four-stage order, as expected by the model; also that the four hypothesized stages blend into each other, so that they cannot be distinguished. Illumination, for example, may not occur; an idea may enter consciousness gradually.

As for incubation, comparisons of a group requested to take a break from a problem with a control group asked to work without interruption on the same problem, have been inconclusive. The assumption was, that if taking a break improved performance, then incubation must have occurred during the break. 'The results from laboratory studies of incubation are at most mixed', writes Robert Weisberg, who is sceptical about the reality of unconscious processing, in his wide-ranging survey of creativity research published in 2006. 'It has been extremely difficult to demonstrate consistently within a single study even that taking a break facilitates problem solving, so one never gets to the question of whether unconscious processing might be the cause of that facilitation.'

If unconscious processing is hard to study scientifically, even harder to investigate is the role of dreams in creativity. As everyone knows from personal experience, dreams resist definition. In *The Oxford Book of Dreams*, editor Stephen Brook notes that he began work by scouring the world's literatures for interesting dreams, and then tried to sort them according to definitions and criteria. But he soon abandoned such classification and resorted instead to categorization by content. 'For instance, how exactly does one distinguish, even in literature, between dream, daydream, hallucination, and reverie?' Kekulé's dream snakes could belong in any of these four categories.

There is no difficulty in studying the physiology of dreaming with various techniques that measure eye movement and the metabolic activity of the brain, as well as the effects on dreaming of drugs (like L-Dopa) and damage to different parts of the brain. For some decades after the discovery in 1953 of REM (Rapid Eye Movement) sleep and its clear connection with dreaming, it looked as if dreaming was simply the result of oscillating brain chemicals and had nothing to do with thoughts in the mind. 'The content of dreams may be totally devoid of "meaning"...they may just be noise', wrote the immunologist (and Nobel laureate) Peter Medawar in 1964.

More recently, however, it has become clear that dreams occur in non-REM sleep, too, and therefore that the REM state is not the physiological equivalent of the dream state. L-Dopa can enhance the frequency and vividness of dreams massively, without having any effect on REM sleep. 'The current neuroscientific evidence gives us every reason to take seriously the radical hypothesis'—first proposed by Freud in 1899—'that dreams are motivated phenomena, driven by our wishes', writes the neuroscientist and psychoanalyst Mark Solms.

Subjects can of course report their dreams when they become conscious again, at least to some extent. The real problem comes with the fact that dreaming can never be manipulated in the laboratory towards creative activities, because a subject who is dreaming cannot consciously take part in an experiment. To study dreams and creativity, psychologists are obliged, therefore, to depend on self-reports by exceptionally creative individuals. We shall look at two crucial examples of dreams: one by a poet, Coleridge, which appears not to be genuine, the other by a scientist, Otto Loewi, which provides solider evidence for unconscious processing than Kekulé's dream.

In 1797, Coleridge wrote the poem 'Kubla Khan: Or, A Vision in a Dream', beginning with its celebrated lines:

> In Xanadu did Kubla Khan
> A stately pleasure-dome decree:
> Where Alph, the sacred river, ran
> Through caverns measureless to man
> Down to a sunless sea.

Since the poem was only a fragment, 'a psychological curiosity' according to Coleridge, he prefaced it with the following explanation of its genesis when it first appeared in print in 1816, at the urging of his friend Byron:

In the summer of the year 1797, the Author, then in ill health, had retired to a lonely farm house between Porlock and Linton, on the Exmoor confines of Somerset and Devonshire. In consequence of a slight indisposition, an anodyne had been prescribed, from the effect of which he fell asleep in his chair at the moment that he was reading the following sentence, or words of the same substance, in *Purchas's Pilgrimage*: 'Here the Khan Kubla commanded a palace to be built, and a stately garden thereunto: and thus ten miles of fertile ground were inclosed in a wall.' The author continued for about three hours in a profound sleep, at least of the external senses, during which time he has the most vivid confidence, that he could not have composed less than two or three hundred lines; if that indeed can be called composition in which all the images rose up before him as things, with a parallel production of the correspondent expressions, without any sensation of consciousness of effort. On awaking he appeared to himself to have a distinct recollection of the whole, and taking his pen, ink, and paper, instantly and eagerly wrote down the lines that are here preserved. At this moment he was unfortunately called out by a person on business from Porlock, and detained by him above an hour, and on his return to his room, found, to his no small surprise and mortification, that though he still retained some vague and dim recollection of the general purport of the vision, yet, with the exception of some eight or ten scattered lines and images, all the rest had passed away like the images on the surface of the stream into which a stone had been cast, but, alas! without the after restoration of the latter.

Whether Coleridge was actually asleep, or in a reverie; whether he had taken opium, as was his wont, or some other drug; whether 'the person from Porlock' existed or was a convenient excuse for the failure of his imagination; indeed whether his account is essentially true or heavily Romanticized—has long been in question. The long gap between the poem's composition and its publication (almost 20 years) adds to the doubts. In 1953, the scholar Elisabeth Schneider examined all of the surviving evidence in Coleridge's manuscripts and letters, and came to the conclusion that 'Kubla Khan' was composed in a much more conventional manner, not in a dream but in various highly conscious drafts, as already mentioned in the introduction. Another Coleridge scholar, Richard Holmes, while not discounting the dream altogether, noted in 1982: 'it is difficult to accept that the chanting, hypnotic, high finished language of "Kubla Khan" is *literally* as Coleridge dreamt it'.

We cannot know for certain how important a daydream was to the making of the poem. Perhaps the best evidence comes not from the Coleridge's own account or from his manuscripts but from a letter written by John Keats to his brother after meeting Coleridge for the first time in 1819:

—I walked with him a[t] his alderman-after-dinner pace for near two Miles I suppose. In those two Miles he broached a thousand things—let me see if I can give you a list—Nightingales, Poetry—on Poetical sensation—Metaphysics—Different genera and species of Dreams—Nightmare—a dream accompanied by a sense of touch—single and double touch—A Dream related—First and second consciousness—...Monsters—the Kraken—Mermaids—southey [*sic*] believes in them—southeys [*sic*] belief too much diluted—A Ghost story...

Judging from Keats's letter, and other reports of Coleridge's far-ranging conversational style, his mind was so agile and preoccupied with dreams and fantasies that he may have drawn relatively little distinction between the dreaming and the waking state. In the words of a modern poet, Tony Harrison: 'I don't dream. I dream all day, I think that's why.'

Otto Loewi was a pharmacologist and physiologist, today mainly remembered for his contributions in the field of chemical transmission of nerve impulses. By experimenting on a pair of isolated frogs' hearts in 1920, Loewi was able to show that a chemical neurotransmitter, which he later identified as the substance acetylcholine, was involved in nerve transmission, in addition to the already understood electrical impulses. In 1936, Loewi and Henry Dale shared the Nobel Prize in physiology or medicine, 'for providing the first evidence that the signals sent across synapses from one neuron to another in the autonomic nervous system are carried by specific chemical transmitters', writes Eric Kandel, a recent Nobel laureate who works on the biochemistry of memory.

According to Loewi, he first thought of the idea of chemical neurotransmitters during a discussion with a friend in 1903. However, he was unable to think of an experiment that would test the idea, and forgot about it. In the meantime, in 1918, he designed an experiment for quite different purposes using two frogs' hearts, which he kept beating in salt solutions in order to discover whether or not they emitted any chemical substance. He published the results in the scientific literature.

Two years later, he had a dream, which he carefully described in 1960 as follows:

> The night before Easter Sunday of that year [1920] I awoke, turned on the light, and jotted down a few notes on a tiny slip of thin paper. Then I fell asleep again. It occurred to me at six o'clock in the morning that during the night I had written down something most important, but I was unable to decipher the scrawl. The next night, at three o'clock, the idea returned. It was the design of an experiment to determine whether or not the hypothesis of chemical transmission that I had uttered 17 years ago was correct. I got up immediately, went to the laboratory, and performed a simple experiment on a frog heart according to the nocturnal design.

In a nutshell, Loewi took one frog's heart with its nerves, and a second heart without its nerves. He then stimulated the vagus nerve of the first heart for a few minutes, causing its beats to slow down. The salt solution from this heart he then transferred to the second heart, and its beats too slowed

down, even though it had no vagus nerve. A chemical emitted into the salt
solution by the nerves in the first heart had to be capable of acting on the
second heart. The same was true when Loewi repeated the experiment, this
time accelerating the beat of the first heart, and then the beat of the second
heart.

He concluded:

> The story of this discovery shows that an idea may sleep for decades in the
> unconscious mind and then suddenly return. Further, it indicates that we
> should sometimes trust a sudden intuition without too much scepticism. If
> carefully considered in the daytime, I would undoubtedly have rejected the
> kind of experiment I performed. It would have seemed likely that any
> transmitting agent released by a nervous impulse would be in an amount
> just sufficient to influence the effector organ. It would seem improbable
> that an excess that could be detected would escape into the fluid which
> filled the heart. It was good fortune that at that moment of the hunch I did
> not think but acted immediately.

Thus, in Loewi's case, it seems clear that an unconscious idea (his 1903 theory)
was combined with a conscious idea (arising from his 1918 experiment) in
a dream to create a new and highly significant idea. While we have only
his own word for the dream experience, the sequence of his thoughts is backed
up by his published record, and there seems little reason—unlike Kekulé's
dream (or for that matter Coleridge's dream)—to doubt the centrality of
Loewi's dream to his discovery. That said, it remains almost unique in the
annals of science. A century after Poincaré, the working of unconscious
processing in exceptional creativity is still, fundamentally, an enigma awaiting
a satisfactory explanation.

CHAPTER 4

BLUE REMEMBERED
WEDNESDAYS

For scientists, savant talents constitute a challenge. How can individuals who are so impaired in their general mental functioning that they need to be looked after by others, nevertheless show specific skills in one domain that are spectacularly better than those possessed by most individuals of high intelligence? What do the answers tell us about mental functioning generally and what light is thrown on the nature of the disorder, autism, that constitutes this background? ... For specialists in the areas for which the talents are shown, the skills raise questions on the very basis of their speciality. Do the talents of a musical savant have anything in common with the creative precocity of, say, Mozart? Have the spectacular drawing skills of artistic savants any connections with creative painting? What have calendar savants' talents got to do with 'real' mathematics?

Michael Rutter, in his foreword to Beate Hermelin's *Bright Splinters of the Mind: A Personal Story of Research with Autistic Savants*, 2001

T he word savant originally referred to a learned person, generally a distinguished scientist, epitomized by the brilliant and far-ranging French scholars, such as the mathematician Joseph Fourier who accompanied Napoleon Bonaparte's expedition to Egypt two centuries ago. Today, in striking contrast, 'savant' is normally applied to individuals of below-average IQ—formerly known as 'idiot savants'—who display an amazing untutored talent, often involving inexplicable feats of memory, in a restricted field such as calendrical or arithmetical calculation, foreign language learning, music, or art. At first glance, the old meaning of 'savant' and the current one seem quite unrelated, but they have more in common than might appear. Savant syndrome, as it is now defined, cuts across talent, intelligence, creativity, and genius, as well as psychopathology and unconscious processing, and raises puzzling questions about the human mind to which there are as yet no clear answers.

Among the wide variety of savants studied by the experimental psychologist Beate Hermelin and colleagues in her recent book *Bright Splinters of the Mind*, are Christopher, a linguistic savant; Noel, a musical savant; and Richard, an artistic savant. (Full names are deliberately withheld by Hermelin.) To describe them briefly will show how intriguing savant syndrome is.

When Christopher's intelligence was tested at the age of fourteen, his IQ on perceptual-spatial problems was comparable to that of an eight year old, in other words an IQ of 57, whereas his verbal IQ tested just below 100 (the average for his age, by definition). He briefly attended an ordinary school, but could not cope with class work and eventually went to live in a sheltered community, where he took up gardening. Though not formally diagnosed as autistic, he demonstrated autistic behaviour, such as avoiding eye contact with others and seldom showing any strong emotions about anything, unless it concerned language learning. Here, uniquely, he was full of enthusiasm. He could understand, talk, read, write, and translate from Danish, Finnish, French, German, Greek, Hindi, Italian, Norwegian, Polish, Portuguese, Russian, Spanish, Swedish, Turkish, and Welsh; and he was keen to acquire further languages.

Noel had an IQ of 57, when tested at 19, and showed almost no capacity for spontaneous speech. At a school for children with severe learning difficulties, he made no contact with other children, and after leaving this school, he was admitted to a residential centre for people with autism. He had no formal training in music, and no musical instrument at home, only access to a piano at school, on which he would play by ear music that he had obsessively memorized at home by listening to the radio. Yet, he was able to give his testers an almost note-perfect rendering of a harmonically complex 64-bar piano composition by Edvard Grieg, 'Melody' (Opus 47 No. 3), only twelve minutes after hearing it for the first time, plus a second, near perfect performance after a gap of 24 hours during which he did not hear the piece again. Noel was far more accurate than a professional pianist who had encountered the piece for the first time too: Noel played 798 notes, of which only eight per cent were wrong, as compared with only 354 notes played by the professional pianist, of which 80 per cent were wrong.

Richard, when aged eleven, was found to have a reasoning ability similar to that of a normal three and a half year old; a later test gave a verbal IQ of

47 and a non-verbal IQ of 55. Severely physically handicapped from an early age and extremely myopic, he never played with toys or with other children, and lived at home with his devoted parents. However, he showed artistic talent at the age of four, using oil-based crayons on paper, drawing mainly landscapes, either from photographs or from memory. Over the years he held open exhibitions of his paintings in many countries, often attended by himself and his father, and his work was sold to a wide audience. 'To the question why a mentally handicapped autistic individual with severely impaired vision should enthusiastically pursue the creation of pictures, there is of course no conclusive answer', comments Hermelin.

Clearly, these three savants are remarkable people. In a sense, despite their below-average IQs, they should be called 'talented', or even 'gifted', like the participants selected in the 1920s by Lewis Terman for his Stanford University study of high-IQ children. For example, they fit pretty well the three criteria for giftedness laid down by the psychologist Ellen Winner in her study *Gifted Children*. They were 'precocious' in their chosen domain (languages, music, or art), that is, they developed in their domain well ahead of the achievement expected at their age. Second, they showed 'an insistence on marching to their own drummer', by mostly teaching themselves in their own way without much help from adults. Third, they had 'a rage to master': an intense and obsessive motivation to acquire a particular skill. As Winner observes: 'Gifted children, especially the extreme ones we call prodigies'—such as Mozart (though not Einstein or any of the other eight geniuses in Part II, with the possible exception of Champollion)—'are far more like savants than like hard-working but otherwise normal children'.

Yet, at the same time, the three savants fit the three main diagnostic criteria for autism defined as a disorder by the cognitive psychologist Uta Frith in her book *Autism: Explaining the Enigma*, following the recommendations of the influential *Diagnostic and Statistical Manual* of the American Psychiatric Association. Relative to their developmental level, judged by their age, Christopher, Noel, and Richard showed all three of the following abnormal behaviours: a qualitative impairment in reciprocal social interaction, for example, a lack of personal relationships; a qualitative impairment in verbal and non-verbal communication, such as a delay in the acquisition of language or a lack of varied, spontaneous, make-believe play; and a markedly restricted repertoire of activities and interests, which related almost exclusively to their focus on developing their particular talent.

Autism (the word derives from the Greek word *autos*, meaning 'self'), like talent and giftedness, is not well defined in psychology. Indeed, some psychologists view autism as too diverse a phenomenon to be properly defined, including as it does both savants and the occasional Nobel Prize winner—even perhaps some aspects of Einstein's behaviour, such as his lack of interest in personal relationships, as well as fictional characters like the detective Sherlock Holmes, the monster Frankenstein, and the *Star Trek* spaceman Mr Spock. Hence the fact that it is now often known not as just 'autism' but as 'autism spectrum conditions' (ASC). These cover: 'classical' autism, as first defined in the United States by Leo Kanner in 1943; Asperger's syndrome, defined in Germany by Hans Asperger in 1944; high-functioning autism, which is similar but not identical to Asperger's; and a last catch-all category known as pervasive developmental disorder—not otherwise specified (PDD-NOS).

There is much uncertainty, too, about what proportion of autistic individuals can be said to be savants, since robust epidemiological data do not exist. Frith suggests that about ten per cent of autistic individuals have 'areas of excellence...not counting unusual rote memory skills', and her close collaborator Francesca Happé agrees with this, on the basis of 'estimates from surveys of parents and carers'. Hermelin, however, thinks that one in ten is likely to be too generous, arguing for less than one per cent: 'one or two in 200 of those within the autistic spectrum disorder can justifiably be regarded as having a genuine talent'. What is not in doubt, is that the proportion of the talented is much higher in ASC than in other developmental or intellectual disabilities (for instance, attention deficit hyperactivity disorder)—a fact that has led to some intensive research and much theorizing as to why this should be so. Why should the below-average IQ, combined with the narrow focus, of most autistic individuals have any connection with extraordinary talent?

Some clue may lie in the reaction of an autistic person to a well-known French painting of c. 1635, *The Cheat with the Ace of Diamonds* by Georges de la Tour, which appears on the cover of Frith's book and is discussed in her text. (See next page.) The normal person's response to this work is to try to read the minds of the four people, and construct a drama out of their situation. The cards (including the ace of diamonds) held behind the back of the gentleman on the left show that he is cheating. The eyes of the seated lady in the centre and the standing servant woman, who both look askance at the man, lead the viewer to infer that both of these women know that the man is cheating.

In addition, the lady gestures at him with her hand. But it is not clear from his own averted gaze whether or not the man knows that the lady knows he is cheating. The young gentleman on the right, seated in front of his money, placidly contemplating his cards, seems from his expression to be unaware of the cheating. The viewer is therefore kept in suspense as to the card players' next move. Perhaps the lady will challenge the cheat? Or maybe she will collude with him to gain advantage over the young man? Or possibly the young man will spot the cheating in time? 'The painter has led us to make only some attributions of mental states but he leaves the outcome open', comments Frith.

Then, she reports the startlingly opposed reaction of a young woman with high-functioning autism, A. C., who wrote to her after reading the discussion in her book. By e-mail, A. C. commented:

> On the cover of your book there's a picture of some people playing cards. I remember looking at the picture for something like an hour, figuring out how smooth the pigments of the paints the artist [used] had to be, and the quality of brushes, and how greatly developed the sub-economy at that time must have been to demand that quality of painting and of reproduction of the actual textures of the fabrics in the characters' clothes, and of course this is the most obvious thing about the painting, the high realism and the skill of the artist, and then I read inside the book, and I was like, What the hell?

There's this whole 'soap opera' that the 'normal' person is supposed to pick on first, and this person cheating, and that person knows, and that other person doesn't, etc. it's nuts!

The conclusion Frith draws from this alternative analysis is that people with autistic spectrum conditions do not automatically think about mental states—in her word they do not 'mentalize'. In fact they find this normal view of the world abnormal, rather as colour-blind people cannot really imagine how other people see the world in colour. 'In this sense they are mind-blind. Of course, it is just as difficult for us to imagine what it is like to be mind-blind as it is for the autistic person to imagine what it is like to be a mind-reader', writes Frith. 'The example provided by A. C. suggests that mind-blindness should not be seen in a purely negative light. It is at least debatable which is more appropriate when looking at a painting: creating a soap opera or deriving an objective analysis of the physical features of the painting?' Abstract art, of course, offers all of us—the non-autistic and the autistic viewer—only the second option.

There is a consensus among autism researchers that mind-blindness lies at the heart of ASC, because it accounts well for the impaired and the intact social and communicative behaviour of autistic individuals. 'They treated people as if they were things', Kanner observed in his initial diagnosis of the condition. For example, an autistic child may step on another child on the floor, treating him or her as a lifeless object, because the autistic child has no ability to mentalize: to imagine that the second child may have a mind like its own. He may also respond literally to a question like 'Can you pass the salt?' by saying merely 'Yes', without understanding the implied meaning of the question.

There is much less agreement as to why mind-blindness should predispose autistic individuals to be talented. In a survey published in 2009, Happé and a collaborator reviewed three possibilities.

'First, it might be argued that individuals with ASC free up both mental and time resources that so-called "neurotypicals" use on tracking and remembering social content, and that these may contribute to talent development', the authors write. 'If reallocation of neural and cognitive resources from social to other (savant-skill relevant) processing explains the association between ASC and talent, we might expect an inverse correlation between social interest and savant talent within ASC, and perhaps within the general population.' Put simply, the less extraverted an autistic person is, the more likely he is to be a savant, as suggested by the stereotype of eccentric geniuses or artists unaware of those around them. But there is little evidence to support this correlation, and no evidence of a causal direction. As the authors caution: 'those with exceptional talent may find it harder to find similar peers with whom to make close friendships, or may have to spend time in practice that limits socializing hours'.

'Second, difficulty tracking the mental states of others may contribute to the *originality* expressed in a developing talent.' Undoubtedly, peer pressure can stifle original thinking in children, through the influence of stereotypes, clichés, and advertising images; it is also a powerful force in the adult world, including the intellectual world. 'People with ASC, on the other hand, may be oblivious to what others think, what is considered the fashionable or correct mode of thought or how others perceive them or their work.' But if they do show originality, it does not follow that what they create is talented, in the sense of being an advance on existing thinking. As both Kanner and Asperger emphasized in their initial accounts of ASC, what is original can be simply bizarre or maladaptive. One of Kanner's autistic children, when asked to subtract four from ten, answered: 'I'll draw a hexagon.' Another was deeply perplexed as to why the history sheets for the study were all headed 'The Johns Hopkins Hospital'. Since all the histories were taken at the hospital, why was it necessary to have its name printed on every sheet?

'Third, mind-blindness for one's *own* mind may be relevant to talent development.' Self-consciousness—too great an awareness of one's working methods—can easily inhibit the production of talented work. This is one reason why many artists do not like to discuss their creativity, lest it somehow desert them. Interviews with leading performers, such as actors and sportsmen, are often surprisingly unrevealing—not merely because they do not want to give away their secrets, but also because they resist reflecting on their talent. 'If people with autism are less self-aware in some ways, this might be advantageous for those skills best developed through implicit learning... Interestingly, level of implicit learning (unlike explicit learning) is unrelated to IQ, and unimpaired in intellectually disabled groups.'

Apart from mind-blindness, there are two other widely considered theories as to why autism might predispose to talent. One of these suggests that the executive dysfunction of individuals with autism, that is the absence of top-down control that accounts for their general lack of common sense, may paradoxically help some of them to develop the narrow skills typical of savants. The other proposes that autistic individuals prefer to process information by focusing on detail rather than the whole picture, the gestalt: by beginning with the trees, rather than the wood, they are able to build up the bigger picture, rather like joining up pieces in a jigsaw puzzle without help from the picture on the box. 'In the social world there is no great benefit to a precise eye for detail', writes the autism researcher Simon Baron-Cohen, 'but in the worlds of maths, computing, cataloguing, music, linguistics, engineering, and science, such an eye for detail can lead to success rather than failure'. The success of Silicon Valley depends on the love of detail among its 'geekish' software developers.

Executive dysfunction is seen at its most extreme in dementia, where individuals lose the capacity to concentrate and are readily distracted and unable to make decisions, eventually becoming incapable of looking after themselves. It also occurs in many other clinical disorders, like attention deficit hyperactivity disorder. In autistic individuals, it manifests itself, both in life and in standard tests, in repetitive actions and speech, such as hand flapping and echolalia, and in difficulties with forward planning, shifting from old habits, and producing new responses to adapt to unexpected demands. The popular stereotype is of the absent-minded professor, cut off from the everyday world, who requires a devoted companion to look after his practical needs. Precisely how executive dysfunction might foster talent in ASC, but no talent in those with other disorders, is still largely unknown, for lack of sufficient reliable studies of individuals, although a neurological mechanism has been proposed by the neuroscientist Allan Snyder, involving reduced frontal functioning.

By contrast, focus on detail among the autistically talented is supported by a mass of evidence. The preoccupation of the autistic woman A. C. with the surface details and painterly technique of De la Tour's *The Cheat with the Ace of Diamonds*, rather than its meaning, is typical. So is the work of the amazing savant artist Stephen Wiltshire, who as a child drew the exact positions of girders lying around demolition sites as fluently as the structures and ornaments of celebrated buildings like St Paul's Cathedral. 'It is characteristic of the savant memory (in whatever sphere—visual, musical, lexical) that it is prodigiously retentive of particulars. The large and small, the trivial and momentous, may be indifferently mixed, without any sense of salience, of foreground versus background', writes the neurologist Oliver Sacks in 'Prodigies', one of his fascinating case studies of savant syndrome.

Some of the most compelling evidence about attention to detail comes from studies of children with absolute musical pitch. Hermelin, for example, compared ten boys from a school for able autistic children with ten normal children. Neither group was aware of the names of musical notes, so each note was paired with a picture of an animal, the name of which identified the note. The two groups were first familiarized with the animal note names, and then asked to identify unknown notes, minutes after familiarization, and again a week later, without further familiarization. The autistic participants identified significantly more notes than the controls, in fact more musical notes after seven days than the controls could identify after two and a half minutes.

Still more revealing was a further experiment in which the two groups were asked to disassemble musical chords. Hermelin describes the procedure:

> This time the children were shown four new pictures of different animals. They were again told that each of these animals had a favourite note. Then each of the four notes was sounded and they were told 'this is the camel's favourite note', etc. After going through this procedure several times with appropriate note/animal pairings, chords containing only three of the previously heard four notes were played. Before this, the children were told: 'You will now hear three of the four animal notes together, but this time the favourite note of one of the animals will be left out. Can you show me which animal's note is missing?' This was a difficult task, as it not only required the children to identify the three notes contained in the chord, but also to remember the one note that the chord did not contain. Nevertheless, the children with autism gave more correct responses than the control children whose performance was at chance level. The group difference proved statistically significant.

Very likely, the 19-year-old musical savant Noel, mentioned earlier, had developed his chord disassembly skill highly while listening to music on the radio, which is what enabled him to play the notes in the chords of Grieg's 'Melody' so accurately.

Musical savants cannot match the recall of musical geniuses, though. There are numerous instances of Mozart's astonishing memory. One of the most famous occurred in Rome in 1770, when he and his father visited the Sistine Chapel to hear the traditional singing of the *Miserere* during Holy Week. The score of this late Renaissance work by Gregorio Allegri had been kept secret by the Vatican musicians on pain of excommunication. The fourteen-year-old Mozart copied it down overnight from memory and (according to his devoted sister Nannerl) returned the following day with his copy under his hat, so as to make a discrete check that it was note perfect.

With numbers, however, the savants rival or even excel great mathematicians in calculating skill. 'Lightning calculators' whose feats have been described in the literature include Thomas Fuller, Jedediah Buxton, Zerah Colburn, Johann Martin Zacharias Dase, Henri Mondeux, Vito Mangiamele, Jacques Inaudi, Pericles Diamondi, and Shakuntala Devi, an Indian and one of the few women. Many have come from humble backgrounds and were probably autistic: Fuller was a slave in eighteenth-century Virginia; Buxton a simple-minded labourer; and Colburn the son of a carpenter; the boy's calculating ability was discovered in 1810 by his father when he overheard the five-year-old Zerah multiplying numbers while playing among the wood shavings in the family workshop. According to a survey by F. D. Mitchell, 'skill in mathematical calculation is… independent of general education; the mathematical prodigy may be illiterate or even densely stupid, or he may be an all-round prodigy, and veritable genius'. Although the methods of lightning calculators vary, so far as they can be understood, calculators are usually divided into two groups: the so-called early/auditory and the late/visual, according to the age at which they develop—before, or after, they learn written numeration—and how they represent numbers mentally. 'Auditory calculators "hear" the numbers in their heads when calculating, and their calculation is often associated with some verbalization or exaggerated motor activity', write Fitzgerald and James in *The Mind of the Mathematician*. 'By contrast, visual calculators "see" the numbers mentally and stay relatively quiet while calculating.'

Daniel Tammet, a present-day savant with Asperger's, belongs to the second group, and is one of the more remarkable of lightning calculators. In 2004, at the Oxford Museum of the History of Science, he publicly recalled the number π to 22,514 decimal places over a period of 5 hours 9 minutes and 24 seconds, thereby setting a British and European record and raising money for the National Society for Epilepsy, from which condition he suffered as a child. He can also multiply and divide large numbers in his head at astonishing speed. In addition, he is able to learn languages from scratch within weeks, and has invented his own language, which he calls Mänti. In 2005, he appeared on live television in Reykjavik, conversing passably with two interviewers in Icelandic for nearly a quarter of an hour, a mere week after beginning to learn the language. Apart from Icelandic, Tammet has taught himself French, Finnish, German, Spanish, Lithuanian, Romanian, Welsh, Estonian, and Esperanto.

But perhaps the most significant aspect of Tammet's story is his articulateness. The majority of savants have been unable to explain their talent, either because their ASC means that they lack the necessary communication skills or because they do not understand it themselves, or for both reasons. (Colburn, as a child, would 'cry and be distressed', when questioned.) Tammet, on the other hand, has worked closely with neuroscientists and psychologists interested in his condition, given dozens of press interviews, and written a classic book, *Born on a Blue Day: A Memoir of Asperger's and an Extraordinary Mind*. A foreword by the psychiatrist Darold Treffert, who has spent four decades studying savants (of whom he estimates a mere 100 living examples are prodigies), informs us that: 'Such first-person explanations of savant syndrome are extremely rare, in fact nearly non-existent...Daniel, uniquely, provides an exceptionally insightful account of his mental capacities.'

The surprising opening words of the book provide a hint of how Tammet manages his memory feats with both numbers and words: 'I was born on 31 January 1979—a Wednesday. I know it was a Wednesday, because the date is blue in my mind and Wednesdays are always blue, like the number nine or the sound of loud voices arguing.' Such 'synaesthesia' takes many forms apart from 'seeing' words, symbols, and sounds; other synaesthetes hear smells, taste sounds, and hear images, for example. This neurological phenomenon, first observed by Francis Galton in the nineteenth century, but then neglected, is now of deep interest to scientists. As Simon Baron-Cohen remarks in a second foreword to *Born on a Blue Day*, Tammet's autism, combined with his synaesthesia, may together account for his rare talents in mathematics and languages. '[If] we assume they are independent, the probability of someone having both synaesthesia and autism is vanishingly small.' He speculates that Daniel's synaesthesia 'gives him a richly textured, multi-sensory form of memory, and his autism gives him the narrow focus on number and syntactic patterns'.

Tammet himself compares his relationship with numbers to the relationship most people have with language. We think of words not as separate items, but as belonging to an interconnected web of words. 'When someone gives me a number, I immediately visualize it and how it relates to other numbers', he says. The particular colours and textures of numbers are crucial to his memorizing and manipulating of numbers in lightning calculation. He gives an example: 'For me, the ideal lumpy number is 37. It's like porridge. So 111, a very pretty number, which is 3 times 37, is lumpy but it is also round. It takes on the properties of both 37 and 3, which is round.' In general, he says, 'When I multiply two numbers together, I see two shapes. The image starts to change and evolve, and a third shape emerges. That's the answer. It's mental imagery. It's like maths without having to think.'

This fluid process sounds somewhat like the creative collaboration between unconscious and conscious processing described by the mathematician Poincaré in the previous chapter, and it may be relevant that Poincaré had some synaesthesia: he saw the letters of the alphabet in colour. Unlike most autistic savants, Tammet is also creative, notably in his invention of a language, perhaps partly because he is synaesthetic. A link between synaesthesia and creativity seems possible to synaesthesia researchers like Cretien van Campen, Richard Cytowic, and V. S. Ramachandran—although slippery to measure and far from proven. According to one study, synaesthesia is seven times more common in creative people than in the general population. But in another study, which tested 223 students at a fine arts academy in The Netherlands, Van Campen, working with an art teacher, found a gradual distribution of synaesthesia scores ranging from 0 to 100 per cent. In his book *The Hidden Sense: Synaesthesia in Art and Science*, Van Campen concludes that 'the question "Are you a synaesthete or a non-synaesthete?" should be reformulated as "How strong is your synaesthesia?"'

The evidence from highly creative individuals is certainly thought provoking. The physicist Feynman, the composer Messiaen, the painter Van Gogh, and the writer Nabokov, all reported synaesthetic experiences, as mentioned in the introduction. So have a few other major creative figures mentioned by Van Campen and by Cytowic in his book *The Man Who Tasted Shapes*.

In Feynman's case, he saw equations in colour during his celebrated lectures on physics. 'As I'm talking, I see vague pictures of Bessel functions from Jahnke and Emde's book, with light-tan *j*'s, slightly violet-bluish *n*'s, and dark brown *x*'s flying around. And I wonder what the hell it must look like to the students.' Messiaen saw music in colours and forms and heard music in colours. Inspired by the flight of a dark blue-tufted bird across the fantastically shaped red, orange, and violet rocks of Bryce Canyon in the United States, Messiaen gave the following schematic instruction to performers of his composition *From the Canyons to the Stars*: 'Woodwind and brass, the massive theme of red-orange rocks. "Contracted chordal resonance" (red and orange), mode three 1 (orange and gold), "transposed chord inversions" (yellow, mauve, red, white, and black) convey the different colours of the stones.' Van Gogh's experience also concerned music. In 1885, he took piano lessons in order to acquaint himself with the subtleties of colour tone. But his elderly music teacher despatched him as a madman when he noticed that his pupil was constantly comparing the sounds of the piano keys with Prussian blue, dark green, dark ochre, cadmium yellow, and other colours. As a painter, Van Gogh compared painting with pencils to playing the violin with a bow. Finally, Nabokov wrote extensively about synaesthesia in his autobiography *Speak, Memory*, as follows:

> The confessions of a synaesthete must sound tedious and pretentious to those who are protected from such leakings and draughts by more solid walls than mine are. To my mother, though, this all seemed quite natural. The matter came up, one day in my seventh year, as I was using a heap of old alphabet blocks to build a tower. I casually remarked to her that their colours were all wrong. We discovered then that some of her letters had the same tint as mine and that, besides, she was optically affected by musical notes. These evoked no chromatisms in me whatsoever.

Personal accounts such as these, combined with surveys of various kinds, psychological tests in the laboratory, and brain scanning of synaesthetes and non-synaesthetes, have produced a crop of conflicting theories about what causes synaesthesia, none of which is generally accepted. As yet, the field is not even as far advanced as the study of autism. In fact, psychologists are divided over a basic question: whether synaesthesia should be regarded as an abnormal or a normal brain function. Already, though, it seems clear that both autism and synaesthesia contribute in extremely complex and interactive ways to savant syndrome, talent, creativity, and even genius.

CHAPTER 5

THE LUNATIC, THE LOVER, AND THE POET

[Shakespeare] had Theseus propose a common psychological basis for the madness of the lunatic and the creativity of the poet. Now if the genes that predispose people to madness can also cause positive attributes such as enhanced creativity, then there would be a force keeping them in the gene pool. Madness would persist in our species because, although it is disadvantageous in itself, it is closely linked to a trait—creativity—which is highly advantageous.

Daniel Nettle, *Strong Imagination: Madness, Creativity and Human Nature*, 2001

F our centuries ago, in his great comedy *A Midsummer Night's Dream*, Shakespeare intuited that mental illness, passion, and artistic creativity had something in common, as mentioned earlier. 'The lunatic, the lover, and the poet/ Are of imagination all compact', says Theseus, the king. 'One sees more devils than vast hell can hold;/ That is the madman. The lover, all as frantic,/ Sees Helen's beauty in a brow of Egypt./ The poet's eye, in a fine frenzy rolling,/ Doth glance from heaven to earth, from earth to heaven.' Theseus concludes: 'Such tricks hath strong imagination ...'

This idea has recurred throughout the ages, and has a compelling hold on our contemporary imagination. Aristotle is said to have asked: 'Why is it that all men who are outstanding in philosophy, poetry, or the arts are melancholic?' As examples, he cited Homeric, Sophoclean, and mythological heroes like Ajax and Bellerophon, and historical figures such as the philosophers Empedocles, Plato, and Socrates. (According to legend, Empedocles died by throwing himself into the crater of Mount Etna, seeking divine status.) In the nineteenth century, at the time of the Romantic Movement, the lives and works of Lord Byron, Robert Schumann, and

Vincent van Gogh—each of them self-destructive—came to epitomize a link between insanity and genius. In the twentieth century, three of America's leading artistic figures, Ernest Hemingway, Sylvia Plath, and Jackson Pollock, took their own lives as a result of depression—and so, in Britain, did Virginia Woolf. Scientists as a group show less mental illness. Nevertheless, a 1990s survey by the psychiatrist Felix Post based on the biographies of 291 exceptionally creative individuals, came to the conclusion that, judged by modern diagnostic standards, Einstein and Faraday suffered from 'mild' psychopathology, Darwin and Pasteur from 'marked' psychopathology, and Bohr and Galton from 'severe' psychopathology, along with a number of other major scientists. Darwin, for example, endured decades of unexplained illness, which seems to have been caused by his anxiety about the public reception of his theory of natural selection.

The dramatic stories told about these individuals tend to distort the overall picture of mental illness and creativity. Anecdotes can easily give the impression that mental instability is a *sine qua non* of exceptional creativity; a notion that is perhaps nourished by the average person's desire to explain away exceptionally creative achievement. For every such example, however, it is not difficult to find a counter-example of an exceptionally creative artist or scientist who shows none of the symptoms of psychopathology. Among the ten studied in Part II, there is evidence of psychopathology in five of them: Champollion, Curie, Darwin, Einstein, and, of course, Woolf; but no evidence in the other five: Cartier-Bresson, Leonardo, Mozart, Ray, and Wren. (Mozart's periods of melancholy are usually attributed to his financial worries or to his poor physical health.)

Only by studying the mental health of substantial groups, whether of past or of living highly creative individuals, can psychologists try to reach a valid conclusion about whether Shakespeare's intuition was correct or not. We shall examine three studies of different types of artistic creativity from three different periods: fine artists in the Italian Renaissance during the fourteenth–sixteenth centuries; British poets during the age of Romanticism in the eighteenth–nineteenth centuries; and American writers in the second half of the twentieth century.

The Renaissance has canonical status as one of the greatest flowerings of creativity in history. Nonetheless, the period gives the overall impression of a dearth, rather than an excess, of psychopathology, especially when compared to the equally canonical Romantic period. While key Renaissance artists like Botticelli, Brunelleschi, Leonardo, Raphael, and Titian, undoubtedly come down to us as strong personalities, they do not appear to have regarded themselves as isolated, tortured geniuses having a tendency towards self-destruction, with the possible exception of Michelangelo; in fact only one of them, the lesser painter Rosso Fiorentino, was reported to have committed suicide, and this report has subsequently been disproved.

The psychologist Andrew Steptoe (known for his insightful study of Mozart's Italian operas) set out to investigate the personalities of the Renaissance artists, so far as possible, by analysing the biographies presented in the first art history of the period, the painter Giorgio Vasari's classic *Lives of the Most Excellent Painters, Sculptors, and Architects*, first published in Italian in the middle decades of the sixteenth century. 'The book allows us to enquire about the characteristics Vasari identified in the great artists of his own time and the recent past', writes Steptoe. 'Did he see the most creative individuals as disturbed, melancholic, and unconventional, or in other terms? These issues call for statistical treatment of Vasari's writing, since it is all too easy to use selective quotations to identify eccentricities and foibles.'

Vasari's book is divided into three parts, covering early, middle period, and contemporary artists. The information in Part I—up to about 1400—is generally accepted to be very unreliable, given the paucity of facts available to Vasari when writing two or three centuries later. Much of it is borrowed from classical authors or stereotypical, such as the story that Giotto painted a spider so life-like that his master was deceived and tried to flick it off the picture, which recurs in the biographies of other painters, some of them Chinese artists. Steptoe's study therefore excludes Part I of Vasari's work and confines itself to the biographies in Parts II and III, covering 123 later artists—that is, 83 painters, 38 sculptors, and 22 architects (many individuals having more than one craft)—who include the best-known figures of the Renaissance.

There is also the problem of Vasari's personal reliability. His factual errors have long been known to scholars. It is Vasari who incorrectly claims that Rosso Fiorentino committed suicide, and that Leonardo left the head of Christ in *The Last Supper* unfinished. But these errors matter less in a study of personality than the question of Vasari's point of view: whether or not he selected from and sanitized his sources to create a picture in line with his underlying agenda that artists were professionals, not mere artisans, worthy of the respect accorded to established professions such as the law, the church, and medicine. There is some evidence that he did. On the other hand, there are sufficient eccentricities and undesirable traits mentioned in Vasari's *Lives* to suggest that the biographies can be taken mainly at face value. Even his favourite artists were 'just as likely to be tarred with negative attributes such as pride or fecklessness as the other artists', in Steptoe's words. Also significant is the fact that the biographies were taken seriously, not sceptically, by Vasari's contemporaries, who themselves knew much about the artists he described.

Steptoe scrutinized the biographies for references to each of 42 different characteristics, including general traits such as honesty and pride, along with features such as melancholy and eccentricity, which are widely thought to form part of an 'artistic temperament'. Inevitably, the material available did not always prove accommodating to his imposed lines of enquiry, and so Steptoe eventually adopted the following broader categories:

(a) High ability: references to exceptional talent, natural ability, inventiveness, and genius, excellence, and originality (terms like *ingegno*, *divino*, *virtù*, *invenzione*).

(b) Studiousness: references to a deep knowledge of art, and to study of other artists, nature, and the ancients.

(c) Hard work: comments on the exceptional hard-working attitude of the artist.

(d) Critical remarks: negative comments about the artist, such as complaints about a lack of inventiveness or excessive reliance on study.

(e) Sociability: descriptions of the artists as socially adept, charming, gregarious, and amusing.

(f) Courteousness: honourable, obliging, generous, and kind to others (terms like *gentilezza*).

(g) Sophisticated: comments on the artist being cultivated, graceful, and at home in educated circles.

(h) Moderate: moderate and temperate in habits.

(i) Unworldly: absent-minded, saintly, careless about material things.

(j) Depressive: references to melancholy, gloom, reclusiveness, and social withdrawal.

(k) Oddities of character: features such as eccentricity, bizarre actions, and descriptions of highly temperamental behaviour.

(l) Unworthy: reference to a range of undesirable characteristics including licentiousness, villainy, jealousy, and fecklessness.

(m) Conceit: descriptions of the artist as proud or jealous of others.

The most common character trait among the Renaissance artists turns out to be studiousness—found in 48 out of the 123 artists (39 per cent). The next most common is courteousness (at 31 per cent). Depressive tendencies and oddities of character are relatively uncommon, as are sophistication and unworldliness. 'There is little here to endorse the presence either of a melancholic temperament, or of the hypersensitive alienated creature of modern conceptualizations', notes Steptoe. Perhaps, though, these characteristics may have been a feature of the elite minority of truly great artists, in other words the subset of painters, sculptors, and architects judged by Vasari to have exceptionally high ability? Not so: after Steptoe has separated out this group and repeated the analysis, the initial pattern becomes even more evident. The elite group is now seen to be more studious, courteous, sociable, and moderate in its habits, than the majority of the artists, with no higher incidence of depressive tendencies or eccentric behaviour. And after Steptoe has repeated the analysis with the still more select group of eleven artists known to be Vasari's favourites (Masaccio, Brunelleschi, Donatello, Leonardo, Raphael, Andrea del Sarto, Rosso Fiorentino, Giulio Romano, Perino del Vaga, Francesco Salviati, and Michelangelo), the pattern becomes yet more pronounced. It appears that the greatest artists of the Renaissance were neither notably unconventional nor notably temperamental, but on the contrary studious, hard-working, courteous, sociable, and sophisticated. This is indeed how Leonardo appears to art historians during the period of the 1480s–90s, when he worked at the court of the duke of Milan and painted The Last Supper— apart perhaps from his well-known failure to finish most of his works.

'If this was the case, then psychological disturbance, unconventionality, or other aspects of the "artistic personality" cannot be intrinsic to creativity', concludes Steptoe. In Renaissance Italy, these attributes presumably did not aid an artist's struggle to achieve a dependable income and social respect. From the late eighteenth century onwards, by contrast, they seem to have conformed better to social expectations of the artist and thereby helped to generate and maintain public interest in art. Picasso would surely not enjoy his current pre-eminent reputation among twentieth-century painters, had he not displayed extremes of unconventionality and temperament, in stark contrast to his nearest rival Henri Matisse.

A second biographical survey, this time of 36 British and Irish poets born between 1705 and 1805, suggests an utterly different relationship between psychopathology and creativity. 'It can be seen that a strikingly high rate of mood disorders, suicide, and institutionalization occurred within this group of poets and their families', writes the psychiatrist Kay Redfield Jamison, who conducted the survey, in her book *Touched with Fire: Manic-Depressive Illness and the Artistic Temperament*.

The group embraces all of the standard names of the period—William Blake, Robert Burns, Lord Byron, John Clare, Samuel Taylor Coleridge, William Cowper, Thomas Gray, John Keats, Sir Walter Scott, Percy Bysshe Shelley, William Wordsworth, and others—as well as less well-known poets like Leigh Hunt, James Clarence Mangan, and Joanna Baillie. Although the sample size was much smaller than that in Steptoe's Renaissance survey, the sources for research on the poets were more plentiful than for the artists, since they included letters, medical records, and family histories, in addition to biographical works and of course the poets' published works. All these were examined for symptoms and patterns of depression, mania, hypomania, and mixed states, taking into account other psychiatric or medical illnesses (for example, Keats's tuberculosis) that might confuse a diagnosis.

Jamison diagnoses Scott as a possible sufferer from recurrent depression. She notes: 'At various times described himself as suffering from a "disposition to causeless alarm—much lassitude—and decay of vigour and intellect", a *morbus eruditorum* [scholars' disease], and a "black dog" of melancholy.' Byron, she thinks, almost certainly suffered from manic depression (bipolar disorder). 'Recurrent, often agitated, melancholia. Volatile temperament with occasional "paroxysms of rage". Mercurial and extravagant; worsening depressions over time. Strong family history of mental instability and suicide.' Then she quotes Scott's powerful letter about his great friend Byron, after Scott had read the third (and most personally revealing) canto of Byron's just-published *Childe Harold's Pilgrimage* in 1816. Scott's words recall Shakespeare's words on the commingling of lunacy and poetry in 'strong imagination'. He writes of Byron:

> We gaze on the powerful and ruined mind which he presents us, as on a
> shattered castle, within whose walls, once intended for nobler guests,
> sorcerers and wild demons are supposed to hold their Sabbaths. There is

something dreadful in reflecting that one gifted so much above his fellow-creatures, should thus labour under some strange mental malady that destroys his peace of mind and happiness, altho' it cannot quench the fire of his genius. I fear the termination will be fatal in some way or other, for it seems impossible that human nature can support the constant working of an imagination so dark and so strong. Suicide or utter insanity is not unlikely to close the scene.

Strictly speaking, Byron died in Greece in 1824 of a fever. But it is clear from the record of his last days that his fear of insanity sapped his will to live, so that his death was really a form of suicide, as Scott had predicted.

Two of the 36 poets—Thomas Chatterton and Thomas Lovell Beddoes—did commit suicide. Six, including Clare and Cowper, were committed to lunatic asylums or madhouses. More than half of the 36 showed strong evidence of mood disorders, like Byron. Jamison's comparisons of the group with the mental illness of the general population of the period show that the poets were more than five times as likely to have committed suicide, at least 20 times more likely to have been committed to an asylum or madhouse, and 30 times more likely to have suffered from manic depressive illness. This latter group includes, apart from Byron, Blake, Coleridge, and Shelley. Only 7 out of the 36 poets—less than a quarter—show no indication of a significant mood disorder, and they are not among the most celebrated. No wonder the poet Burns—whom Jamison thinks was probably a sufferer from cyclothymia, the least serious form of mood disorder—wrote that: 'The fates and character of the rhyming tribe often employ my thoughts when I am disposed to be melancholy. There is not, among all the martyrologies that ever were penned, so rueful a narrative as the lives of the poets.'

Our third survey involves twentieth-century writers, and was the first scientific attempt to diagnose the relationship between creativity and psychopathology in living writers. Over several years, beginning in the early 1970s, the psychiatrist Nancy Andreasen (who began her career as a professor of Renaissance literature), and co-workers at the University of Iowa, conducted structured interviews, based on systematic psychiatric diagnostic criteria, with writers in residence at the established and respected Iowa Writers' Workshop. She also interviewed a control group whose occupations did not require high levels of creativity, matched for education and age with the writers. Each person was interviewed separately, not in a group. Initially, there were 15 writers and 15 controls, but this group later expanded to a total of 30 writers and 30 controls—just short of the 36 dead poets studied by Jamison. Needless to say, the interviewed writers (who remain anonymous in the published study) were not at the exceptional level of Jamison's poets. However, some had received national acclaim in the United States, while others were graduate students or teaching fellows of the workshop. (Iowa Writers' Workshop graduates have won 16 Pulitzer Prizes since 1947; faculty members have included John Berryman, John Cheever, Robert Lowell, and Philip Roth.)

Andreasen began with a working hypothesis that the writers themselves would be generally healthy, psychologically speaking, but have a higher incidence of schizophrenia in their family than would the control group. She was aware from reliable studies of adopted children born to mothers with schizophrenia compared to the adopted children born to mentally normal mothers, that schizophrenia was known to be inherited; ten per cent of the adopted children of schizophrenic mothers are themselves schizophrenic, despite growing up in a normal environment, as compared to an incidence of schizophrenia in the general population of less than one per cent. Moreover, inherited schizophrenia was evident to Andreasen in the families of Einstein, James Joyce, and Bertrand Russell; Einstein's first wife had some mental illness, and one of his sons was a schizophrenic who spent much of his adult life in a mental asylum. Inherited schizophrenia had been reported, too, by an Icelandic psychiatrist among the relatives of successful individuals listed in Iceland's Who's Who. The general opinion among psychiatrists in the early 1970s was that the genetic tendency towards schizophrenia might express itself either in a severe form, as an illness, or in a mild form, as creativity.

Notwithstanding this theory, Andreasen's interviews showed that not a single one of the 30 Iowa Workshop writers had any of the symptoms of schizophrenia. Instead, the majority—80 per cent of them, as compared to 30 per cent of the control group—met her formal diagnostic criteria for a major mood disorder: either bipolar illness or unipolar depression. (The percentage in the control group is surprisingly high, given the typical percentage for the general population, which is between five and eight per cent.) Most of these writers had received treatment, in the form of hospitalization, or outpatient medication, or psychotherapy. She also found a significantly higher incidence of mood disorders and creativity in the first-degree relatives (parents and siblings) of the writers, than among the first-degree relatives of the controls. But when Andreasen offered this evidence contradicting her own working hypothesis for publication, no scientific journal would initially accept it, because of the consensus about schizophrenia and creativity. It eventually appeared in print in 1974.

Looking back on her pioneering study in her book *The Creating Brain* (2005), Andreasen felt that it confirmed 'two apparently conflicting, but prevailing, ideas about the nature of creativity and its relationship to mental illness'.

The first, espoused by Lewis Terman in his 1920s study at Stanford University, says Andreasen, 'is that gifted people are in fact super-normal or superior in many ways'. The same might be said of the Renaissance artists in Steptoe's study (far more creative though they were than Terman's subjects). 'My writers certainly were', writes Andreasen. 'They were charming, fun, articulate, and disciplined. They typically followed very similar schedules, getting up in the morning and allocating a large chunk of time to writing during the earlier part of the day. They would rarely let a day go by without writing. In general, they had a close relationship with friends and family.' But on the other hand, Andreasen's writers—like the dead poets in Jamison's study—also manifested the view of madness and creativity similar to Shakespeare's in *A Midsummer Night's Dream*. 'Many definitely had experienced periods of significant mood disorder. Importantly, though handicapping creativity when they occurred, these periods of mood disorder were not permanent or long-lived.' Moreover, the mood disorders could possibly be productive. 'In some instances, they may even have provided powerful material upon which the writer could later draw, as a Wordsworthian "emotion recollected in tranquillity".'

Creative individuals are generally ambivalent about this last notion. None has claimed to be able to produce work of enduring value when seriously depressed. But few have wished to be entirely free of their demons, fearing their own sterility. Their attitude towards their illness is, not surprisingly, complex. While they are under no illusion that their mental illness produces their creativity, they suspect that it is an inseparable companion that must be accepted if not welcomed. 'It's something they manage to live with and to produce with', says the polymathic Jonathan Miller, who trained as a doctor and became an opera director. '[But] the idea that you have to be in some way disordered to produce or that it's an advisable state of mind is...nonsense.'

The poets Rainer Maria Rilke and Tony Harrison confirm this, as quoted in the introduction. When the artist Edvard Munch (painter of *The Scream*) was told that psychiatric treatment could rid him of many of his troubles, he responded: 'They are part of me and my art. They are indistinguishable from me, and it would destroy my art. I want to keep those sufferings.' Virginia Woolf wrote in her diary after decades of on-and-off psychological turmoil: 'I believe these illnesses are in my case—how shall I express it?—partly mystical . . . I lie quite torpid, often with acute physical pain . . . Then suddenly something springs . . . Ideas rush in me.' T. S. Eliot—whose best poetry was written under mental stress, including periods of nervous breakdown—noted that: 'Poetry is not a turning loose of emotion, but an escape from emotion, it is not the expression of personality, but an escape from personality. But, of course, only those who have personality and emotions know what it means to want to escape from these things.' The Nobel Prize-winning mathematician and economist John Nash, whose paranoid schizophrenia became the subject of the book and movie *A Beautiful Mind*, when asked by an incredulous fellow mathematician 'How could you believe you are being recruited by aliens from outer space to save the world?' replied: 'Because the ideas I had about supernatural beings came to me the same way that my mathematical ideas did. So I took them seriously.' Even Einstein recognized the necessity of accepting psychological lows as well as highs in his search for a theory of general relativity, which made him gravely ill in 1917. Later he reflected: 'The years of anxious searching in the dark, with their intense longing, their alternations of confidence and exhaustion and the final emergence into the light—only those who have experienced it can understand that.'

Before the psychiatrist John Cade's accidental discovery of lithium salts in 1948 for treating mania, and the discovery of other drugs such as reserpine and chlorpromazine in the 1950s for controlling schizophrenia, sufferers had little choice but to come to terms with their illness. Once reliable drugs were available, creative people had to decide upon the advantages and disadvantages of taking them.

Robert Lowell took lithium in the late 1960s, and found himself both relieved from breakdown and more poetically productive. But he told the neurologist Oliver Sacks: 'my poetry has lost much of its force'—and it is true that his later poems, post-lithium, are not as highly regarded by critics as his earlier work. With others, too, there does appear to be a trade-off between quantity and quality, according to a 1979 study of artists with manic depression (bipolar disorder) who were given lithium carbonate by the psychiatrist Mogens Schou. Taking lithium can allow someone to work again, but at some cost to insights obtained during manic highs. As the poet Gwyneth Lewis (the first National Poet of Wales) remarks in an essay, 'Dark gifts', written for the collection *Poets on Prozac*:

> Only two of my eight books have been written while taking antidepressants, so I find it very difficult to distinguish between the effect of the medication and a development of my own style away from ornamentation and towards greater simplicity (which, of all literary effects, requires the most skill and is the most difficult to achieve). Even if it was proven that antidepressants adversely affected my ability as a poet, I'd still take them. After being a zombie for months, being able to write at all is a miracle, and that participation in the creative discipline, rather than a more objective measure of excellence, is the bottom line for me.

To psychologists, the issue of productivity versus excellence is of compelling interest for the light it sheds on the nature of genius. While mania without doubt increases productivity, might it also sometimes improve quality too? If a creative person has a sustained burst of energy and self-confidence, it would seem reasonable that this should have a positive influence on his or her work. On the other hand, mania is likely to preclude the operation of the critical faculty essential for exceptional creativity, which edits with cool detachment what has been created passionately. There are many great artists, even Shakespeare, who produced a considerable number of mediocre works, which they should probably have done better to suppress.

In other words, simply put, does madness enhance or diminish genius? With this in mind, the psychologist Robert Weisberg analysed in two separate studies the output of two major artists: the compositions of Robert Schumann and the poems of Emily Dickinson. Both of them have been retrospectively diagnosed as sufferers from manic depression (bipolar disorder), though this is less certain for Dickinson than for Schumann. He attempted suicide more than once and ended his short life in a mental asylum, where he starved himself to death in 1856; Dickinson had a more conventional and somewhat longer life, but became a recluse for almost two decades before her death in 1886. Almost all of her poetry was published posthumously. Living in the nineteenth century, both Schumann and Dickinson predated the availability of scientific psychiatric treatment.

'Periods of remarkable creativity, productivity, and high spirits were woven into the otherwise frighteningly sad fabric of Schumann's life', remarks Jamison in *Touched with Fire*. Between the years 1829 and 1851, he more or less alternated between moods of hypomania and depression, judging from his doctors' records, his letters, the letters of those who knew him, and other historical documents. Naturally, it is not possible to diagnose his mood at all times, and a particular mood may also have lasted for less than a whole year. Nevertheless, a dominant mood can be established for most of the years of Schumann's creative period.

The number of his compositions in each year does not track these moods exactly, but there are two peaks, in 1840 and 1849: manic years when he composed 25 or more works—far more than in any other year. The first of these peaks, Schumann's 'year of song', corresponded with his marriage to Clara Wieck. The average number of his compositions in the years of hypomania is approximately five times the average number in the years of depression.

To assess the compositions' quality, rather than their number, Weisberg counted the number of available recordings for each composition; the more recordings there were, the higher the quality of the composition. He could have chosen other measures, such as the number of appearances of a work in concert programmes, or the assessments of experts, such as conductors, musicians, musicologists, or critics. The number of recordings per composition has the advantage that it is both convenient to measure, and correlates well with other measures, for example, the frequency with which a work is discussed in critical analyses of music. Hence, the number of recordings per composition is more than simply a measure of the popularity of the composition.

'If Schumann's periods of mania improved his thought processes, then compositions produced during his manic years should be recorded more frequently, on average, than compositions produced during the depressive years', notes Weisberg. But his analysis does not support this hypothesis. The average number of recordings per composition from Schumann's manic years, taken together, is actually about the same as the average number from his depressive years, taken together. Indeed, the peak number of recordings relates to a year of depression, *not* to a manic year. The implication is, that although Schumann was highly motivated to compose in his manic years, and he therefore composed far more works at this time, his motivation did not improve the quality of his creativity.

Dickinson and her poetry were subjected by Weisberg and a co-worker to a similar kind of analysis of quantity and quality of poems written during manic, depressed, and neutral years, as defined by external evidence, such as

Dickinson's correspondence. Most of her poems were written in an eight-year period between 1858 and 1865, when she was 28–35 in age; after this period, the tide of her composition ebbed. They fall into two four-year phases, divided by an emotional crisis. This time, the measure of quality was the number of appearances of a poem in more than a dozen compendia of poetry published during the twentieth century, instead of numbers of musical recordings. As with Schumann, there are found to be large differences in quantity of poetic output, with manic years resulting in high output. Unlike Schumann, however, there is some evidence that the poems produced during manic years were of higher quality. So the results for Dickinson do not agree with those for Schumann: instead they provide some support for the idea that mania can increase creativity, although the shorter span of Dickinson's major productivity—eight years as compared to Schumann's more than 20 years—makes the Dickinson analysis less rigorous and convincing.

To establish a definitive connection between mental illness and creativity is impossible, at present. Psychologists and psychiatrists assess it very differently. All accept, with Shakespeare, that there is something about madness that can inform our understanding of genius—especially among poets. 'It seems that the age-old notion that genius is related to madness was not entirely unfounded, even if some invalid *explanations* have been offered', writes R. Ochse in his balanced survey of studies on genius. Many accept that the relationship arises from natural selection, which must surely favour creativity as an advantageous evolutionary trait. But for now, there is no agreement on the detail of where creativity's connection with madness actually lies.

PART II

TEN BREAKTHROUGHS
IN ART AND SCIENCE

CHAPTER 6

LEONARDO DA VINCI

The Last Supper

One who was drinking and has left the glass in its position [has] turned his head towards the speaker. Another twisting the fingers of his hands, turns with stern brows to his companion. Another with his hands spread shows the palms, and shrugs his shoulders up to his ears, making a mouth of astonishment. Another speaks into his neighbour's ear and he, as he listens, turns towards him to lend an ear while holding a knife in one hand, and in the other the loaf half cut through. Another as he turns with a knife in his hand upsets a glass on the table. Another lays his hands on the table and is looking. Another blows his mouthful. Another leans forward to see the speaker shading his eyes with his hands. Another draws back behind the one who leans forward, and sees the speaker between the wall and the man who is leaning.

Leonardo da Vinci, 'Notes on *The Last Supper*', undated but probably 1495–97

The artworks and notebooks of Leonardo da Vinci are famously dense with puzzles and mysteries. But *The Last Supper*, Leonardo's best-known painting after the *Mona Lisa*—and the only one still *in situ*—suffers from a disadvantage unique in his oeuvre. Despite being among the most familiar paintings in the history of art, *The Last Supper* started to disintegrate even before the death of Leonardo in 1519, less than two decades after its completion around 1498. The experimental technique he adopted for richness of tone and colour, and also so that he could paint the mural slowly and reflectively (unlike the rapid brushwork required in fresco painting), soon led to the paint's flaking from the walls of the refectory of the monastery of Santa Maria delle Grazie in Milan. The 'restoration' of the painting, including drastic cleaning, retouching, and some extensive repainting, began during the sixteenth century and continued for some four centuries, sometimes with disastrous results. By the nineteenth century, it had become a standard lament of critics that the surviving painting was a mere shadow of Leonardo's magnificent conception. Thus, any assessment of *The Last Supper* unavoidably came to be based on shifting ground, since the original work had effectively ceased to exist.

Its present-day appearance, following a comprehensive, two-decade restoration programme completed in the late 1990s, is astonishingly—even shockingly—different from its familiar image. 'For centuries our grasp of *The Last Supper* has been hazy, obscured by myth and rather mystifying beliefs arising from the work's universal appeal', observes the chief restorer Pinin Brambilla Barcilon. 'This, as well as the painting's profoundly innovative realism, has bequeathed to us an *idea* of the original work.' She and her team removed dark grime and layers of paint added after the 1490s to reveal what remains of Leonardo's brushstrokes. In the process, the colours radically altered, and became much less bright; and the postures, gestures and facial expressions of Jesus Christ and most of the twelve apostles emerged considerably changed.

For example, the legend that Leonardo left the face of Christ unfinished has been exploded by the restorers' discovery that the original face was highly finished. So much for the myth-making of the artist Vasari, Leonardo's first biographer, who stated that Leonardo believed himself 'incapable of achieving the celestial divinity the image of Christ required'. Moreover, the tendons in the apostle Judas Iscariot's neck, as he tenses at Christ's disturbing words about betrayal, are clearly suggested in the restored painting, confirming Leonardo's scientific study of anatomy, which began in the late 1480s according to his notebooks.

Inevitably, the latest restoration is controversial. Opinions about *The Last Supper*, and the method of its creation, have had to be significantly modified. However the longstanding view of it, as expressed by the influential art historian E. H. Gombrich in *The Story of Art*, basing his view on the mid-twentieth century appearance of the painting, is unlikely to be revised.

'Even in its ruined state, *The Last Supper* remains one of the great miracles wrought by human genius.'

The life of its creator, by contrast, is frustratingly little restored by research: it is still dependent on Vasari's brief, somewhat unreliable account and a handful of contemporary documents—since Leonardo's notebooks, for all their sprawling wonders, tell us virtually nothing about his *modus vivendi*. Amazingly, they never once mention the major artist Andrea del Verrocchio, in whose workshop the novice Leonardo trained for perhaps half a decade. For the first three decades of Leonardo's life in Vinci and Florence, before he left for Milan, possibly in 1482, 'all we know for certain about his career and his itinerary are a few dates, a few facts, often questionable ones', notes a recent Leonardo biographer, Serge Bramly. During the 1480s, his first decade in Milan, hard information is if anything even more scarce. In the following decade, even as Leonardo neared the height of his artistic fame, nothing certain can be said about the date of commissioning of *The Last Supper*, other than that it probably lies between 1493 and 1495.

Research in the Tuscan archives shows that Leonardo's paternal family were not artists but rather lawyers, hailing from the village of Vinci and making their name and fortune in Florence over several generations, with the exception of his grandfather, who lived as a country squire in Vinci. Leonardo, born in Vinci in 1452, was the first son of the notary Ser Piero da Vinci and a young, unmarried farmer's daughter Caterina, with whom he had an affair. Ser Piero married another woman that same year (the first of his four wives), while Caterina married the following year, probably with the assistance of Ser Piero. The illegitimate Leonardo seems to have been brought up by his grandparents and an uncle, not his natural parents, given that he appears in his grandfather's tax declaration in 1457 as a *bocca*—a mouth to feed, and again in 1469, in a tax declaration by his grandmother. Only after their deaths, apparently, did he move from Vinci to Florence under the charge of his father, who declared him as a dependent in the city in 1470.

Nothing is known of his early education in Vinci. Presumably, he was taught to read and write and do arithmetic (not his strong point as an adult despite his fascination for mathematics), and began to develop the habit of left-handed mirror writing he would use throughout his notebooks. Latin tuition was not included, given the fact that he began to teach himself the language from scratch in his late thirties. Since printing had only just been invented, he would have had no access to books. Exposure to the visual arts would most likely have been restricted to the sacred art in the local church. But Leonardo seems to have shown promise in this direction, judging from an intriguing undated anecdote told by Vasari.

Ser Piero had been given a plain wooden shield made by one of his peasants with the request that he have it painted in Florence. He passed it to his son to decorate. The result was said to have been a terrifying monster with poisonous breath, inspired by the head of the Medusa, 'emerging from a dark and broken rock', made out of 'crawling reptiles, green lizards, crickets, snakes, butterflies, locusts, bats, and other strange species'. (In his notebooks, Leonardo noted that to make an invented animal such as a dragon seem natural, the artist should draw 'for the head that of a mastiff or hound, for the eyes a cat, and for the ears a porcupine, and for the nose a greyhound, and the brows of a lion, the temple of an old cock, the neck of a terrapin'.) When the shield was ready, Leonardo invited his father to collect it. But instead of simply handing it to him, he prepared the room theatrically by dimming the light and placing the shield on his easel. An unthinking Ser Piero entered, was 'immediately shaken', and stepped back. Leonardo told him: 'This work has served the purpose for which it was made.' His father, shrewd lawyer that he was, must have been impressed, because he purchased a second, simple shield for the peasant (showing 'a heart pierced by an arrow'), and 'secretly' sold Leonardo's shield to some merchants for 100 ducats, who then sold it on to the Duke of Milan for 300 ducats. One suspects that no part of this money reached his bohemian son who, being illegitimate, had no prospect of a bourgeois career such as the legal profession of his forefathers.

Whether or not Leonardo was already apprenticed to Verrocchio when he made the monstrous shield is left vague by Vasari. We do not know at what age he became an apprentice, but it probably happened quite late for those days: some time between 1469, when Leonardo seems to have left Vinci for Florence at the age of 17, and 1472, when his name appears in the account book of the painters' confraternity, the Compagnia di Santa Luca. What is certain, if we rely on Vasari, is that it was Ser Piero who introduced his son to his 'very good friend' Verrocchio by showing him some of Leonardo's drawings and urgently begging his advice on the boy's prospects as an artist.

Verrocchio was an inspired choice of master for a budding polymath. He was not in the very first rank of Renaissance artists, but he had diverse talents. Like some other artists, for instance, Filippi Brunelleschi and Lorenzo Ghiberti, he had begun as a goldsmith: an art that required both skill in drawing, engraving, modelling and carving, and techniques as varied as polishing gemstone and working molten metal. In 1471, to the excitement of all Florence including a watching (perhaps assisting) Leonardo, Verrocchio was responsible for making a two-ton gilded copper ball, designed by the late Brunelleschi, and erecting it atop the cupola of the cathedral of Santa Maria del Fiore. Then in his mid-thirties, Verrocchio was already established as the official sculptor of the Medici family, following the death of Donatello in 1466. Although sculpture would be his best-known achievement, his draughtsmanship—with a decided bent towards drawing from nature—was much admired by other artists. His bustling workshop was wide-ranging: apart from sculpture, Verrocchio and Co. produced paintings, metalwork, chests, armour, and theatrical costumes, machinery, and sets (an important interest of Leonardo when he moved to Milan and designed machines and pageants for court entertainments and carnivals). In addition, Verrocchio had a number of assistants, which made the workshop a meeting place for young artistic talent and a crucible for new ideas. Leonardo in his notebooks may have given Verrocchio no direct credit, but he plainly learnt an enormous amount from working under him.

The two Renaissance artists Leonardo most admired were probably Giotto, who died in 1337, and Masaccio, who died young in 1428. In an outline of the history of art written in his notebooks around 1490, Leonardo singled them out for praise:

> The painters after the Romans...always imitated each other, and from age to age continually brought their art into decline. After these came Giotto the Florentine, who (not content to imitate the works of Cimabue, his master) being born in the solitary mountains inhabited only by goats and similar animals, and being guided by nature towards this art, began to draw upon the rocks the actions of the goats of which he was the keeper; and thus began to draw in this manner all the animals found in this countryside; after much study he surpassed not only the masters of his own age but all those of many centuries past. After this, art receded because all imitated existing paintings, and thus it went on from one century to the next until Tomaso the Florentine, nicknamed Masaccio, showed by perfect works how those who take for their guide anything other than nature—mistress of the masters—exhaust themselves in vain.

This emphasis on observing nature, so important to Leonardo in both his art and his writings on art, found expression in his earliest known drawing, now in the Uffizi Gallery in Florence. Unusually for him, it is dated in his hand 'day of Saint Mary of the Snow/day of 5 August 1473', making it the first dated landscape study in Western art. Drawn in pen and ink, with flicks of golden paint from a brush, a panorama of the Tuscan hills, quite possibly around Vinci, falls precipitously down to the plain. It is easy to believe that the drawing was based on early memories of wandering in the hills as a boy, like Giotto with his goats. Everything appears to be in movement: the light and shadow moving over the slopes, the leaves on the trees stirring in the wind, water cascading downwards. Already, says Kenneth Clark in his study *Leonardo da Vinci*, Leonardo had mastered an original technique for capturing the effects of light that did not resemble the formal style of the period, such as that found in Verrocchio's paintings. 'There is a kind of genial recklessness about the touch which does not suggest the painstaking goldsmith's apprentice.'

The drawing is reminiscent in turn of another famous early evocation of nature by Leonardo, which is written rather than drawn. It describes his discovery of a cave in the hills—whether real or allegorical we have no means of knowing from the context. Around 1480, he noted:

> Driven by an ardent desire and anxious to view the abundance of varied and strange forms created by nature the artificer, having travelled a certain distance through overhanging rocks, I came to the entrance to a large cave and stopped for a moment, struck with amazement, for I had not suspected its existence. Stooping down, my left hand around my knee, while with the right I shaded my frowning eyes to peer in, I leaned this way and that, trying to see if there was anything inside, despite the darkness that reigned there; after I had remained thus for a moment, two emotions suddenly awoke in me: fear and desire—fear of the dark, threatening cave and desire to see if it contained some miraculous thing.

This potent combination of motives—fear and desire—is what makes many of Leonardo's paintings, including the *Mona Lisa*, *The Last Supper*, and especially his final painting *St John the Baptist*, so disturbing. It is no accident that Leonardo's paintings are among the most vandalized in the history of art. Sigmund Freud, in his essay on Leonardo, judged him to be a thoroughly abnormal mind.

There are hints of his power even in his earliest known paintings, made under Verrocchio's direct influence. Around 1473–74, so far as we know,

Leonardo painted an *Annunciation*, with a winged angel and a Madonna on a walled garden terrace, and then, around 1476, one of the two angels in Verrocchio's *Baptism of Christ*. In the *Annunciation*, nature is heavily stylized —although the angel's wings are based, unconventionally, on a bird's wings (later crudely lengthened to canonical proportions by overpainting)—yet the dark trees silhouetted against the light-grey sky are suffused with twilit mystery. In the *Baptism*, Leonardo's angel is subtle and grave beside Verrocchio's simple and sunny angel. Indeed, X-rays show that Leonardo painted the face with many very thin layers of paint, unmixed with white lead, whereas his master used the conventional white for highlighting the contours of the angel's face. Having seen his apprentice's sophistication, an angry Verrocchio 'would never touch colours again', claimed Vasari (probably with exaggeration).

Leonardo's highly probable homosexuality was surely a factor in his developing power to disturb—difficult though it is to assess. Homosexuality was well known among artists and intellectuals in Florence—one artist openly acknowledged his nickname Il Sodoma—and partly tolerated by the authorities, despite the censure of the church. In April 1476, court records show that Leonardo was among four young men formally accused of sodomy with a 17-year-old apprentice goldsmith who was apparently a notorious prostitute, but the charges were dropped in June for lack of proof. During the rest of his life, Leonardo never gave certain proof of his sexuality. However, there is no record of any woman in his life, nor any female friendship, and the two male companions he lived with, first Salai and later Francesco Melzi, were handsome youths. There is also an almost total absence of references to women in his notebooks. As for his art, he unquestionably showed a preference for the male over the female nude. Homosexuality 'is implicit in a large section of his work, and accounts for his androgynous types and a kind of lassitude of form', in Clark's view. 'We cannot look at Leonardo's work and seriously maintain that he had a normal man's feelings for women. And those who wish, in the interest of morality, to reduce Leonardo, that inexhaustible source of creative power, to a neutral or sexless agency, have a strange idea of doing service to his reputation.'

It is not known exactly when Leonardo left Verrocchio's workshop and set up on his own—most likely some time in 1477–78. Probably he hung on there, knowing that he lacked Verrocchio's (and his father Ser Piero's) hard head for business, required by a successful artist in the competitive atmosphere of mercantile Florence. Although his talent was never in doubt, the next few years until he left for Milan were a struggle and not highly productive of painting. Dating Leonardo's work from this period is tricky; but he seems to have completed only two or three paintings, and left two others unfinished—all of them promising, yet none reaching the level of his later paintings. By contrast, his drawings were wonderfully fresh, lively, and spontaneous. Comparing them with his paintings, one senses a conflict between his desire to innovate and his fear of rejecting academic tradition (that tendency to imitate earlier painters he privately excoriated). The study Leonardo rapidly sketched for what is known as The 'Benois Madonna', roughly dated 1478–80, shows a mother and child of ineffable charm interacting with the playfulness of a Mozart duet. However, the finished painting—heavy drapery, haloes, and all—is stodgy and lifeless, with a weakly sentimental Madonna and a frankly monstrous baby.

All of the paintings from this first decade, bar Leonardo's imaginative portrait of a young woman Ginevra de' Benci, are on religious themes, from his Annunciation of 1473–74 to his unfinished St Jerome of around 1480 and his Adoration of the Magi of 1481. There are obvious reasons for this, given the prevailing Florentine academic tradition of Christian painting, plus the need for an artist to obtain commissions from powerful religious institutions and wealthy, pious aristocrats. However, the religious orthodoxy, as well as the artistic orthodoxy, must have cramped the development of Leonardo's style. Vasari cautiously implies that Leonardo was not a believer in the God of the Catholic church of his time, and from his notebooks there is no evidence that he believed in life after death. 'He was not . . . a religious-minded man', states Clark firmly, unlike his contemporary Michelangelo. As an artist, Leonardo 'has generally been regarded as of dubious orthodoxy in Christian terms, if not an actual atheist', writes a current Leonardo expert, Martin Kemp. Significantly, in my view, in tackling The Last Supper Leonardo chose a moment of high human drama—Christ's announcement of his future betrayal—rather than the more avowedly religious scene tradition-ally chosen by painters: Christ's sharing of the bread and wine in the Eucharist.

There are broad hints of Leonardo's interest in depicting the Last Supper as early as 1481, almost a decade and a half before he actually began his mural.

A vigorous pen-and-ink sketch from 1481 shows a single figure, Christ-like, sitting in front of a plate, and near it five men debating at a table: one of them pointing his finger at another, who rests his chin on his hand, two who listen either attentively or dreamily, and a fifth who has stood up and rested one hand flat on the table while open-handedly gesturing at the speaker in apparent disagreement. It is an 'argumentative *Last Supper*', as Kemp aptly observes. (Typically for Leonardo, the rest of the sheet diverges, with sketches of naked male figures in conversation and movement; a Madonna and child; and a diagram of a hygrometer.)

In the *Adoration of the Magi*, too, the connection to *The Last Supper* is there, if differently expressed. Among the crowded ring of faces in the foreground gazing at the Virgin Mary and her baby, the cynosure of almost all eyes, there are some who distinctly resemble those of the apostles in *The Last Supper*. Joseph, behind Mary, grimaces emphatically in a gesture that prefigures the face of the apostle Andrew; one of the bearded magi with his hand raised to his forehead looks like an early version of the apostle Peter; and a beautiful young man seen in profile anticipates the apostle Philip. The picture's overall composition—with its iconographically unconventional placing of the Virgin and child beneath a tree, and its allegorical background—though not similar to *The Last Supper*, was considered revolutionary in the late fifteenth century, and was much admired by other artists. They included Sandro Botticelli, Raphael, who stood awestruck in front of the *Adoration*, and even Michelangelo, who seems to have borrowed some elements from Leonardo's crowd of faces for his ceiling in the Sistine Chapel. It seems reasonable to conjecture that such fervent professional appreciation helped to give Leonardo the confidence to break with convention in his composition for *The Last Supper*.

The *Adoration* was abandoned near the end of 1481 and never completed. Failure to finish his artistic projects became something of a Leonardo signature, though with some notable exceptions (including *The Last Supper*). There are many contemporary references to his dilatoriness. Vasari states (inaccurately) that 'he began many projects but never finished any of them'. Pope Leo X, who wished to commission a work from Leonardo, was dismayed to find the artist immediately preoccupied with distilling oils and herbs for the varnish. 'Alas, this man is never going to do anything, for he starts to think about finishing the work before it is even begun!' the pope exclaimed (according to Vasari). Michelangelo taunted Leonardo with the failure of his project to sculpt a giant horse for the Duke of Milan: 'You who made a model of a horse you could never cast in bronze and which you gave up, to your shame.'

The reason for incompletion, according to Vasari, was Leonardo's artistic perfectionism. This may be true of *The Adoration of the Magi*. 'To have carried the *Adoration* any further without depriving it of magic would have taxed even Leonardo's genius...the whole subject is conceived in a spirit opposed to clear statement. It is an allegory', writes Clark. On the other hand, the monks who commissioned the work appear from the records to have stopped paying Leonardo in September 1481, for reasons unknown, and they did not claim the unfinished work, as they were entitled to do, had Leonardo himself defaulted. We do not really know whether the artist or the patron killed the project.

Another reason, overlooked by Vasari, since it became obvious only in the nineteenth century with the publication of Leonardo's notebooks, is certainly his astonishingly diverse interests. Leonardo's polymathy shaded into dilettantism, in which he was easily distracted from a project in hand by other fascinating problems. In 1501, a contemporary in Florence, the head of the Carmelite monks, despaired in a letter: 'the life that Leonardo leads is haphazard and extremely unpredictable, so that he only seems to live from day to day'. A characteristic sheet from his notebooks, dated around 1509, shows studies for subjects as various as the release mechanism of a water clock, the human oesophagus, and a costume design. Over and over again, Leonardo doodles the words 'di mi se mai, di mi se mai'. 'Di mi se mai fu fatta alcuna cosa' is Italian for 'Tell me if anything was ever done.' Once, he noted to himself in despair: 'Like a kingdom divided, which rushes to its doom, the mind that engages in subjects of too great variety becomes confused and weakened.'

The move to Milan, which falls some time between September 1481 and April 1483 (when Leonardo is known to have begun work there on the painting that eventually became known as the '*Virgin of the Rocks*'), was intended to secure Leonardo a salaried position at court, unavailable in republican Florence, which would allow him to indulge his expanding interests in art and science without the pressure of having to sell his work. It began with an approach to Milan's ruler Ludovico Sforza, probably in the form of a begging letter setting out Leonardo's qualifications, though it is not clear whether the letter that survives was actually sent.

The most surprising aspect of this document is that almost all of it is concerned not with art but with military engineering—a field in which Leonardo had hitherto not had much experience. Nothing daunted, he situates himself in the tradition of artist-architects and engineers like

Giotto, Brunelleschi, Donato Bramante (already in Milan), and indeed Verrocchio. The letter offers to design, for example, bridges, tunnels, siege engines, mortars, catapults, and armoured vehicles—all of which Leonardo shrewdly perceived would interest a ruler then embroiled in war. Only at the end does he come to his usefulness in peacetime, as an architect of public and private buildings, and aqueducts. Finally he adds, seemingly almost as a throwaway: 'I can carry out sculpture in marble, bronze, and clay; and in painting can do any kind of work as well as any man, whoever he be. Moreover, the bronze horse could be made that will be to the immortal glory and eternal honour of the lord your father of blessed memory and of the illustrious house of Sforza.'

Leonardo's attraction to military engineering and war was genuine, not merely a ploy to gain the ear of a powerful ruler. He enjoyed inventing lethal and original machines for destroying the enemy and his environ-ment, in the tradition of his admired predecessor Archimedes. There is ample evidence of this in his notebooks, despite Vasari's being unaware of it when writing his biographical account in the mid-sixteenth century. In 1502, Leonardo was even appointed 'family architect and general engineer' to the notorious Cesare Borgia, captain-general of the papal armies. There was a misanthropic streak in Leonardo, which revelled in conflict, horror, and apocalypse. Yet, his love of killing machines certainly makes a perplex-ing contradiction with his lack of personal aggression, so far as we know, and his unquestionable love of nature and especially animals. As Vasari famously records, Leonardo had the reputation of purchasing caged birds from street sellers and then setting the creatures free.

In practice, his military machines made little impression in Milan, judg-ing from the silence about them in the historical record. Apart from the ill-fated bronze horse, and a small amount of architecture, most of his practical inventiveness for the Sforzas went into designing ingenious pageants and masquerades, of which sadly little evidence remains. After a longish period of making himself accepted in Milan, by the 1490s 'he was regarded as an ornament of the court, a man who could discourse on an astonishing variety of things, a wit with a ready fable for every occasion, and a master chef of visual treats for sophisticated palates', writes Kemp.

Independently of the court, Leonardo pursued scientific studies in earn-est. From the notebooks, it is clear that he read very widely (including eventually in Latin) and pestered his knowledgeable Milanese friends with questions. His investigation of anatomy, begun in Florence, is the most important part of this programme, from the point of view of his painting, in particular the human figures in *The Last Supper*. His earliest dated anatomical drawings, from 1489, are a sequence of studies of the human skull, as part of his attempt to discover the location of the soul. He also examined the eye and many other parts of the human body. His iconic drawing, showing a spread-eagled naked man fitted into a circle and a square, known as a *Proportional Study of a Man in the Manner of Vitruvius*, dates from this period. And his portrait of Cecilia Galerani (the mistress of Ludovico Sforza), known as *Lady with an Ermine*, painted some time in the late 1480s, shows how much he had now understood of the bony structure of the subject's hand as she holds the creature.

How much Leonardo's study of science—and of mathematics from the mid-1490s onwards—really improved his painting, is debatable. His mastery of chiaroscuro is as fine in some works painted before he scientifically studied the eye, optics, light, and shade, as it is in others painted after these studies. His understanding of the golden ratio (detectable in the *Mona Lisa*) was sharpened by his friendship with the mathematician Luca Pacioli, who came to Milan in 1496 while Leonardo was working on *The Last Supper*. Yet, Leonardo never noted that the golden ratio was in his mind while actually painting. The four tapestries on the walls in *The Last Supper* diminish in size with distance from the viewer according to what appear to be harmonic ratios, as found in the tonal intervals of a musical octave. Yet, Leonardo never noted this fact; moreover his deployment of perspective as a whole in the painting is very far from being mathematically precise. A set of numbers written along the edge of a sheet with drawings of the *The Last Supper* was once thought to define the system of proportions used in planning the painting's background. But it is now evident from many other similar sheets that the numbers are simply a record of expenses! The relationship between intuition and calculation in painting is a subtle one, never formulaic. In about 1514, Leonardo made an acute note on the point while criticizing Michelangelo (without naming him) for his overemphasis on anatomy in painting. 'O anatomical painter, beware, lest in the attempt to make your nudes display all their emotions by a too strong indication of bones, sinews and muscles, you become a wooden painter.'

The Last Supper seems to have been commissioned for the refectory of the Dominican monastery of Santa Maria delle Grazie not by the friars themselves but by Ludovico Sforza, around the time he was officially invested as the Duke of Milan in 1494, after the death of his young nephew Gian

Galeazzo Sforza (whom Ludovico may have poisoned). The duke was friendly with the prior of the monastery, Vincenzo Bandello, and used to dine there twice a week at the prior's table. So he must have personally witnessed the creation of Leonardo's painting, beginning with the lunettes above the main scene showing heraldic symbols of the Sforza family.

Leonardo was not short of direct artistic precedents. In Florence alone, a Last Supper was painted by Andrea del Castagno in the 1440s, by Pietro Perugino in 1480, and by Domenico Ghirlandaio in the early 1490s. In all three examples, the composition is very similar: Jesus and eleven apostles are depicted behind the dining table, while Judas is separated from them in front of the table. And so is the atmosphere: the apostles sit formally, without much animation, wearing haloes, in luxurious physical surroundings. It required courage for Leonardo to break with this solemn and static tradition, and make the scene real, by portraying Jesus and all twelve apostles seated together as one would expect, behaving as flesh-and-blood individuals, in comparatively austere surroundings.

Early in the planning, it seems from the limited evidence, he toyed with using the traditional position for Judas. There is very little in the way of surviving preparatory studies for *The Last Supper*—nothing like the substantial preparatory studies for the *Adoration of the Magi*—and some of what does exist has been questioned by experts. However, three undated drawings show Judas separate from the rest of the group. One is in red chalk not in the style of Leonardo but bearing what appears to be his handwritten labels for the apostles, though many suspect it to be a forgery; the other two drawings (mentioned above in connection with mathematical proportions), are in pen and ink in Leonardo's style without any accompanying writing, and are undoubtedly genuine.

These sketches from the notebooks, minimal as they are, were 'clearly of capital importance in realizing *The Last Supper*', writes Pietro Marani in his detailed study of the painting published in 1999 at the time of completion of its latest restoration. Marani perceptively describes the two sketches as follows:

> The largest study at the top shows a grouping of eight or nine apostles with Christ, with Judas seated on the viewer's side of the table. The scene is set against a wall with a row of support arches for a vault...[The] vault must have been conceived as a means of harmonizing the scene with the actual architecture of the refectory. Leonardo's mobile, darting use of pen and ink enlivens the drawing, which is intentionally abbreviated in defining the

figures, only barely suggested by a few hatched lines. To the right, the second drawing on the sheet depicts a slightly larger-scale grouping of Christ, John, Peter, and Judas at the moment Christ announces the betrayal and passes the sop to Judas. Christ's left arm is represented simultaneously in two different positions like a frame sequence: extended in the act of picking up the bread, and bent in the gesture of handing it to Judas. Judas rises and leans forward to take the bread. The poses of the other two apostles are most unusual: John is almost thrown bodily over the table with Christ's left arm resting on his back; and Peter raises his left hand to his forehead, perhaps incredulous at Christ's revelation. Leonardo manages to give Christ a moving, resigned expression with just a few lines and two or three ink spots.

Four further drawings, considerably more finished, show individual apostles: Philip, and James Major, for certain; Judas, and either Bartholomew or Matthew, less certainly. The first two are easily recognizable in the finished painting, from both their features and the angle of view, the other two less so; Judas has a beard in the painting, for example, whereas in the drawing the figure is clean-shaven, though the angles of the two heads are similar. Some of these drawings (and no doubt other drawings that do not survive) were almost certainly taken from life. Leonardo himself made notes on his extensive searches, sketchbook in hand, for interesting human types in the streets of Milan, including visits to a public bathhouse, taverns, and the occasional brothel. He also noted that he wished to make a portrait study of 'the young count, the one attached to Cardinal del Mortaro', for his figure of Christ, and to use a certain Alessandro Carissimi of Parma as the model for Christ's hand. Near the end of his life, in 1517, he reportedly told a reliable visitor that the figures in The Last Supper were portraits from life 'of several people of very high stature from the court and Milan of that period'.

As for the reactions of the individual apostles, Leonardo was generally guided by his belief that: 'Painted figures must be done in such a way that the spectators are able with ease to recognize through their attitudes the thoughts of their minds.' His brief planning notes on various possible Last Supper figures (unnamed), quoted at the head of this chapter, conform to this belief. However, Leonardo followed the notes only partially in applying them to particular apostles as the painting took shape on the wall. Here creative unity took over from prior calculation. The apostle Andrew does indeed 'with his hands spread show the palms, and shrug his shoulders up to his ears, making a mouth of astonishment'. Peter does indeed vigorously 'speak into his neighbour's ear'—that is, into John's ear—but the knife for cutting bread mentioned by Leonardo is appropriately placed in Peter's hand, not John's. Judas, rather than turning with a knife in his hand and upsetting a glass, holds a bag (presumably containing the 30 traitorous pieces of silver) and upsets the salt (visible in early copies of the original painting but now unrecognizable). Other gestures mentioned in the notes, such as an apostle twisting the fingers of his hands, another choking on his food, and yet another holding a half-raised glass, were omitted altogether, perhaps as being too quotidian for so heroic a scene.

The gestures and movements are of course dramatically expressive. 'There is so much order in this variety, and so much variety in this order, that one can never quite exhaust the harmonious interplay of movement and answering movement'—Gombrich's view. Clark, on the other hand, is rather less persuaded: '[The] movement is frozen. There is something rather terrifying about all these ponderous figures in action; something of a contradiction in terms in the slow labour which has gone into the perfection of every gesture.' In other words, the spontaneity of gesture, movement, and feeling so immediate in Leonardo's few notebook drawings of *The Last Supper* has evaporated in the painting. I personally tend more towards Clark than Gombrich on this important issue. But then all viewers of *The Last Supper* must constantly remember that they are not seeing exactly what Leonardo painted. The expressions on the faces of the apostles have suffered severely over five centuries from the ravages of time and restorers. The proper balance between feeling and gesture in the figures is no longer there, except perhaps in the faces of Christ and one or two of the apostles, such as Philip.

Not much is known of Leonardo's working method after he started on the wall of the refectory. He wrote nothing about it in his surviving notebooks. But something can be gleaned from the work of restorers. On top of a final layer of fine plaster, termed *intonaco* in fresco painting, it is known that Leonardo laid down a priming coat of white lead, to act as a highly reflective support for his pigments mixed with organic binder. There is some evidence that he then made sketches on the intonaco in red chalk, traces of which have been found in almost imperceptible quantities. He also made some incisions in the intonaco to mark the perspective lines of the ceiling and the left wall. But unlike in fresco painting, the intonaco was allowed to dry, and then painted. Leonardo's new technique was 'more akin to egg tempera painting on a gessoed panel' than fresco painting, writes Kemp.

Fortunately, there are several eyewitness accounts of the artist himself at work on his painting. The best is by Matteo Bandello, the nephew of the prior of the monastery. In 1554, he published a novella, in which he tells of how, as a boy, he would see Leonardo arrive early in the morning and climb the scaffolding. In Bandello's words:

> He sometimes stayed there from dawn to sundown, never putting down his brush, forgetting to eat and drink, painting without pause. He would also sometimes remain two, three, or four days without touching his brush, although he spent several hours a day standing in front of the work, arms folded, examining and criticizing the figures to himself. I also saw him, driven by some sudden urge, at midday, when the sun was at its height, leaving the Corte Vecchia, where he was working on his marvellous clay horse, to come straight to Santa Maria delle Grazie, without seeking shade, and clamber up onto the scaffolding, pick up a brush, put in one or two strokes, and then go away again.

A second good source is the dramatic poet Giovanni Battista Giraldi, who published a text, also in 1554, with references to Leonardo, based on information obtained from his father, who had watched the painter at work on *The Last Supper*. Giraldi tells the well-known story—also told by Vasari— of a characteristically Leonardesque delay in completing the painting. The impatient prior of Santa Maria delle Grazie, having already complained once without effect to Leonardo's paymaster, eventually told the duke in exasperation: 'There is only the head of Judas still to do, and for over a year now, not only has Leonardo not touched the painting, but he has only come to see it once.' Ludovico Sforza, impatient himself (judging from a letter about the delay in his archives dated June 1497), summoned the artist and asked for an explanation. An unabashed Leonardo responded that he had in fact spent the year, night and morning, in a notorious part of Milan studying ruffians (and who knows what else?), searching for the perfect model for Judas. 'But I have not yet been able to discover a villain's face corresponding to what I have in mind. Once I find that face, I will finish the painting in a day. But if my research remains fruitless, I shall take the features of the prior who came to complain about me to Your Excellency and who would fit the requirements perfectly.' The duke laughed, but appreciated the serious point at issue, and agreed to let Leonardo take more time. The face of Judas was eventually painted, although sadly it is today too damaged to see fully what Leonardo was striving so doggedly to achieve.

These two stories, by Bandello and Giraldi, complement each other well, and have the ring of truth. One can easily believe that Judas Iscariot, of all the characters around the supper table, would have exerted the most trenchant hold on Leonardo's imagination, which was driven, as he once wrote of his visit to the dark cave, by the allied emotions of fear and desire. *The Last Supper*, with its commingling of treachery, compassion, and love, was the perfect subject for such a complex, tortured perfectionist.

CHAPTER 7

CHRISTOPHER WREN

St Paul's Cathedral

An Architect ought to be jealous [suspicious] of Novelties, in which Fancy blinds the Judgment; and to think his Judges, as well those that are to live Five Centuries after him, as those of his own Time. That which is commendable now for Novelty, will not be a new Invention to Posterity, when his Works are often imitated, and when it is unknown which was the Original; but the Glory of that which is good of itself is eternal.

Christopher Wren, 'Tract I', date unknown, in *Parentalia: or, Memoirs of the Family of the Wrens*, posthumously published in 1750

Architecture, by its very nature, is more collaborative a discipline than the majority of the arts and sciences—partly because it is both an art and a science. Architects depend on many others, from financiers to engineers, in order to realize their visions. Buildings, however novel and original they may appear at the time of construction, are usually known to the public by their function or by the name of their patron, not their architect. Only a handful of architects become associated with their buildings in perpetuity, as artists do with their works or scientists with their theories and experiments.

Christopher Wren is one of them. His buildings in London, Oxford, and Cambridge—notably the Royal Hospital at Greenwich, the Sheldonian Theatre, and Trinity College Library (also known as the Wren Library)—immediately bring his name to mind. Above all, there is St Paul's Cathedral, probably London's most celebrated landmark. As striking today as it was to Wren's contemporaries three centuries ago, St Paul's will always be linked with him in the public mind. The Latin inscription above his undecorated black slab of a tombstone in St Paul's crypt, placed there by his son after Wren's death in 1723, is indeed apt: 'LECTOR, SI MONUMENTUM REQUIRIS, CIRCUMSPICE' ('Reader, if you seek a monument, look around you').

The design and construction of St Paul's was groundbreaking in at least three ways, which might be regarded as breakthroughs in architecture. First, unlike the medieval or Renaissance cathedrals such as Westminster Abbey or St Peter's Basilica in Rome, St Paul's was the work of only one architect, and was built in his lifetime—indeed Wren was the only one of the original team to see the building completed. Second, unlike previous architects, Wren was a distinguished scientist (though the word scientist had yet to come into use) and a skilled draughtsman, who personally conceived and oversaw both the structural and the aesthetic aspects of the building, from the foundations to the carvings on the walls. Lastly, unlike earlier domed buildings, St Paul's was finished with a unique 'triple' dome supporting its lantern, which had no precedent in the history of architecture and has not been repeated. The dome's ingenious—even revolutionary—structure, and its grandeur, were made feasible by Wren's knowledge of science and art, and are generally considered to lift his building into the realm of the greatest architecture.

Yet St Paul's has always had its professional critics, and few visitors to the cathedral admire its entirety. Many aspects are conventional, and some are the result of flawed compromises. The English crown, the Anglican Church, and the Gothic tradition in English architecture all exercised their influence, compelling Wren to make changes against his wishes. Structural and technical problems forced him to adopt solutions that were sometimes against his architectural principles. 'St Paul's embodies the exertions of one outstandingly brilliant and self-reliant mind—a mind which was receptive and inventive to the end', wrote the leading architectural historian John Summerson in his 1953 biography of Wren. But, he added, 'It is not a perfect building. It does not, from every point of view, fall into a wholly satisfying unity.'

Wren's career was a lifelong dialectic between orthodoxy and unorthodoxy, both in his ideas and in his behaviour. Orthodoxy beckoned from his intimate childhood relationship with the crown and church. His father Christopher and his uncle Matthew were well-established, high-church clergymen in the immediate circle of King Charles I and Archbishop Laud. In the early 1620s, Matthew Wren had been chaplain to Prince Charles, who after becoming monarch made him dean of Windsor in 1628—a position to which his younger brother Christopher succeeded in 1635. Christopher's children, including his son Christopher, therefore passed their childhood in the royal environs of Windsor Castle, cocooned in comfort and privilege.

But in 1642, when the boy was ten, with the outbreak of civil war between the king and Parliament, this gilded world was shattered. Matthew Wren, now Bishop of Ely, near Cambridge, was immediately arrested and incarcerated in the Tower of London, where he remained until the Restoration of Charles II in 1660. The deanery at Windsor was ransacked by parliamentary troops, and Dean Wren decamped with his family to his parish in the Wiltshire countryside, where they sat out the war. In 1646, however, after the defeat of the king, the delinquent dean was deprived of his Wiltshire living in favour of a Puritan preacher, and found himself homeless. Fortunately for the Wrens, they were offered refuge in a rectory at Bletchingdon near Oxford by the local clergyman, William Holder, who had married Susan Wren, the dean's third daughter. Dean Wren never recovered his former position, dying in 1658, unlike Matthew Wren, who flourished after the Restoration and provided his nephew with his very first architectural commission, in 1663.

Christopher Wren never spoke of this turbulent period in his teens and twenties, and wrote no journal or memoir of his life, so we are obliged to speculate on its effects. For one thing, it apparently made him remarkably circumspect about religion. Ironically, almost nothing is known of the religious views of the builder of one of England's greatest cathedrals. For another, it seems to have reinforced the conventional appeal of positions of wealth and status, which is inevitably strong among architects who depend on the rich and powerful for patronage. By contrast, Wren's profound attraction to science and its rational truths in this period may have acted as an antidote to the political and social turmoil. Finally, it may be that his extreme early restlessness as a scientist and inventor—shifting between extraordinarily diverse fields without bothering to complete or publish his discoveries—derived to some extent from anxiety about his security during his highly uncertain youth.

Wren's interest in science revealed itself as a schoolboy, long before his interest in buildings. He designed a sundial, the first of several, and at the age of thirteen, in 1645, he invented a calculator of the movements of the heavenly bodies, which he called a *panorganum astronomicum* and dedicated to his father with a description composed in his already fluent Latin.

No doubt Dean Wren was encouraging, judging from his extensive 1650s scientific marginalia in books (now in the Bodleian Library, Oxford) studied by the historian Jim Bennett, which show a 'well-informed and widely read interest in mechanics and natural philosophy' despite an entrenched theological opposition to the heliocentric theory of Copernicus, even a century after its publication in 1543. Encouraging too was Holder, who taught Wren his first mathematics. But it was a well-connected royalist physician, a friend of Holder named Charles Scarburgh, who became Wren's first professional scientific mentor, especially in mathematics and medicine. Initially introduced to Scarburgh as a patient in about 1647, Wren stayed at the doctor's London home for months, maybe more than a year. Aged only about 15, he joined in the weekly meetings of a small group of experienced men discussing 'physick, anatomy, geometry, astronomy, navigation, staticks, magneticks, chymicks, mechanicks and natural experiments'. Groups such as Scarburgh's, in London and Oxford, inspired by Francis Bacon's belief in experimentation rather than Aristotelian speculation, would lead to the formation of the Royal Society just over a decade later, after the Restoration, with Wren as a key founding member.

Some doubt surrounds the exact date in the late 1640s when Wren became a student at Oxford University. Wren's son writes 1646, when Wren was 14, which is surely too early. Others generally favour 1649. Yet on 30 January 1649, King Charles I was publicly beheaded by Parliament, and his royalist supporters trembled for their lives. According to Wren biographer Lisa Jardine, the limited surviving evidence (two letters, one by Wren) suggests that the youth was sent out of the country secretly in March 1649 by his anxious father in the company of a family friend, the clergyman John Wilkins, who was officially touring continental Europe, and did not return to England until December. On the other hand, there is absolutely no reference to these travels by Wren or any of his friends or acquaintances after the Restoration, which seems hard to understand, since Wren lived into his nineties. That said, if Wren really did spend nine months abroad in 1649, it would certainly solve 'one of the long-standing mysteries about his later career,' writes Jardine, 'how a man who had never seen the great new buildings of Europe could have embarked so confidently on an architectural career shortly after the Restoration.'

Whatever the truth, by 1650 Wren was residing not far from his family in Bletchingdon at Wadham College, Oxford, where Wilkins had been appointed the warden by the parliamentarians in 1648, after a purge of royalist heads of colleges. Enthusiastically supported by the liberal and tolerant Wilkins, who made himself the centre of a club of experimenters, Wren would remain in Oxford until 1657, latterly as a fellow of All Souls College, and return to Oxford as the Savilian professor of astronomy in 1661 for a period after the Restoration. These years, until his early thirties, would lay the basis for his scientific reputation, which prompted Isaac Newton to call Wren one of the three 'foremost geometers of the previous generation' in his *Principia Mathematica*, in recognition of Wren's experimental work on the laws of motion.

'Wren's science has been neglected', wrote Bennett in *The Mathematical Science of Christopher Wren* in 1982. This is still largely true. Wren's architectural achievements eclipse his scientific work in the 1650s and early 1660s to such an extent that some books on Wren devote merely a few pages to him as a scientist, while well-known biographical encyclopaedias of scientists omit Wren altogether. As for the relevance of his science to his architecture, this is widely accepted but still underdetermined. 'Although the evidence of his writings on architecture can be used to establish a link between Wren's scientific background and his architectural thinking, it is for the most part in terms of his approach to the study of history and his empirical definition of beauty', writes the editor of Wren's writings, Lydia Soo. 'Determining a definite link between his mind-set as an experimental scientist and as a practising architect is much more difficult.' Even in the curvature of the dome of St Paul's, the relationship between Wren's knowledge of mathematics and of masonry is controversial.

Wren's scientific research ranged more broadly than any of his Oxford contemporaries, who included such brilliant and wide-ranging experimenters as Robert Boyle and Robert Hooke. For example, he applied mathematics to astronomy, cosmology, meteorology, mechanics, surveying, and the search for longitude. He took up microscopy, and made exquisite drawings of minute creatures, such as a flea and a fly's wing, some of which eventually appeared in Hooke's pioneering *Micrographia*, published in 1665. He injected poison into animals to show that it followed the circulation of the blood—an idea discovered by Charles I's physician William Harvey—which soon led to the first (disastrous) attempts at blood transfusion by others. He also invented a number of devices, notably a double-writing instrument to make exact copies of documents, which proved successful. Throughout, his emphasis was on experiment rather than theory, the tangible rather than the invisible, and results that might be useful to society.

Some idea of his practicality—which would come to the fore in his later architecture—can be sensed from Boyle's description of Wren's drug injection experiment on a large dog in 1656, watched by a select group in Oxford. 'His way...was briefly this: First, to make a small and opportune incision over that Part of the hind leg, where the larger Vessels that carry the Blood, are most easy to be taken hold of: then to make a Ligature upon these Vessels, and to apply a certain small Plate of Brass...almost of the Shape & Bigness of the Nail of a Man's Thumb, but somewhat longer.' This plate had four little holes in the sides, near the corners, through which Wren passed threads that he tied securely around the vein, and a narrow aperture down the middle, almost as long as the plate, in which he could insert a lancet. Wren then made 'a Slit along the Vein, from the ligature towards the Heart, great enough to put in at the slender Pipe of a Syringe; by which I had proposed to have injected a warm Solution of Opium in Sack, that the Effect of our Experiment might be the more quick and manifest'. Then, Boyle reported, 'our dexterous Experimenter having surmounted the Difficulties, which the tortured Dog's violent Strugglings interposed, conveyed a small Dose of the Solution or Tincture into the opened Vessel...'. The poor dog was rapidly stupefied by the narcotic circulating in its blood from leg to brain, and looked as if it might not survive. But in fact the animal not only recovered, it became famous; and was eventually stolen from Boyle's house.

With such credentials, the young Wren was a natural candidate for a professorship at Gresham College in the City of London. The college had been founded 60 years before, in 1597, under the terms of the will of Sir Thomas Gresham, a leading financier in Elizabethan times. In exchange for £50 a year and free college lodgings, Gresham professors—in divinity, law, physic, rhetoric, music, geometry, and astronomy—were expected to give weekly public lectures to the citizens of London, emphasizing practice over theory, and speaking in both Latin and English (unlike in Oxford, where the lectures were in Latin). In 1657, Wren—probably promoted by Wilkins—was appointed Gresham professor of astronomy, and moved from Oxford to London. He served there for four years, interrupted by the military

occupation of the college buildings during the collapse of the Commonwealth following the death of Oliver Cromwell in 1658, when all but the
professor of physic prudently withdrew from their lodgings then mired in
the army's stink. (This professor had 'prepar'd his Nose for Camp Perfumes'
while acting as physician to Cromwell's army in Scotland, and had 'excellent Restoratives in his Cellar', a friend in London vividly warned Wren,
who had retreated to Oxford.)

In his first Gresham lecture, the only one that survives, Wren gives by far
the most extensive available account of his scientific views at a time of
intellectual revolution. Despite his conventional background, and his immersion in the Latin classics, he showed himself willing to reject ancient
authority. Near the beginning he states: 'the Mathematical Wits of this Age
have excell'd the Ancients, (who pierced but to the Bark and Outside of
Things) in handling particular disquisitions of Nature, in clearing up History, and fixing Chronology'. He also rejects his father's outmoded view of
Copernicus: 'the apparent Absurdity of a moving Earth makes the Philosophers contemn it, tho' some of them taken with the Paradox, begin to
observe Nature, and to dare to suppose some old Opinion false; and now
began the first happy Appearance of Liberty to Philosophy, oppress'd by
the Tyranny of the Greek and Roman Monarchies'. This was probably not a
sentence Wren would have chosen to deliver in public a few years later,
after the return of King Charles to the throne.

The Royal Society, the modern world's first scientific institution, was
conceived at Gresham College on the afternoon of 28 November 1660,
when twelve men, including Wren, Wilkins (the prime mover), and Boyle,
met in the lodgings of the professor of geometry. In 1662, it was given a
royal charter by Charles II. Wren remained an active fellow for the rest of
his life, serving as its third president in the 1680s, often attending its
meetings and periodically publishing in its journal, *Philosophical Transactions*.
Yet, his relationship with the society was an ambivalent one, not whole-
heartedly committed, especially as his involvement with architecture deepened from the late 1660s onwards.

In 1661, for example, Wren—now back in Oxford (where experimental
philosophers were viewed with some suspicion by churchmen)—was invited
by the Royal Society, at the personal request of the king, to provide some of his
microscopic drawings of creatures and a model globe of the Moon, based on
his telescopic observations in the 1650s made with a moving-wire eyepiece
micrometer of his own invention. Wren presented the globe personally to

Charles II, inscribed with a flattering dedication, without showing it first to the Royal Society; and subsequently failed to make another globe at the society's request. (The royal globe is now lost, but appears in the foreground of Wren's portrait hanging in the Sheldonian Theatre in Oxford.) That same year, at the request of the first president, Lord Brouncker, Wren analysed at length, and imaginatively, the possible experiments that might be performed for the entertainment of the king on his inaugural visit to the Royal Society. However, he showed a certain impatience with the purpose of the occasion, making the shrewd comment to Brouncker that: 'certainly Nature in the best of her Works is apparent enough in obvious Things, were they but curiously observ'd; and the Key that opens Treasures, is often plain and rusty, but unless it is gilt, 'twill make no Show at Court'. In the early years of the Restoration, Wren the scientist and Wren the royalist (and future royal architect) clearly co-existed in a state of creative tension.

The beginnings of Wren's architectural career date from this time, though it is at least possible that he helped Wilkins with his plans for an unbuilt scientific 'college' at Oxford in the mid-1650s. We know from a passing reference in a letter written to Wren in 1661—there is no other evidence—that the king had requested Wren to help survey the fabric of Old St Paul's with a view to repairing it. He also received a formal offer from the government to become the surveyor in charge of some important naval fortifications at Tangier in Morocco (a Portuguese territory handed over to Charles II when he married Catherine of Braganza). As an inducement to accept, Wren was also offered the much more appealing position of 'Surveyor-General of the King's Works'—the king's official architect—upon the death of the current incumbent.

From today's perspective, it may seem strange that Charles II thought of Wren as any kind of architect, since he had built nothing by 1661 and was a professor of astronomy at Oxford. Yet in seventeenth-century England, architecture did not exist as a profession—in fact, the first English architecture school dates from only 1847; the single recognized English architect was Inigo Jones, who worked for Charles I and died in 1652. The main qualification for designing buildings in this age was a knowledge of mathematics, which Wren certainly had as a leading geometer. His mathematical expertise, according to his son, was the main reason why he received the Tangier offer (not to mention, of course, the loyalty of the Wren family to the king).

More surprising, really, is Wren's own desire to consider architecture as a career, given that it did not feature in his scientific work of the 1650s, except tangentially through surveying. While an architectural career would certainly continue to involve science, it would be bound to lead him in a direction very different from astronomy. In the face of Wren's own silence, Summerson speculates convincingly on his motives:

> To many scientific minds, the crystallization of theory in papers and books is concrete enough. To Wren it was not ... [Architecture] absorbed all his capacities—his love of concrete exposition in models as well as his feeling for Roman design and language, his power of geometrical analysis as well as his love of decorative precision in drawing, his faculty for inventing practical homely devices as well as for estimating the strength of a vault. It was the complete answer.

In the event, Wren deftly declined the Tangier request in 1661 while retaining the goodwill of the king, by pleading ill health. The job went to a professional surveyor, Sir Jonas Moore, who became extremely wealthy—far wealthier than Wren ever did—and later the driving force behind the building of the Royal Observatory at Greenwich, designed in the 1670s by Wren.

His first completed architectural commission came not from the king but from his high-church uncle: the chapel of Matthew Wren's old college in Cambridge, Pembroke, beneath which the reinstated Bishop of Ely would finally be laid to rest in 1667, in a vault designed by his nephew. The scheme for the chapel, including a wooden model—the first of dozens Wren would build, perhaps partly inspired by his scientific background—was ready by May 1663, when building began; the chapel was consecrated some two years later. It was not ambitious, but it was well crafted and thoroughly classical (without any hint of the Gothic style typical of Cambridge buildings), with a street facade based on engravings of a classical temple facade published in 1611 in an English edition of a Renaissance architecture textbook by Sebastiano Serlio. Wren's role in the project was probably a limited one, subservient to his formidable uncle's wishes, since there is no reference to the chapel in his son's memoir *Parentalia*.

Concurrently with Pembroke Chapel, Wren began designing his first major building, intended for secular Oxford University functions such as the degree ceremonies then held in the unsuitable surroundings of the University Church. On completion in 1669, it was called the Sheldonian Theatre, after Gilbert Sheldon, warden of All Souls College at the time of the Restoration, later chancellor of the university and Archbishop of Canterbury, who paid for its entire construction cost. Sheldon knew Wren at

All Souls and may have discussed the project with him as early as 1659, but the first announcement of Wren's scheme was not until April 1663, when he presented a model of it to the Royal Society.

There was no English precedent for such a building. Wren therefore went back to ancient Rome and modelled his design along the lines of the D-shaped Theatre of Marcellus, begun by Julius Caesar and completed by Augustus in 13 BC, making its dramatic focus the chancellor's seat at the curved centre of the D. He knew the Roman original from an engraving in Serlio's textbook, but he frequently departed from his Renaissance source. 'The archetypal Renaissance secular facade has three zones: the basement, which supports, the main storey, and the attic', notes Kerry Downes, the current editor of Wren's architectural drawings. 'Here Wren simply left out the main storey. The treatises give examples of facades without basements or without attics, but no warrant for having both of these with no middle. Wren, like the good experimenter he was, tried it. And no bolt came from heaven.' The final result may not have been as impressive as he hoped—the Sheldonian has plenty of critics—but it certainly sprang from his self-assurance in modifying the classical original, not from the ignorance of immaturity.

For the roof of the Sheldonian, there was no classical precedent, since the ancient Romans used only temporary awnings. The 70-foot span of the design was too wide to be bridged by single timbers. So Wren, determined to avoid inappropriate Gothic vaulting or supporting columns that would ruin the classical effect, created a new type of covering. With the help of a fellow Savilian professor, the geometer John Wallis, designer of a so-called 'geometrical flat floor', Wren constructed a flat ceiling visible to the audience, fashioned from overlapping timbers supported from above by invisible wooden trusses made of shorter sections held in place by their own weight and secured by carefully positioned iron bolts and plates. So strong was this ceiling that the university's Clarendon Press was able to store its books in the attic space between the ceiling and the topmost roof of the building.

Designing the Sheldonian must have made Wren acutely conscious of his lack of actual contact with classical architecture, as opposed to illustrations of it in books. In the early 1660s, he was yet to travel beyond England (unless we accept the idea that he visited the Continent in 1649). Wren therefore decided to spend some months in 1665–66 in the France of Louis XIV, observing the churches, palaces, and other buildings of Paris and Versailles, and the chateaux in the countryside, including buildings still under construction and the unfinished Louvre, while getting to know a number of French scientists who like him were interested in architecture.

A particular draw in Paris was the presence of the great Gianlorenzo Bernini, a celebrity who had come from Rome at the invitation of the king to present his drawings for the Louvre. Sadly, the meeting was dissatisfying, as Wren described in a letter home: 'Bernini's Design of the Louvre I would have given my Skin for, but the old reserv'd Italian gave me but a few Minutes View; it was five little Designs in Paper, for which he hath receiv'd as many thousand Pistoles; I had only Time to copy it in my Fancy and Memory.' Nevertheless, the encounter with an established master must surely have made a strong impression on a rising star. 'He learned from Bernini that architecture was more than just a profession for master-builders or a hobby for gentlemen', argues Wren biographer Adrian Tinniswood. 'It was a vocation, and like any vocation, it required commitment. And—if you were good enough—it promised power and status.'

Wren returned to London in March 1666. The immediate result of his French exposure was that he proposed a dome for the restoration of Old St Paul's, influenced by the dome of the Church of the Sorbonne in Paris designed by Jacques Lemercier and the dome of St Peter's Basilica in Rome. In a report dated 1 May 1666, Wren told the royal commission on St Paul's, established in 1663: 'I cannot propose a better Remedy, than by cutting off the inner Corners of the Cross, to reduce this middle Part into a spacious Dome or Rotundo, with a Cupola, or hemispherical Roof, and upon the Cupola, (for the outward Ornament) a Lantern with a spiring Top, to rise proportionably, tho' not to that unnecessary Height of the former Spire of Timber and Lead burnt by Lightning.' The new dome and lantern could be constructed around the remains of the existing tower, which could afterwards be dismantled, Wren further suggested, thereby saving both money in scaffolding, and avoiding public despond at the destruction of the familiar tower.

In 1561, lightning had destroyed the spire of the medieval St Paul's started by the Normans and completed in 1327 (on the site of three earlier cathedrals dating back to 604). In the century since then, the fabric of Old St Paul's had decayed substantially, apart from some

recladding of the nave and transepts and the construction of a magnificent classical portico at the west end (still the main entrance to the
cathedral), all undertaken by Inigo Jones at the behest of Charles I in
the 1630s; in the Commonwealth period, after the civil war, the
cathedral had been used as a military barracks and stables for horses,
with disastrous effects. By the time of the Restoration in 1660, parts of
the building had either collapsed or were in imminent danger of
collapse.

Wren's proposals, which he worked up as coloured drawings in his
rooms in Oxford that summer of 1666, were not immediately accepted,
because the royal commission still hoped to repair, rather than rebuild,
St Paul's. But at a site meeting on 27 August 1666, 'after much contest'
(according to the diarist John Evelyn, one of the commissioners, who
backed his friend Wren), the dome idea predominated, subject to studies
of the foundations.

Within barely a week of this decision, there was no longer much question
about whether to rebuild or not, for large parts of the cathedral were now
completely beyond repair, after being ravaged by the Great Fire of London
at the beginning of September. The fire, burning for four days, reduced
almost everything within the old walls of the City to smouldering ruins: an
area of some 373 acres (150 hectares). It destroyed 13,200 houses and
rendered 80,000–100,000 inhabitants homeless, forcing them to camp
out in the fields around the City's boundaries. In addition to the cathedral,
87 parish churches were devastated.

For Wren, the calamity proved to be his making as an architect. Although
his amazingly prompt plan for restructuring the City, stimulated by the
contemporary remodelling of Paris by Louis XIV, was rejected as too radical
by the City's fathers and residents, he was appointed by Charles II to the six-
man rebuilding commission. Three commissioners were chosen by the
king, and three by the Corporation of London, one of whom was Wren's
friend Hooke, who was already an experienced surveyor. Money for
rebuilding was to come from a government tax on coal brought into the
port of London. Decades of imposing this tax, reluctantly renewed by
successive Parliaments until 1716, would in due course pay for most of the
construction of St Paul's.

Rebuilding the parish churches began in 1670, well before the cathedral.
Between then and the end of his life, Wren—ably assisted by Hooke and
later by Nicholas Hawksmoor—oversaw the rebuilding of 51 parish

churches in London, chiefly in the City. Each church presented its own problems and required its own design solution, not to speak of negotiations with its vestry about their desire to outdo neighbouring churches in the size and decoration of their church's rebuilt tower and steeple. This intensive church building programme taught Wren some of the difficulties he would face with St Paul's, and allowed him time and space to experiment. In 1673, for instance, he designed a beautiful dome for the light-filled St Stephen's church in Walbrook—widely regarded as his finest City church still in existence—supported on a series of eight equal arches springing from slender columns. The dome was made of wood, though resembling masonry, unlike the interior masonry dome of St Paul's, which also rests on eight arches and far more substantial columns. Yet, the St Stephen's dome can be seen as a trial run for the much more complicated and demanding cathedral dome, built three decades later.

The new churches also compelled Wren to consider how to meet the requirements of congregational worship, emphasized by the Anglican Church since the Reformation in the previous century, which attached more importance to the pulpit and the sermon than the ritual at the altar (beloved of Wren's high-church uncle Matthew). 'The Romanists, indeed, may build larger Churches, it is enough if they hear the Murmur of the Mass, and see the Elevation of the Host, but ours are to be fitted with Auditories', Wren noted in his ever-practical way. 'Concerning the placing of the Pulpit, I shall observe...A moderate Voice may be heard 50 Feet distant before the Preacher, 30 Feet on each Side, and 20 behind the Pulpit, and not this, unless the Pronunciation be distinct and equal, without losing the Voice at the last Word of the Sentence, which is commonly emphatical, and if obscur'd spoils the whole Sense.' Wren was determined to make the new St Paul's an effective space for congregational worship, unlike the medieval Gothic cathedrals.

After a further collapse at the west end of Old St Paul's in 1668, during an attempt to repair Inigo Jones's fire-cracked portico, the dean and chapter finally agreed to demolish the cathedral, with the permission of the king, and follow the recommendations of Wren. 'What we are to do next is the present Deliberation, in which you are so absolutely and indispensably necessary to us, that we can do nothing, resolve on nothing without you', the dean wrote to Wren in Oxford. The following year, 1669, the 36-year-old professor of astronomy, while retaining his position in Oxford until 1673—presumably as an insurance policy against failure as an architect—was officially appointed as both the king's architect ('Surveyor-General of the King's Works') and the cathedral's architect ('Surveyor of the Fabrick'): positions he would retain for half a century, almost until his death.

Demolition began at the east end in 1668 and required many years of arduous labour; it was not finally completed at the west end until the mid-1680s. To increase the pace, Wren, in the best tradition of the Royal Society, experimented with gunpowder. The explosives demolished the pillars supporting the old tower with dramatic success, but were abandoned after a near-accident with flying debris, in favour of a battering ram of the type used in military siege operations, swung back and forth on ropes by 30 men. At length, in the mid-summer of 1675, sufficient ground had been cleared for a foundation ceremony. Soon after, it is famously said (as reported by Wren's son in *Parentalia*), Wren was laying out the position of the dome on the ground. Needing a stone to mark the centre, and not wishing to leave the spot, he called for a labourer to bring one. When he turned it over, it happened to be a piece of a charred gravestone, 'with nothing remaining of the Inscription but this single word in large Capitals, RESURGAM' ('I shall rise again'). Today, the prescient Latin word appears boldly beneath a carving of a phoenix rising from the ashes on the south facade of the cathedral.

The six years between Wren's appointment as architect of the new St Paul's in July 1669 and the beginning of construction in June 1675 were crucial ones for the design of the cathedral. Sketches, drawings, plans, elevations, sections, and wooden models were made by him and his assistants; reviewed by the king, the commissioners, and the St Paul's chapter; rejected, revised, rejected again, revised again; and finally approved. But it would be wrong to imagine that the entire design was fixed when construction began, even in its fundamentals, as one might expect with a modern building of the importance of St Paul's. Far from it. Although establishing the precise sequence of the design and construction process is tricky on the basis of the documents and models that survive (many were undoubtedly destroyed or lost over some four decades of work), because they are seldom dated and the hands of the different draughtsmen are not certain, it is clear that Wren's design continued to evolve long after 1675, often creatively and sometimes radically.

In *Building St Paul's*, the architectural historian James Campbell identifies eight key differences between the so-called Warrant design (see above), which received the royal warrant in May 1675, and the cathedral as completed in 1711. In 1675:

> 1. The layout of the pillars and towers around the dome crossing is different. 2. No crypt is shown. 3. The walls are thinner. 4. The transepts end in rectangular porches [rather than semicircular porticoes]. 5. The section shows no screen walls above the aisles, meaning that the buttresses supporting the roof would have been visible from outside the cathedral. 6. The west end is much simpler, without the extensions that hold the Consistory Court, Library, Morning Chapel, and Trophy Room. 7. The towers are different, and the portico is similar to the one Inigo Jones built for Charles I. 8. The Warrant design features an extraordinary dome.

Compared to the St Paul's we know today, the Warrant design seems a hotchpotch, and its dome has a peculiar and slightly absurd spire. One cannot believe that Wren seriously intended to build the design as drawn in 1675; it must have been intended primarily to silence his critics, as we shall now see by tracing the steps in its evolution.

Let us begin at the beginning of the design process, in 1669. Part of what is known as the First Model design, presented to Charles II in 1670, survives in the cathedral's Trophy Room in the form of an oak and pear wood model of a nave/choir with its domed entrance vestibule missing. The overall design bears no resemblance to either Old St Paul's or the Warrant design. The dome is placed at the west end, not over the centre of the church, and separate from the nave; and there are no aisles, but instead a series of open arcades at ground level, loggias probably based on the design of Andrea Palladio's Italian basilica at Vicenza, according to the scholar Gordon Higgott. Presumably these arcades were intended to be shelters for those who had formerly carried on their trade in the nave of Old St Paul's, such as booksellers. It seems from *Parentalia* that Wren was responding to a brief requesting a moderate-sized, affordable building with good acoustics for congregational worship. But his model pleased no one (except perhaps Wren), being regarded by some as deviating too much 'from the old Gothick Form' and by others as 'not stately enough'. Wren was asked by the commissioners to come up with a different design. The First Model did not go to waste, however, as it reappeared in 1676, in modified form (and without the dome and vestibule) in Wren's design for Trinity College Library in Cambridge.

The design that now emerged was totally different, and without precedent in England. Known as the Greek Cross design, it may have been inspired by early designs for St Peter's Basilica. It shows the cathedral in the shape of a Greek cross with an enormous central dome and lantern supported by eight piers having complete circulation around them and four arms separated by Baroque concave elevations. Thus it has no nave and transept, as in a conventional cross-shaped church like Old St Paul's, and the choir is simply the arm on the east side of the dome. 'The idea of congregational assembly as the main purpose of a church could hardly be more firmly, more geometrically, expressed', remarks Summerson.

The Greek Cross design was approved in November 1672 by the king, who authorized the building of a model large enough for a man to stand inside it. With the addition of a library vestibule and a grand portico, Inigo Jones style, at the west end in February 1673, the design was turned into the superb Great Model that stands in the cathedral's Trophy Room today. Built on a scale of 1:24, it is 13 feet (3.95 m) high, 13 feet 1 inch (3.97 m) wide and 20 feet 1 inch (6.36 m) long. Plastered and painted both inside and out, and including miniature statues, it cost over £500 by the time it was finished in early 1674. Wren was thrilled, and 'in private Conversation, always seem'd to set a higher Value on this Design, than

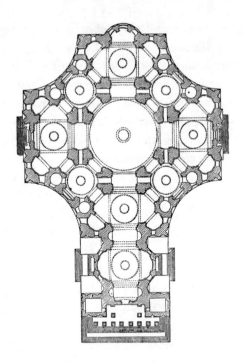

any he had made before or since', according to his son. (See plan of the
Great Model above.)

Its rejection by the St Paul's clergy, in 1674, therefore came as a heavy
blow. Essentially, the chapter thought the design 'not enough of a Cathedral-fashion' (*Parentalia*). In other words, they wanted a recognizable nave,
transept, aisles, and choir. Moreover, they wanted a choir that could be built
separately, and put to use well before the rest of the cathedral—which was
plainly impossible with the Greek Cross design.

After a failed appeal to the king, Wren had no choice if he wanted his
cathedral but to compromise—at least on paper. He therefore created the
Warrant design of 1675, which offered everything required by the chapter,
and a dome with a Gothic-looking spire. But according to his son's memoir,
having obtained the royal warrant, Wren seems to have received permission from the king, informally, to make such changes during construction
as he should see fit. He was also canny enough to make sure that construction of different parts of the cathedral proceeded simultaneously, fearing
that otherwise, once the choir was complete, the funds would run out. At
the same time, again according to *Parentalia*, Wren 'resolved to make no
more Models, or publickly expose his Drawings, which (as he had found by

Experience) did but lose Time, & subjected his Business many Times, to incompetent Judges'. Whether authorized or not, Wren's eventual changes were very substantial, as listed by Campbell above; so in the end, he got his way in most matters by patiently waiting. But it is not true that there were no more models; the building accounts show that over 70 models were made, including large-scale structural models of the dome in stone in 1693. Nor is it the case that Wren managed to avoid showing any drawings to the commissioners, although he unquestionably played his cards close to his chest, especially with regard to the dome.

The foundations, the walls, the porticoes, the piers, the crossing, the roof, the buttresses, the stairways, and many other parts of the cathedral, all presented Wren with problems requiring imaginative solutions and in some cases compromise. Most famously, he surrounded the roof level of the building with a screen wall to conceal his use of flying buttresses: a sham structure according to purists, yet certainly necessary for aesthetic reasons. The giant portico at the west end, shown as one storey of columns in the Warrant design, had to become two storeys, because Wren could not procure blocks of Portland stone long enough to span the intercolumnia- tions of the entablature. But it is of course the dome and lantern, the construction of which took over a decade from 1697 to 1710, that attract the most attention.

Wren's most basic problem was as follows: a dome that looked right to a worshipper inside the cathedral would look puny on the London skyline, and yet a dome with the right external silhouette would look like a chimney to those standing underneath it. Hence, he needed a double dome. While there were precedents for this, such as the double domes of St Peter's in Rome, Florence Cathedral, and Persian architecture, Wren knew that his foundations and piers, which were already showing differential settlement in the 1680s, could not stand the weight of two brick domes. So while the inner dome could be made of brick, the outer dome had to be much lighter, made of wood covered in lead. Yet, a wooden dome could not support the weight of the planned heavy stone lantern visible both from the outside and from the inside while looking up through the oculus at the top of the inner dome. A wooden lantern was ruled out as insufficiently impressive, and also liable to rot.

Wren's eventual solution was therefore his ingenious triple dome. Its inner dome is an almost hemispherical shell made of bricks about 18 inches (46 cm) thick, which supports nothing other than its own weight. Above it,

but not resting on it, is a hollow brick cone between the inner and outer domes, invisible from below, cut off at the top to reveal light streaming through windows (invisible from outside) located just below the lantern. This cone serves two functions: to support the weight of the stone lantern (about 700 tons), and to support the timber framework that holds up the timber outer dome and its lead covering. The invisible brick cone, unlike the visible screen wall, is therefore a key structural element. 'The real elegance of Wren's solution is that it allowed the structural and aesthetic aspects of the [dome] design to be developed independently of each other', write James Campbell and Robert Bowles, a consulting engineer to the cathedral, in *St Paul's: The Cathedral Church of London, 604–2004*. (See the section through the cathedral above, drawn in 1755.)

The concept required faith to conceive and courage to execute. In October 1708, after completing the brick cone and the stone lantern, but before starting on the outer dome, there was an unofficial ceremony on the scaffolding atop the brick cone, high above London. Christopher Wren junior, accompanied by the master mason and his son, laid the final stone on the lantern. Wren senior, by now 76 and too frail to climb to the top, watched from below.

There has long been a debate among architects and architectural historians, mathematicians, and engineers, about how far Wren relied on stone models in deciding upon stable curvatures for the inner dome and the brick cone, and how far he calculated the correct curvatures from geometry and the structural theory developed by Hooke and himself in the 1670s. (The curvature of the outer dome, weighing relatively little, could be decided from purely aesthetic considerations.) Probably both experiment and theory played a part, but the empirical evidence from the stone models was the more important, given the infancy of structural mechanics in Wren's day.

Nor, frustratingly, do we have any clear evidence as to how Wren came up with his idea of the invisible brick cone, since neither he nor his son wrote a single word on the subject. The only certainty is that the triple-dome structure—roughly indicated in some undated surviving drawings—post-dates the Warrant design of 1675. There was a sort of architectural forerunner in the triple dome of the Baptistery at Pisa, completed in the fourteenth century, but the Baptistery's brick cone was clearly visible from the outside; and anyway it is uncertain if Wren was aware of the Italian building or not. He must have pondered the problem for many years after he discovered in the 1680s that the St Paul's foundations would not support a second brick dome—driven by his determination to create the particular outer dome profile and lantern that pleased him as an artist. No doubt he discussed it at length, too, with the masons and other craftsman who would realize his grand vision.

Most probably, the triple-dome solution struck Wren some time after the building of the stone models of the inner dome in 1693. Like all breakthroughs, it was the product of long experience and passionate involvement, made possible, in Wren's case, by a rare combination of scientific and aesthetic perception.

CHAPTER 8

WOLFGANG AMADEUS MOZART

The Marriage of Figaro

I don't know, but it seems to me that in an opera the Poesie must always be the obedient daughter of the Music.—Why are Italian comic operas so popular everywhere?—in spite of their wretched texts!—even in Paris, where I saw it myself. Because the Music reigns supreme—which makes one forget everything else. Therefore an opera that is well designed must please all the more; where words are written expressly for the Music and not merely to suit some miserable rhyme here and there...It is so much better if a good composer, who understands something about the stage and can make a suggestion here and there, is able to team up with an intelligent Poet and create a true Phoenix.

Wolfgang Amadeus Mozart in a letter to his father Leopold, 1781

During its first run in Vienna in 1786, Mozart's three-hour opera *Le Nozze di Figaro*, known in English as *The Marriage of Figaro*, received so many encores that the length of each performance was almost doubled. Within a week of the premiere, the Holy Roman Emperor Joseph II, a deep admirer of Mozart's music, was obliged to issue a general order for all operas permitting encores only of the arias and not of the longer ensembles.

Since then, *The Marriage of Figaro* has alternated with *Don Giovanni* as the most popular Mozart opera. Connoisseurs—not least Mozart himself— have long considered it to be among his finest artistic achievements. For many people, *Figaro* is not just the greatest of all social comedies but may scale the summit of perfection attainable in the operatic medium. It is no accident that a production of *Le Nozze di Figaro* was chosen to inaugurate the Glyndebourne festival of opera in 1934.

For this supreme stature Mozart certainly cannot be given all of the credit. *Le Nozze di Figaro* was closely modelled on an enormously successful French play, *La Folle Journée, ou Le Mariage de Figaro*, written by Pierre-Augustin Caron de Beaumarchais, first produced in Paris at the Comédie Française in 1784. The play's adaptation into a libretto was carried out by the Italian poet Lorenzo da Ponte, then working in Vienna, who went on to collaborate with Mozart on *Don Giovanni* in 1787 and *Così Fan Tutte* in 1790, and thereby became the leading opera librettist of his generation.

Beaumarchais had no personal input into the creation of *Figaro*, although he may have advised on its Paris production in 1793. As for Da Ponte, how much of the final libretto was written by him and how much created by Mozart's suggestions and modifications cannot be definitively established, given the surprisingly meagre surviving evidence. (There is not a single letter between Mozart and Da Ponte, for instance.) Yet, it is clear enough from reading Beaumarchais's somewhat dated play, which today is not much performed outside France, and also from the lack of any lasting literary achievement by Da Ponte beyond his three Mozart librettos, that the contributions of the two writers, while crucial, cannot account for why *The Marriage of Figaro* has become a staple of the opera repertory in Europe and America. Unquestionably, it is the music that breathes life into the opera today, rather than the characters and their utterances— notwithstanding the central character Figaro's deserved status as an Every-man. Mozart's score, listened to on its own, without any attempt to follow the entertaining but bewildering plot of Beaumarchais/Da Ponte, or even without the barest knowledge of the story, is endlessly enjoyable and invigorating. To hear it sung as part of a stage production, by a cast who are also good actors, is an overwhelming experience.

The originality of the opera lies in its exceptionally close and inventive integration of action, thought, language, song, and instrumental music. Before *Figaro*, librettists and composers of the period, including Mozart in *Idomeneo* (1781), had already broken with the conventional restrictions on movement, content, and form accepted in opera seria—that is, opera based on a serious theme, usually classical or mythological. For example, in the late 1760s/early 1770s they phased out the conventional static da capo aria, in which a single character was permitted to reflect on his or her feelings repetitively, as favoured by earlier composers of opera seria, notably George Frederick Handel (though Handel could be innovative, too). In another liberating development, Italian opera buffa—comic opera, based on contemporary life—flourished from the 1760s in the hands of composers such as Giovanni Paisiello and Domenico Cimarosa.

The Marriage of Figaro went much further, however, and made what amounted to a breakthrough. For the first time in either opera seria or buffa, ensembles were allowed to equal, and even dominate, arias. Of its 28 numbers, half were written for ensembles rather than for the solo voice: a proportion of ensemble singing unprecedented in eighteenth-century opera. The expressive effect was radical, a bit like the move from silent films into talkies. 'It brought a new dramatic and psychological realism to the medium. Instead of taking characters and their emotions at their own word, so to speak, audiences could now see and evaluate them in a variety of social contexts', comments the musicologist Basil Deane. 'This above all was the great opportunity that Da Ponte's libretto offered to Mozart—the opportunity of presenting fully rounded characters in a range of evolving situations. The composer understood this, and by musical genius transformed the already brilliant concept of Da Ponte into one of the great masterpieces of dramatic art.'

No one will ever be able to explain Mozart's alchemy fully. But we can still obtain considerable insight into his transformation of the Beaumarchais/Da Ponte story by first going back to his prodigiously musical childhood in the 1760s, when he became enchanted with Italian opera, some 20 years before composing The Marriage of Figaro, and then following the twists and turns of his engagement with opera up to 1786.

As a child and youth, Mozart never attended a school or college, and had no musical tuition outside of his family, apart from some voice lessons in London in 1764–65, aged eight or nine, from the castrato Giovanni Manzuoli and some counterpoint studies with the composer Padre Martini in Bologna in 1770. Instead, his education and upbringing from his birth in Salzburg in 1756 until his early twenties were rigorously directed by his father Leopold, a professional musician and composer at the court in Salzburg, who was without doubt the greatest single influence on his life.

Leopold Mozart came from a family of artisans long resident in the south German city of Augsburg. His father was a bookbinder, his mother the daughter of a weaver. The eldest of six surviving children, Leopold was apparently intended for the Catholic priesthood, but he felt an inner resistance. After attending a Jesuit gymnasium, where he became known for his singing and violin playing, he dropped out of school, aged 16, on the early death of his father in 1736. The following year, he resumed formal education at the Benedictine University in Salzburg, but in 1739 was expelled for want of application and poor attendance. He took a position with a prominent canon of Salzburg Cathedral as a chamberlain and musician. From there, in 1743, he moved to the court orchestra as a violinist, began teaching violin and later keyboard to the choirboys of the cathedral oratory, composed both sacred and secular music prolifically, wrote a classic teaching text on the violin in 1756, and in 1763 was appointed deputy Kapellmeister. He never moved back to his native Augsburg, residing in Salzburg until his death in 1787.

Leopold's youthful decision not to return after his father's death developed into a rift with his mother, which seems to have soured his adult life and in turn distorted his affection for his son. When Leopold married in 1747, he chose a woman from a place near Salzburg, Anna Maria Pertl, whose family had more musical talent than the Mozarts, but who was living in near poverty as a result of the premature death of her father leaving heavy debts. In retaliation, Leopold's mother refused to give her eldest son the dowry she gifted to all of her other children when they married. He never received the money, despite requests, and during the last ten years of her life, there was a grim silence between mother and son. When, in 1763, Leopold brought little Wolfgang and his sister Maria Anna to perform in Augsburg, near the beginning of their celebrated tour of Germany, France, England, Holland, Belgium, and Switzerland in 1763–66, the children's grandmother refused to attend the concerts.

Much ink has been lavished by Mozart scholars on Leopold's character and its effect on Wolfgang and his music. The father's ambivalent, often contemptuous, attitude to the bewigged nobility on whose patronage he always depended—which was certainly shared by the son—informs a sarcastic aside in Leopold's book on the violin. Of the instruments' ornamented scrolls he writes: 'The beautifully "curled" lion's head can improve the tone of a violin just as little as a fancifully curled wig can improve the intelligence of its living wig stand. Yet in spite of this, many a violin is

valued simply for its appearance, and how often does it happen that
clothes, money, pomp, and especially the curled wig is that which turns a
man into a scientist, counsellor, or doctor?' But it is mainly from Leopold's
copious, and sometimes shockingly manipulative, letters that his complex
personality really emerges. A typical example is his well intentioned if
cynical advice on friendship written to Wolfgang in 1777, after his trusting
son left Salzburg on a tour of Germany in search of a position at another
court:

> My son, to find *one man in a 1000* who is your true friend for reasons other
> than self-interest *is one of the greatest wonders of this world*. Examine all who call
> themselves your friends or who make a show of friendship and you'll find
> the reason why this is so. If they're not motivated by self-interest on their
> own account, then they'll be acting in the interests of some other friend
> whom they need; or they are your friends so that by singling you out they
> can annoy some third party.

Did Leopold Mozart nurture Wolfgang's astonishing talent for the benefit
of his son, or more for his own benefit? Speaking for the defence, H. C.
Robbins Landon regards Leopold as being 'in many respects his son's most
perceptive and sympathetic critic, friend and adviser. It would have been
better if Wolfgang had heeded his father's advice on many matters'.
Whereas Maynard Solomon, for the prosecution, remarks: 'true to the
deep-rooted outlook of the artisan class from which he sprang, Leopold
Mozart regarded his son as his personal economic resource and insurance
against the calamities of old age'. Ample documentary evidence can be
adduced to support both positions.

What is beyond argument is that Leopold's able and indefatigable
impresario role gave his son a uniquely wide ranging and precocious
musical education between his first performances for royalty in Munich
and Vienna in 1762, aged six, and his return to Salzburg from his final visit
to Italy in 1773. Thus in London, in 1764, Wolfgang played for King George
III and his family at Buckingham House. His father described the occasion
in a long letter home to Salzburg:

> The king gave him not only works by [Georg Christoph] Wagenseil to play,
> but also [Johann Christian] Bach, [Carl Friedrich] Abel and Handel, all of
> which he rattled off *prima vista* [at sight]. He played the king's organ so well
> that everyone rates his organ playing far higher than his harpsichord
> playing. He then accompanied the queen in an aria that she sang and a
> flautist in a solo. Finally he took the violin part in some Handel arias that

happened to be lying around and played the most beautiful melody over the simple bass, so that everyone was utterly astonished. In a word, what he knew when we left Salzburg is a mere shadow of what he knows now.

Mozart's first published composition—two violin sonatas—dates from this year. It appeared in Paris. Other compositions, including arias and symphonies, quickly followed. Four years later, in Vienna, at the tender age of twelve he made his first attempt to compose an opera. On a hint from the Emperor Joseph II, immediately picked up by Mozart's ambitious father, Mozart wrote *La Finta Semplice* (The Pretended Simpleton), a three-act opera buffa, using a libretto by Marco Coltellini based on a text by Carlo Goldoni. The intention was to produce the opera in Vienna. But it foundered embarrassingly at the first rehearsal, rejected by the singers, musicians, and theatre management. Mozart's youth, his imperfect command of Italian, and his inexperience in depicting the battle of the sexes, not to speak of envy and intrigue from others (described with fury by Leopold Mozart in a lengthy letter to Salzburg), went against him. The Vienna production was abandoned; nevertheless the opera was mounted in Salzburg in 1769. Today, its interest is mainly historical, in demonstrating Mozart's incipient ability to compose for the stage. 'The lively finales leave little room for vocal characterization of person or situation, yet there are anticipations of the magic to come—Simone's arrival in the Act I finale, like Figaro's in the Act II finale, and a beautiful G major plea for forgiveness (here by the women) near the end as in the Act IV finale of *Figaro*', to quote *The New Penguin Opera Guide*.

La Finta Semplice was a rare misjudgement by Leopold, who now shrewdly propelled his protégé towards Italy, the fountainhead of opera, so as to let him acquire the experience he lacked in Vienna and Salzburg. Between 1769 and 1773, Wolfgang, shepherded by his father, visited Italy three times, making a striking impression on leading Italian composers, musicians, and singers. In 1770, he composed his first opera seria, *Mitridate, Re di Ponto* (Mitridate, King of Pontus), from a libretto by Vittorio Amedeo Cigna-Santi based on a French tragedy by Jean Racine, which was premiered in Milan to great acclaim. In 1772 came another opera seria, *Lucio Silla* (Lucius Sulla), from a libretto by Giovanni de Gamerra based on the classical story of the Roman dictator Sulla, which also premiered in Milan, though with less success.

Mozart improved his knowledge of Italian and learned an enormous amount about the mechanics and art of opera from composing these two works for singers at the top of their field. Above all, he realized the necessity—for practical and aesthetic reasons—of adapting his music to the capabilities of a particular artiste. In both operas, the all-important arias had to be tailored, which meant that the scores could not be completed until the singers were physically present in Milan. The tenor playing Mitridate, Guglielmo d'Ettore, required his opening aria to be rewritten three times. In *Lucio Silla*, the prima donna Anna de Amicis, who became very fond of Mozart, arrived only three weeks before the first performance, while the totally inadequate tenor playing the title role, a late substitute, had a mere eight days to rehearse; he was therefore given just two undemanding arias, which undoubtedly diminished the opera's impact. 'The writing and performance of *Lucio Silla* was in many ways a traumatic and tense time for Wolfgang', writes the conductor and Mozart expert Jane Glover. 'But, as was often to be the case in his later life, he thrived on this sort of energy.' Famously, the overture for *Don Giovanni* is said to have been finished by Mozart only on the day of its first public performance in 1787.

His next opera, *La Finta Giardiniera* (The Pretended Gardener), an opera buffa commissioned in 1774 for the Munich Carnival, shows how much Mozart had gained from his sojourns in Italy. The weak libretto, of uncertain authorship (it may have been written by Giuseppe Petrosellini), had been set to music by a leading Italian composer, Pasquale Anfossi, about a year earlier. Mozart was clearly aware of Anfossi's version and aimed to improve on it. Both composers adopt most of the structures found in opera buffa of the 1760s, while abandoning the now-unfashionable da capo aria. But Mozart's music is superior. Comparing the same setting of words by Anfossi and Mozart, Michael F. Robinson finds Mozart's music 'better shaped', with 'greater contrasts', and 'a more imaginative use of the instruments'. He explains:

> The violins do not merely come into prominence when filling in the gaps between vocal phrases, as in Anfossi's case. They start a phrase . . . They also carry a phrase forward, taking the melodic line over from the voice. Instruments and voice therefore come into partnership during this passage and together mould the music. Such interactions are of course common in Mozart's later operas and their appearance here and in other places in *La Finta Giardiniera* are signs of his growing maturity as a composer.

This is especially evident in the finale to Act II, which is linked to the three previous arias by orchestral sections or accompanied recitatives. It continues for 26 minutes—as compared with less than 20 minutes for the great Act II finale in *Figaro*.

No Mozart opera was performed after *La Finta Giardiniera* until his first operatic masterpiece *Idomeneo* in 1781—a gap of six years. We can ignore his two-act serenata, *Il Re Pastore* (The Shepherd King), performed virtually as a cantata with a minimum of scenery and movement in Salzburg in 1775. The reason for this fallow period is that Mozart was mostly stuck in Salzburg, where there was no theatrical or operatic tradition. Of course he composed many other works during this time, notably his revolutionary piano concerto No. 9, K271, but his yearning for opera was compelled to go unfulfilled.

In September 1777, a frustrated Mozart resigned his position as concert-master to the Archbishop of Salzburg and set off to look for a patron in a musical capital city (accompanied by his mother since his father was obliged to remain at court). Opera was at the front of his mind. From Munich he wrote home in October: 'I have an inexpressible desire to write an opera again... Whenever I hear people talk about an opera, whenever I'm in the theatre and just hear the tuning of the instruments—oh, I get so excited, I'm totally beside myself.' From Mannheim, in February, he sounded the same note to his father: 'Don't forget my wish to write operas. I'm envious of everyone who writes one. I could literally weep with frustration whenever I hear or see an aria. But Italian, not German, serious, not buffa.' And from Paris, in August 1778, compelled by his mother's sudden death and his father's imprecations to confront the possibility of having to return to Salzburg, he wrote disgustedly to a friend of his father:

> Salzburg is no place for a man of my talent!—In the first place, the people associated with the orchestra are not respected, and secondly one hears nothing—there's no theatre there, no opera!—and even if they wanted to perform an opera, who'd sing in it?—For 5 or 6 years the Salzburg orchestra has been rich in all that is useless and unnecessary but very poor when it comes to what's necessary and entirely lacking in what's most indispensable of all...

Some months later, in January 1779, Mozart was reluctantly back in his home city, officially appointed as court and cathedral organist while unofficially seeking commissions elsewhere. He was fortunate in that the theatre began to expand during his last two years in Salzburg. Two travelling troupes of players successively took up residence and gave German-language performances at the Ballhaus. They were led by two of the era's leading directors, Johann Heinrich Böhm and Emanuel Schikaneder. Mozart and his circle became friendly with both men. He composed some music for Böhm, including a fragment of a singspiel known as

Zaide; and Böhm in his turn mounted a production in Augsburg of Mozart's *La Finta Giardiniera* in a German translation. For Schikaneder, at his father's urging, Mozart wrote an aria; and in 1791 Schikaneder wrote the libretto for Mozart's last opera *Die Zauberflöte*. In addition, Mozart learned much about stagecraft from these Salzburg productions based on French and Italian models, which would enrich his Viennese operas of the 1780s, including *Figaro*.

Mozart's main hope of composing an Italian opera currently lay in Munich, where the court, under the artistic Karl Theodor, elector from 1778, was notably committed to music and opera, and included many Mozart advocates. The commission came at last in the late summer of 1780. The subject, chosen by the court, was from ancient Greek mythology: the story of Idomeneus, king of Crete, who is forced to sacrifice his own son as a result of a vow to the gods, made while shipwrecked on his return from fighting in the Trojan wars, to sacrifice the first person he meets if he is saved. The librettist for this opera seria, chosen by Mozart, was Gianbattista Varesco, court chaplain at Salzburg, whose task was to base his Italian libretto on a French lyric tragedy, *Idomenée*. Having obtained some weeks of leave from Salzburg to complete the opera and oversee its production in January 1781, Mozart left for Munich in early November. Leopold Mozart remained in Salzburg to act as an intermediary with Varesco, a versifier who had no experience of writing for the theatre.

The exchanges between son and father in letters during these three months of separation show them at their best, creatively collaborating to solve issues of characterization and dramatic action, which required drastic alteration of Varesco's original libretto. Still, Leopold cannot avoid warning Wolfgang not to break too many conventions in his music. 'I advise you when composing to consider not only the musical, but also *the unmusical public*', he writes from Salzburg. 'You must remember that to every *ten real connoisseurs* there are a *hundred ignoramuses*. So do not neglect the so-called *popular* style, which tickles *long ears*.'

Idomeneo does indeed break many of the rules of opera seria, and begins to display Mozart's genius for ensemble composing, especially in the quartet between the king, his doomed son, and the two women who love him. In *Lucio Silla*, Mozart's trio was really a duet-plus-one, in *Zaide* his quartet was a duet-plus-one-plus-one, whereas in *Idomeneo* his quartet manages to be both four separate voices and a unity. 'With brilliant control, Mozart focuses first on one character and then on another, bringing his or her musical line into sharp relief against the background of those of the others', writes Glover, 'and the audience thus has the impression of hearing and comprehending four strands of wretchedness at the same time; and the moments of shared suffering are heart-stopping.'

Even so, the opera did not secure a position for Mozart at the court in Munich. Why is unclear, since there is no evidence. It may be that his father was right about the need to avoid being too original with the music, because there are no diaries, letters, or significant reviews mentioning the three Munich performances of *Idomeneo* in early 1781. Or possibly Mozart had already settled in his mind that his future lay in Vienna, where the music-loving Joseph II, who had supported him in the 1760s, at last became sole ruler on the death of his co-regent mother Maria Theresia (a Mozart detractor) in November 1780.

At any rate, in March 1781 Mozart moved to Vienna on the orders of his employer, the Archbishop of Salzburg, Count Hieronymus Colloredo, who was staying there on a visit to Joseph and his court. After disagreements about his status at court and his opportunities to perform in Vienna, Mozart made his notorious break with Colloredo in May. Shortly after, he was unceremoniously dismissed by the archbishop's chief chamberlain Count Arco, who literally booted his employee out with a 'kick up the arse' (according to Mozart). Leopold Mozart, predictably horrified by the career implications, tried to make his son apologize, but Wolfgang for the first time in his life refused to obey his father. In a flurry of recriminatory letters (all of which from Leopold were later destroyed, presumably by Mozart's wife), Wolfgang at length told his father indignantly: 'It is the heart that ennobles man; and though I am not a count, I have probably more Honour in me than many a count; and whether I am dealing with a lackey or a count, if he insults me, he is a scoundrel.' The sentiment is one that Beaumarchais might easily have put into the mouth of his Figaro, whose defiant soliloquy against his employer Count Almaviva in the final act of the play includes the following words: 'Nobility, wealth, rank, high position, such things make a man proud. But what did you ever do to earn them? Chose your parents carefully, that's all.'

Relations between father and son never regained their previous intimacy. Two years after the 1781 break, Wolfgang wrote to Leopold: 'I hope I don't need to say that I care very little for Salzburg and nothing whatsoever for the archb., and that I shit on both of them—and that it would never in my life enter my head to go there specially, if you and my sister weren't there.'

Soon after, along with his new wife Constanze, he paid just one final visit to Salzburg in an attempted reconciliation with his father and sister, which failed. He had married in Vienna in 1782, greatly against the wishes of Leopold, who informed his son that he should expect no paternal financial support. The bad blood between Leopold and his mother over his marriage in the 1740s now haunted his treatment of his son.

It is sometimes imagined that Mozart did not suffer for his work, because the humour, charm, and beauty of his music appear to have emerged from his head so effortlessly, even miraculously. The writer of the play *Amadeus*, Peter Shaffer, who also wrote the screenplay of Milos Forman's influential film *Amadeus*, states categorically: 'There is really not the slightest evidence, either in his own voluminous correspondence or in accounts of him by contemporaries, that Mozart ever suffered for his art.' The film reflects this surprising view in its controversial portrayal of Mozart's personality as essentially frivolous, insouciant, and ribald.

If by 'suffering', we mean mental pain and anguish, then surely Mozart experienced plenty of it throughout his adult life, as his letters alone plainly demonstrate. The death of his mother in Paris in 1778, the break with his father in 1781, his estrangement from his sister (whom he did not meet after 1783), the collapse of his income in the late 1780s, the bad health of his wife and himself, are all key examples of his suffering, not to mention his rejection by his first love, the singer Aloysia Weber, and the humiliations of his employment at the Salzburg court.

Whether his sufferings found their way into his music is naturally not so evident. Yet at the very least, we can be sure that Mozart suffered through moving to Vienna in pursuit of his art, in that he traded a secure (if underpaid) niche in Salzburg for the constant and anxious uncertainties of freelance composing at a time when almost all composers of note held permanent positions. One also can hardly avoid seeing some of Mozart's personal struggles reflected in his works, such as his courting and marrying of Constanze in 1781–82 while writing his singspiel *Die Entführung aus dem Serail* (*The Abduction from the Harem*), and also the ugly and violent feelings of Figaro and Count Almaviva—admittedly present in Beaumarchais's original but given much greater depth and nuance by Mozart. A lot of the music of *The Marriage of Figaro* is far from serene in its beauty. Perhaps, in the final analysis, whether or not Mozart suffered for his art comes down to the sensitivity and integrity necessary to create enduring art in any culture. Situations that caused Mozart acute suffering would have been brushed off as mere inconveniences by a man less creative and more willing to compromise than he was. His constitutional inability to rest on his laurels is why he evolved into a great composer during the last decade of his life.

After his long years of disappointment in Vienna, following the failure of his first opera there in 1768, Mozart's moment had arrived. Joseph II, now sole monarch, was not only supportive of opera in general, he also disliked opera seria and actively encouraged comedy: in the form of German singspiel until 1783, thereafter Italian opera buffa. (All 59 operas produced at Vienna's imperial Burgtheater between 1783 and Joseph's death in 1790 were Italian comic operas, mostly by Italian composers, with Paisiello the most popular.) Moreover, Joseph treated Mozart, along with many other composers, with more respect than the average aristocrat, especially as he had known him as a boy prodigy. 'Mozart had been fêted by the highest in Europe while still a child, but Joseph was the only monarch who would accord even a fraction of that dignity to an adult', notes Andrew Steptoe.

As important, the Viennese nobility, old and new, were music lovers. Frivolous though Vienna was in its entertainments and general attitude to the arts, it took music seriously. The social scene was therefore most congenial for a performer like Mozart, and to begin with financially very rewarding. His early letters from Vienna to his father and others show him in touch with many aristocrats and music patrons, one of whom, Baron Wetzlar, became the godfather of the Mozarts' first child and in 1783 introduced him at his house to his future librettist Da Ponte. 'Despite Mozart's immense productivity and devotion to his work he was not isolated from the world,' writes Solomon, 'and the richness and variety of his social contacts and friendships is extraordinary to contemplate.'

By coincidence, both Da Ponte and Mozart arrived in Vienna in the same year, 1781. On the recommendation of the composer Antonio Salieri, a fellow Italian who had been working in Vienna since 1766, Da Ponte was appointed poet at the Burgtheater in 1783, when Joseph II revived opera buffa. Conscious of his lack of theatrical (as opposed to literary) experience, Da Ponte persuaded a local poet, Gianbattista Varese, to share with him what was said to be a valuable collection of some 300 Italian texts. In his acerbic memoirs published decades later, Da Ponte described his disappointment: 'Poor Italy! What stuff they were! They had no plot, no characters, no interest, no scenic effects, no charm of language or style, and though they were written to make people laugh, one would rather have thought they had been written to make people weep.'

Mozart, too, was then researching suitable Italian librettos, and had come to a similar conclusion. In May, just after meeting Da Ponte, he wrote an important letter to his father in Salzburg:

> Well, the Italian opera buffa has started again here and is very popular...I have looked through at least a hundred librettos and more, but I have scarcely found a single one with which I am satisfied; that is to say, so many alterations would have to be made here and there, that even if a poet would undertake to make them, it would be easier for him to write a completely new text—which indeed it is always best to do. Our poet here is now a certain Abbate Da Ponte. He has an enormous amount to do in revising pieces for the theatre and has to write *per obbligo* an entirely new libretto for Salieri, which will take him two months. He has promised me after that to write a new libretto for me. But who knows whether he will be able to keep his word—or will want to? For, as you know, these Italian gentlemen are very civil to your face. Enough, we know them! If he is in league with Salieri, I shall never get anything out of him. But indeed I would dearly love to show what I can do in an Italian opera! So I have been thinking that unless Varesco is still very much annoyed with us about the Munich opera [*Idomeneo*], he might write me a new libretto for seven characters... The most essential thing is that on the whole the story should be really *comic*; and, if possible, he ought to introduce *two equally good female parts*, one of these to be *seria*, the other *mezzo caratere* [a 'mixed' character], but both parts equal *in importance and excellence*. The third female *character*, however, may be entirely buffa, and so may all the male ones, if necessary. If you think that something can be got out of Varesco, please discuss it with him soon.

Intriguingly, such a threesome is reminiscent of the three women at the centre of *The Marriage of Figaro*: Countess Almaviva (a seria character), her maid Susanna (a *mezzo caratere*), and the governess Marcellina (a buffa character). So Mozart apparently had such a combination in mind long before he got to work on Da Ponte's *Figaro* libretto in 1785.

In the meanwhile, he had to bide his time, working on various opera-related compositions that provided useful experience. From Salzburg, Varesco, egged on by Leopold Mozart, somewhat reluctantly sent an outline of a possible opera buffa, *L'oca del Cairo* (The Goose of Cairo). It involved a huge mechanical goose, to be used like a Trojan horse by a lover to rescue his beloved, who had been locked in a tower by her fool of a father. A doubtful Mozart worked slowly on the music for some months in 1783 and then abandoned the story—before reaching the scene with the goose but after writing an opening duet 'worthy, in its freshness and charm, of Susanna and Figaro', according to Alfred Einstein. Around the same time, he produced an overture leading to a quartet, two arias and a trio for a second opera buffa, *Lo Sposo Deluso* (The Deceived Bridegroom), from a libretto by an unnamed 'Italian poet', which may or may not have been the libretto promised to him by Da Ponte—before abandoning this too. And in addition, 'Mozart put his foot in the door of the Burgtheater, as it were', writes Tim Carter, by composing three arias for an opera by Anfossi staged in June 1783 (two of which were performed).

At least three new operas by other composers influenced Mozart in the run-up to *Figaro*. The most important was Paisiello's *Il Barbiere di Siviglia* (The Barber of Seville), performed at the Burgtheater in August 1783. This became the theatre's most popular opera in the 1780s, with 60 performances in all. Based on the first play in Beaumarchais's Figaro Trilogy, *Le Barbier de Séville*, published in 1775—*Le Mariage de Figaro* is the second—its tremendous Viennese success undoubtedly triggered Mozart and Da Ponte's initial interest in tackling the second play. A year later, in August 1784, came the premiere of another Paisiello opera, *Il Re Teodoro in Venezia* (King Theodore in Venice), with remarkably real human characters—as in *Figaro*—instead of the stereotypes of *commedia dell'arte*. Many musical details in Mozart's opera show the influence of Paisiello's operas. Lastly, just before Christmas 1784, Mozart heard *La Fedeltà Premiata* (Fidelity Rewarded) by Joseph Haydn—a composer he keenly admired—performed in German before Joseph II and the whole court. 'In this opera there are two fascinating and brilliant finales (Acts I and II), multi-movement sections which in their tonal and vocal instrumental richness, length and psychological complexity surpass anything that had been written by Italian composers', writes Robbins Landon. 'Mozart was to turn the style of these Haydn finales into something even more spectacular—in Acts II, III, and IV of *Figaro*.'

It is not known exactly when in 1785 Da Ponte began work on the libretto of *The Marriage of Figaro*, nor how long it took Mozart to compose all the music. Mozart wrote almost nothing on the process, being extremely busy and also somewhat estranged from his father, and so we must rely on the not entirely reliable memoirs of Da Ponte. He credits Mozart with suggesting the play to him in conversation, and then claims: 'I set to work accordingly, and as fast as I wrote the words, Mozart set them to music. In six weeks everything was in order.' While this seems like a tall order, modern scholarship, based on Mozart's autograph manuscript—the first two acts of which are in Berlin, while the third and fourth are in Krakow—has revealed that the score was initially noted in a kind of musical shorthand, showing the essential instruments and all the vocal parts. For this, six weeks would be plausible. Given that Mozart told his father very briefly on 2 November 1785 that he was up to his eyes in the opera, this draft score was probably written in October and November, followed by a full score completed in April 1786.

Both Da Ponte and Mozart were aware that Beaumarchais's play was politically sensitive. In France, it had caused an uproar when it was at last performed in 1784; the theatre was besieged from eight o'clock in the morning by a crowd of 5000 people that crushed to death three enthusiastic theatregoers, in 'what was probably the most spectacular success of any opening night in history', writes one of its translators, the playwright John Wells. (King Louis XVI read the manuscript in 1782 and said that the Bastille would have to be demolished before the play could be performed in public, while Napoleon later declared it part of the mechanism of the French Revolution.) In Vienna, an attempt by Schikaneder to stage it in German had provoked the following instruction from Joseph II in January: 'since this piece contains much that is objectionable, I therefore expect that the Censor shall either reject it altogether, or at any rate have such alterations made to it that he shall be responsible for the performance of this play and for the impression it may make'. In the event, the theatrical performance was cancelled, but the censor permitted the play to be printed.

Da Ponte claims that he obtained permission for the opera in a personal interview with the emperor, by assuring him that he had 'omitted or cut anything that might offend good taste or public decency'. He also titillated Joseph's interest by mentioning the beauty of the music. 'I ran straight to Mozart, but I had not yet finished imparting the good news when a page of the emperor's came and handed him a note', commanding the composer to bring his score to the palace. When Mozart played various selections, Joseph II was apparently bowled over.

Apart from these 'political' changes—most significantly the deletion of Figaro's tirade against the aristocracy, government, and censorship in the play's last act—Da Ponte was forced for artistic reasons to make considerable further cuts and changes, while preserving most of the plot. In his preface to the libretto, he calls it an 'extract' from the play, rather than an 'adaptation', but still apologizes for its length:

> for which we hope sufficient excuse will be found in the variety of threads
> from which the action of this play is woven, the vastness and grandeur of
> the same, the multiplicity of the musical numbers that had to be made in

order not to leave the actors too long unemployed, to diminish the vexation and monotony of the long recitatives, and to express with varied colours the various emotions that occur, but above all in our desire to offer as it were a new kind of spectacle to a public of so refined a taste and such just understanding.

'A new kind of spectacle' is indeed what Da Ponte and Mozart had created. In general terms, it is clear that all the ensembles are modelled closely on the work of Beaumarchais; the arias are in a few cases poetically developed from speeches in the play but are most often the invention of Da Ponte; while the new introspection of the characters in the libretto is throughout amplified and deepened by the music of Mozart. Presumably, as in *Idomeneo*, Mozart required many changes in the libretto, but these have to be inferred from the finished work by musicologists in the absence of documentary evidence. To take just one exquisitely ironic example, the seduction duet in Act III ('Crudel! Perchè finora') between a lustful Count Almaviva and a deceptively willing Susanna, seems to involve a brilliant interpolation by the composer. Carter explains:

In the second quatrain, where the Count and Susanna have alternate lines, the feminine endings of the Count's questions are firmly answered by Susanna's masculine '-ò' endings. Furthermore, the insinuating '-ai' rhymes well match the Count's intentions and are complemented by the suave melodic lines of Mozart's setting. However, at least one feature of this setting does not seem attributable to Da Ponte. Mozart indulges in a delicious 'yes-no' game as Susanna muddles her answers to the Count. This lies outside the metrical scheme of the verse and thus is probably Mozart's invention.

As to Mozart's compositional process, we can only speculate. 'When some grand conception was working in his brain he was purely abstracted, walked about the apartment and knew not what was passing around,' his wife Constanze told Mary Novello in 1829, 'but when once arranged in his mind, he needed no Piano Forte but would take music paper and whilst he wrote would say... "Now, my dear wife, have the goodness to repeat what has been talked of", and [my] conversation never interrupted him.'

In 1786, the first production of *Figaro* at the Burgtheater was 'both a triumph and a disappointment', says Solomon. Apart from the exceptional length of the encores, mentioned earlier, 'those in the orchestra I thought would never have ceased applauding, by beating the bows of their violins against the music desks', wrote the Irish tenor Michael Kelly (who sung two roles in the production) in his memoirs, published in 1826. Yet, opinion was divided, among the cognoscenti and the general public, as Leopold Mozart had privately predicted to his daughter. Da Ponte in his memoirs claimed *Figaro* was a success with both groups but admitted that it provoked 'doubts, reserves, and headshakings [among] the other maestros and their partisans'. Count Zinzendorf, a barometer of taste, noted in his diary for 1 May merely: 'at 7 o'clock to the opera *Le Nozze di Figaro*, the poetry by Da Ponte, the music by Mozhardt. Louise in our box, the opera bored me'. Mozart himself, who wrote nothing about the performances, did not make as much money as he had reasonably hoped. Perhaps the public expected a sensation, having heard about the play's reputation in Paris and its banning in Vienna, and was 'disappointed that the opera was not more inflammatory', as Steptoe suggests. There were nine performances in all—a respectable but by no means rapturous response. *Figaro* was not heard again in Vienna for three years, when it began to catch on.

In less fashionable Prague, where it was staged in 1787, it caused a furore. 'Here they talk of nothing but—"Figaro"; nothing is played, blown, sung and whistled but—"Figaro"; again and again it is—"Figaro"; it's all a great honour for me', Mozart excitedly wrote to a friend in Vienna. But in Italy, despite a few performances, his opera did not enter the regular repertory.

By the time it was produced in Paris, in 1793, and London, in 1812, Mozart was dead. The 1812 production, revived in 1813, 1816, and 1817, was in Italian. The first production in English, at Covent Garden in 1819, made radical alterations, with the plot drastically simplified, the Count becoming a speaking role, many changes to the arias, and the more complex action-ensembles removed and converted into dialogue—all apparently on the grounds that the original was too complex to be followed by English ears. This bowdlerized version held sway on the English stage for about two decades until the first, largely faithful English production at Covent Garden in 1842. Today the debate continues about whether *Figaro* should be performed in English, for the sake of the audience's comprehension, or in Italian, for the sake of Mozart and Da Ponte's phoenix-like fusion of music and poetry.

CHAPTER 9

JEAN-FRANÇOIS CHAMPOLLION

Decipherment of Egyptian Hieroglyphs

Hieroglyphic writing is a complex system, a script all at once figurative, symbolic, and phonetic, in one and the same text, in one and the same sentence, and, I might even venture, in one and the same word.

Jean-François Champollion,
Précis du système hiéroglyphique des anciens Égyptiens, 1824

Ancient Egypt has exerted a powerful influence on the world of learning for well over two millennia, beginning with the Greek historian Herodotus. Yet, accurate knowledge of the language and script of the pharaohs was completely lost in classical antiquity, when hieroglyphic writing fell into disuse. No Greek or Roman writer knew how to read hieroglyphs.

Only in the past two centuries has Egyptology become a recognized discipline, since the discovery of the Rosetta Stone by French soldiers at Rosetta in Egypt in 1799. Two decades later, in 1822—a hundred years before the discovery of Tutankhamun's tomb almost to the day—Jean-François Champollion, after years of research, cracked the Egyptian hieroglyphic code. Within a matter of months, he made a great civilization start to speak in its own voice. During the 1820s, Champollion translated a mass of inscriptions on tombs, temples, obelisks, and papyri, and established the chronology of the pharaonic dynasties, which turned out to be far older than suggested by the Bible. Without his breakthrough, the story of Tutankhamun could not have been told. While most branches of science like to salute a particular individual as a founding figure, with varying degrees of justification, Champollion fully deserves the appellation 'father' of Egyptology.

His moment of breakthrough was worthy of the Romantic Movement of his time, the age of Byron and Beethoven. It is said—as described by Champollion's German biographer Hermine Hartleben long after his death—that towards noon on 14 September 1822, he rushed from his house in Paris to the nearby National Institute, where his elder brother and mentor worked as an ancient historian, flung some drawings of Egyptian inscriptions onto a desk in his brother's office, and cried: 'Je tiens l'affaire!' But before he could explain his achievement, he collapsed on the floor in a coma. For an instant, his brother feared he was dead. Taken home to rest, Champollion apparently did not wake until the evening five days later, when he plunged into work again. On 27 September, he gave a historic lecture at the Royal Academy of Inscriptions and Literature announcing his breakthrough, which was published in October under the title *Lettre à M. Dacier, relative à l'alphabet des hiéroglyphes phonétiques*, as a paper addressed to the academy's permanent secretary, Bon-Joseph Dacier.

Champollion's eureka experience sounds exaggerated, and might be dismissed as implausible, were it not for the fact that it fits his well-documented lifelong obsession with ancient Egypt and its literature. It conceals, however, an important truth: Champollion's breakthrough was stimulated not only by his own solo studies of the Rosetta Stone and the Egyptian scripts from about 1814 but also by the prior published research of the polymath Thomas Young. Working across the Channel in England, Young took the first crucial steps towards a decipherment, which appeared in print in 1815–19, including a lengthy and pioneering article on Egypt in the *Encyclopaedia Britannica*. Champollion, though, always adamantly denied that reading Young's work had led to his breakthrough. In his own first major publication on the hieroglyphs, the classic *Précis du système hiéroglyphique des anciens Égyptiens* of 1824, Champollion polemically stated that in the same period as that of Young's research, 'without having any knowledge of the opinions of M. le docteur Young', he had arrived at 'more or less similar results' by independent methods.

The controversy that erupted between the two men, and their many distinguished supporters, has rumbled ever since—somewhat like the debate surrounding the role of Isaac Newton, his rival Robert Hooke, and several others in the discovery of gravity. Champollion versus Young does not die, because the dispute can have no simple resolution. Instead, it sheds a fascinating light on what defines a creative breakthrough, the interplay between science and art in discovery, the virtues and drawbacks of polymathy versus specialization in research, and the role of personality in creativity, since Champollion and Young were extremely unalike in family background, intellectual training, and temperament. For example, Young never went to Egypt, and never wanted to go. In founding an Egyptian Society in London in 1817, to publish as many ancient inscriptions and manuscripts as possible, so as to aid the decipherment, Young coolly remarked that funds were needed 'for employing some poor Italian or Maltese to scramble over Egypt in search of more'. Champollion, by contrast, had long dreamt of travelling to the land of the pharaohs and immersing himself in its past and present culture, ever since he saw the hieroglyphs as a youth in Grenoble. When he finally got there, in 1828–29, he was able to pass for a native, given his swarthy complexion and his excellent command of Arabic. 'I am Egypt's captive—she is my be-all', he wrote to his brother from beside the Nile.

Champollion was born in 1790, in the small town of Figeac, in the Quercy region of southwest France. His father had settled in Figeac as a moderately successful bookseller, after abandoning a hard life as an itinerant pedlar in his native Valbonnais, an Alpine region south of Grenoble. His mother, surprisingly for the wife of a bookseller, could not read or write. She bore Jean-François, the baby of the family, at the age of 46, after a gap of eight years since her last child and her recovery from a paralysing illness. Although a healthy baby, he would suffer from poor health for most of his life and die at the premature age of only 41. His ever-present awareness of his own mortality seems to have spurred his fanatical drive for immortality.

Jean-François did not attend school until the age of almost eight and stayed mainly within the family home. The French Revolution had closed the schools of the *ancien régime*, which were run by the religious orders, and made the streets unsafe for children; Figeac's guillotine was located in a square within earshot of the Champollion house. His parents seem to have neglected him, while his three sisters and brother spoiled the boy to some extent, which may have contributed to the 'violent mood swings and tantrums' characteristic of him in his early years and even as a grown man.

Yet, surrounded by his father's books, and encouraged by his devoted brother Jacques-Joseph (twelve years his senior, whose own education had been badly disrupted by the revolution), the boy quickly learned to read and demonstrated an exceptional ability for learning languages. However, he had trouble with writing and spelling, probably because he had taught himself by copying words from books and confused writing with drawing—an early hint of his later fascination with the pictographic nature of hieroglyphs.

In 1798, when a new school opened, Jean-François became a pupil, but did not last long there. His dislike of formal discipline and mechanical methods of teaching, and his aversion for mathematics, persuaded his brother to find the boy a private tutor, a former Benedictine monk, who developed his interest in languages and natural history. But this man found his evidently gifted pupil unpredictable. He reported to Jacques-Joseph: 'There are days when he appears to want to learn everything, others when he would do nothing.'

After two years of private tuition, Jean-François left Figeac in 1801 and moved 200 miles away to Grenoble, where his brother was now working for a small company run by cousins of his father. He never again saw his mother, who died in 1807. Grenoble would become his home, more than Figeac and Paris, for most of the next two decades, and the place where he would first encounter ancient Egypt and fall in love with his subject. Within a few years the two brothers, publicly distinguished as 'Champollion-Figeac' (Jacques-Joseph) and 'Champollion le jeune' (Jean-François), were well known in Grenoble for their antiquarian interests, not to speak of their sympathy for Republican politics.

According to family legend—there is no archival evidence—the Egyptian love affair began when the boy was eleven, in the autumn of 1802. During an inspection of Champollion's new *lycée* by Joseph Fourier, the prefect of the department of the Isère (headquarters Grenoble), Fourier learned of Jean-François's interest in Egypt and invited him to the prefecture to see his collection of Egyptian antiquities. Besides being a celebrated mathematician and physicist, Fourier had been a key official in Egypt during Napoleon Bonaparte's ill-fated 1798 expedition, before returning from Cairo in 1801 to be appointed prefect by Napoleon. At their meeting, the precocious schoolboy is said to have been tongue-tied but inspired by the sight of Fourier's unreadable hieroglyphs.

Maybe in reality Jean-François was part of a school group, or the meeting occurred much later (in 1809, as suggested by the archives). Whatever the truth, there is no question that by 1804 he was assisting Jacques-Joseph—who had become well known to Fourier—with research for Fourier's extensive preface to the first volume of the grand, colour-illustrated report of Napoleon's Egyptian expedition, *Description de l'Égypte* (a series finally completed only in 1828, the year that Champollion reached Egypt). By 1807, after graduating brilliantly from his *lycée*, Champollion le jeune was taken seriously enough to lecture on Egypt to Grenoble's scholarly academy, which immediately elected him a member at the age of 16. And by 1809, having studied Oriental languages and Coptic at university in Paris—and tackled the Rosetta Stone for the first time in 1808—he was back in Grenoble as an 18-year-old professor of ancient history at the city's new university, appointed along with his brother, who became professor of Greek literature. Already, he had drafted his first book on ancient Egypt, a survey of existing knowledge of its civilization published in 1814, with some preliminary remarks on the Rosetta Stone, preparatory to beginning his full attack on the ancient Egyptian writing system.

But before delving into his decipherment, we too need a survey of earlier research into ancient Egypt's scripts, however brief. To decipher the Egyptian hieroglyphs in the period 1814–24 required Champollion, and his rival Young, to sweep away centuries of erroneous thinking, dating back to classical antiquity, while building on a handful of genuine insights from various scholars.

The civilization of the pharaohs—dating from about 3000 BC—had gone into eclipse some 2000 years before Champollion, when it was conquered by Alexander the Great (who founded Alexandria) in 332 BC and came under the Hellenistic rule of the Ptolemaic dynasty, named after Alexander's general, Ptolemy I. Such was its ruined magnificence, however, that the Greeks and Romans, especially the Greeks, regarded ancient Egypt with a paradoxical mixture of reverence for its wisdom and antiquity, and contempt for its 'barbarism'. The very word hieroglyph derives from the Greek for 'sacred carving'. Egyptian obelisks were taken to ancient Rome and became symbols of prestige; today, thirteen obelisks stand in Rome, while only four remain in Egypt.

The classical authors generally credited Egypt with the invention of writing (though Pliny the Elder attributed it to the Mesopotamian inventors of cuneiform). But none of them, so far as is known, learned to speak and write Egyptian, despite the fact that hieroglyphic inscriptions continued to be written until AD 394. They preferred to believe, as Diodorus Siculus wrote in the first century BC, that Egyptian writing was not phonetic, 'not built up from syllables to express the underlying meaning, but from the appearance of the things drawn and by their metaphorical meaning learned by heart'. In other words, the hieroglyphs were conceptual or symbolic, not alphabetic like the Greek and Latin scripts—a crucial distinction in the story of the decipherment. Thus, a hieroglyphic picture of a hawk represented anything that happened swiftly; a crocodile symbolized all that was evil.

By far the most important classical authority was an Egyptian magus named Horapollo (Horus Apollo) supposedly from Nilopolis in Upper Egypt. His treatise, *Hieroglyphika*, was probably composed in Greek, during the fourth century AD or later, and then sank from view until a manuscript was discovered on a Greek island in about 1419 and became known in Renaissance Italy. Published in 1505, the book was hugely influential: it went through 30 editions, one of them illustrated by Albrecht Dürer, was studied by Champollion in 1806, and even remains in print.

Horapollo's readings of the hieroglyphs were a combination of the (mainly) fictitious and the genuine. Young called them 'puerile...more like a collection of conceits and enigmas than an explanation of a real system of serious literature'. For instance, according to the esteemed *Hieroglyphika*:

> [W]hen they wish to indicate a sacred scribe, or a prophet, or an embalmer, or the spleen, or odour, or laughter, or sneezing, or rule, or judge, they draw a dog. A scribe, since he who wishes to become an accomplished scribe must study many things and must bark continually and be fierce and show favours to none, just like dogs. And a prophet, because the dog looks intently beyond all other beasts upon the images of the gods, like a prophet.

—and so on. As we now know, thanks to Champollion, there are elements of truth in this, mixed with absurdity: the jackal ('dog') hieroglyph writes the name of the god Anubis, who is the god of embalming, a smelly business (hence Horapollo's meaning 'odour'?); and a recumbent jackal writes the title of a special type of priest, the 'master of secrets', who would have been a sacred scribe and considered something of a prophet; while a striding jackal can also stand for an official, and hence perhaps for a judge.

The Arabs who occupied Egypt in 642 with the coming of Islam had a marginally more accurate understanding of the hieroglyphs because they at least believed that the signs were partly phonetic, not purely symbolic. (Their attribution of phonetic values was wrong, however.) But this belief did not pass from the Islamic world to the European. Instead, fuelled by Horapollo, the Renaissance revival of classical learning brought a revival of the Greek and Roman belief in the hieroglyphs as symbols of wisdom. The first of many scholars in the modern world to write a whole book on the subject was a Venetian, Pierius Valerianus. He published it in 1556, and illustrated it with delightfully fantastic 'Renaissance' hieroglyphs.

The most famous of these interpreters was the Jesuit priest Athanasius Kircher, whose works were thoroughly studied by Champollion. In the mid-seventeenth century, Kircher became Rome's accepted pundit on ancient Egypt. But his voluminous writings took him far beyond 'Egyptology'; 'sometimes called the last renaissance man' (notes the *Encyclopaedia Britannica*), and dubbed 'the last man who knew everything' in a recent academic study, Kircher attempted to encompass the totality of human knowledge. The result was a mixture of folly and brilliance—with the former easily predominant—from which his reputation never recovered.

In 1666, Kircher was entrusted with the publication of a hieroglyphic inscription on a small Egyptian obelisk in Rome's Piazza della Minerva. This had been erected on the orders of Pope Alexander VII to a design by the sculptor Bernini (it stands to this day, mounted on a stone elephant, encapsulating the concept 'wisdom supported by strength'). Kircher gave his reading of a *cartouche*—i.e., a small group of hieroglyphs in the inscription enclosed by an oval ring—as follows: 'The protection of Osiris against the violence of Typho must be elicited according to the proper rites and ceremonies by sacrifices and by appeal to the tutelary Genii of the triple world in order to ensure the enjoyment of the prosperity customarily given by the Nile against the violence of the enemy Typho.' Today's accepted reading of the cartouche is simply the name of a pharaoh, Wahibre (Apries), of the 26th dynasty!

By contrast, Kircher genuinely assisted in the rescue of Coptic, the language of the last phase of ancient Egypt, by publishing the first Coptic grammar and vocabulary. The word Copt is derived from the Arabic *qubti*, which itself derives from Greek *Aiguptos* (Egypt). The Coptic script was invented around the end of the first century AD, and from the fourth to the tenth centuries Coptic flourished as a spoken language and as the official language of the Christian church in Egypt; then it was replaced by Arabic, except in the church, and by the time of Kircher, the mid-seventeenth century, Coptic was headed for extinction, though it was still used in the liturgy—as the Oriental languages student Champollion regularly heard for himself at a Coptic church in Paris in 1807–09. During the eighteenth century, however, several European scholars acquired a knowledge of Coptic and its alphabet. Its standard form consists of 24 Greek letters plus 6 signs borrowed from pharaonic Egypt (from the demotic script, one of the three scripts on the Rosetta Stone, as we shall see). This scholarly knowledge of Coptic—unparalleled in Champollion's case—would prove essential in reconstructing the probable ancient Egyptian language, during the nineteenth-century decipherment of the hieroglyphs.

Wrong-headed theories about Egyptian writing flourished throughout the eighteenth-century Enlightenment. For example, a Swedish diplomat, Count Palin, suggested in three publications that parts of the Old Testament were a Hebrew translation of an Egyptian text—which was a reasonable conjecture —but then tried to reconstruct the Egyptian text by translating the Hebrew into Chinese. This was not quite as crazy as it sounds, given that both Egyptian hieroglyphs and Chinese characters have a strong conceptual and symbolic element; the existence of the Chinese script, and also a particular structural link between it and hieroglyphic, would in fact offer an important clue in deciphering Egyptian in the more cautious hands of Champollion, Young, and others. But Palin went way too far with his hieroglyphic extravaganza.

The first 'scientific' step in the right direction came from an English clergyman. In 1740, William Warburton, the future Bishop of Gloucester, suggested that all writing, hieroglyphic included, might have evolved from pictures, rather than by divine origin. Abbé J. J. Barthélemy, an admirer of Warburton, then made a sensible guess in 1762 that obelisk cartouches might contain the names of kings or gods—ironically, on the basis of two false observations (one being that the hieroglyphs enclosed in the oval rings were different from all other hieroglyphs). Finally, near the end of the eighteenth century, a Danish scholar, Georg Zoëga, hazarded that some hieroglyphs might be, in some measure at least, what he called 'notae phoneticae', Latin for 'phonetic signs', representing sounds rather than concepts in the Egyptian language. The path towards decipherment was at last being cleared.

And now we reach a turning point: the arrival of Napoleon's invasion force in Egypt in 1798 (which the 19-year-old Jacques-Joseph Champollion had hoped to join), and the discovery of the Rosetta Stone. The word cartouche, as applied to Egyptian hieroglyphs, dates from this fateful Eastern East–West encounter. The oval rings, easily visible to the soldiers on temple walls and elsewhere in Egypt, reminded them of the cartridges (*cartouches*) in their guns.

Fortunately, the French military force was almost as interested in culture as in conquest. A large party of savants including Fourier, Champollion's later mentor, accompanied the army; there were also many artists, who illustrated the elephantine volumes of the *Description de l'Égypte*. When a demolition squad of military engineers discovered the Rosetta Stone while rebuilding an old fort in the village of Rashid (Rosetta) in the Nile Delta, the officer in charge recognized its importance and sent it to the savants in Cairo. Copies of the inscription were made and distributed to the scholars of Europe during 1800—a remarkably open-minded gesture considering the politics of the period. But the stone itself was captured by the British army in 1801 and sent to London.

From the moment of discovery, it was clear that the inscription on the stone was written in three different scripts, the bottom one being the Greek alphabet and the top one—unfortunately the most damaged—being Egyptian hieroglyphs with visible cartouches. Sandwiched between them was a script about which little was known. It plainly did not resemble the Greek script, but it seemed to bear at least a fugitive resemblance to the hieroglyphic script above it, though without having any cartouches. Today we know this middle script as *demotic*, a development (*c.* 650 BC) from a cursive form of writing known as hieratic used in parallel with the hieroglyphic script from as early as 3000 BC (hieratic itself does not appear on the Rosetta Stone). The name derives from Greek *demotikos*, meaning 'in common use'—in contrast to the sacred hieroglyphic, which was essentially a monumental script. The term demotic was first used by Champollion, who refused to import Young's earlier coinage, 'enchorial', which Young had adopted from the description of the second script given in the Greek inscription: *enchoria grammata*, or 'letters of the country'.

The first step towards decipherment was obviously to translate the Greek inscription. This turned out to be a decree issued at Memphis, the principal city of ancient Egypt, by a general council of priests from every part of the kingdom assembled on the first anniversary of the coronation of the young Ptolemy V Epiphanes, king of all Egypt, on 27 March 196 BC. Greek was used because it was the language of court and government of the descendants of Ptolemy, Alexander's general. The names Ptolemy, Alexander, and Alexandria, among others, occurred in the Greek inscription.

The eye of would-be decipherers was caught by the very last sentence of the Greek version. It read: 'This decree shall be inscribed on a stela of hard stone in sacred [i.e., hieroglyphic] and native [i.e., demotic] and Greek characters and set up in each of the first, second and third [-rank] temples beside the image of the ever-living king.' In other words, the three inscriptions—hieroglyphic, demotic, and Greek—were equivalent in meaning, though not necessarily 'word for word' translations of each other. This was how scholars first knew that the stone was a bilingual inscription: the kind most sought after by decipherers, a sort of Holy Grail of decipherment. The two languages were clearly Greek and (presumably) ancient Egyptian, the language of the priests, the latter being written in two different scripts—unless the 'sacred' and 'native' characters concealed two different languages, which seemed unlikely from the context. (In fact, as we now know, the Egyptian languages written in hieroglyphic and demotic are not identical, but they are closely related, like Latin and Renaissance Italian.)

Since the hieroglyphic section was so damaged, attention focused on the demotic. In 1802, two scholars, a distinguished French Orientalist, Sylvestre de Sacy (one of Champollion's teachers in Paris in 1807–09), and a student of De Sacy, the Swedish diplomat Johan Åkerblad, adopted similar techniques. They searched for a name, such as Ptolemy, by isolating repeated groups of demotic symbols located in roughly the same position as the eleven known occurrences of Ptolemy in the Greek inscription. Having found these groups, they noticed that the names in demotic seemed to be written alphabetically, as in the Greek inscription—that is, the demotic spelling of a name apparently contained more or less the same number of signs as the number of letters in its assumed Greek equivalent. By matching demotic sign with Greek letter, they were able to draw up a tentative alphabet of demotic signs. Certain other demotic words, such as 'Greek', 'Egypt', and 'temple', could now be identified using this demotic alphabet. It looked as though the entire demotic script might be alphabetic like the Greek inscription.

But in fact it was not, unluckily for De Sacy and Åkerblad. Young was sympathetic: '[They] proceeded upon the erroneous, or, at least imperfect, evidence of the Greek authors, who have pretended to explain the different modes of writing among the ancient Egyptians, and who have asserted very distinctly that they employed, on many occasions, an alphabetical system, composed of 25 letters only.' Taking their cue from classical authority, neither De Sacy nor Åkerblad could get rid of his preconception that the demotic inscription was written in an alphabetic script—as against the hieroglyphic inscription, which both scholars took to be wholly non-phonetic, its symbols expressing ideas, not sounds, along the lines of Horapollo's *Hieroglyphika*. The apparent disparity in appearance between the hieroglyphic and demotic signs, and the suffocating weight of European tradition that Egyptian hieroglyphs were a conceptual or symbolic script, convinced the two scholars that the invisible principles of hieroglyphic and demotic were wholly different: the hieroglyphic had to be a conceptual/symbolic script, the demotic a phonetic/alphabetic script.

Except for one element. De Sacy deserves credit as the first to make an important suggestion: that the foreign names inside the hieroglyphic cartouches, which he naturally assumed were Ptolemy, Alexander, and so on, were also spelt alphabetically, as they were in the demotic inscription. He was led to this by some information given to him by one of his pupils, a student of Chinese, in 1811. The Chinese script was at this time generally thought in Europe to be a primarily conceptual script like the hieroglyphs. Yet, as this student pointed out, foreign (i.e., non-Chinese) words and names, had to be written *phonetically* in Chinese with a special sign to indicate that the Chinese characters were being reduced to a phonetic value without any conceptual value. (English-speakers indicate some foreign words in writing English with their own 'special sign'—italicization.) Were not Ptolemy, Alexander, and so on, Greek names foreign to the Egyptian language, and might not the car-touche be the ancient Egyptian hieroglyphic equivalent of the special sign in Chinese? But as for the rest of the hieroglyphs—all those not enclosed in cartouches—De Sacy was convinced they were undoubtedly non-phonetic.

This was the state of play when both Champollion and Young—who had so far contributed nothing to the decipherment—independently launched an intensive study of the Rosetta Stone in 1814; indeed they had a brief correspondence on the subject in 1814–15, in which Young offered to help Champollion correct his reproductions of the Rosetta Stone by reference to the original in the British Museum. Ideally, we should now examine the steps in Champollion's thinking between 1814 and the publication of his breakthrough *Lettre à M. Dacier* in 1822. Unfortunately, this is impossible, since, unlike Young, Champollion published next to nothing in this period and left few records of his thinking, other than letters to his brother.

From these letters it is clear that Champollion was forced to give up work on hieroglyphic decipherment for almost two years in the period 1816–18, as a result of his political and financial difficulties following the collapse of Napoleon's regime in 1815 and the return of the monarchy. His support for Napoleon cost him (and his brother) dear, since he was exiled to Figeac in March 1816 and did not return to Grenoble for 19 months—well after his more diplomatic brother, who then obtained a post for himself in Paris. Having of course lost his position at the university, and having refused to leave his home city for a proffered professorship at Turin University, Champollion became a Grenoble schoolteacher in 1818 and later a librarian, too; he also got married. There was some respite in 1819–20, when he was again able to take to take up Egyptology in earnest, but his health troubled him. In 1821, after the death of his father, who had become an alcoholic, he once more became embroiled in politics, joining (bloodlessly) in a popular uprising against the ultra-royalist prefect of the Isère in March 1821. Charged with treason, he was acquitted of any wrongdoing, but was effectively ousted from Grenoble and compelled to join Jacques-Joseph in Paris in July 1821. Here, in August, his ever-loyal brother arranged for him to give a lecture at the Academy of Inscriptions. He then settled to the intensive study that within about a year led to his breakthrough of September 1822.

There is, however, a single brief publication by Champollion from this troubled period—and it is revealing. In April 1821, while still in Grenoble, he published a fascicle consisting of seven pages and seven plates illustrating 700 hieroglyphic and hieratic signs from various Egyptian monumental and manuscript sources, under the title *De l'écriture hiératique des anciens Égyptiens*. It announced three significant conclusions, based on his comparison of hieroglyphic and hieratic (the cursive script from which demotic derives). First, hieratic 'is no more than a simple modification of the hieroglyphic system, and differs from it only in the form of its signs'. In other words, hieroglyphic was the origin of hieratic (and hence of demotic). Second, hieratic 'is not in any way alphabetical'. Third, hieratic characters 'are signs of things and not sounds'.

His first conclusion was correct, and had already been published by Young in 1815 and repeated in 1819 in his *Encyclopaedia Britannica* article. In a published letter to De Sacy, Young noted a 'striking resemblance', not spotted by any previous scholar, between some hieratic and demotic signs and what he called 'the corresponding hieroglyphics'—not only in the Rosetta Stone but also in some papyrus manuscripts published in the *Description de l'Égypte*.

Champollion's second 1821 conclusion—that hieratic was 'not in any way alphabetical'—contradicted the published work of De Sacy, Åkerblad, and Young, and was likely to be incorrect since they had shown that demotic (derived from hieratic) almost certainly contained alphabetic elements. In the same letter to De Sacy, Young wrote in 1815: 'I am not surprised that, when you consider the general appearance of the [demotic] inscription, you are inclined to despair of the possibility of discovering an alphabet capable of enabling us to decipher it; and if you wish to know my "secret", it is simply this, that no such alphabet ever existed.' Young's logical conclusion was that the demotic script consisted of 'imitations of the hieroglyphics . . . mixed with letters of the alphabet'. It was neither a purely conceptual or symbolic script nor an alphabet, but a *mixture* of the two. As Young added later (in the *Encyclopaedia Britannica*), employing an analogy for demotic that perhaps only a polymath such as he could have come up with, 'it seemed natural to suppose, that alphabetical characters might be interspersed with hieroglyphics, in the same way that the astronomers and chemists of modern times have often employed arbitrary marks, as compendious expressions of the objects which were most frequently to be mentioned in their respective sciences'. A modern, non-scientific example of the same idea would be symbols, such as $, £, %, =, +, in other words 'compendious hieroglyphics' that represent concepts non-phonetically, and often appear adjacent to alphabetic letters.

Champollion's third conclusion—which implied that hieroglyphic, as well as hieratic, represented 'things not sounds' (since hieratic was derived from hieroglyphic)—was bound to be incorrect, if his second conclusion (about there being no alphabeticism in hieratic) was incorrect. Presumably, in mid-1821, Champollion still had faith in the hoary classical notion that all the Egyptian scripts were conceptual rather than phonetic.

His published denial of any phoneticism in the Egyptian scripts was a serious error; and it seems as if Champollion soon realized this, because he is alleged to have made strenuous efforts to withdraw all copies of his 1821 publication, suppress the incorrect text, and redistribute only the plates. The allegation is probably true, given the subsequent rarity of the publication; the fact that Champollion presented only the plates to Young, who was unaware of the text; and, most telling of all, that Champollion chose to make no reference of any kind to the embarrassing 1821 publication in his *Lettre à M. Dacier* of 1822. Clearly, in the year that elapsed between August 1821 (when Champollion's lecture at the academy in Paris was based on his incorrect Grenoble publication) and his September 1822 announcement, Champollion changed his mind and decided that there was, after all, a phonetic element in the Egyptian scripts. The question then becomes, what caused his radical change of mind?

It was now, settled in Paris in 1821–22, that Champollion definitely studied Young's article in the *Encyclopaedia Britannica*, by his own admission. (In a letter written from Grenoble to his brother in Paris around the time of the article's publication in 1819, he urged Jacques-Joseph to obtain Young's article from London 'straight away'.) In his 1824 *Précis*, Champollion asked the world to believe that Young's published work did not substantially influence his own independent thinking, as already mentioned. While this claim is conceivably true, given Champollion's long and passionate study of the subject since 1808 and the genius of his intuitions into hieroglyphic post-1822, it nevertheless strains credulity. Far more likely is that Champollion is a superlative example of Arthur Koestler's statement in *The Act of Creation*: 'Once one embraces an idea and lives with it day and night, one can no longer bear the thought that

she, the idea, has formerly belonged to someone else; to possess her completely and be possessed by her, one must extinguish her past.'

In my view, unprovable as it may be, Young's 1819 article, and his earlier
communications to De Sacy and others, compelled Champollion to em-
brace the existence of phoneticism in the Egyptian scripts. Young's article
saliently publishes what he calls 'something like a hieroglyphic alphabet' in
the form of a short list of hieroglyphs representing 'Sounds', along with a
second list of demotic signs labelled 'Supposed enchorial alphabet', modified from those suggested by Åkerblad. Moreover, Champollion was well
aware (as admitted in his *Précis*) that Young's rudimentary hieroglyphic
'alphabet' had been derived from the cartouches of Ptolemy and the Ptolemaic Queen Berenice, by attempting to match each hieroglyphic sign in a
cartouche with its equivalent alphabetic letter in the Greek spelling of the
names. Surely, having critically digested Young's published works and
accepted some of his ideas, however reluctantly, Champollion was now
primed to take his own first correct original step.

It came in January 1822, when he saw a copy of an obelisk inscription
sent to the National Institute in Paris by an English traveller and collector
William Bankes, who had had the obelisk removed from Philae (near
Aswan) and transported to Bankes's country house at Kingston Lacy in
Dorset, where it still stands. The importance of the obelisk was that it was
bilingual. The base-block inscription was in Greek, while the column
inscription was in hieroglyphic script. This, however, did not make it a
true bilingual, a second Rosetta Stone, because the two inscriptions did not
match. Notwithstanding, in 1818, Bankes realized that in the Greek letters
the names of Ptolemy and Cleopatra, Ptolemaic queen, were mentioned,
while in the hieroglyphs two (and only two) cartouches occurred—presumably representing the same two names as were written in Greek on the
base. One of these cartouches was almost the same as a long cartouche on
the Rosetta Stone identified by Young as Ptolemy with a title:

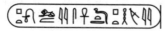

Rosetta Stone   Philae Obelisk

—so the second obelisk cartouche was likely to read Cleopatra. In sending a
copy of the Philae inscription to Young and other scholars, including the
National Institute, Bankes pencilled his identification of Cleopatra in the
margin of the copy.

Unfortunately for Young, the copy that came to him contained a significant error. The copyist had expressed the first letter of Cleopatra's name
with the sign for *t* instead of *k*. So, says Young, 'as I had not leisure at the
time to enter into a very minute comparison of the name with other
authorities, I suffered myself to be discouraged with respect to the application of my alphabet to its analysis'. In other words, Young had an unlucky
break here; but he was also undermined by his lifelong polymathic tendency to spread himself too thin.

Champollion, after years of frustration, was not about to be diverted
from study of Egypt by other interests and duties. He took the new clue—
without giving any acknowledgment to Bankes or Young (in his *Lettre à M.
Dacier*)—and ran with it. Just as Young had done, he decided that a shorter
version of the Ptolemy cartouche on the Rosetta Stone spelt only Ptolemy's
name, while a second, longer cartouche must involve some royal title,
tacked onto Ptolemy's name. Again as Young had done, Champollion
assumed that Ptolemy was spelt alphabetically, and thus, following Bankes's
identification, that the same applied to Cleopatra on the obelisk from
Philae. He proceeded to guess the phonetic values of the hieroglyphs in
both cartouches:

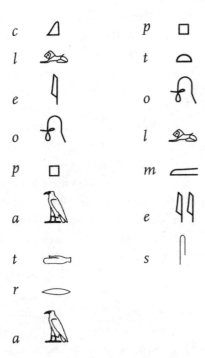

There were four signs in common, those with the phonetic values *l, e, o,* and *p,* but the phonetic value *t* was represented differently in the two names. Champollion deduced correctly that the two signs for *t* were what is known as *homophones,* that is, different signs with the same sound (compare in English **J**ill and **G**ill, **C**atherine and **K**atherine)—a concept that Young was also aware of. The real test of the decipherment, however, was whether these new phonetic values, when applied to the cartouches in other inscriptions, would produce sensible names. Champollion tried them in the following cartouche:

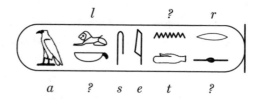

Substitution produced *Al?se?tr?.* Champollion guessed the name Alksentrs = (Greek) Alexandros [Alexander]—again the two signs for *k/c* (◯ and ⟋) are homophonous, as are the two different signs for *s* (—•— and ⎮). Using his growing alphabet, Champollion went on to identify the cartouches of other rulers of non-Egyptian origin: Berenice (already tackled, though with mistakes, by Young), Caesar, and a title of the Roman emperor, Autocrator. It was quickly obvious to him that many more identifications would now follow. The hieroglyphic code, after two enigmatic millennia, was beginning to break.

From many more such Graeco-Roman names written in hieroglyphs, Champollion worked out a table of phonetic signs, in the manner of Young's 'hieroglyphic alphabet', but much fuller and more accurate than his rival's, which he published in the *Lettre à M. Dacier.* (His portrait painted at this time shows him proudly holding this table.) However, at this juncture Champollion did not expect his phonetic values to apply to the names of indigenous, Egyptian-origin rulers (the pharaohs, pre-Alexander), which he persisted in thinking would be spelt non-phonetically. Even less did he expect his initial 'decipherment' to apply to the entire Egyptian writing system, beyond merely the names of rulers, which he continued to think must function by representing 'things not sounds'.

This belief is transparent in his introductory paragraph in 1822, which states: 'I hope it is not too rash for me to say that I have succeeded in demonstrating that these two forms of writing [hieratic and demotic] are neither of them alphabetic, as has been so generally thought, but *ideographic,* like the hieroglyphs themselves, that is to say, depicting the *ideas* and not the *sounds* of the language.' Yet, when he republished the original *Lettre* in 1828, he crucially modified this passage to read: 'neither of them <u>entirely</u> alphabetic, as has been so generally thought, but <u>often also</u> *ideographic*, like the hieroglyphs themselves, that is to say, <u>sometimes</u> depicting the *ideas* and <u>sometimes</u> the *sounds* of the language'. As Young had grasped the mixed nature of demotic in 1815, so now Champollion understood that hieroglyphic, too, was a mixture of conceptual ('ideographic') signs and phonetic signs.

The vital shift in Champollion's thinking—pivotal to his decipherment—occurred between his celebrated lecture of September 1822 and April 1823, when he announced his full decipherment to the Academy of Inscriptions. He never said what finally changed his mind, but this time the inspiration was certainly his own—nothing to do with Young, who in fact died in 1829 still mistakenly believing that hieroglyphic was essentially a conceptual script with phonetic elements only for spelling foreign names.

Probably a combination of factors was at work. For one thing, it struck Champollion that on the Rosetta Stone there were only 66 distinct signs among the 1419 hieroglyphic characters; if the hieroglyphs truly were symbols of words and ideas, then many more than 66 signs would have been expected, each one representing a different word. The small ratio of signs to characters implied instead a small set of phonetic signs mixed with other signs standing for whole words. For another thing, he learnt with surprise from a newly published French grammar of Chinese that there were phonetic elements not only in foreign names written in Chinese characters but also in indigenous Chinese words.

But very likely the most influential factor was that Champollion was thrilled to discover he could apply his phonetic alphabet to indigenous Egyptian names and words with results that made sense. An inscription he received from Egypt in September 1822 began the revelation. It came from the temple of Abu Simbel in Nubia and contained intriguing cartouches. They appeared to write the same name in a variety of ways, the simplest being:

He easily recognized the last two signs as having the phonetic value *s*. From his knowledge of Coptic, he guessed that the first sign had the value *re*, which was the Coptic word for 'sun'—the object apparently symbolized by the sign. Was there an ancient Egyptian ruler with a name that resembled

R(e)?ss, he wondered. Champollion, steeped in his passion for ancient Egypt, promptly thought of Ramesses, a king of the nineteenth dynasty listed in a well-known Greek history of Egypt written by a Ptolemaic historian, Manetho. If this guess was correct, then the sign must have the phonetic value *m*. (Champollion assumed hieroglyphic did not represent vowels, except in foreign names.)

A second hieroglyphic cartouche further suggested he was on the right track:

Of these three signs, two were 'known'; the first, an ibis, symbolized the god Thoth (inventor of writing). Then the name must be Thothmes, a king of the eighteenth dynasty also mentioned by Manetho. The Rosetta Stone appeared to confirm the value of . The sign occurred there, again with , as part of a group of hieroglyphs with the Greek translation 'genethlia', meaning 'birthday'. Immediately, Champollion was reminded of the Coptic word for 'give birth', 'mise'. (He was only half correct about the spelling of Ramesses: does not have the phonetic value *m*, as he thought, its value is the *bi*consonantal *ms*, as implied by the Coptic 'mise'. Champollion was not yet aware of this complexity.)

Having accepted that hieroglyphs were a mixture of phonetic signs and word signs, Champollion was in a position to decipher the second half of the long cartouche of Ptolemy, the king's title, on the Rosetta Stone:

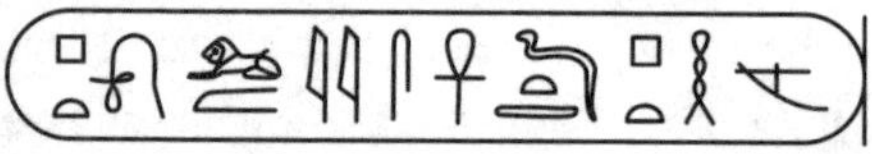

On the basis of the Greek inscription, the meaning of the entire cartouche was 'Ptolemy living for ever, beloved of Ptah' (Ptah was the creator god of Memphis). In Coptic, the word for 'life' or 'living' was 'onkh'; this was thought to be derived from an ancient Egyptian word 'ankh' represented by the sign (a word sign). The next signs presumably meant 'ever' and contained a *t* sound, since the sign was now known to have the phonetic value *t*. With assistance from Greek and Coptic, the could be assigned the phonetic value *dj*, producing a rough ancient Egyptian pronunciation *djet*, meaning 'for ever'. (The other sign was silent, a kind of classificatory word sign called a determinative; it symbolized 'flat land'.)

The first of the remaining four signs ⬚𓊪𓏏 was now known to stand for *p* and the second for *t*—the initial two sounds of Ptah; and so the third sign could be given the approximate phonetic value *h*. The fourth sign—another word sign—was therefore assumed to mean 'beloved'. Once again, Coptic came in useful to assign a pronunciation: the Coptic word for 'love' was known to be 'mere', and so the pronunciation of the fourth sign was probably *mer*. Thus, to sum up, Champollion arrived at the following rough approximation of the famous cartouche (guessing at the unwritten vowels): *Ptolmes ankh djet Ptah mer*—'Ptolemy living for ever, beloved of Ptah'.

The complexity of the hieroglyphic system is obvious from these few examples, and is encapsulated by Champollion's statement at the head of this chapter. It would take him the rest of his short life to establish its main features by brilliantly applying his decipherment to thousands of inscriptions, both in Europe and in Egypt itself. 'So poor Dr Young is incorrigible?' Champollion wrote scornfully to his brother from the Valley of the Kings in 1829. 'Why flog a mummified horse? . . . May the doctor continue to agitate about the alphabet while I, having been for six months among the monuments of Egypt, I am startled by what I am reading fluently rather than what my imagination is able to come up with.' Passionate as ever until the very end, Champollion created many enemies (most of them Frenchmen such as De Sacy). Partly for this reason, and partly because of the complexity of the hieroglyphic system, his decipherment was not generally accepted until the second half of the nineteenth century.

As for its beginning, Young indisputably made the first, and most difficult, moves towards the decipherment in 1814–19, which prepared the ground for Champollion's breakthrough in 1822–23. By sticking intransigently to his claim of sole authorship, Champollion achieved his ambition of becoming known as *the* decipherer of the Egyptian hieroglyphs. But in doing so he lost his good name, rather like Newton in physics, who denied any credit to others. While Champollion fully deserves to be called a genius, his reputation will forever be tainted by his hubris towards Young.

CHAPTER 10

CHARLES DARWIN

Evolution by Natural Selection

Thus, from the war of nature, from famine and death, the most exalted object which we are capable of conceiving, namely, the production of the higher animals, directly follows. There is grandeur in this view of life, with its several powers, having been originally breathed into a few forms or into one; and that, whilst this planet has gone cycling on according to the fixed law of gravity, from so simple a beginning endless forms most beautiful and most wonderful have been, and are being, evolved.

Charles Darwin, *On the Origin of Species by Means of Natural Selection*, 1859

The theory of evolution by natural selection was conceived by Charles Darwin and secretly scribbled down in his notebooks fully two decades before he published it. In the final months of 1838, the 29-year-old bachelor was a rising star in London's scientific world, secretary to the Geological Society, and shortly to be elected a fellow of the Royal Society, busy networking and building on the intellectual reputation he had gained by his round-the-world voyage in 1831–36 as the naturalist on HMS *Beagle*. Yet, within months of the birth of his theory, he abruptly got married to his quiet cousin Emma Wedgwood and produced the first of ten children; abandoned the metropolis for the country as soon as he could;

and in less than a decade transmuted himself into a reclusive but highly respectable gentleman–scientist anchored like a barnacle to his house and 'laboratory' garden in the village of Down outside London: the sage Darwin best known to posterity. Not until mid-1858 was its retiring author winkled out of his shell by the appearance of a rival theory and forced to publish—first in a scholarly journal and then, in late 1859, in his book *On the Origin of Species by Natural Selection*. Darwin's extraordinary delay in going public—coupled with his exceptionally staid and conventional life after the adventurous peregrinations of his *Beagle* voyage—have proved endlessly intriguing for well over a century. Both are integral to his discovery of natural selection.

In his *Autobiography*, written in the 1870s and originally intended only for his family, Darwin offers the following laconic account of the theory's conception and early development:

In October 1838, that is, fifteen months after I had begun my systematic enquiry, I happened to read for amusement [Thomas] Malthus on *Population*, and being well prepared to appreciate the struggle for existence which everywhere goes on from long-continued observation of the habits of animals and plants, it at once struck me that under these circumstances favourable variations would tend to be preserved and unfavourable ones to be destroyed. The result of this would be the formation of new species. Here, then, I had at last got a theory by which to work; but I was so anxious to avoid prejudice, that I determined not for some time to write even the briefest sketch of it. In June 1842 I first allowed myself the satisfaction of writing a very brief abstract of my theory in pencil in 35 pages; and this was enlarged during the summer of 1844 into one of 230 pages, which I had fairly copied out and still possess.

This copy a seriously unwell Darwin gave to his wife, with instructions that it be edited and published by one of his many scientific friends and associates in the event of his early death. At the time, not a single person except his wife had been allowed to read his ideas about species and evolution, barely a hint of which he included in the 'Journal of Researches' generally known as the *Voyage of the Beagle* that Darwin published in 1839 and in a second edition in 1845.

No doubt his delay in publishing the theory was influenced by the decision of his eminent physician and naturalist grandfather Erasmus Darwin to wait some two decades before risking publication of *his* celebrated book on evolution, *Zoonomia: or the Laws of Organic Life*, in two volumes in 1794–96, which appeared in Dublin rather than London. In 1792, aged 61, Erasmus had written a letter to his son Robert about his manuscript (quoted by Charles when writing a biography of his grandfather): 'I am studying my "Zoonomia", which I *think* I shall publish ... as I am now too old to fear a little abuse.' The published book, comments his grandson, 'was honoured by the Pope by being placed in the "Index Expurgatorius"'—as would happen in due course to his own *On the Origin of Species*. From the first inklings of his controversial theory in the 1830s, Darwin had a well-founded fear of both scientific and social ostracism, were he to publish prematurely.

Zoonomia and its author blasphemously rejected divine authority, the supposedly six millennia of earth's history since the Creation in 4004 BC, and the biblical account of the origin of species in which each species is an independent creation of God. In place of creationism, Erasmus Darwin propounded a mixture of materialism and metaphysical speculation. For example, this vision of the evolution of animal species from a primal aquatic ancestor:

> Would it be too bold to imagine, that in the great length of time since the earth began to exist, perhaps millions of ages before the commencement of the history of mankind, would it be too bold to imagine, that all warm-blooded animals had arisen from one living filament, which THE GREAT FIRST CAUSE endowed with animality, with the power of acquiring new parts, attended with new propensities, directed by irritations, sensations, volitions, and associations; and thus possessing the faculty of continuing to improve by its own inherent activity, and of delivering down these improvements by generation to its posterity, world without end!

The language and ideas may have been intoxicating, yet the book was not scientific, since it proposed no mechanism for evolution. The Romantic poet Coleridge, an early convert to Erasmus's works, later strongly rejected them and coined 'darwinizing' as a word to describe wild theorizing. Thomas Young, who knew Erasmus personally, noted sympathetically but critically in 1815 that 'much ingenuity, much practical knowledge, and much absurdity' were combined in the *Zoonomia*. 'To follow [its] theories would be useless, but some of [its] hypothetical assertions require to be noticed, for their singularity and boldness.' Charles Darwin himself, having greatly admired *Zoonomia* as a medical student in his teens, was 'much disappointed' when he reread it as an adult in search of ideas for his own theory in the 1830s—'the proportion of speculation being so large to the facts given'. Nevertheless, Erasmus's speculative tendency would reappear in grandson Charles, informed and moderated by an insatiable hunger for facts; and, unlike in *Zoonomia*, it would change the world.

Erasmus died in 1802, seven years before Charles was born. Something of a tyrant towards his family (his first wife died of alcohol poisoning, and a son committed suicide), he had compelled his son Robert, Charles's father, to become a physician, much against the young man's wishes. But Robert Darwin managed to combine a successful medical practice of wealthy and titled patients with a ruthless head for investment; for half a century, until his death in 1848, he was the most significant financier in the Shropshire region around his home in Shrewsbury. In 1796, he married Susanna, the eldest daughter of the potter Josiah Wedgwood, and by 1800 he had built a large house in Shrewsbury, The Mount, where his children grew up. Thus Charles, the fifth of six sons and daughters, born in 1809, was surrounded by the comforts and conventions of the country gentry throughout his up-bringing. It was also an affectionate, if somewhat clannish family. The only shadow on his childhood was the death of Charles's mother when he was eight, but this seems to have left relatively little imprint on him, probably because he was taken in hand by two doting sisters and a close elder brother.

About his formal education in the schools of Shrewsbury (and later at university in Edinburgh and Cambridge), Darwin was consistently negative. In his sixties, he told his psychologist cousin Francis Galton in answer to a questionnaire: 'I consider that all I have learnt of any value has been self-taught.' Shrewsbury's well-known school run by Dr Samuel Butler (grand-father of the author of *The Way of All Flesh*), concentrated on the classics, which held almost no appeal for Charles, and ignored any kind of science, which already interested both him and his brother. 'The school as a means of education to me was simply a blank', Darwin wrote in his notably honest autobiography. When he was taken away from Shrewsbury School by his father in 1825 after seven years, 'I believe I was considered by all my masters and by my father as a very ordinary boy, rather below the common standard in intellect.'

No pronounced talent for studying a particular subject (and no hint of any genius) was evident: a situation that might be said to have persisted even as late as Darwin's arrival on board the *Beagle* at the age of 22. The sole exception was perhaps a childish taste for natural history. But this was mainly a passion for collecting—shells, minerals, coins, insects, and so forth (less so beetles until his university days)—not found in any other Darwin sibling, 'which leads a man to be a systematic naturalist, a virtuoso, or a miser'. Otherwise, looking back, Darwin could discern only some traits in his character that promised well and are certainly manifest in his extremely wide-ranging, hard-working, and rigorous scientific career: 'I had strong and diversified tastes, much zeal for whatever interested me, and a keen pleasure in understanding any complex subject or thing.'

For his part, Dr Darwin had apparently discerned in his son the makings of a successful doctor, despite his own unhappy medical training. He despatched Charles and his brother to study medicine in Edinburgh in late 1825. From the outset, Darwin felt unmotivated by most of the lectures. The constant upsetting exposure to blood, corpses, suffering, and death was not mitigated by his never-strong religious faith. Dissection disgusted him, and so he did not learn it, to his later regret. The experience of watching two 'very bad' operations, one of them on a child (of course well before anaesthesia), drove him from the operating theatre in horror. After learning in the summer of 1826 from family talk—not from his father—that he could expect to inherit a considerable fortune, Darwin ceased to consider his course of medical study a professional necessity during his second year at Edinburgh. It was probably around this time that his father angrily scolded him: 'You care for nothing but shooting, dogs, and rat-catching, and you will be a disgrace to yourself and all your family', as Darwin recalled in old age with deep mortification.

In lieu of medicine, he gave his best energies to natural history. He had earlier taken lessons in skinning and stuffing birds from a freed slave who acted as a taxidermist for the university's natural history museum. Now he attended assiduously the exciting meetings of the undergraduate Plinian Society and became friendly with one of its stalwarts, Robert Grant, a well-travelled doctor who was fascinated by microscopic tidal creatures. Grant was also a closet materialist and evolutionist, who knew the great Parisian biologist Jean-Baptiste Lamarck, and keenly admired his controversial belief in transmutation of species, as well as the views of Lamarck's English counterpart, Erasmus Darwin. Confessing himself to Erasmus's grandson on field trips to the coast near Edinburgh, Grant encouraged Darwin to study sea-mats (*Flustra*) by lending him a microscope, which led to two small discoveries by Darwin delivered as papers at a meeting of the Plinian in March 1827. Later in the meeting, another member provoked a ruckus by outrageously maintaining that 'mind as far as one individual's sense and consciousness are concerned, is material'—causing his paper to be struck from the society's minutes. While Darwin mentions his own papers in his autobiography, he is silent about the censored paper. Here was his first personal warning of the dangers of unorthodox scientific thinking about man in public.

Not long after this meeting, Darwin gave up his medical training for good and left Edinburgh. His father, 'very properly vehement against my turning into an idle sporting man', suggested that he consider becoming a country clergyman: an undemanding position that would conventionally allow him to carry on his researches as a naturalist. Although Darwin was already doubtful about some of the dogmas of the faith, he persuaded himself of his belief in the Anglican Creed after reading some works of theology, and arrived at Christ's College, Cambridge to study for a BA degree in divinity in early 1828.

Cambridge science, then known as natural philosophy, was a citadel of religious orthodoxy (and ordained scientists) in the form of 'natural theology': the belief that science should consist of investigating the evident harmony and beauty of the natural world in order to demonstrate the existence and good-ness of its Maker. *Natural Theology: or Evidences of the Existence and Attributes of the Deity*, published in 1802 by the late William Paley, a fellow of Christ's College, was the key text of this creed, which Darwin now formally studied with deep attention. Another important believer was William Whewell, master of Trinity College from 1844–66, whom Darwin knew personally. Whewell's influential *History of the Inductive Sciences* stated categorically that: 'Species have a real existence in nature, and a transition from one to another does not exist'— ironically in 1837, the very year in which Darwin would begin to believe precisely the opposite about transmutation.

'During the three years which I spent at Cambridge my time was wasted, as far as the academical studies were concerned, as completely as at Edinburgh and at school', writes Darwin in his autobiography. Yet his informal contacts with academics and others in the university during this period, combined with his reading of two popular books by the natural philosopher John Herschel, and the naturalist and South American traveller Alexander von Humboldt, would prove the making of Darwin as the naturalist of the *Beagle*. The Cambridge professor of botany John Stevens Henslow, a devout natural theologian, selflessly encouraged Darwin's pas-sion for natural history, while the professor of geology, Adam Sedgwick, an even more devout believer, initiated him into field geology during a trip through Wales in the summer of 1831. Last but not least, Darwin's cousin William Darwin Fox, a fellow undergraduate at Christ's and a future coun-try clergyman, introduced him to beetle collecting, which quickly became an all-consuming pursuit. 'I can remember the exact appearance of certain posts, old trees, and banks where I made a good capture', Darwin enthused half a century later. Beetles, more than any other creature, started Darwin down the path towards natural selection. 'Bug-hunting was the Trojan horse of Victorian agnosticism', writes a modern editor of On the Origin of Species (John Burrow, a recent fellow of Christ's).

It was Henslow who recommended Darwin to the Admiralty for the Beagle voyage in August 1831, while his protégé was geologizing in Wales with Henslow's Cambridge colleague Sedgwick. Robert FitzRoy, the volatile captain of this official surveying vessel, wanted a gentleman companion on board able to pay his own way, who could also double as a naturalist. He liked the look of Darwin, except for his nose, which he thought betrayed lack of energy and determination. Darwin's father and sisters were initially firmly opposed to FitzRoy's startling and risky proposal. But after careful persuasion by a Wedgwood uncle (appealed to by a desperate Charles) whom his father trusted, Robert Darwin gave in gracefully and agreed to finance his son's entire expedition. As Darwin amusingly recalled, 'The voyage of the Beagle has been by far the most important event in my life, and has determined my whole career; yet it depended on so small a circumstance as my uncle offering to drive me 30 miles to Shrewsbury, which few uncles would have done, and on such a trifle as the shape of my nose.'

After two months' delay (a miserable time for a waiting Darwin) to allow for a refit of the ship and fair weather, HMS Beagle sailed from Devonport on 27 December 1831. She crossed the Atlantic, stopping at the Cape Verde Islands, to the coast of Brazil, travelled down the eastern coastline of South America to Tierra del Fuego and the Falkland Islands, then up the western coast to the Galapagos Islands, crossed the Pacific via Tahiti to New Zealand and Australia, and returned to England via Keeling Island, Mauritius, South Africa, Saint Helena, and Brazil, making landfall at Falmouth on 2 October 1836.

Although the entire voyage lasted almost five years, Darwin himself was at sea for only 18 months—much to his relief, as he was abominably seasick and loathed the ocean. While the ship doggedly surveyed the coasts of South America for the government in London, its quasi-official naturalist periodically got off it to rove the land on foot and horseback with a gun, geological hammer, and collecting boxes. In Argentina, living among the gauchos of the Pampas in 1833, Darwin got caught up in the war of extermination waged against nomadic Indians by General Rosas, and witnessed the struggle for existence between races at its most vicious. In the Andes, he went on a four-month expedition in mid-1835.

To begin with, he was more geologist than biologist. The *Voyage of the Beagle* opens with geology: a description of the volcanic landscape of the Cape Verde Islands with its apparently sterile lava plains, and volcanism's effect on the islands' soil, flora, and fauna, so utterly unlike the English landscape of Shrewsbury or Cambridge. Indeed geology was fundamental to Darwin's research throughout the voyage. For in the first decades of the nineteenth century, geology had demonstrated how inconceivably ancient the earth must be—hundreds of millions of years old or more—which even a creationist like Sedgwick was obliged to admit. As Darwin started to perceive dimly during the later stages of his voyage, this great lapse of time revealed by geology might explain the origin of species without resort to creationism.

On the Origin of Species emphasizes the crucial point about geological time in robust language:

> It is hardly possible for me even to recall to the reader, who may not be a practical geologist, the facts leading the mind feebly to comprehend the lapse of time. He who can read Sir Charles Lyell's grand work on the Principles of Geology, which the future historian will recognize as having produced a revolution in natural science, yet does not admit how incomprehensibly vast have been the past periods of time, may at once close this volume. Not that it suffices to study the Principles of Geology, or to read special treatises by different observers on separate formations, and to mark how each author attempts to give an inadequate idea of the duration of each formation or even each stratum. A man must for years examine for himself great piles of superimposed strata, and watch the sea at work grinding down old rocks and making fresh sediment, before he can hope to comprehend anything of the lapse of time, the monuments of which we see around us.

Lyell's three volumes of his *Principles of Geology*, published in 1830–33, were constant cabin reading for Darwin on board the *Beagle*. Volume one was gifted to him by FitzRoy (who was keenly interested in the subject) before they sailed, while the other two volumes were sent to him during the voyage. Although Sedgwick was publicly scathing about Lyell's palaeontology, and Henslow advised Darwin to read volume one but 'on no account to accept the views therein advocated', Darwin lapped it up and became Lyell's first scientific disciple. He and Lyell were in touch during the voyage, and on his return to England, they became friends and strong advocates of each other's ideas, despite Lyell's hesitation in fully accepting Darwin's theory of natural selection during the 1860s.

The key idea that the *Principles* imparted to Darwin was the gradualism of geological processes, which of course came to underpin his view of evolution.

Gradualism—first propounded by James Hutton in the 1790s—was an idea directly opposed to the catastrophism favoured by creationists, who believed in the biblical account of the Flood. Whewell dubbed Lyell's view of geological processes—the weathering effects of sea, wind, and rain, the activity of volcanoes, and even the occurrence of earthquakes —'uniformitarianism': the idea being that the processes acted uniformly throughout earth's history, neither faster nor slower than today. In other words, the present was the key to the past, and the earth was a self-balancing, non-progressive system. In particular, the landmasses had experienced periods of gradual elevation making mountain ranges, and gradual subsidence making ocean basins, which were continuing even in modern times, followed by reversals in direction of movement. As Darwin gazed on the Cape Verde landscape, the coastlines of Patagonia and Chile, the peaks of the Andes, and the coral islands of the Pacific and Indian Oceans, he excitedly viewed them through Lyell's eyes as examples of past and present oscillations of elevation and subsidence.

Thus, after experiencing in February 1835 a devastating earthquake and its elevating effects on the coastline of Chile, carefully measured on land and at sea by FitzRoy (using depth soundings), Darwin became convinced that an extensive series of earthquakes—a phenomenon long familiar in Chile— had been responsible for much grander elevation over geological time. So much so, as he later discovered, that fossil remains of marine organisms could be observed in slate on the heights of the Cordillera at some 13,000 feet above sea level. 'With this additional instance [of an earthquake] fresh before us, we may assume as probable, according to the principles laid down by Mr Lyell, other small successive elevations', he records in the *Voyage*. 'The elevation of the land to the amount of some feet during these earthquakes, appears to be a paroxysmal movement, in a series of lesser and even insensible steps, by which the whole west coast of South America has been raised above the level of the sea.'

This Lyellian idea, concretely reinforced by Darwin's eyewitness evidence of elevation by the 1835 earthquake (which he regarded as perhaps the most 'deeply interesting' sight of his entire voyage), helped to suggest a solution to one of many puzzles about fossils in South America. Why had he discovered frequent fossils in the rocks of the coastline of eastern South America, including fascinating examples of extinct giant quadrupeds, yet virtually no fossils in the rocks of the western coastline? Not only no fossils, but no recent deposits sufficiently extensive to last for even a short geological period.

The contrast between the two coastlines struck Darwin forcibly. It could not be attributed to chance, given the months of effort he had devoted to exploring both coastlines, and it begged for a scientific explanation.

Darwin's tentative answer was that in recent times the east coast had experienced first subsidence and then elevation, whereas the west had only been elevated, without much (or perhaps any) period of subsidence. On the east coast, fossils had been formed because subsidence of the sea bottom had proceeded at a rate that nearly balanced the rate of supply of sediment from degradation of the land, allowing the sea to remain shallow and thus favourable for life, and the formation of a fossil layer thick enough to resist degradation when it was subsequently elevated to produce the current coastline. On the west coast, by contrast, no fossils were formed because any deposits on the sea bottom were degraded by the action of coastal waves and muddy streams entering the sea, as sea bottom was gradually elevated to become coastline. 'I am convinced that all our ancient formations, which are rich in fossils, have thus been formed during subsidence', Darwin wrote much later in the *Origin*. Other contemporaneous geologists came to the same conclusion about fossil formations in diverse parts of the world.

The idea had the further advantage of helping to explain one of the gravest and trickiest objections Darwin would face in convincing himself and others of the truth of natural selection rather than creationism. (The problem persists today, and was called 'palaeontology's trade secret' by the palaeontologist Stephen Jay Gould.) Why was the world's fossil record so imperfect, with so few examples of the gradual change in species through geological time expected in line with Lyell's uniformitarian theory? One important reason, said Darwin, had to be that fossils would not be laid down during periods of land elevation, only during periods of subsidence, ensuring that numerous species would not be preserved in the geological record.

Other fossil puzzles in South America included the anatomical relationship evident between some extinct and living species, and the cause of species extinction, which seemed to have been of recent occurrence, since many of the extinct fossils were found in deposits containing fossils of still existing molluscs. In his *Voyage*, Darwin ruminates: 'It is impossible to reflect without the deepest astonishment, on the changed state of this continent. Formerly it must have swarmed with great monsters, like the southern parts of Africa'—he meant the elephant, rhinoceros, hippopotamus, and so on—'but now we find only the tapir, guanaco, armadillo, and capybara.' Although Darwin was unable to solve these puzzles during his tour, they set him thinking about how the different species that closely resembled each other, either across epochs or across geographical regions, might share a common ancestor, rather than being independent of each other as required by creationists.

The Galapagos Islands famously focused Darwin's thinking on species. But at the time of his visit in October 1835, his observations created more confusion than clarity in his mind. The tortoises, birds, trees, and other wildlife of this Pacific archipelago were not identical on the various islands, even though the islands were only a few miles apart and had the same physical conditions. Unfortunately for Darwin, he had assumed in advance of arrival that the same species would be identical on different islands, and he discovered their revealing differences rather late in his collecting, partly by talking to the locals, who claimed to be able to identify which island a particular tortoise came from by the shape of its shell. Only when Darwin's bird collection was examined back in London by an expert ornithologist, John Gould, did it become clear to Darwin just how subtle the distinctions between different islands were, notably in the beak structure of his finch collection. Were the finches really different species or merely varieties of one species? Recalling this experience in the *Origin*, Darwin wrote: 'I was much struck how entirely vague and arbitrary is the distinction between species and varieties.'

On board the *Beagle*, some six months after leaving the Galapagos, heading home for England in 1836, Darwin took a first careful look at his puzzling collection from the archipelago. He allowed himself a cautious and ambiguous catalogue note:

> When I recollect, the fact that from the form of the body, shape of scales & general size, the Spaniards can at once pronounce, from which Island any tortoise may have been brought, When I see these islands in sight of each other, & possessed of but a scanty stock of animals, tenanted by these birds, but slightly differing in structure & filling the same place in Nature, I must suspect they are only varieties. The only fact of a similar kind of which I am aware, is the constant asserted difference—between the wolf-like Fox of East and West Falkland Islds.—If there is the slightest foundation for these remarks the zoology of Archipelagoes—will be worth examining; for such facts would undermine the stability of Species.

Intended for his eyes only, this note was his very first written hint of his newly formed doubts about the permanence of species.

Back at The Mount in Shrewsbury in early October 1836 after five years' absence, Darwin was once again embraced by his family. On greeting him, his doctor father turned to his sisters and said: 'Why, the shape of his head is quite altered.' Whatever the truth of this observation—neither father nor son really believed in phrenology—Darwin certainly knew that his *mind* had been broadened by his travels. He was, however, unsure in what way to apply this unique experience to his future life and career. To become a clergyman was clearly now out of the question given his scientific passion and religious questioning. He was unable to see himself as a professional academic, as his family thought he might. To remain with his father and sisters in conventional Shrewsbury was never an option. So he had either to go back to Cambridge for further studies or to move to London.

Since his *Beagle* collections were all with the ever-supportive Professor Henslow in Cambridge—periodically sent there by ship during the long voyage—Darwin took lodgings in Cambridge for a few months, then in March 1837 moved to London. Not only would he be physically close to professional experts, societies, and institutions in the capital such as Gould, the Geological and Zoological societies, and the British Museum, to his brother, and to friends like Lyell, Darwin also probably sensed that he needed the freer intellectual atmosphere of London to begin thinking through his unorthodox ideas. His travels had made him acutely aware of the necessity of studying the works of relevant experts, in order to coun-teract his speculative tendency 'to fill up the wide gaps of knowledge, by inaccurate and superficial hypotheses', as he remarks on the final page of the *Voyage of the Beagle*, which he completed in London during 1837 (though it was not published until 1839).

In July that year, Darwin opened the first of four notebooks on 'Trans-mutation of Species', covering a two-year period, and at the head of the first page wrote the title *Zoonomia*, in homage to his grandfather's treatise on evolution. A year later, in July 1838, he started the first of two more note-books on 'Man, Mind and Materialism', which conclude around August 1839. In his autobiography, he claims: 'I worked on true Baconian principles, and without any theory collected facts on a wholesale scale, more especially with respect to domesticated productions, by printed enquiries, by conversations with skilful breeders and gardeners, and by extensive reading.' His fanatical fact collecting continued throughout the 1840s and 50s, right up to the publication of the *Origin*, indeed almost until his death in 1882.

The years 1837–39, and especially the intense reading of the closing months of 1838, were the crucial ones in the conception of natural selec-tion, as already mentioned. Darwin scholars have therefore pored over this period's often pithy but hieroglyphic notes in minute detail for decades. Key advances in Darwin's thought have emerged from their detective work—along with retreats, detours, impasses, and blunders. However, the most significant result has been the gradual understanding that Darwin's achievement was realized 'not in a golden moment of insight but in the slower process of constructing an original point of view'.

The remark is from *Darwin on Man: A Psychological Study of Creativity*, an analysis of Darwin's early notebooks by the psychologist Howard Gruber, together with an annotated transcription by the historian of science Paul Barrett. Gruber also makes another interesting observation: 'The pandemonium of Darwin's notebooks and his actual way of working, in which many different processes tumble over each other in untidy sequences—theorizing, experimenting, casual observing, cagey questioning, reading, etc.—would never have passed muster in a methodological court of inquiry among Darwin's scientific contemporaries.' So much for the 'true Baconian principles' remembered by Darwin in the 1870s. But then, as will often be apparent in this book, creators seldom recall accurately their own creative processes.

The entry for 21 September 1838 in the first 'Man, Mind, and Materialism' notebook describes a provocative dream of execution:

> Was witty in a dream in a confused manner. Thought that a person was hung & came to life, and & then made many jokes about not having run away & having faced death like a hero, & then I had some confused idea of showing scar behind (instead of front) (having changed hanging into his head cut off) as kind of wit showing he had honourable wounds. All this was kind of wit.—I changed I believe from hanging to head cut off (there was the feeling of banter and joking) because the whole train of Dr Monro experiment about hanging came before me showing impossibility of person recovering from hanging on account of blood, but all these ideas came one after other, without ever comparing them. I neither doubted them nor *believed* them.—Believing consists in the comparison of ideas connected with judgement. [What is the Philosophy of Shame & Blushing?]

This captures something of the fluid and nimble associations in dreaming and thinking, and their relationship to rational thought. Darwin gives no interpretation of the dream, apart from his final remark about shame in square brackets, which he added later. Nevertheless, many writers on Darwin, such as Gruber and Darwin's chief modern biographers Adrian Desmond, James Moore, and Janet Browne, have felt compelled to see the dream as an expression of Darwin's fear of persecution. In this view, the execution of the dreamer pictured an increasingly anxious conflict between

Darwin's worry about being condemned for his heretical ideas, and his desire that they bring him immortality. By choosing decapitation rather than hanging, the dreamer appears to improve his chances. (The gruesome reference to Monro is to Alexander Monro (III), Darwin's most disliked lecturer in his anatomy class at Edinburgh more than a decade earlier.)

A week later, on 28 September 1838, he began to read Malthus's *Essay on the Principle of Population* in its sixth edition. First published in 1798 as a riposte to French Revolution utopianism, and widely quoted, debated, and attacked since then—not least by Lyell in his *Principles of Geology*—its basic thesis would have been long familiar to Darwin, though he had not yet referred to it in writing. Malthus claimed that the human population expanded geometrically (doubling every 25 years on average), while agricultural production increased only arithmetically. Therefore the population must ineluctably be controlled in the struggle for sustenance and reproduction by such checks as famine, epidemics, wars, abortion, infanticide, contraception, or at best moral self-restraint in the form of late marriage and sexual abstinence. Society, said Malthus, must recognize this underlying statistical cause of misery and vice, and look for logical ways to alleviate them.

What Darwin now perceived was that the human struggle was also found in the animal and plant kingdoms. The harmony and beauty of nature seen by the Cambridge 'natural theologians' was in reality a persistent illusion. 'It is difficult to believe in the dreadful but quiet war lurking just below the serene facade of nature', Darwin memorably noted in March 1839.

His mind had been prepared to see this by observing the fecundity and variety of nature, first among the beetles of Cambridgeshire, then during his voyage around the world. The violent competition between the races in South America, New Zealand, and Australia had also made an indelible impression. In addition, earlier in 1838, he had become sensitized by reading of the biologist C. G. Ehrenberg's recent discoveries concerning the incredible rate of reproduction of micro-organisms. 'One invisible animalcule in four days could form 2 cubic stone', Darwin noted, apparently days before he began to read Malthus.

On 28 September, he noted in his third 'Transmutation' notebook, directly after some comments on Malthus: 'One may say there is a force like a hundred thousand wedges trying [to] force every kind of adapted structure into the gaps in the oeconomy of nature, or rather forming gaps by thrusting out weaker ones ... The final cause of all this wedging, must be to sort out proper structure, & adapt it to change.' In other words, those varieties of a species that could best adapt and so wedge themselves into their environment would survive at the expense of less effective varieties, and thereby gradually change the species. Malthus's deadly checks on human population had been silently transmuted by Darwin into a creative principle of development in plants and animals.

It was a flash of insight. Yet it cannot be said to have produced in Darwin a rush of understanding of the origin of species. The very next entry in his notebook switches to the curiosity of monkeys and baboons, while subsequent entries deal with other matters for well over a month. Not until some time in November 1838 (the exact date is unclear) does he return to the subject and note laconically: 'Three principles will account for all (1) Grandchildren like grandfathers (2) Tendency to small change especially with physical change (3) Great fertility in proportion to support of parents.'

Here Darwin has defined the three elements of his mechanism for evolution, which he would later call 'natural selection': heredity, variation, and great fertility. None of these was original to him. The transmission of characteristics from generation to generation by heredity was widely known and accepted. The ability to artificially select variations in domesticated species had long been familiar to breeders. The idea of great fertility leading to the struggle for existence was the doctrine of Malthus. What was original to Darwin was his synthesis of the three principles so as to explain how varieties could give rise to new species without the intervention of God.

In the introduction to the *Origin*, he gives an exquisitely concise summary of his new view of nature:

> As many more individuals of each species are born than can possibly survive; and as, consequently, there is a frequently recurring struggle for existence, it follows that any being, if it vary however slightly in any manner profitable to itself, under the complex and sometimes varying conditions of life, will have a better chance of surviving, and thus be *naturally selected*. From the strong principle of inheritance, any selected variety will tend to propagate its new and modified form.

Even in 1859, Darwin treated natural selection as a hypothesis, subject to future scientific confirmation. He could offer no mechanism at all to explain either heredity or variation (explained today by the accuracy of self-replication of DNA with rare inaccuracies), and had simply to assume their operation. And he had major difficulties in explaining in evolutionary terms, for example, the imperfection of the fossil record, the absence or

PLATE 1 Portrait of Leonardo da Vinci attributed to Francesco Melzi, *c.* 1508.

PLATE 2 Bust of Sir Christopher Wren by Edward Pierce, c. 1673.

PLATE 3 (*above*) Portrait of the Mozart family by Johann Nepomuk della Croce, 1780-81. From left to right: Maria Anna (Nannerl), Wolfgang Amadeus, and Leopold Mozart; the oval portrait shows Mozart's deceased mother, Anna Maria.

PLATE 4 Daguerreotype of Charles Darwin and his eldest son William, 1842. This is the only known photograph of Darwin with a member of his family.

PLATE 5 Portrait of Jean-François Champollion attributed to Mme de Rumilly, *c.* 1823. He holds his hieroglyphic/demotic 'alphabet'.

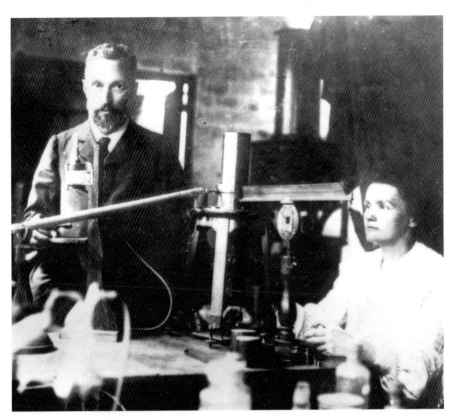

PLATE 6 (*above*) Photograph of Pierre and Marie Curie, late 1890s, with the piezoelectric electrometer used to measure radioactivity.

PLATE 7 Photograph of Virginia Woolf, 1925.

PLATE 8 Photograph of Satyajit Ray by Marc Riboud, 1956. Ray, shown with his cameraman Subrata Mitra, is making *Aparajito*, the second film of the Apu Trilogy.

PLATE 9 Photograph of Henri Cartier-Bresson by René Burri, 1959.

PLATE 10 Photograph of Albert Einstein, *c.* 1906, at the Swiss Patent Office, Bern.

rarity of transitional varieties between species, the complexity and perfection of organs such as the eye, and the apparently functionless beauty of structures such as the peacock's tail. Nor could he legitimately exclude from the purview of his theory the sensitive subject of human evolution (though he deliberately avoided it in print until after the publication of the *Origin*). Above all, his theory dismantled creationism. No wonder, back in 1838, he felt a severe need to accumulate as much evidence as possible before presenting natural selection to a potentially critical public.

In the two decades between his discovery and its publication, Darwin and Down House became an important centre for elegant and subtle experimentation on plants and creatures, especially insects, and the focus of a worldwide spider's web of correspondence with experts, collectors, and scientists as far afield as the Americas and Australia. Among the numerous lines of enquiry he pursued, Darwin devoted eight years, 1846–54, to a gruelling study of barnacles, in order to convince other scientists of his authority in writing about species and their correct classification. He did not travel again as he once had on the *Beagle*, mainly for health reasons though partly by design; but world travellers such as his friend Joseph Hooker, later director of Kew Gardens, were regular visitors to Down. By persistence, flattery, and exploitation of his growing reputation, Darwin charmed and cajoled others into giving or lending him the specimens he needed.

In 1856, the naturalist Alfred Russel Wallace, who was then working in Southeast Asia, wrote to Darwin enclosing his published paper, 'On the law that has regulated the introduction of new species.' Darwin replied cautiously from Down that he had been thinking on the same subject for 20 years, and began a brief but cordial correspondence. Little did he suspect that in 1858 Wallace would have virtually the same idea of natural selection as he had in 1838. It struck Wallace while he was lying in bed in the Malay Archipelago with a bout of malaria. Amazingly, it was stimulated by his having read Malthus (though in his case twelve years previously, rather than concurrently as with Darwin). Wallace promptly mailed a paper outlining his idea to Darwin and asked him to forward it to Lyell. A profoundly embarrassed Darwin was now compelled to publish, or forever lose his priority. And so, in 1858, in the journal of the Linnean Society, two papers by Darwin and by Wallace appeared together, having been swiftly presented to the society by Darwin's friends Hooker and Lyell without the permission of the faraway Wallace. Fortunately, Wallace took it very well when informed by Darwin, and always gave Darwin the chief credit for the theory. '[F]or I have not the love of *work*, *experiment* and *detail* that was so pre-eminent in Darwin, and without which anything I could have written would never have convinced the world', Wallace accurately observed three decades later.

In truth, without the advocacy of scientific friends such as Hooker and Thomas Henry Huxley, Darwin's theory, however copiously researched, might not have convinced Victorian Britain. The *Origin* was a stiff and unillustrated read, and its retiring and respectable author had few skills as a public speaker and none as a polemicist. He was intentionally absent, for example, from the celebrated bruising 1860 debate over evolution at the University Museum in Oxford between science (represented by Huxley) and religion (represented by Bishop Samuel Wilberforce), chaired by an equivocal Henslow. 'I would as soon have died as tried to answer the Bishop in such an assembly', Darwin admitted to Huxley afterwards in a letter. Several key scientists were unsympathetic to natural selection. Herschel mocked the theory as 'the law of higgledy-piggledy'; Lyell was dubious about its applicability to man; the geologist Sedgwick and the palaeontologist Richard Owen were trenchantly opposed. For decades, well into the next century, and even today, natural selection would remain controversial, either in whole or in part, though there can be no modern scientist who denies the existence of evolution. The philosopher John Stuart Mill's 1862 verdict on Darwin soon after publication of the *Origin* remains perceptive: 'He has opened a path of inquiry full of promise, the results of which none can foresee.'

CHAPTER 11

MARIE CURIE

Discovery of Radium

A great discovery does not leap completely achieved from the brain of the scientist, as Minerva sprang, all panoplied, from the head of Jupiter; it is the fruit of accumulated preliminary work. Between the days of fecund productivity are inserted days of uncertainty when nothing seems to succeed, and when even matter itself seems hostile; and it is then that one must hold out against discouragement. Thus without ever forsaking his inexhaustible patience, Pierre Curie used sometimes to say to me: 'It is nevertheless hard, this life that we have chosen.'

Marie Curie, *Pierre Curie*, 1923

The discovery and isolation of radium in 1898–1902 by Marie Curie, collaborating with her husband Pierre Curie, is frequently regarded as a story of elemental simplicity. In fact, it was the result of a complex interaction between physics and chemistry, involving exact observation, subtle thinking, cutting-edge technology, brute-force methods, extreme dedication, and good luck. The heroic legend that has naturally grown up around her name—epitomized by Albert Einstein's comment that 'Marie Curie is, of all celebrated beings, the only one whom fame has not corrupted'—has emphasized the simplicity. But the complexity is more interesting from the perspective of understanding scientific creativity, which in Curie's case led to the remarkable award of two Nobel Prizes: the first in physics in 1903, the second in chemistry in 1911. How did a Polish woman, Manya Sklodowska, from an insignificant scientific background, who did not begin studying science at university level until she was 24 years old, come to merit such a unique double accolade as a result of only a few years of research into radioactivity?

Her upbringing in Poland was undoubtedly crucial to her success. Warsaw, where she was born in 1867, was under Russian rule throughout her youth. In 1815, at the Congress of Vienna after Napoleon's defeat at Waterloo, Poland came under the joint control of Russia, Prussia, and Austria; Tsar Alexander I of Russia was named 'King of Poland'. The Russian regime was the harshest of the three dominant powers. Two Polish uprisings against it in 1830 and 1863 failed, the second after a year and a half's fighting with the Russian army. Thousands of the resistance were killed or exiled to Siberia; about a hundred thousand Poles fled the country and settled abroad, chiefly in France. The leaders of the uprising were hung from the ramparts of Warsaw's Alexander Citadel, their corpses left to rot for months in 1864, not far from the Sklodowski home.

Several of the Sklodowski family fought in the two uprisings. Manya's grandfather, a physics and chemistry professor, was in the artillery in 1830. Captured by Cossacks, and forced to march barefoot for 140 miles to a prison camp in Warsaw, he was lucky to escape with his life. A paternal uncle was twice wounded in the 1863 uprising and got away to France; a maternal uncle was sent to Siberia for four years.

The Siberian exile's sister—Manya's mother Bronislawa—and Manya's father Wladyslaw, did not actually fight but were leading members of the unarmed, intellectual resistance, as distinguished school teachers. Wladyslaw Sklodowski had been unable to attend Warsaw University, because it was temporarily closed after the 1830 uprising, but he studied biology unofficially in Warsaw and later managed to take a degree in mathematics and physics from the University of St Petersburg. Back in Warsaw he became a poorly paid assistant teacher in a private school and got married; his talented wife worked her way up to become headmistress of the city's only private school for girls. In 1868, he was appointed assistant director of a government-run 'gymnasium', and his wife abandoned her teaching position. His salary improved, and he was given an apartment in the school building for his growing family of four daughters and a son; but the post brought him under the diktat of Russian educational officials at a time of severe repression.

In all Polish schools under Russian domination the Polish language was banned in communications between teachers and pupils, and in the gymnasia even private conversations between pupils were supposed to be in Russian. The Russian language was mandatory in education, to the extent that lessons in Polish as a language had to be carried out in Russian. Banned, too, was the teaching of Polish literature and history, except in so far as history supported a triumphalist view of Russia's past. In general, the Russian professors in the gymnasia treated their Polish pupils as 'enemies', Curie recalled in her autobiography in the 1920s. At her girls' gymnasium in the late 1870s and early 1880s, they were constantly spied upon: 'the children knew that a single conversation in Polish, or an imprudent word, might seriously harm, not only themselves, but also their families'.

School and education were a consuming passion for Manya and her siblings as the offspring of teachers, and their excellent marks in class were taken for granted at home. Born in the schoolhouse where her mother taught, she spent her earliest years in the schoolhouse of her father. Her very first school was the one where her mother had recently been headmistress, but she was soon moved to another private school closer to home run by a formidable woman patriot determined to give her pupils instruction in their own culture despite the watchful eyes of Russian schools inspectors. A double curriculum was required—a false one for the authorities, the real one for the students, with maximum time given to Polish language, history, and geography. All the students knew, for example, that a period of 'home economics' really meant Polish history. The strain on both staff and students of maintaining this double life was considerable, especially on Manya, the best in her class at speaking Russian, who would be called upon to recite when a Russian inspector paid the school a dreaded visit.

Manya graduated from her gymnasium in 1883, aged 15, first in her class, like her brother Jozef and sister Bronia before her, and was awarded a gold medal. Her achievement is remarkable, given her troubled home life during these years. When she was about four, her adored mother had contracted tuberculosis—which meant no kisses or caresses for Manya as a child. To make matters much worse, her father had been dismissed from the gymnasium in 1873—most likely because of a conflict with his tyrannical Russian superior—and lost both his salary and his apartment. He was compelled to turn the family's new quarters into a boarding school, crowded with noisy students. Probably as a result, typhus infected the household. Both Bronia and her sister Zosia, the eldest child of the Sklodowskis, caught the disease; Bronia survived but Zosia succumbed in 1874, not yet in her teens, devastating her ailing mother. In 1878, after a long period of expensive treatment and declining health, Bronislawa died, pushing her ten-year-old daughter Manya into 'a profound depression' (her own later words). The widowed Wladyslaw was left alone with little money and four children. Ten years later, he wrote of his wife's death in a poem: 'When she left, my whole world turned into a cemetery.'

Nevertheless, he and his wife, stimulated by the patriotic fervour of the time, had inculcated in Manya the austere combination of determination to succeed, passion for knowledge, and moral conviction that would define Marie Curie's career. 'Thanks to her father she lived in an intellectual atmosphere of rare quality known to few girls of her age', wrote Eve Curie, Marie's second daughter, in *Madame Curie*, her 'authorized' posthumous biography. Marie herself wrote of her mother: 'With all her intellectuality she had a big heart and a very high sense of duty. And, though possessing infinite indulgence and good nature, she still held in the family a remarkable moral authority.'

After finishing school, there was a year's break for Manya staying in the country, away from the crowded Warsaw apartment, as a guest of Sklodowski relatives and friends. It was a period of indolence and pleasure, literature, music, and dancing, summer and winter sports, such as she would never again experience, which shone in her memory as an adult. After one all-night ball, at dawn she recalled throwing away some new shoes of russet leather, because their soles had ceased to exist.

Back in Warsaw at last in 1884, she faced the lack of higher educational options for women, and of course the need to make a living. She began to take courses, including science courses, at a clandestine academy for women, where the teaching was at first done at home and then increasingly in supportive city institutions; by 1889–90, despite official repression, this so-called 'Flying (or Floating) University' had a thousand women enrolled. She also gave private tuition to school students but without making much money. Eventually she was compelled to sign on as a governess. An initial experience with a family of lawyers disgusted her, however she persisted after coming to an agreement with her elder sister Bronia. The money she earned as a governess would go to help Bronia train as a doctor in Paris. Once her sister was established there, Manya would join her in France and begin university study. This distant prospect would make her present wage slavery bearable.

For some three and a half years, from 1886–89, Manya Sklodowska was a governess living with wealthy families in the country away from Warsaw, sometimes descending into the bleakness of despair at the futility and ignominy of her position but consoling herself through letters exchanged with family and friends. Cruel as this position was for a young woman with her mind, at least there was plenty of time for solitary study, and it was now that she decided on science as her future. Initially drawn to literature and sociology, she turned resolutely towards a serious programme of study in mathematics and physics, using textbooks picked up at random bolstered by correspondence with her scientifically minded father. 'This method could not be greatly productive, yet it was not without results. I acquired the habit of independent work', she reflected in her autobiography decades later. However discouraging the isolation may have been at the time, it unintentionally helped to prepare her for her coming solitary studies in a Paris garret.

In late 1888, she wrote to a cousin: 'it seems to me that I am coming out of a nightmare...First principle: never let one's self be beaten down by persons or by events.' In practice, another three years passed by before Manya arrived at the Sorbonne to study science. Her sister Bronia, who married a fellow Polish medical student in 1890, was keen to welcome her in Paris that year, but Manya surprisingly demurred. 'For one thing, [she] always had trouble travelling to strange new places', suggests Curie biographer Susan Quinn. For another, various commitments were holding her back in Warsaw. Her father had finally retired and needed her support (though he strongly advocated her Paris plan); a tortured romance with a man she had met in 1886 as a governess was smouldering; the Flying University was at its zenith, offering congenial intellectual company; and a cousin who had studied with the chemist Dmitri Mendeleev in Russia had offered her the chance to use his laboratory at the Museum of Industry and Agriculture. Instead of going to Paris, she spent a year or so living with her father and giving private tuition, while mixing with patriotic student friends, gaining some limited trial-and-error experience in physics and chemistry through experiments described in her books, and finally putting an end to her love affair. Then, in November 1891, about to turn 24, she took the train from Warsaw to Paris. Although she fully intended to return to her family in Poland at the end of her studies, in fact she would never again reside in her home country.

To begin with in Paris, she lived with her sociable doctor sister and brother-in-law, but very soon sought solitude and freedom, so that she could concentrate fiercely on her studies. Like many another Polish student (as she emphasizes in her autobiography), she rented cheap rooms. One of them, under the roof of a six-storey apartment block, was within easy walking distance of her laboratory and the Sorbonne. Conditions were spartan:

> The room I lived in was in a garret, very cold in winter, for it was insuffi-ciently heated by a small stove which often lacked coal. During a particu-larly rigorous winter, it was not unusual for the water to freeze in the basin in the night; to be able to sleep I was obliged to pile all my clothes on the bedcovers. In the same room I prepared my meals with the aid of an alcohol lamp and a few kitchen utensils. These meals were often reduced to bread with a cup of chocolate, eggs, or fruit. I had no help in housekeeping and I myself carried the little coal I used up the six flights.

But she then adds, no doubt mentally comparing her more physically comfortable, yet desperate existence as a Polish governess:

> This life, painful from certain points of view, had, for all that, a real charm for me. It gave me a very precious sense of liberty and independence. Unknown in Paris, I was lost in the great city, but the feeling of living there alone, taking care of myself without any aid, did not at all depress me. If sometimes I felt lonesome, my usual state of mind was one of calm and great moral satisfaction... All my mind was centred on my studies, which, especially at the beginning, were difficult.

Enrolled as Marie, rather than Manya, Sklodowska, she was one of 23 women who joined the sciences faculty of the Sorbonne in 1891, out of more than 1825 new science students. But at no point in her own accounts of her student life does she mention that hers was a male-dominated academic world. Indeed, when she was famous, she never encouraged feminist attempts to cite her as an example to other women. 'It isn't necessary to lead such an anti-natural existence as mine', her daughter Eve quotes Marie Curie as telling her more militant female admirers. 'I have given a great deal of time to science because I wanted to, because I loved research... What I want for women and young girls is a simple family life and some work that will interest them.'

In the 1890s, scientific research was burgeoning at the Sorbonne, if no longer leading the world as France had done at the beginning of the century. (In physics, Germany was at the leading edge; in the first half of the twentieth century it would be Britain.) Among the 16 professors who taught the Polish newcomer in the years 1891–94, eight conducted research that justifies an entry in the current *Dictionary of Scientific Biography*. They included the physicist and pioneer of colour photography Gabriel Lippmann (a Nobel Prize winner in 1908), the mathematician and aviator Paul Painlevé (a future French minister of war) and, most brilliant of all, Henri Poincaré, who would play a small but significant role in the study of radioactivity. Marie Sklodowska relished their lectures and laboratory demonstrations, and flourished despite the initial handicap imposed by her lack of introductory preparation in Poland. In July 1893, by dint of fanatical study, she ranked first in the examination for the *licence ès sciences*, and in July 1894 second in the exam for the *licence ès mathématiques*.

It was probably Lippmann who arranged her first scientific research, during early 1894. In a constricted corner of his laboratory, she set about analysing the magnetic properties of various steels on behalf of the Society for the Encouragement of National Industry. There she was visited by a Polish professor of physics, Jozef Kowalski, and his wife, who happened to be in Paris on their honeymoon. (He and Manya had first met in Poland in a house where she was governess—which suggests that those years were not quite as barren of intellectual companionship as she implied.) Seeing her unsatisfactory working conditions, Kowalski arranged an introduction to another young but already much respected physicist working on magnetism at the School of Physics and Chemistry of the City of Paris (EPCI), a new municipal institution close to the Sorbonne, though less prestigious. Perhaps he would have facilities suitable for her in his laboratory.

Pierre Curie, eight years older than Marie, made an immediate impression on her at their first meeting. 'Upon entering the room I perceived, standing framed by the French window opening on the balcony, a tall young man with auburn hair and large, limpid eyes. I noticed the grave and gentle expression of his face, as well as a certain abandon in his attitude, suggesting the dreamer absorbed in his reflections. He showed me a simple cordiality and seemed to me very sympathetic', she wrote years after his death. The dreamer image coincides with Pierre's own idea of himself written in his journal when he was 21: 'We are obliged to eat, drink, sleep, laze, love; this is to say, to touch the sweetest things in life, and yet not succumb.

What is necessary, in doing all that, is to make the anti-natural thought to which one has devoted one's self remain dominant and continue its impassable course in one's poor head. One must make of life a dream, and of that dream a reality.' A family photograph of a languid Pierre next to his vivacious physicist brother Jacques, probably taken in their twenties, confirms the picture of a dreamer. After Pierre's death through absent-mindedness in a Paris traffic accident in 1906, his doctor father's first words on hearing the tragic news were: 'What was he dreaming of this time?'

The similarities in background between Marie and Pierre were striking. Both the Sklodowskis and the Curies were families with more education than money. In both cases, a love of science—and a father's unfulfilled desire to be a scientist—had been passed on to the children. Furthermore, the idealistic convictions combined with anti-establishment politics of both fathers had damaged their career prospects. Characteristically, the unmaterialistic Pierre was charmed, rather than put off, by his first visit to Marie's student garret.

Nonetheless, there was an important difference in the families' attitudes to education, which perhaps has a bearing on Pierre's dreaminess and Marie's drive as scientists. Pierre was never sent to school, whereas Marie was a prize pupil, keen to come top of the class in whatever she studied. The Curie parents recognized their son's dreaminess early and educated him at home, allowing him to pursue his interests and progress at his own pace. One result of this haphazard process was that he was precociously knowledgeable about science and geometry (he passed the Sorbonne's *licence ès sciences* exam at only 18), but had virtually no training in literature or classics. As a youth, he took 'time to look, to see everything around him with his own eyes, to form a complete and intimate bond with things which he retained for the rest of his life, and which rendered him incapable of this hasty, superficial, and insipid understanding one acquires from books', wrote the grieving physicist Paul Langevin, Pierre's and Marie's close friend, after Pierre's premature death.

After much conversation, in and out of the laboratory, and a spell of vacation in Warsaw for Marie in mid-1894, Pierre persuaded Marie to stay in France, and they married in mid-1895, shortly after Pierre defended his long-delayed doctoral thesis at the Sorbonne and was created a professor at his nearby institute, the EPCI. Marie, now considering her own doctoral thesis, obtained authorization to work with her new husband in his laboratory, while pragmatically preparing for an examination that would allow her to teach science to young girls (and therefore entitle her to call herself 'professor').

September 1897 saw the birth of their first child Irène (later to win a Nobel Prize in chemistry as Irène Joliot-Curie for her work on artificial radioactivity). At the same time Pierre's mother died, and his widowed father came to live with them and his new granddaughter. The couple were faced with the immediate dilemma of how to take care of the baby without Marie's giving up research. 'Such a renunciation would have been very painful to me', she writes in her autobiography, 'and my husband would not even think of it; he used to say that he had got a wife made expressly for him to share all his preoccupations. Neither of us would contemplate abandoning what was so precious to both.' Happily for the couple, Pierre's father took charge of the infant during the hours when they were teaching or doing research, with the help of a hired servant.

The true beginning of the Curies' collaboration falls on 16 December 1897, with Marie's first entry in the joint laboratory notebook, following some notes by Pierre on crystals. For her doctoral thesis she had decided to examine the puzzling rays emitted by the salts of uranium. The project was intended to be entirely her own, yet almost immediately Pierre joined her as co-researcher. Their handwriting alternates throughout their notebooks over the next few years. Not only was there a constant exchange of ideas between the couple, there was also 'an exchange of energy', said Poincaré, 'a sure remedy for the temporary discouragements faced by every researcher'.

Uranium's radiation had been discovered in Paris in late February 1896, during the first year of the Curies' marriage, by Henri Becquerel, working alone in his private laboratory at Cuvier House, his residence in the grounds of the Museum of Natural History. His research was provoked, somewhat curiously, by the very recent discovery of a new and mysterious radiation in Germany. In December 1895, Wilhelm Röntgen had startled the world with his eerie 'photograph' of the bone structure of his wife's hand and the dark outline of her wedding ring. In Röntgen's experiment, an electrified high-vacuum discharge tube created 'cathode rays' (now known to be streams of electrons), which bombarded the glass walls of the tube and made the glass glow in a darkened room. What Röntgen decided to call X-rays were produced during this luminescence. Their invisible presence was indicated by a singular fact: when the glowing tube was covered in black cardboard so that no light could escape, a nearby screen coated with a luminescent mineral (a barium salt) glowed—and continued to glow, amazingly, even when this detector screen was moved to an adjacent room. X-rays could clearly penetrate both cardboard and walls. When they were announced in France to the Academy of Sciences in January 1896, Poincaré speculated (wrongly as it turned out) that the luminescence accompanying the invisible X-rays might be related to the well-known luminescence of certain minerals. Becquerel heard Poincaré's announcement and became curious enough to reactivate his interest in research, dormant for the past five years. He had long been intrigued by luminescence, whether it was the instantaneous fluorescence or the longer-lasting phosphorescence. Perhaps fluorescent and phosphorescent minerals emitted invisible, as well as visible, radiation?

Becquerel tested a number of luminescent minerals in the form of a thin crystalline layer on top of two sheets of very heavy black paper wrapped around an unexposed photographic plate, by placing them in bright sunshine for several hours. His idea was that neither sunlight nor fluorescence would be able to fog the plates because of the paper, but that any 'invisible fluorescence'—in other words the emission of rays similar to X-rays—should be detectable as dark patches on the plate.

With uranium salts, he discovered that the paper was not opaque to radiation from the mineral; part of the photographic plate was fogged by a dark silhouette of the mineral layer. He therefore assumed that sunlight had stimulated the emission of invisible rays from the uranium. But then a period of several cloudy days intervened. A disappointed Becquerel held back some of the prepared plates, with their uranium coatings, and stored them in a closed laboratory drawer. When he developed them anyway, he got a shock. Instead of finding very weak shadows from the uranium layers as he anticipated, 'the silhouettes appeared with great intensity. I thought at once that the action must have been going on in darkness', Becquerel excitedly reported to the Academy on 2 March 1896, the very next day. He had discovered radioactivity. (Sylvanus Thomson made the same discovery in London in the same week, but Becquerel went public first.)

Why he chose to develop these stored plates—thereby providing a celebrated example of accidental discovery—Becquerel did not explain. 'Whether this represents simple thrift, an innate thoroughness, or an overriding curiosity, it was the lucky action that sent him forward', writes the historian of radioactivity Alfred Romer. Becquerel went on to make other significant discoveries with uranium in 1896. Although some of his reasoning was mistaken, he correctly concluded—unlike two other researchers at the time—that his (and Poincaré's) original hypothesis did not hold good: the invisible radiation from uranium was *not* related to luminescence. Becquerel was forced to accept that the radiation was an unfamiliar type of energy, stored within uranium, not externally supplied by exposure to light. How the element stored energy, he could not understand; he merely termed it 'invisible phosphorescence'.

By the time the Curies took up uranium rays in late 1897, Becquerel had temporarily lost interest in them, as had most other researchers. (X-rays seemed more exciting.) Marie and Pierre naturally read and pondered Becquerel's problematic publications in the proceedings of the Academy during 1896–97; later Becquerel would present some of the Curies' work to the Academy, since they were not members; and in 1903, Becquerel and the Curies would share the Nobel Prize. Yet in no sense were the Curies mentored by Becquerel, especially as they inhabited very different social worlds. Becquerel was an establishment insider at the Academy of Sciences, the third of a scientific dynasty of Becquerels; the Curies were the ultimate outsiders, neither of whom would ever fit in at the Academy.

They were, however, surely influenced by Lord Kelvin. As a pioneer of electromagnetism, he was an admirer of Pierre and his brother Jacques's 1880s work on piezoelectricity, had welcomed an instrument sent to him by Pierre, corresponded warmly with him, and visited Pierre in his Paris laboratory in 1893. Working from his Glasgow laboratory, Kelvin and his collaborators published two papers on uranium's electrical effects, in December 1896 and March 1897, which have a bearing on the initial approach of the Curies. Electricity, rather than photography *à la* Becquerel, would be the key to their measuring and analysing uranium rays—and to their eventual discovery of radium.

To be fair to Becquerel, he had been the first to discover that the invisible rays discharged electrified bodies, as well as affecting photographic plates. Somehow, uranium made air conduct an electric current. (Ionization of the air molecules was yet to be understood in 1896.) Observing the deflection of a charged gold-leaf electroscope—the traditional technique for measuring electric charge—Becquerel attempted to define the strength of uranium radiations by timing the angle between the gold leaves of the electroscope as they lost their charge and collapsed together: the faster the collapse, the larger the electric current, and hence the stronger the radiation. It was significant work, but not very precise, and incapable of quantifying the tiny currents of the order of a millionth of a millionth of an ampere that the Curies would succeed in measuring in 1898.

Pierre Curie designed the far more sensitive current-measuring instrument that Marie would patiently employ: an electrometer combined with a piezoelectric quartz balance. The latter was something of a family speciality; not only was piezoelectricity discovered in 1880 by Pierre and Jacques Curie, the balance had also been the subject of Jacques Curie's doctoral thesis in 1889.

The principle of the new device was fairly simple, even if its operation was extremely finicky. When Marie's granddaughter Hélène Langevin-Joliot was asked to demonstrate it in the twenty-first century she replied: 'Impossible! No one at the [Curie] Institute has the sleight-of-hand or the concentration to do it. In fact, I know of no one alive who has this skill.'

In essentials, the apparatus consisted of a condenser (ionization chamber); an electrometer to measure differences in electric potential; and a piezoelectric quartz crystal. Piezoelectric crystals have the property of producing a minute electrical polarization across their crystal faces when mechanically stressed. In this case small weights suspended from the bottom of the crystal produced the polarization. The substance to be tested was spread as a fine powder on the bottom plate of the condenser, which was connected to one pole of a 100-volt battery. The top plate was connected to one terminal of the electrometer, and the other terminal to the top of the quartz crystal. (The bottom of the crystal was earthed, as was the other pole of the battery, thus making a complete electric circuit.)

During operation, the slow increase in electric charge on both plates caused by the ionization of the air in the condenser was counterbalanced by the increase in charge of the quartz crystal generated by gradually adding weights to it. The balance point was detected by the electrometer. This was made of a rotating blade of aluminium suspended from a conducting platinum wire with a small mirror below it; a beam of light falling on the rotating mirror produced a spot of light on a graduated glass scale. When the spot fell on the centre of the scale (regarded as zero), the charges on the top plate of the condenser and on the piezoelectric quartz crystal were exactly equal.

The trick was to keep the spot of light in the centre as the experiment proceeded. Remaining as still as possible, with one hand Marie had to add weight after weight to the crystal and with the other hand start and stop a chronometer, while continually monitoring the movement of the spot of light with her eyes. After time T from the beginning of the experiment, the amount of charge Q on the plate of the condenser was equal to the charge on the crystal. The current flow caused by the radiation was then given by the flow of charge per second, i.e., Q divided by T. 'In this way the amount of electricity passing through the condenser in a given time, the intensity of the stream (current), may be measured', Marie remarked in an experimental demonstration at the Sorbonne in 1899.

Described like this, or in the neutral tones of one of the Curies' scientific papers published in these early years, the whole investigation sounds straightforward enough, given sufficient practice with the tricky instrumental technique. In fact, their working conditions at the EPCI were unpromising from the start: an uncomfortable and very cold laboratory, lack of money for equipment, and poor access to mineral samples—not to speak of the difficulties of leaving a baby only a few months old at home. The condenser was built out of leftover wooden grocery crates, into which the Curies fitted two metal plates eight centimetres in diameter and three centimetres apart. Minerals had to be scrounged from four generous colleagues. It was not until early February 1898 that the measuring apparatus and supplies were ready for Marie to begin serious work on her doctoral thesis.

In the first weeks she worked alone, without Pierre. As rapidly as possible, she measured the ionization current in air produced by several dozen minerals, elements such as phosphorus, and metals such as gold. Very soon it became clear that compounds of uranium and of thorium produced the largest currents—more than 100 times larger than the least active substances (including gold). On 17 February 1898, Marie had her first encounter with the ore pitchblende, a mineral form of uranium oxide so-called for its pitchy lustre, containing many chemical compounds, from which the pure element uranium had been isolated in 1789. Certain types of pitchblende (notably from the mines of Joachimsthal in today's Czech Republic) produced the highest ionization current of all, 83 millionths of a millionth of an ampere—some three times more active than the black oxide of uranium, at 27 millionths of a millionth of an ampere.

After some intense research, on 12 April the Academy heard its first, very concise, report from 'Mme Sklodowska Curie' (alone), presented by her old teacher Lippmann. Entitled 'Rays emitted by compounds of uranium and thorium', the report began with the barest of nods to Becquerel, then described her electrical technique and listed the currents she had measured for two or three dozen active minerals. In the middle came a prescient statement: 'Two minerals of uranium, pitchblende (a uranium oxide) and chalcolite (uranyl copper phosphate) are much more active than uranium itself. This fact is most remarkable, and suggests that these minerals may contain an element much more active than uranium.' She added: 'I prepared chalcolite from pure reagents according to the procedure of Debray; this artificial chalcolite is no more active than other uranium salts.' Natural chalcolite registered a current of 52 millionths of a millionth of an ampere, as opposed to only nine millionths of a millionth of an ampere for artificial chalcolite. The presence of a highly active mystery substance in natural chalcolite was therefore obvious.

The report concluded with a somewhat less prescient theoretical statement: 'To interpret the spontaneous radiation of uranium and thorium, one could imagine that all space is constantly traversed by rays analogous to Röntgen rays but more penetrating and unable to be absorbed except by certain elements with high atomic weight such as uranium and thorium.' Both Marie and Pierre Curie were at this time inclined to believe that the energy radiated from uranium came from *outside* rather than inside the atom, and they would continue to think this, even as late as 1905.

The first observation of pitchblende's ionization current is probably the nearest that Marie Curie came to experiencing a eureka moment (as dramatically depicted in the 1944 Hollywood film *Madame Curie*, needless to say). Marie certainly implied as much in an article she wrote in 1904 for the general public curious about her Nobel Prize: 'This observation astonished me greatly. What explanation could there be for it? How could an ore, containing many substances which I had proved inactive, be more active than the active substances of which it was formed? The answer came to me immediately: the ore must contain a substance more radioactive than uranium and thorium, and this substance must necessarily be a chemical element as yet unknown.' While her later account may have benefited from hindsight, it is supported by a story told by her sister Bronia. Around the time of the discovery in 1898, Marie came to see her and told her in a 'restrained, ardent voice', according to Eve Curie's biography: 'You know, Bronia, the radiation that I couldn't explain comes from a new chemical element. The element is there and I've got to find it. We are sure! The physicists we have spoken to believe we have made an error in experiment and advise us to be careful. But I am convinced I am not mistaken.' In further support, we have her laboratory notebook. On the day of the experiment, 17 February, there is no comment on it, as if she doubts the experiment's veracity. Instead, she retests the equipment, and for the next few days the notebook shows her to be taken up with making comparisons of pitchblende with various substances. In each new measurement the pitchblende registers as unusually active. Such careful checks are consistent with both her astonishment and other scientists' warnings to be cautious.

The obvious next step was to try to isolate the unknown chemical element. Pierre now joined Marie full time, despite his being more a physicist than a chemist. They thought that isolation would require perhaps a few weeks. In the event it took them, and Marie in particular, a few years; and also determined the course of her entire life.

With the help of the head of the chemistry laboratory at the EPCI, Gustave Bémont, the Curies developed a purification method involving both fractional distillation and chemical treatment of pitchblende. By July 1898, they had a substance about 400 times more active than uranium. In addition, it was clear from the chemical analysis that there were at least two new elements in pitchblende, not just one, the first of which separated from the ore along with bismuth, the second along with barium.

Unable to separate the new element from bismuth chemically, they submitted the mixture to a colleague for spectroscopic analysis. Every chemical has a characteristic spectrum (dependent on its atomic or molecular structure). Even though this last technique proved inconclusive— spectra are frequently hard to resolve into their constituent lines—the Curies had enough confidence in the rest of their analysis to announce the new element to the Academy in mid-July, this time via Becquerel himself. He reported their words: 'If the existence of this new metal is confirmed, we propose to call it *polonium* from the name of the country of origin of one of us.' The title of their joint paper, 'On a new radioactive substance contained in pitchblende', marked the earliest use of 'radioactive' as a scientific term.

The paper also brought Marie an encouraging prize from the Academy, the Prix Gegner, citing her old work on the magnetic properties of steel and, more cautiously, her latest work on radioactivity. The prize money helped to buy a shipment of pitchblende from Joachimsthal in October. The autumn was spent trying to isolate the second unknown element from barium. But although their sample was eventually 900 times more active than uranium, it refused to be separated. This time, however, its spectrum displayed one clear line that could not be assigned to any known element.

'The intensity of this line increases . . . at the same time as the radioactivity; that, we think, is a very serious reason for attributing it to the radioactive part of our substance', the Curies reported to the Academy on 26 December in an historic paper written with their unassuming colleague Bémont. 'The new radioactive substance certainly includes a very large portion of barium; in spite of that, the radioactivity is considerable. The radioactivity of radium then must be enormous.'

The name of the new element had first appeared in writing in Pierre's hand: just one word, 'radium', scrawled in the middle of a page of the laboratory notebook in heavy ink on 20 December 1898. Marie, too, made the same note, but at home, in a school notebook covered in grey linen. It was sandwiched between 'Irène can walk very well, and no longer goes on all fours' (17 October) and 'Irène has fifteen teeth!' (5 January).

From this time, for the next three or four years, Marie became basically a chemist, implacably determined to obtain a pure sample of radium out of pitchblende, which would convince the scientific world of the existence of the new radioactive element beyond any shadow of doubt. Pierre, by contrast, reverted to his natural role as a physicist, fascinated by the nature of radioactivity. Other physicists and chemists joined the field, too, notably Ernest Rutherford, Frederick Soddy, and William Crookes, in addition to the rejuvenated research of Becquerel.

Tons of brown mine residue from Joachimsthal, left behind after the extraction of pitchblende and mixed with forest pine needles, were now imported by rail into the Curie laboratory. They were laboriously purified in an abandoned, leaky-roofed shed, once used for dissection by medical students, and its adjoining yard—the only facilities that the EPCI was able to spare its future Nobel laureates. Conditions were primitive. When the chemist Wilhelm Ostwald saw the shed, he noted that it looked like 'a stable or potato cellar and if I had not seen the worktable with the chemistry equipment I would have thought it was a hoax'. The physicist Rutherford, another visitor, thought that 'it must be dreadful not to have a laboratory to play around in'.

Marie Curie herself admitted that with better facilities she could probably have accomplished the isolation of radium in about a year. 'Yet it was in this miserable old shed that we passed the best and happiest years of our life, devoting our entire days to our work', she writes in her autobiography. 'Often I had to prepare our lunch in the shed, so as not to interrupt some particularly important operation. Sometimes I had to spend a whole day mixing a boiling mass with a heavy iron rod nearly as large as myself. I would be broken with fatigue at the day's end. Other days, on the contrary, the work would be a most minute and delicate fractional crystallization, in the effort to concentrate the radium.' What she does not record—unlike her daughter Eve in her biography—is that Pierre became so tired of the interminable struggle that he was ready to abandon the purification. Marie's commitment was, however, absolute.

Some nights, leaving their sleeping child in the care of Pierre's old father, they would return to the shed. On all sides they looked joyfully upon the luminous silhouettes of bottles and capsules containing their preparations. 'It was really a lovely sight and one always new to us. The glowing tubes looked like faint, fairy lights', Marie records.

The end product, in mid-1902, was a tenth of a gram of pure radium chloride—a minute one-fiftieth of a teaspoonful. But it was enough, as Marie announced to the Academy in July, for her to determine the atomic weight of radium as 225 (very close to today's value 226) and to place radium below barium in Mendeleev's periodic table of the elements, in the column of alkaline earth metals. (By 1910, working with another chemist, she had prepared the pure metal.) For isolating radium, she received her second Nobel Prize in 1911. Pure radium became a standard of comparison for other radioactive substances, not least those used in radiotherapy. 'It is not an exaggeration to say today that [the isolation of radium] is the cornerstone on which the entire edifice of radioactivity rests', wrote the physical chemist and Nobel laureate Jean Perrin in 1924.

Yet it has to be said that the theoretical explanation of radioactivity largely eluded both Marie and Pierre Curie—as it had Becquerel, with his bent towards luminescence. At the very time the Curies were studying radium, a revolution was taking shape through the work of Rutherford, Soddy, and others. Arising from their careful study of the radioactivity of thorium—largely neglected by the Curies—Rutherford and Soddy proved that radioactive elements were transmuting themselves into other elements, some of these products being radioactive, others not. Nervously, then with increasing confidence, Rutherford and Soddy proposed in 1902 a modern, scientific form of the outlandish, long-discredited idea of alchemy. Mendeleev had been wrong to regard every chemical element as indivisible and intransmutable, said Rutherford and Soddy. By 1904, it was becoming clear to all researchers that the energy of radioactivity came not from external radiation, as the Curies suspected, but from inside the atom, from its disintegration to form new elements. In the decade or so following the discovery of radium in 1898, the concepts of radioactive decay, half-life, isotopes, and radioactive series were born. As we now know, for example, uranium decays via a series of elements—including the commonest isotope of radium (Ra-226) that decays into radon with a half-life of 1602 years—to form a stable isotope of lead.

Even in their Nobel Prize lecture of 1905 (delivered by Pierre on behalf of them both), the Curies still preferred their old hypothesis that radioactive substances borrowed energy from external radiation. 'It is not absurd to suppose that space is constantly traversed by very penetrating radiations which certain substances would be capable of capturing in flight', said Pierre. He admitted, though, that transmutation was the 'more fertile' hypothesis. Possibly transmutation struck him and Marie as a threat to their years of obsession with proving the existence of radium as a new and stable element. If so, it would scarcely be the first example in science of an investment in one idea by a genius preventing him or her from appreciating a seminal idea put forward by another.

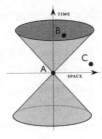

CHAPTER 12

ALBERT EINSTEIN

Special Relativity

'An hour sitting with a pretty girl on a park bench passes like a minute, but a minute sitting on a hot stove seems like an hour.'

Albert Einstein's explanation of relativity given to his secretary to relay to reporters and other laypersons

Einstein created his theory of special relativity in May-June 1905, while he was also working at a full-time job as a patent clerk. From conception of the idea to completion of his article, 'On the electrodynamics of moving bodies', took a mere five or six weeks, Einstein told a biographer decades later, in 1952. 'But it would hardly be correct to consider this as a birth date, because the arguments and building blocks were being prepared over a period of years, although without bringing about the fundamental decision.'

For his 70th birthday, in 1949, Einstein attempted to analyse how his mind came up with such new and world-changing ideas as relativity. He recalled his first scientific experience, at the age of four or five. His father showed him a magnetic compass, and Albert saw how the compass needle determinedly pointed in one particular direction, even though no one had touched it. Here was the first of many encounters with the concept of a field—in this case the earth's magnetic field—which produced seemingly magical action at a distance. The conflict with his unconscious childish assumption that you have to touch an object to make it move provoked wonder and puzzlement, which made a lasting impression. 'Something deeply hidden had to be behind things.'

'For me it is not dubious that our thinking goes on for the most part without the use of words and beyond that to a considerable degree unconsciously. For how, otherwise, should it happen that sometimes we "wonder" quite spontaneously about some experience?' Einstein wrote. 'This "wondering" seems to occur when an experience comes into conflict with a world of concepts which is already sufficiently fixed in us. Whenever such a conflict is experienced hard and intensively it reacts back upon our thought world in a decisive way. The development of this thought world is in a certain sense a continuous flight from "wonder".'

As with the magnetic compass, so with light. Special relativity would arise from the 16-year-old Einstein's similar, if far more abstract, struggle to understand what was hidden behind the electromagnetic wave nature of light. A simple thought experiment with a ray of light would lead to a new sense of wonder and conflict in Einstein's mind. From this experience, after ten years of mental incubation, would suddenly blossom forth his new theory of space and time.

In the Einstein family tree, there was not much tendency towards wonder, and no hint of any intellectual distinction. Indeed Einstein himself insisted in old age that 'exploration of my ancestors . . . leads nowhere' in explaining his particular bent. His father Hermann was an easy-going businessman who was not very successful in electrical engineering and his paternal grandfather a merchant, while his mother Pauline, a fine piano player but otherwise not gifted, also came from a business family, which ran a profitable grain concern and was wealthy. Although both sides of the family were Jewish, neither was orthodox nor were they devoted to reading the Hebrew scriptures. Hermann and Pauline Einstein were thoroughly assimilated and non-observant Jews ('entirely irreligious', according to their son).

Nor was there much sign of distinction in Einstein as a child. Albert was born in Ulm, the city northeast of Buchau, on 14 March 1879, the first of two children, the second being a daughter, known as Maja. He was a quiet baby, so quiet that his parents became seriously concerned and consulted a doctor about his not learning to talk. But when Maja was born in November 1881, Albert is said to have asked promptly where the wheels of his new toy were. It turned out that his ambition was to speak in complete sentences:

first he would try out a sentence in his head, while moving his lips, and only then repeat it aloud. The habit lasted until his seventh year or even later. The family maidservant dubbed him 'stupid'.

His first school was a Catholic one in Munich, where the Einstein family had shifted from Ulm in 1880. Albert was the only Jew in a class of about 70 students. But he seems to have felt anti-Semitism among the teachers only in the religious education classes, not in the rest of the school curriculum. One day the teacher brought a long nail to the lesson and told the students that with just such nails Christ had been nailed to the cross by the Jews. Among the students, however, anti-Semitism was commonplace, and though it was not vicious, it encouraged Albert's early sense of being an outsider, a feeling that would intensify throughout adulthood into old age and undoubtedly foster his scientific unorthodoxy. As he would famously remark in an article written when he was about 50, 'I am truly a "lone traveller" and have never belonged to my country, my home, my friends, or even my immediate family, with my whole heart.'

Academically he was good yet by no means a prodigy, both at this school and at the Luitpold Gymnasium, his high school in Munich from the age of nine and a half. But Einstein showed hardly any affection for his schooling up to and including his time at the gymnasium, and in later life he excoriated the system of formal education in Germany of his day. He disliked games and physical training, and detested anything that smacked of the military discipline typical of the Prussian ethos of northern Germany. In 1920 he even told a Berlin interviewer that the school matriculation exam should be abolished. 'Let us return to Nature, which upholds the principle of getting the maximum amount of effect from the minimum of effort, whereas the matriculation test does exactly the opposite.'

Part of his problem lay in the heavy emphasis in the German gymnasia— as in British 'public' schools of the period—on the humanities; that is, on classical studies and to a lesser extent German history and literature, to the detriment of modern foreign languages. (This meant that Einstein's command of French was not fluent and that he would never be confident in speaking English, still less in writing it; nor did he learn Hebrew, to his later regret.) Science and mathematics were regarded in the gymnasia as the subjects with the lowest status.

But the main problem with school was probably that Albert was a confirmed autodidact. 'Private study' is a term that frequently pops up in his early letters and adult writings on education. To the average young student, such an idea is an invitation to indiscipline—maybe a chance simply to shirk—but for the young Einstein, studying at his own whim was his chief means of becoming educated. His sister Maja recalled that even with noisy company around him, Albert could 'lie down on the sofa, pick up a pen and paper, precariously balance an inkwell on the backrest, and engross himself in a problem so much so that the background noise stimulated rather than disturbed him'. His physicist friend for four decades, the Nobel laureate Max Born, recalled that: 'Einstein expressed over and over again the thought that one should not couple the quest for knowledge with a bread-and-butter profession, but that research should be done as a private spare-time occupation. He himself wrote the first of his great treatises while earning his living as an employee of the Swiss Patent Office in Bern...What he did not consider, however, [was that] to be able to practise science as a hobby, one has to be an Einstein.'

From a relatively early age he began reading mathematics and science books simply out of curiosity; at college in Zurich he ranged very widely in his reading, including the latest scientific journals, way beyond what was prescribed by the professors; and as an adult he never read books simply because they were said to be classics, only if they appealed to him. Maybe there is a parallel here with Isaac Newton, an eclectic reader who neverthe-less does not seem to have read many of the great names of his or earlier times. 'Einstein was more of an artist than a scholar; in other words, he did not clutter up his mind too much with other people's ideas', in the words of the astronomer Gerald Whitrow.

His first scientific experience had occurred with the magnetic compass shown to him by his father. Then, when he was twelve, he experienced 'a second wonder of a totally different nature' while working through a small book of Euclidian plane geometry—as had Galileo at the age of 17. The 'lucidity and certainty' of the geometrical proofs, based on Euclid's ten simple axioms (for example, a circle can be constructed when its centre, and a point on it, are given), made a second deep impression, and set Einstein thinking for the rest of his life on the true relationship between mathematical forms and the same forms found in the physical world. The very word geometry, he noted, was from the Greek for 'earth-measuring', which implied that mathematics 'owes its existence to the need which was felt of learning something about the behaviour of real objects'.

At the same time, he began reading popular science books brought for him by a poor medical student, Max Talmud, who would be given lunch once a week by his parents—among the few Jewish customs that the Einsteins did observe. *Kraft und Stoff* (Force and Matter) by Ludwig Büchner and the series *Naturwissenschaftliche Volksbücher* (Science for the People) by Aaron Bernstein set Einstein on course to be a scientist. A secondary effect of reading the books was to kill off Albert's incipient belief in orthodox religion. Just before he delved into them, he had suddenly turned highly religious. He stopped eating pork, started singing hymns with great fervour (and even composed a few), and began preparing with a rabbi to become a bar mitzvah on the Sabbath following his thirteenth birthday. But the science books—although they did not attack religion as such—convinced him that much of the Bible was untrue, and induced a 'suspicion against every kind of authority', including authorities in physics, which would last until his dying day.

At the Luitpold Gymnasium, things came to a head in 1894, when Albert was 15. A new class teacher informed him that 'he would never get any-where in life'. When Einstein replied that surely he 'had not committed any offence', he was told: 'Your mere presence here undermines the class's respect for me.' For the rest of his life, Einstein would be known for a mocking way with words that was sometimes biting and would always be at odds with his later saintly image. It was bound to get under the skin of authority figures—whether they were Germans, fellow Jews or, in later life, Americans. He very often mocked himself too, referring to his 'impudence' and remarking to a friend after he became famous: 'To punish me for my contempt for authority, Fate has made me an authority myself.'

At home, too, all was not going well. In 1893, after a battle with larger companies, the Einstein company had failed to get a contract for lighting an important part of Munich, and the next year the decision was made to liquidate the company and set up a new one in Italy. Maja moved to Italy with her parents, but her brother was left alone in Munich with some distant relatives in order to take his matriculation exam. Meanwhile the beloved Einstein home was sold and quickly demolished by developers under his eyes.

The combination of disruptions at school and at home seems to have been too much for Albert, who would never refer to this unhappy period. Without consulting his parents, he got a doctor (Talmud's elder brother) to state that he was suffering from exhaustion and needed time off school, and convinced a teacher to give him a certificate of excellence in mathematics. The school authorities released him. Just after Christmas 1894, he left Munich and headed south to Milan to face his surprised parents.

Einstein did not return to the disliked Luitpold Gymnasium, and a year later rejected his German nationality, presumably to avoid military service, becoming stateless until he was accepted as a Swiss citizen in 1901. Instead, he stayed at home in Italy and pursued his own course of private study. It prompted a third key experience of wonder, some time during 1895–96, when he was 16. While daydreaming, he conducted a thought experiment about how it would appear if he could chase a beam of light and catch up with it. What would light look like if it were 'at rest' relative to an observer? It would take him ten years to find a satisfactory answer to this question.

That autumn he sat the exam early for the Swiss Polytechnic in Zurich—probably the leading centre for the study of science in central Europe outside of Germany. He failed. However, his excellence in mathematics and physics was recognized and he was encouraged to try again the following year after further schooling. On the advice of a Polytechnic professor, he went to the cantonal school in Aarau, some 30 miles west of Zurich, which was based on the liberal ideas of the Swiss educational reformer Johann Heinrich Pestalozzi. Here Albert boarded happily with the family of one of the school's teachers and started a teenage romance with their daughter. When he took the school's final exam, which qualified him to begin study in Zurich in late 1896, he wrote a revealing essay, 'My plans for the future.' It announced his desire to study the theoretical part of physics because of 'a personal gift for abstract and mathematical thought and a lack of fantasy and practical talent', and concluded significantly: 'Moreover, there is a certain independence in the profession of science that greatly appeals to me.'

Switzerland became integral to Einstein's life, during this formative intellectual period, which was also the time of his first love affair with his fellow physics student Mileva Marić, the Serbian woman who became his first wife. If there was anywhere that Einstein would have been inclined to call 'home' during his peripatetic career, it would have to be Switzerland—not his native Germany or the United States, his place of exile from Germany after 1933.

In his youthful letters, his love of hiking in the Swiss mountains is transparent. It is hard to resist the feeling that the solitude of the Alpine peaks and the clarity of the stars at night must have influenced his scientific theorizing. While living in America, he wrote that, 'creating a new theory is not like destroying an old barn and erecting a skyscraper in its place. It is rather like climbing a mountain, gaining new and wider views, discovering unexpected connections between our starting-point and its rich environment.

But the point from which we started out still exists and can be seen, although it appears smaller and forms a tiny part of our broad view gained by the mastery of the obstacles on our adventurous way up.'

Thus, around 1895, Einstein would start from Newton's laws of motion and James Clerk Maxwell's equations of electromagnetism, and ascend via the theory of special relativity in 1905 to the heights of the field equations of general relativity in 1915. He achieved this not by overturning Newton or Maxwell, but rather by subsuming them into a more comprehensive theory, somewhat as the map of a continent subsumes a map of an individual country.

To understand how Einstein came to special relativity, we need to digress a little into the work of Newton, Maxwell, and his nineteenth-century contemporaries, and even Galileo, whom Einstein regarded as the 'father of modern science' for his insistence on doing physical, quantitative experiments, using projectiles and falling weights, to test his theories. It was their scientific ideas that provoked Einstein to wonder about the nature of space, time, light, and gravity.

Galileo was the first to state the mechanical principle of relativity. He put it so beautifully in a famous thought experiment conducted in his *Dialogue Concerning the Two Chief World Systems* (1632), that the description is worth quoting in full:

> Shut yourself up with some friend in the main cabin below decks on some large ship, and have with you there some flies, butterflies, and other small flying animals. Have a large bowl of water with some fish in it; hang up a bottle that empties drop by drop into a narrow-mouthed vessel beneath it. With the ship standing still, observe carefully how the little animals fly with equal speed to all sides of the cabin. The fish swim indifferently in all directions; the drops fall into the vessel beneath; and, in throwing something to your friend, you need throw it no more strongly in one direction than another, the distances being equal; jumping with your feet together, you pass equal spaces in every direction. When you have observed all these things carefully (though there is no doubt that when the ship is standing still everything must happen in this way), have the ship proceed with any speed you like, so long as the motion is uniform and not fluctuating this way or that. You will discover not the least change in all the effects named, nor could you tell from any of them whether the ship was moving or standing still.

In other words, the unmoving passengers on the moving ship have a velocity relative to the land, but relative to the ship they have no velocity.

With reference to the ship they are at rest and feel no force acting upon them, provided that the ship is not accelerating forwards (or turning) and provided they stay below decks away from air currents. For a modern equivalent, think of long-distance air travel in a jet at a speed of many hundreds of miles per hour. During most of the flight at high altitude, unless there is bad weather, while seated and not looking out of the window one has hardly any physical sensation of the aircraft's movement, and walking up the aisle feels the same as walking down the aisle or across the aircraft. (In fact, the aircraft's engines are constantly doing work against the force of gravity, so the motion of the aircraft is not exactly uniform as in Galileo's idealized moving ship.)

It may seem only a short step from Galileo's discoveries to Newton's laws of motion, remarked Einstein in 1927. But, he pointed out, Galileo's mechanics were formulated to refer to a body's motion as a whole, whereas Newton's laws of motion were able to answer the question: 'How does the state of motion of a mass-point change in an infinitely short time under the influence of an external force?'

Newton's laws, incorporating Galileo's experimental work and combined with Newton's own theory of gravitation, were published in his *Principia Mathematica* in 1687. This revolutionary book succeeded in unifying the motions of planetary and earthly bodies with one set of equations that could predict—given any body's mass, velocity, and direction of motion—exactly how it would subsequently move under a known force. The Newtonian, mechanical view of the universe would dominate physics for the next two centuries.

Newton's first law is simply stated. In his own words (translated from the original Latin): 'Every body perseveres in its state of being at rest or of moving uniformly straight forward, except in so far as it is compelled to change its state by forces impressed.' In modern language: a body continues in a state of rest or uniform motion in a straight line unless it is acted upon by external forces. This can also be called the principle of inertia; inertia being the property of matter that causes it to resist any change in its motion. Newton, like Galileo (but not Aristotle), perceived that an object at rest and an object moving uniformly can both be treated by physics in the same way—an idea with profound implications which is not obvious to common-sense thinking.

His second law was entirely his own. In modern language: the rate of change of momentum of a moving body is proportional to and in the same direction as the force acting on it. In other words, if you push a mass twice as hard you will accelerate it (that is, change its momentum) at twice the rate, and plainly objects try to move in the direction in which you push them, not at some angle to your push. It is the second law that explains why Galileo's cannon balls allegedly dropped from the Leaning Tower of Pisa fell together at the same velocity from his tower, despite their different masses.

Newton's third law is somewhat counter-intuitive. It makes clear that while you sit in a chair, the chair exerts an upwards force on you to balance your weight pushing down on it. And the same is true in the heavens, said Newton: while the earth exerts a gravitational tug on the moon, keeping it in orbit, the moon, for its part, tugs on the earth, creating the tides in the oceans. In the words of the *Principia*: 'To any action there is always an opposite and equal reaction; in other words, the actions of two bodies upon each other are always equal and always opposite in direction.'

To calculate gravity—Newton's second great contribution to mechanics— he postulated the existence of an invisible force acting between masses, proportional to the sizes of the masses and inversely proportional to the square of the distance between them. In the case of the sun, which is nearly 400 times further from the earth than the moon is from the earth, the inversely proportional factor diminishing the gravitational force is about 400 squared (16,000)—but this enormous diminution is compensated by the vastly greater mass of the sun as compared to the moon (the sun-to-moon mass ratio is 30,000,000). And so the earth remains in orbit around the sun.

Newton's gravitational force acted at a distance through space faster even than the speed of light, which was first measured experimentally in 1676 at about 140,000 miles per second (quite close to its current value, 186,000 miles per second). This force was totally unlike the push and pull exerted on masses in physical contact with forces, as in the projectile experiments of Galileo. Such instantaneous 'action at a distance', with no mechanical explanation, naturally worried Newton, but he could see no alternative to it.

Another weakness in his grand structure was that it required the existence of absolute time and space. To quote Newton again: 'Absolute, true, and mathematical time, in and of itself, and of its own nature, without reference to anything external, flows uniformly... Absolute space, of its own true nature without reference to anything external, always remains homogeneous and immovable...' In other words, a passenger on a ship moves relative to the ship, the ship moves relative to the land, the earth moves relative to the Sun—and everything physical moves relative to a universal reference frame of space–time, which is 'at rest'. But what is the nature of this universal reference frame? Newton had no real answer. 'God informed Newton's creed of absolute space and absolute time', writes Newton biographer, James Gleick. And Newton must have had some doubts about the correctness of absolute time and space, for he also noted in the *Principia*: 'It may be, that there is no such thing as an equable motion, whereby time may be accurately measured. It may be that there is no body really at rest, to which the places and motions of others may be referred.' To the young physics student Einstein, a similar speculation would prove highly stimulating in creating special relativity.

Nevertheless, looking back to his student days in Zurich, in 1940 Einstein described the Newtonian basis of physics at the end of the nineteenth century as 'eminently fruitful' and 'regarded as final':

> It not only gave results for the movements of the heavenly bodies, down to the most minute details, but also furnished a theory of the mechanics of discrete and continuous masses, a simple explanation of the principle of the conservation of energy and a complete and brilliant theory of heat. The explanation of the facts of electrodynamics [the physics of moving electric charges] within the Newtonian system was more forced; least convincing of all, from the very beginning, was the theory of light.

Unlike mechanics and heat, electricity, magnetism, and light were not so amenable to a Newtonian mechanical treatment. Newton had done brilliant though incomplete work on light, which he reluctantly published in 1704 in his *Opticks*. His splitting and recombination of white light with prisms into the colours of the rainbow, which established that light is a mixture of colours, was merely the most famous of his numerous important optical experiments. But his preference for regarding light rays as streams of particles, or 'corpuscles', as opposed to seeing light as a wave (first proposed by Christiaan Huygens in 1678), was a serious stumbling block to Newton's comprehension of light. Reflection, refraction, and diffraction could be explained only with difficulty by a corpuscular theory. Though Newton knew this, and in some respects favoured a wave theory, he nevertheless put his great authority behind corpuscles, which therefore dominated the thinking of physicists long after his death in 1727. 'He was justified in sticking to his corpuscular theory of light', thought Einstein in 1940, given the insecure foundation of the wave theory during Newton's age.

After 1800, however, light waves gradually took precedence over corpuscles. Thomas Young demonstrated that a light beam, when passed through two narrow double slits to create two beams, *interfered* with itself to produce a regular pattern of light and dark areas on a screen. This was an astonishing fact: light shining on light could produce more light, which was expected, but it could also produce dark, which was not at all anticipated. It had to be that the bright areas were due to the coincidence of two wave peaks, while the dark ones were due to the superimposition of a wave peak and a wave trough, thus cancelling the light. Further experiments on interference were done by Augustin Fresnel, who also studied examples of the polarization of light—a phenomenon possible only with waves. Fresnel concluded that light was a transverse wave which vibrated at right angles to its direction of propagation, like the ripples when a stone is dropped into a pond and the water itself moves *vertically* while the wave's energy spreads horizontally from the central point of impact, or somewhat like the spreading of a rumour from stationary gossiper to stationary gossiper so that the rumour propagates from one place to another, to use Einstein's amusing analogy. (Sound waves, by contrast, are longitudinal waves, in which air is compressed and rarefied in the same direction as the sound propagates.) By the middle of the nineteenth century, all physicists were persuaded that light was a transverse wave.

But what was the substance that transmitted the wave energy when, for example, the sun's light radiated through empty space to reach the earth? This problem had not bedevilled the corpuscular theory: the corpuscles were assumed to pass through the vacuum like bullets through air. The only apparent wave-based solution was a perplexing one.

Since they believed in the mechanical view of nature, leading physicists in the second half of the nineteenth century were forced to conclude that there existed a mysterious undetectable medium, the ether, which permeated the entire universe, filling all the interstices between matter. The ether must be the transmission medium for light waves. Yet this entailed some contradictory properties. For various respectable physical reasons, the ether had to be 'absolutely stationary, weightless, invisible, with zero viscosity, yet stronger than steel, and undetectable by any instrument'—in the words of a modern theoretical physicist, Michio Kaku. Not surprisingly, during the early twentieth century, beginning with Einstein, the ether would be abandoned as an implausible concept.

Nevertheless, in the 1850s, accepting the ether, James Clerk Maxwell set out to establish what exactly it was that was vibrating transversely in a light wave. Maxwell's work is highly mathematical, which makes it impossible to comprehend fully without mathematics, but his most important insights and results can be summarized.

Maxwell drew on the discoveries of Michael Faraday and Lord Kelvin about the associated phenomena of electricity and magnetism, such as the electric currents induced by moving magnets and, conversely, the magnetism generated by electric currents, which suggested the physical reality of electric and magnetic *fields*. He derived a set of differential equations describing a new concept: an electromagnetic wave. (See diagram opposite.) The energy of such a wave is contained in two fields, the electric and the magnetic, which are polarized transversely at right angles to each other, while the wave itself propagates at right angles to the plane of polarization. When Maxwell calculated his wave's theoretical speed of propagation from his equations he was thrilled to discover that it coincided with the latest experimental estimate for the speed of light. He thus inferred that light was probably an electromagnetic wave and published this idea in his *Treatise on Electricity and Magnetism* in 1873.

A decade or so later, Heinrich Hertz began looking for physical evidence of Maxwell's waves. In 1888, he confirmed their existence experimentally; and showed that radio waves, light, and radiant heat were all electromagnetic waves whose behaviour was described by Maxwell's equations, and that they all travelled at the speed of light. Thus, in electrodynamics—if not in mechanics and gravity—there was now no longer any need to take refuge in Newton's instantaneous action at a distance; the electromagnetic field transmitted electrical and magnetic forces at a finite speed, the speed of light.

On the centenary of Maxwell's birth in 1931, Einstein said: 'Before Maxwell people conceived of physical reality...as material points, whose changes consist exclusively of motions...After Maxwell they conceived of physical reality as represented by continuous fields, not mechanically explicable...This change in the conception of reality is the most profound and fruitful one that has come to physics since Newton.'

The main source for Einstein's thinking in his early years in Zurich is his correspondence with his fellow student Mileva Marić, the love letters written between 1897 and the time of their marriage in 1903, which were published only in the 1980s. The letters are peppered with references to the

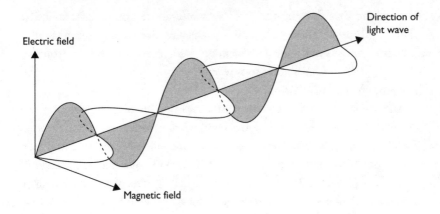

scientific books Einstein was reading on an impressive range of subjects. He thought about not only the electrodynamics of moving bodies, the problem of the ether, and the mechanical principle of relativity, as might be expected of a physicist—but also molecular forces, thermo-electricity, physical chemistry, and the kinetic theory of gases.

Unfortunately for historians, there is not much solid scientific detail in the letters, probably because Mileva avoided science in her replies. So it is hard to penetrate the evolution of Einstein's ideas. Perhaps the closest we get comes in a letter written in the summer of 1899 (while Albert was holidaying in a Swiss hotel with his mother and sister), which says that he is rereading Hertz on the propagation of electric force: 'I'm convinced more and more that the electrodynamics of moving bodies as it is presented today doesn't correspond to reality, and that it will be possible to present it in a simpler way. The introduction of the term "ether" into theories of electricity has led to the conception of a medium whose motion can be described, without, I believe, being able to ascribe physical meaning to it.'

What is clear from the letters, however, is Einstein's dissatisfaction with some of the science teaching at the Swiss Polytechnic. Though he pays tribute to his professors of mathematics, such as Hermann Min-kowski (who thought Einstein a 'lazy dog' as a student but who would develop special relativity mathematically after 1905), he regards his physics professors as behind the times and unable to cope with his challenges to their authority. Without doubt Einstein was extremely precocious among physics students of his age in Zurich, yet still it is astonishing that the physics professors offered no course on Maxwell's seminal, three-decades-old equations. Despite Hertz's experimental justification of Maxwell's electromagnetic theory in 1888, the electromagnetic field was considered too recent and controversial an idea for students in the late 1890s.

After four years of study, most of it 'private', in the summer of 1900 Einstein graduated with a diploma entitling him to teach mathematics in Swiss schools. His real aim was to become an assistant to a physics professor at the Polytechnic, write a doctoral thesis, and enter the academic world as a physicist. But now his ill-concealed 'impudence'—'my guardian angel', as he dubbed it in a letter to Mileva—along with his Jewishness, told against him.

The next two years would be very tough indeed for Albert and Mileva (who had failed to acquire a diploma). He was not offered an assistantship in Zurich, unlike some fellow physics graduates. Nevertheless, he thought continually about physics and managed to publish a paper in the best-known German physics journal, *Annalen der Physik*, in 1901; but the thesis he wrote was not accepted by Zurich University. He was still effectively unknown, and so when he wrote to notable professors offering his services, his letters went unanswered. (One of these professors, the chemist Wilhelm Ostwald, ironically would be the first scientist to nominate Einstein for a Nobel Prize, a mere nine years later.) 'I will have soon graced all the physicists from the North Sea to the southern tip of Italy with my offer!' Albert joked wryly to Mileva in April 1901.

Soon, he was virtually starving, dependent on casual school teaching, and at risk of malnutrition. Then Mileva became pregnant, failed the Polytechnic exam again, and gave birth to a girl, probably named Lieserl, an episode that had to be hushed up. (To this day, no one knows what happened to her.) Einstein's parents had always hotly opposed his proposed marriage and refused their consent; they did not relent until his father lay dying in 1902, his business in bankruptcy, although his mother would never reconcile herself to the marriage. Only Einstein's unshakeable confidence in his own scientific prowess, encouraged by Mileva's single-minded devotion, could have carried him through these desperate two years.

Rescue came in the end from another fellow student at Zurich. Marcel Grossmann, who would later play a significant role in the mathematics of general relativity, suggested Einstein for a job at the Federal Swiss Office for Intellectual Property—the Patent Office—in Bern. Grossmann's father was a friend of the office's long-standing director, who was looking for a patent examiner with the ability to understand inventions in the burgeoning electrical industry. Einstein's knowledge of electromagnetic theory, and his considerable practical exposure to electrical devices through the family business, was deemed sufficient. After an anguished wait of more than a year, in June 1902 he reported for duty as a 'technical expert, third class'—the most junior post of its kind. The Swiss Patent Office would become the somewhat unlikely setting that allowed him to make his name as a physicist.

Just before joining, Einstein formed a small club in Bern with a friend of about the same age, Conrad Habicht, who was studying for a doctorate in mathematics from Zurich University, and an ebullient Romanian student, Maurice Solovine, who had originally answered an advertisement from the impecunious Einstein offering private tuition in physics. As a joke they gave the club a high-sounding name, the Olympia Academy, with Einstein as president, and arranged to meet in the cafés of the city, at music recitals, on long walks at the weekend, or in the Einsteins' small apartment. Besides reading together the physics and philosophy of Ernst Mach, the 'three intellectual musketeers' argued in detail about a recently published book, *Science and Hypothesis*, by Henri Poincaré, and debated the thoughts of Hume, Spinoza, and other philosophers (while also tackling some classic literature, by Sophocles, Racine, and Cervantes). Sometimes Einstein would play his violin.

They also stuffed themselves with as much good food as they could afford, and generally horsed around. Once, for a special treat on Einstein's birthday, Habicht and Solovine bought some caviar. But the president got so caught up in explaining Galileo's principle of inertia that he ate it without noticing. 'So that was caviar', Einstein said, when the other two finally intervened, 'Well, if you offer gourmet foods to peasants like me, you know they won't appreciate it.' Another time, Habicht had a tin plate engraved by a tradesman and fixed it to the Einsteins' door. It proclaimed 'Albert Ritter von Steissbein, President of the Olympia Academy'—meaning roughly 'Albert Knight of the Backside' or maybe something worse (since the rhyming word *Scheissbein* means 'shit-leg'!). Albert and Mileva 'laughed so much they thought they would die', according to Solovine.

The Olympia Academy folded up in late 1904, when Habicht left Bern to take up a job. By then, Einstein had a baby son, Hans Albert. Spending more time at home seems to have spurred him to his incredible intellectual outpouring in 1905.

The first announcement of the work that would change the course of science occurred in late May or early June 1905, when Einstein had been working at the Swiss Patent Office for just short of three years. It came in a now-celebrated letter he wrote—with barely suppressed excitement—to his friend Habicht, informing him that he would soon receive a published paper in the mail, the first of four that Einstein had been working on.

The letter opens (of course originally in German): 'Dear Habicht! Such a solemn air of silence has descended between us that I almost feel as if I am committing a sacrilege when I break it now with some inconsequential babble. But is this not always the fate of the exalted ones of this world?' Then he chaffs his friend for not sending him his doctoral dissertation: 'So what are you up to, you frozen whale... Don't you know that I am one of the 1 ½ fellows who would read it with interest and pleasure, you wretched man?' Then he describes his own papers:

> [The first] deals with radiation and the energetic properties of light and is very revolutionary, as you will see provided you send me *your* paper first. The second paper is a determination of the true size of atoms by way of the diffusion and internal friction of diluted liquid solutions of neutral substances. The third proves that, on the assumption of the molecular theory of heat, particles of the order of magnitude of 1/1000 millimetres suspended in liquids must already perform an observable disordered movement, caused by thermal motion. Movements of small inanimate suspended bodies have in fact been observed by physiologists and called by them 'Brownian molecular movement'. The fourth paper is at the draft stage and is an electrodynamics of moving bodies, applying a modification of the theory of space and time; the purely kinematic part of this paper is certain to interest you.

To a non-scientist, perhaps this laconic, fairly technical description does not sound all that amazing—even when one becomes aware of the fact that Einstein would never again call any of his theories and discoveries (including general relativity) 'revolutionary'. But with hindsight we know that the first of these four papers published in *Annalen der Physik* in 1905 launched the most original scientific theory of the twentieth century, quantum theory—which, unlike relativity, marked a distinct break with the 'classical' physics of Newton and Maxwell—for which Einstein received his Nobel Prize. The second paper, which earned Einstein his doctorate from Zurich, became one of the most frequently cited papers in science, because it stimulated numerous practical applications (notably in petrochemistry). The third yielded the earliest incontrovertible proof that atoms and molecules exist and established Einstein as a founder of modern statistical thermodynamics. The fourth contained the essentials of what would become known as 'special' relativity, which led on to general relativity a decade later. (General relativity incorporates gravity, which is excluded from special relativity.)

All four papers were written in much less than six months in the first half of 1905—with the relativity paper, the final one, received by the journal on 30 June. And we must certainly not forget that in September Einstein added a fifth paper, a three-page coda to the fourth paper, which derived the energy–mass equation $E = mc^2$ that ultimately changed the course of the Second World War. All in all, 1905 was a year of miraculous achievement— an *annus mirabilis*—for a virtual unknown, a patent clerk without personal contact with any of the leading physicists of his day, whose papers cited hardly any previous scientific authors, and who was a mere 26 years old.

No wonder, a century later, physicists and historians are still trying to understand how this scientific marvel transpired. There is no straightforward answer, but it is possible to hazard a few general guesses, before coming to special relativity itself.

Part of the reason for Einstein's success was surely his wide and precocious reading in science, from his mid-teens onwards, fuelled by his voracious curiosity and allied to his unusual capacity to concentrate. His first PhD pupil, Hans Tanner, gave a graphic picture of his supervisor's ability to focus: 'He was sitting in his study in front of a heap of papers covered with mathematical formulae. Writing with his right hand and holding his younger son in his left, he kept replying to questions from his elder son Hans Albert who was playing with his bricks. With the words: "Wait a minute, I've nearly finished", he gave me the children to look after for a few moments and went on working. It gave me a glimpse into his immense powers of concentration.'

In addition, Einstein had an analytical ability worthy of his nearcontemporary, the fictional Sherlock Holmes. Anomalies like the ether were a challenge to him. He 'was intrigued rather than dismayed by apparent contradictions, whether they consisted of experimental results that conflicted with theoretical predictions'—as was the case with his first paper (on the quantum)—'or theories with formal inconsistencies'—as occurred with his fourth paper (on relativity), remarks the physicist John Rigden in his centenary study, *Einstein 1905: The Standard of Greatness*.

In a related vein, Einstein was unwilling to adopt received ideas simply on the authority of a scientist's high reputation. For example, he examined the highly influential works of Ernst Mach, whose *Science of Mechanics* went through 16 editions in three decades. Mach did not accept the concept of the ether or of the atom, neither of which had been physically observed in the nineteenth century, on the philosophical grounds that science should concern itself only with experimentally measurable entities. (When Mach died in 1916, he was among the last major physicists to reject the atomic theory.) Although Einstein did not share Mach's positivist philosophy, he liked Mach's scepticism. '[Einstein] would carefully study Mach's arguments against burdening physics with unnecessary concepts and eventually discard the ether concept, while accepting Mach's criticism of atomism as a challenge and trying to provide evidence for the existence of atoms', write the historians Jürgen Renn and Robert Schulmann.

A further clue to Einstein's success is that he relished debate, even if his ideas got torn apart by his friends Habicht and Solovine. Decades later, now laden with academic honours, Einstein remembered the Olympia Academy of 1902–04 in a letter to Solovine as being 'far less childish than those respectable ones which I later got to know'. It, and Einstein's discussions about science with a few other close friends in Bern, were unquestionably a key stimulus to his thinking in the period leading up to his 'miraculous year'.

The most important of all Einstein's friends at this time was probably Michele Besso (not an 'Olympian'), who was six years older than Einstein: a well-read, quick-witted, and affectionate man whose career as a mechanical engineer did not prosper because of a natural indecisiveness. Einstein got to know Besso at a musical gathering in his first year as a student in Zurich, and they would remain in touch for six decades until Besso's death just a month before Einstein's own. In 1904, at Einstein's suggestion, Besso joined the Patent Office too, and soon the two friends were walking back and forth from the office together discussing physics. Earlier, Besso had been the one who had interested the student Einstein in Mach. Now, he became the catalyst in Einstein's removal of the chief obstacle in formulating relativity theory.

Some time in the middle of May 1905, Einstein tells us that he went to see Besso for a chat about every aspect of relativity. After a searching discussion, Einstein returned to his family's apartment, and during that evening and night he saw the solution to his difficulties. The following day he went back to Besso and straightaway told his friend, without even saying hello: 'Thank you. I've completely solved the problem. An analysis of the concept of time was my solution. Time cannot be absolutely defined, and there is an inseparable relation between time and signal velocity.' His sincere gratitude can be felt in his published acknowledgement to Besso (a relative rarity with Einstein) for his 'steadfastness' and for 'many a valuable suggestion'— especially given the remarkable fact that Einstein's relativity paper contains no bibliographical citations of the works of physicists (not even Newton and Maxwell).

So where *did* special relativity arise from, if not obviously from the work of earlier and contemporary physicists? The physicist Stephen Hawking, in his millennial essay 'A brief history of relativity', tells us that Einstein 'started from the postulate that the laws of science should appear the same to all freely moving observers. In particular, they should all measure the same speed for light, no matter how fast they were moving.' Let us try to unpack these tricky ideas a little.

Near the beginning of *Relativity: The Special and the General Theory* (1916), Einstein's short introduction to his ideas for the general reader, he describes a simple but profound observation reminiscent of Galileo's moving ship. Instead of a ship, you stand at the window of a railway carriage that is travelling uniformly—at constant velocity, not accelerating or decelerating—and let fall a stone onto the embankment, without throwing it. If air resistance is disregarded, you, though you are moving, see the stone descend in a straight line. But a stationary pedestrian, that is someone 'at rest', who sees your action ('misdeed', says Einstein) from the footpath, sees the stone fall in a parabolic curve. Which of the observed paths, the straight line or the parabola, is true 'in reality', asks Einstein? The answer is—both paths. 'Reality' here depends on which frame of reference—which system of coordinates in geometrical terms—the observer is attached to: the train's or the embankment's.

One can rephrase what happens in relative terms as follows, says Einstein: 'The stone traverses a straight line relative to a system of coordinates rigidly attached to the carriage, but relative to a system of coordinates rigidly attached to the ground (embankment) it describes a parabola. With the aid of this example it is clearly seen that there is no such thing as an independently existing trajectory (lit. "path-curve"), but only a trajectory relative to a particular body of reference.' Moreover, there is no such thing as the *absolute* frame of reference for the universe, against which all velocities may be measured, found in 'classical' physics. For Newton, this reference frame was God; for Maxwell, it was the ether. But although

Newton had stated his belief in absolute space and time while creating his laws of motion and equations of gravity, he had later had his own doubts, as mentioned earlier. Einstein's doubts were stronger, and eventually caused him to dethrone absolute space and time. For Einstein, the absolute frame of reference did not exist.

Another, somewhat less familiar, teaser involving relativity concerned electrodynamics. As is well known, an electric charge at rest produces no magnetic field, while a moving charge—that is, an electric current—does generate a magnetic field (Faraday's circular lines of magnetic force around a current-carrying wire). Imagine a stationary electrically charged object with an observer A, also at rest relative to the object; the observer will measure no magnetic field using a compass needle. Now add an observer B moving uniformly to the east. Relative to B's reference system, the charged object (and observer A) will appear to be moving west uniformly; B, using a sensitive compass, will detect a magnetic field around the moving charged object. So, from A's point of view, there is no magnetic field around the charged object, while from B's uniformly moving point of view there *is* a magnetic field.

Anomalies of this kind intrigued Einstein. He was determined to resolve them.

It was his deeply held view that throughout the physical world the laws of mechanics, and indeed the laws of science as a whole, must be the same —'invariant' in scientific language—for all observers, whether the observers are 'at rest' or are moving uniformly, as already mentioned by Hawking. We may choose to describe our car as moving down the motorway at a constant velocity of 70 miles per hour, however, this figure has no absolute significance; it defines our position and speed relative only to the ground and takes no account of the earth's rotational position and velocity around its axis or earth's orbital position and velocity around the sun.

But if this new postulate about the invariance of the laws of nature was physically correct, it must apply not only to moving bodies but also to electricity, magnetism, and light: the electromagnetic wave of Maxwell and Hertz, which by 1905 was known from experiment to move at a constant velocity in a vacuum of about 186,000 miles per second, supposedly relative to the stationary ether. This posed a severe problem. While Einstein was content enough to relinquish the ether, which had never satisfied him as a concept, the constancy of the speed of light was another matter altogether.

Ten years previously, when he was 16, Einstein had reflected on what would happen if one chased light and caught up with it. In 1905 he concluded: 'If I pursue a beam of light with the velocity c (velocity of light in a vacuum), I should observe such a beam of light as a spatially oscillatory electromagnetic field at rest. However, there seems to be no such thing, whether on the basis of experience or according to Maxwell's equations.' To catch up with light would be as impossible as trying to see a chase scene in a movie in freeze-frame: light exists only when it moves, the chase exists only when the film's frames move through the projector. Were we to travel faster than light, Einstein imagined a situation in which we should be able to run away from a light signal and catch up with previously sent light signals. The most recently sent light signal would be detected first by our eyes, then we would see progressively older light signals. 'We should catch them in a reverse order to that in which they were sent, and the train of happenings on our earth would appear like a film shown backwards, beginning with a happy ending.' The idea of catching or overtaking light was clearly absurd.

Einstein therefore formulated a radical second postulate: the speed of light is always the same in all coordinate systems, *independent* of how the emitting source or the detector moves. However fast his hypothetical vehicle might travel in chasing a beam of light, it could never catch it: relative to him, the beam would always appear to travel away from him at the speed of light.

This could be true, Einstein eventually realized in May 1905 after talking to Besso, only if time, as well as space, was relative and not absolute. In order to make his first postulate about invariance compatible with his second about the speed of light, two 'unjustifiable hypotheses' from New-tonian 'classical' mechanics had therefore to be abandoned. The first was that 'the time-interval (time) between two events is independent of the condition of motion of the body of reference'. The second was that 'the space-interval (distance) between two points of a rigid body is independent of the condition of motion of the body of reference'.

Thus the time of the person chasing the light wave and the time of the wave itself are not the same. Time flows for the person at a rate different from that of the wave. The faster the person's vehicle goes, the slower his time flows, and therefore the less distance he covers (since distance trav-elled equals speed multiplied by duration of travel). In Hawking's words, relativity 'required abandoning the idea that there is a universal quantity called time that all clocks would measure. Instead, everyone would have his or her own personal time.' For space, too, there is a difference between the person and the light wave. The faster the person goes, the more his space contracts, and therefore the less distance he covers. Depending on how close the speed of the person's vehicle is to the speed of light, his time dilates and his space contracts in proportion to the time and space of an external observer ('mission control'), according to Einstein's equations of special relativity. However, like the person who drops a stone from a uniformly moving train and sees it fall in a straight line, not a curve, the person who is chasing the light wave does not himself perceive his watch slowing or his body shrinking; only the external observer sees these effects. To the moving person, everything in the vehicle seems normal. This is because his brain and body are all equally affected by his speed. His brain thinks and ages more slowly, and his retina is squashed in the same ratio as the vehicle; hence his brain perceives no change in the size of the vehicle or his body.

These ideas seem extremely alien to us on first encounter because we never travel at speeds of even a tiny fraction of the speed of light, so we never observe any 'relativistic' slowing of time or contraction of space. Human movements seem to be governed entirely by Newton's laws of motion (in which the speed of light is a quantity that does not even appear). Einstein himself had to struggle hard in 1905—hence his need for an intense discussion with Besso—to accept these relativistic concepts so remote from everyday experience.

With space contraction, he at least had the knowledge of a comparable 1890s proposal by Hendrik Lorentz and George FitzGerald, although it had a different theoretical basis from his own and relied on the existence of the ether, a concept that Einstein had of course rejected. But the abandonment of absolute time required a still greater leap of the imagination. Poincaré had questioned the concept of simultaneity in 1902 in his *Science and Hypothesis* (dissected by the Olympia Academy). Poincaré wrote: 'Not only do we have no direct experience of the equality of two times, but we do not even have one of the simultaneity of two events occurring in different places.' Indeed Poincaré seems to have come very close to a theory of relativity just before Einstein, but apparently drew back because its implications were too disturbing to the Newtonian foundations of physics. Simultaneity is a very persistent illusion for us on Earth because we so easily neglect the time of propagation of light; we think of it as 'instantaneous' relative to other familiar phenomena like sound. 'We are accustomed on this account to fail to differentiate between "simultaneously seen" and "simultaneously happening"; and, as a result, the difference between time and local time is blurred', wrote Einstein. Being a generation younger than Poincaré, and having no scientific reputation to lose, Einstein could afford to be radical in his thinking about time.

Yet, despite the strangeness of its predictions, relativity theory was nevertheless built on the mechanics of Galileo and Newton modified by the electrodynamics of Maxwell, as Einstein was in due course at pains to emphasize. This is why, although most modern physicists regard relativity as revolutionary, Einstein himself did not, and reserved that adjective, uniquely in his work, for his quantum theory.

There was a strong reaction to the relativity paper within months of its publication in *Annalen der Physik* on 28 September 1905. German-speaking physicists were polarized by it, and remarkably soon the unknown patent clerk came to be held in an unusual mixture of high esteem and vigorous contempt—a sure sign of the arrival of a radical thinker. This was an early signal of what would happen to relativity and its creator in the world at large after the First World War—as reflected in the fact that in the early 1920s the Swedish Academy considered relativity too controversial even for a mention in Einstein's Nobel Prize citation. (He was awarded the prize mainly for his first 1905 paper, the one on the quantum.) Indeed, the Swedish Academy asked Einstein not to speak on relativity at the award ceremony—a decision overturned in the event by overwhelming public interest, including that of the Swedish king. As the physicist Max Planck memorably remarked at the end of a lifetime's experience of science, 'A new scientific truth does not triumph by convincing its opponents and making them see the light, but rather because its opponents eventually die, and a new generation grows up that is familiar with it.'

Planck was relativity's first and strongest supporter. As professor of physics at Berlin University, he was at the centre of German science and one of the world's leading theoretical physicists. Despite Einstein's view that relativity was a 'modification' of existing work by Galileo, Newton, Maxwell, and Lorentz, Planck was immediately overwhelmed by the new theory's logic and hailed it in 1909 as unique: 'In boldness it probably surpasses anything so far achieved in speculative natural science.' It had 'brought about a revolution in our physical picture of the world, which, in extent and depth, can only be compared to that produced by the introduction of the Copernican world system', the normally cautious Planck enthused. Four years later, he would persuade Einstein to return to his native Germany and work in Berlin, where Einstein would create the theory of general relativity (incorporating gravity) in 1915.

Yet the very first published reaction to relativity, in January 1906, from an experimentalist, was firmly dismissive. For several years, the noted physicist Walter Kaufmann had been accelerating electrons emitted in the radio-active decay of radium to find out how an electron's energy increased with velocity. Relativity theory predicts that at such high energies, besides increasing the velocity of an electron, the energy also goes into increasing its mass. (Indeed, the mass of an electron—or any mass—becomes infinite at the speed of light itself.) But the variation of electron mass with velocity observed by Kaufmann did not seem to agree with the predictions of special relativity. With deliberately dramatic emphasis, Kaufmann declared in *Annalen der Physik* that his results were 'not compatible' with Einstein's fundamental assumptions and fitted better with those of two rival theories.

The junior patent clerk, though jolted, stood firm. While paying tribute to Kaufmann's carefulness, and admitting the other theories' better fit with the experimental data, Einstein responded: 'in my opinion, these theories should be ascribed a rather small probability because their basic postulates concerning the mass of the moving electron are not made plausible by theoretical systems which encompass wider complexes of phenomena'. In Einstein's view, the results of one experiment should not automatically trump a theory, if the theory can be shown to explain a range of other physical data. The best theories make many facts interlock in the structure of science. He was proved right when Kaufmann's experimental technique was refined by another physicist.

Again and again in his subsequent career, Einstein would show breath-taking confidence in the power of his theories when they had apparently been falsified by experimental evidence—and in the vast majority of cases he was vindicated. His mind had the confidence to wonder at paradox but believe in truth. 'Subtle is the Lord, but malicious He is not,' he famously remarked while on a tour of the United States in 1921. He was responding to the breaking news that the president of the American Physical Society, Dayton Miller, had at long last proved that the elusive ether existed and modulated the speed of light—obviously a death blow to relativity, if true. Miller had refined and repeated the celebrated Michelson–Morley experi-ment of 1887 that had failed to detect variation in the speed of light due to the ether, and had now detected a variation. But as with Kaufmann in 1906, so with Miller in 1921, the experimenters were deceived. Their experiments were not designed subtly enough for nature: errors were discovered in due course; the ether was relegated to non-existence; and relativity theory was further reinforced.

Today, after surviving all manner of ever more precise experimental tests, in space as well as on earth, Einstein's special and general relativity are part of the foundations of physics, along with Newton's and Maxwell's laws. After a century's 'continuous flight from wonder'—his striking description of his creative process—Einstein's esoteric thought world has come to seem almost mundane.

CHAPTER 13

VIRGINIA WOOLF

Mrs Dalloway

I am now galloping over Mrs Dalloway, re-typing it entirely from the start, which is more or less what I did with the V.O. [The Voyage Out]—a good method, I believe, as thus one works with a wet brush over the whole, & joins parts separately composed and gone dry. Really & honestly I think it the most satisfactory of my novels (but have not read it cold-bloodedly yet). The reviewers will say that it is disjointed because of the mad scenes not connecting with the Dalloway scenes. And I suppose there is some superficial glittery writing. But is it 'unreal'? Is it mere accomplishment? I think not. And as I think I said before, it seems to leave me plunged deep in the richest strata of my mind. I can write & write & write now: the happiest feeling in the world.

Virginia Woolf, *Diary*, 13 December 1924

L iterary reputations depend on a writer's biography as well as on his or her writing. Among twentieth-century writers, one need only consider the importance of the lives of, say, T. S. Eliot, Ernest Hemingway, Sylvia Plath, or Graham Greene, to their reputations. With Virginia Woolf, the biography is particularly salient, despite the fact that her life was comparatively speaking private and uneventful. It involved few public roles, limited travel—none of it beyond Europe, a single husband, no children, and only one love affair outside marriage, with Vita

Sackville-West (unlike most members of the Bloomsbury Group). Indeed large tracts of her life were comprised of sitting at home in a state of introspection and often mental illness with just a pen and paper for company.

Yet somehow, since her death in 1941, Woolf's life has acquired a prominence that rivals and even eclipses her novels, except among literary academics. The shift in emphasis originated with her courageous suicide, acquired momentum with the publication of her diary in the 1950s and the appearance in 1962 of Edward Albee's play *Who's Afraid of Virginia Woolf?*, and accelerated with the rise of feminism in the 1970s. In 2003, a Hollywood movie loosely inspired by Woolf's breakthrough novel *Mrs Dalloway* depicted not its central character Clarissa Dalloway but rather two fragments of the married life of her creator. Entitled *The Hours* (Woolf's original title for her novel), the film focuses almost exclusively on her mental illness; it begins and ends with her drowning in the river near her home—as if to imply that her 'madness' was the source of her creativity.

Of course, Woolf herself chose to make her life the subject of her fiction to a far greater extent than most novelists. Her troubled Victorian and Edwardian upbringing before she published her first novel *The Voyage Out* in 1915—with its absence of any school or university education, her profoundly ambivalent relationship with her domineering father and do-gooding mother Leslie and Julia Stephen, four devastating family deaths within a decade, and two nervous breakdowns—provided the content, if not the modernist form, for much in her later novels, notably *Jacob's Room* and *To the Lighthouse*. At the same time, her decision to marry the former colonial civil servant Leonard Woolf in 1912 was crucial in preventing her from taking her life and ending her career before it had begun. Initially her lover, Leonard quickly became more her guardian. Then, her extraordinarily candid diary and letters anatomized her day-to-day existence and encounters, enabling researchers to trace numerous creative connections between life and fiction. So precisely and vividly observed are the diary and the letters, along with her equally vivid, posthumously published autobiography, 'Sketch of the past', written in 1939–40, not to mention dozens of significant essays, short and long (especially the highly personal *A Room of One's Own*), that some critics value her non-fiction more highly than her fiction. On the basis of his own autobiography, Leonard Woolf would seem to have agreed with this assessment.

'Virginia Woolf's story is reformulated by each generation', wrote the leading Woolf biographer Hermione Lee in 1996. 'She takes on the shape of difficult modernist preoccupied with questions of form, or comedian of manners, or neurotic highbrow aesthete, or inventive fantasist, or pernicious snob, or Marxist feminist, or historian of women's lives, or victim of abuse, or lesbian heroine, or cultural analyst, depending on who is reading her, and when, and in what context.'

Whatever the stance, any enquirer into Woolf's mind, and the creation of *Mrs Dalloway*, is bound to begin with her family and childhood. No matter how much she tried to break with convention in her novels, they are generally preoccupied with the personalities and ramifications of the influential Victorian family into which Virginia Stephen was born in London in 1882.

Both sides of her family were intimate with empire—the deep background to *Mrs Dalloway*—either as colonial administrators and legal historians of colonial government based in Britain on her father's side (the Stephens), or as civil servants in India and members of the Calcutta gentry on her mother's side (the Pattles). Some of the Stephens were also learned writers and successful journalists.

James Stephen, Virginia's great-grandfather, was a barrister and MP who actively supported the abolition of the slave trade and married William Wilberforce's sister. His son, Sir James Stephen, was a colonial undersecretary, known as 'Mr Over-secretary Stephen' for his influence, who prepared the bill to abolish the trade in 1833. Sir James Stephen's oldest surviving son, Sir James Fitzjames Stephen, was the legal member of the viceroy's council in India before becoming a high court judge. A crusty imperialist as compared with his father and grandfather, 'Uncle Fitzy' sired a branch of the family disliked by his niece Virginia. His seven offspring included a son who became a high court judge in Calcutta and two pious daughters who very likely influenced Woolf's portrayal of the Anglo-Indian official Peter Walsh and the narrow-minded missionary Doris Kilman in *Mrs Dalloway*. The fictional Walsh has an uncontrollable habit of opening and shutting his pocketknife while talking. In her diary for 1918, Woolf notes a visit from her cousin Harry Stephen, the judge, 'who sat like a frog with his legs akimbo, opening and shutting his large knife, & asserting with an egoism proper to all Stephens, that he knew how to behave himself, & how other people ought to behave... The impenetrable wall of the middle-class conservative was never more stolid...'

Another of the Fitzjames Stephen cousins, the writer J. K. Stephen, went violently insane after a brief but brilliant career at Cambridge, and starved himself to death in a mental asylum in 1892. He has even been proposed by one historian as being the murderer Jack the Ripper who terrorized the East End of London in 1888. Virginia, then a mere girl, keenly recalled her cousin's disturbing behaviour as a visitor to Hyde Park Gate during his decline. (J. K. Stephen was treated by the same doctor as would later treat her.) Mental illness seems to have run in the Stephen family, judging from the depressions suffered by her grandfather James Stephen, who wrote to his wife in 1841, presciently in relation to his granddaughter:

> Living alone, I sometimes am oppressed by myself. I seem to come too closely into contact with myself. It is like the presence of some unwelcome, familiar, and yet unknown visitor. This is a feeling for which I have no description in words. Yet I suppose everyone has now and then felt as if he were two persons in one, and were compelled to hold a discourse in which soliloquy and colloquy mingle oddly and even awfully.

His tendency to groan out loud to himself manifested itself in his second surviving son Sir Leslie Stephen, who fully shared what he called the 'irritable and nervous temperament' of the Stephens. Of Leslie Stephen's own children apart from Virginia, his daughter by his first marriage, Laura, had to be sent away to an asylum in the 1890s, while his first son Thoby seems to have made a suicide attempt as a teenager.

In Virginia's youth, Leslie Stephen, who started his career as a Cambridge don, was regarded as one of the great intellectuals of his time, comparable with Thomas Carlyle. A century or so later, he is principally remembered as the prodigious founding editor of the *Dictionary of National Biography*. Between 1882 and 1891, when he resigned on grounds of ill-health, Leslie Stephen edited the first 26 volumes and contributed 378 biographies, in recognition of which he was knighted in 1902. But his main interests lay in philosophy and literature, in which he published, among other books, *History of English Thought in the 18th Century* in 1876 and *English Literature and Society in the Eighteenth Century* in 1904, the year of his death. Although major works, they were not the landmarks that he aspired to write, and in later life he would suffer from chronic and lacerating self-doubt about his achievements, which would sour his relationship with his children, including Virginia, in his final decade.

His first wife was Minny Thackeray, a daughter of the novelist William Makepeace Thackeray. They had one child, Laura, before Minny's sudden death in 1875. Three years later, Leslie Stephen got married again, to a woman who was almost a next-door neighbour in London.

Julia Duckworth had also been widowed by the early death of her partner. She was a daughter of one of the seven Pattle sisters of Calcutta—descendants of a French aristocrat at the court of Marie Antoinette, as Virginia liked to recall—girls then well known in Anglo-Indian circles for their beauty and social connections (and now known for numbering the Victorian photographer Julia Margaret Cameron, *née* Pattle). Julia's first husband, Herbert Duckworth, a lawyer and country gentleman extremely unlike Leslie Stephen, died unexpectedly in 1870, leaving Mrs Duckworth with three very young children, George, Gerald, and Stella: half-brothers and a half-sister to Virginia who would play an important, if generally disconcerting, part in her adolescence and early adulthood.

Except for the loss of her religious faith, Julia Stephen was an archetypal Victorian matriarch, an 'angel in the house': opposed to female suffrage; devoted to her husband; the bright centre of a large family, while assiduously helping the poor and needy. When she died (in 1895, at the age of only 48), 'it was as though on some brilliant day of spring the racing clouds of a sudden stood still, grew dark, and massed themselves; the wind flagged, and all creatures on the earth moaned or wandered seeking aimlessly', Virginia wrote in her autobiography. On the other hand, her daughter honestly added about her mother, 'she was impetuous, and also a little imperious; so conscious of her own burning will that she could scarcely believe that there was not something quicker and more effective in her action than in another's'.

Within a few years of her marriage in 1878, there were eight children in the Stephen household: one by Leslie's first marriage, three by Julia's first marriage, and four from their own marriage, born between 1880 and 1883. The eldest of the foursome, Vanessa, who became the painter Vanessa Bell, was the closest to Virginia, and the only member of the family with whom she felt an unreserved rapport; she inspired Virginia's second novel, *Night and Day*. Her elder brother Thoby, his Cambridge circle of intellectual friends and his premature death from typhoid in 1906 after a trip to Greece, influenced her writing deeply; *Jacob's Room*, her third novel, is modelled on Thoby. With her younger brother Adrian, she had an unfruitful and somewhat awkward relationship.

The family's narrow, six-storey London house, at 22 Hyde Park Gate, South Kensington, is brilliantly evoked by Woolf in her 'Sketch of the past'. Upstairs was her study–bedroom and her father's book-lined study; at the bottom of the house the heavily furnished dining and drawing rooms for meals and social life with her brothers and sisters and her parents' stream of visitors—grand and humble—with whom she was expected to make polite conversation. 'Downstairs there was pure convention; upstairs pure intellect. But there was no connection between them', she emphasizes. The sketch concludes with a paragraph dwelling on this disconnection:

> There were so many different worlds: but they were distant from me. I could not make them cohere; nor feel myself in touch with them. And I spent many hours of my youth restlessly comparing them. No doubt the distraction and the differences were of use; as a means of education; as a way of showing one the contraries. For no sooner had I settled down to my Greek than I would be called off to hear George's [law] case; then from that I would be told to come up to the study to read German; and then the gay world of Kitty Maxse would impinge.

The character Mrs Dalloway—who makes her first appearance in a cameo in *The Voyage Out*—was partly based (according to a letter from Virginia to Vanessa) on Julia Stephen's close friend Kitty Maxse, an elegant, socially gifted woman whose marriage to a political editor in 1890 Mrs Stephen had helped to arrange. Probably the roots of *Mrs Dalloway* as a whole lie here, in the teenaged Virginia Stephen's habit of intense analysis of incompatible individuals and their interactions at 22 Hyde Park Gate. There are multiple disconnections in the novel. Most obvious is the parallel existence of Clarissa Dalloway's privileged world as the middle-aged wife of a conservative politician, and the increasingly deranged world of the young clerk Septimus Smith: two worlds which finally cohere, if they really do, only in the privacy of Mrs Dalloway's mind near the end of the novel. There is the disconnection between her inner feelings and the insincerities she utters to her guests at her party. And throughout the novel there is the disconnection between intellect and emotion, analysis and empathy, as Peter Walsh—the most intelligent character in the novel—ruefully examines his unrequited passion for his old flame Clarissa. All of these disconnections Virginia certainly experienced in a different form in the London house (and on long family holidays at their house in St Ives in Cornwall) in the 1880s and 90s through her parents and siblings, and their visiting relatives, friends, and lovers.

School friends were not part of the picture, since Virginia's early education took place entirely at home. But although the Stephens were unwilling to give daughters a formal education—as was typical of the time, if undoubtedly a cause of resentment for Vanessa and Virginia—the parents encouraged their mental development by giving them lessons and the run of the library. Virginia was soon reading precociously. As early as 1893, Leslie told Julia that the eleven-year-old Virginia 'takes in a great deal and will really be an author in time'. In her autobiography, Woolf remembered that books were a bond between her and her father: 'I was a snob no doubt, and read partly to make him think me a very clever little brat. And I remember his pleasure, how he stopped writing and got up and was very gentle and pleased, when I came into the study with a book I had done; and asked him for another.'

In her mid-teens, she began to concentrate on the classics, taking outside help. She commenced classes in Latin and Greek in the autumn of 1897 with Dr George Warr, translator of Aeschylus and a founder of the Ladies Department of King's College, in Kensington; but did not take the exams. Two years later, she started private lessons with the classics teacher Clara Pater, sister of the art historian Walter Pater, who lived around the corner from Hyde Park Gate. A year after this, she found her ideal teacher, a Cambridge-trained classicist living with her sister in Hampstead, Janet Case, who became a lifelong friend (though a critic of Mrs Dalloway for using style to conceal shallowness). With Case's tuition, Virginia was able to discuss the classics with her brother Thoby, who had gone up to Cambridge in 1899 and immersed himself in Greek. Nevertheless, she often felt isolated. When Thoby returned to Trinity College in 1903, she complained in a letter to him: 'I don't get anyone to argue with me now, and feel the want. I have to delve from books, painfully and all alone, what you get every evening sitting over your fire and smoking your pipe with [Lytton] Strachey etc. No wonder my knowledge is but scant. There's nothing like talk as an educator I'm sure.'

The pros and cons of Woolf's (lack of) education raise interesting questions for her career as a novelist. It is true that Leslie Stephen did not want to spend money on Virginia's education, but it may also be the case that he thought his daughter's health, following her nervous breakdown after the death of her mother, could not cope with a university education. 'Arguably—as she sometimes argued herself—he gave her a better education from his study than she would have had at school or college. And certainly she would not have been the writer she was, with the subjects she chose, if she had had a formal education', thinks Hermione Lee.

Unquestionably, during this unhappy period, from 1897 up to her father's protracted death in 1904, their relationship became exceptionally fraught, as suggested by the tyrannical behaviour of Mr Ramsay in To the Lighthouse. Two years after he lost his wife, Leslie Stephen's step-daughter Stella

Duckworth suddenly died, a few months after getting married. The patriarch now expected Vanessa, aged 17, helped by Virginia, to take over the running of the household and to support him emotionally—but neither daughter was capable of meeting his demands. 'Suppose I, at fifteen, was a nervous, gibbering, little monkey, always spitting or cracking a nut and shying the shells out, and mopping and mowing, and leaping into dark corners and then swinging in rapture across the cage', writes Woolf in her autobiography, 'he was the pacing, dangerous, morose lion; a lion who was sulky and angry and injured; and suddenly ferocious, and then very humble, and then majestic; and then lying dusty and fly pestered in a corner of the cage.' More prosaically, in her diary, on her father's birthday in 1928, she noted that he would have been 96, had he lived. 'His life would have entirely ended mine. What would have happened? No writing, no books;—inconceivable.'

Her half-brother George Duckworth, in his early thirties and still unmarried, socially ambitious and sexually predatory on Virginia, now took it upon himself to arrange the 'coming out' into society of the two Stephen girls. Vanessa, already set on becoming an artist, resisted strongly, but Virginia was initially cooperative. However, she proved something of a disaster at parties: unsuitably dressed, unable to dance, and uninterested in conventional conversation. Still, she was half-fascinated by the shimmer of fashionable, late Victorian society, as she would remain for the rest of her life. 'If you ask me would I rather meet Einstein or the Prince of Wales, I plump for the Prince without hesitation', she remarked in 1936, in a talk to Bloomsbury's Memoir Club, entitled 'Am I a snob?' Some of those she encountered at parties in her late teens and early twenties would later be invited to Mrs Dalloway's fictional party. 'There were originals for some of the people in *Mrs Dalloway*: but very far away—people I last saw ten years ago and even then, did not know well. Those are the people I like to write about', she admitted, quite revealingly, at the time of the novel's publication in 1925, in a letter to the politician Philip Morrell (husband of Lady Ottoline Morrell), who feared that he might be the model for the novel's dull Richard Dalloway or the toadying courtier Hugh Whitbread.

The year 1904 was a pivotal one. Leslie Stephen died in February. In the spring, Virginia travelled to Italy for the first time, with Vanessa and a woman friend. But in May, the strain of the previous few years precipitated a severe breakdown, including a suicide attempt of some kind. When Virginia had recovered over the summer, free at last of her father, she began to write her earliest pieces of published journalism, which would fairly soon earn her a worthwhile income, much of it from book reviews and articles in *The Times Literary Supplement*. Then, in December, all of the Stephen children—Vanessa, Thoby, Virginia, and Adrian—with servants, uprooted themselves from the Victorian ethos of Hyde Park Gate and decamped across London to a shared house in Gordon Square, Bloomsbury, a distinctly unfashionable area in Edwardian London. The Duckworth half-brothers went their own ways: George married into the aristocracy that same year and moved to the country; Gerald continued to build up the Duckworth publishing house that would in due course publish Virginia's first novel.

At the new house, Thoby Stephen's friends from Cambridge became regular visitors, forming the nucleus of the loose association that would gradually become known as the Bloomsbury Group. Saxon Sydney-Turner, Clive Bell (who soon married Vanessa Stephen), Desmond MacCarthy, Lytton Strachey, and later Duncan Grant and Leonard Woolf, were the 'founders', along with the two Stephen sisters and their brother. The keynote of the group—much disapproved of by their parents' friends, such as Kitty Maxse—was a belief in freedom from Victorian convention in talk and behaviour (though not freedom from servants). To capture their liberated conversation in writing was difficult, as Virginia discovered when she became a novelist. Not long before beginning *Mrs Dalloway* in 1922, in a talk on 'Old Bloomsbury', she ironically told the Memoir Club (established in 1920 by Molly MacCarthy) that: 'Talk—even the talk which had such tremendous results upon the lives and characters of the two Miss Stephens —even talk of this interest and importance is as elusive as smoke. It flies up the chimney and is gone.' Her first novel, *The Voyage Out*, is full of conventional dialogue within quotation marks; by the time of *Mrs Dalloway*, much of this has given way to a narrative voice borrowed freely from speech rhythms shorn of conventional speech markers.

Her new life in Bloomsbury was not all amusing highbrow talk and book reviewing. During 1905–07, following the example of her socially conscious Victorian mother, Virginia gave lectures in history and English composition at Morley College, an evening institute for working men and women in south London's Waterloo Road. They were not a great success, and she soon abandoned the lessons as too onerous. But her encounter with a young male 'degenerate poet', Cyril Zeldwyn, obsessed with Keats, would eventually find its way into *Mrs Dalloway*, in which the 'shy, and stammering' literary-minded clerk Septimus Smith falls in love with 'Miss Isabel Pole, lecturing in the Waterloo Road upon Shakespeare.'

She began her first attempt at a novel some time in late 1907, under the unpromising title *Melymbrosia*, and battled through numerous redrafts for more than five years until its acceptance by the publishers Duckworth in 1913. She felt herself to be working in the shadow of established Edwardian male novelists, in particular Arnold Bennett, John Galsworthy, and H. G. Wells, whose solidly crafted literary conventions for establishing character she would progressively reject in favour of more fluid and diffuse techniques. With the death of King Edward VII in 1910, and a widely perceived social shift in relations between masters and servants, husbands and wives, parents and children (epitomized by the Stephen children's exodus from South Kensington to Bloomsbury), 'on or about December 1910 human character changed', she would famously claim in an essay, 'Character in fiction', published in 1924. And so, she said, the depiction of character in novels must also change. '[The Edwardian novelists] have laid an enormous stress upon the fabric of things. They have given us a house in the hope that we may be able to deduce the human beings who live there...But if you hold that novels are in the first place about people, and only in the second about the houses they live in, that is the wrong way to set about it.'

Her own life changed radically around this time, when she accepted Leonard Woolf's proposal of marriage in early 1912. A year or two older than her, from a struggling Jewish family settled in London, Leonard was a friend of her late brother Thoby from his Cambridge days. Having spent more than six years in Ceylon as an effective if somewhat overbearing government official, in 1911 he was considering whether or not to resign the civil service out of disenchantment with colonial life, encouraged by his friend Strachey, who believed he should marry Virginia. On leave from Ceylon in London, he became a tenant in a new Bloomsbury house at Brunswick Square acquired by Virginia and Adrian Stephen in 1911, and there he rapidly wrote an impressive first novel about Ceylon, *A Village in the Jungle*, which was published by Duckworth in 1913.

Some resonant echoes of the marriage are to be found in *Mrs Dalloway*. Peter Walsh, back in London in June 1923 (the date specified in the novel) after five years' government service in India, noticing the powerful new motor cars on the streets, is reminded of the fact that he 'had invented a plough in his district, had ordered wheelbarrows from England, but the coolies wouldn't use them, all of which Clarissa knew nothing whatever about'. Leonard Woolf had put much effort into introducing English ploughs to the often recalcitrant Sinhalese farmers of his district on the southeastern coast of Ceylon, as documented at length in his official diary. No doubt he told the story to Virginia. But neither this, nor any of Leonard's other formative experiences in Ceylon, including *A Village in the Jungle*, were of more than passing interest to his new wife, judging from her diary and letters. (Her biographers, too, follow her lead and neglect Leonard's years in Ceylon and his first novel.)

The detail is a superficial one, but at a deeper level the Virginia–Leonard relationship must have been constantly in her mind when creating the Clarissa Dalloway–Peter Walsh relationship. Clarissa is not Virginia, and Peter is certainly not Leonard. After all, Virginia took the unorthodox step of marrying her 'penniless Jew' (as she referred to him in letters to Bloomsbury friends), whereas in the novel Clarissa rejects the passionate and risky Peter in favour of the safety, comfort, and status of the politician Richard Dalloway. Moreover, Peter is described as belonging to 'a respectable Anglo-Indian family which for at least three generations had administered the affairs of a continent', rather like the Pattles, whereas Leonard had no colonial family connections at all before going to Ceylon in 1904. And yet, immediately following this just quoted phrase about Walsh's background, Virginia adds Peter's inner reflection from his stream of consciousness in characteristic parentheses: '(it's strange, he thought, what a sentiment I have about that, disliking India, and empire, and army ...)'. This contrast, surely, comes straight from Leonard's conflicted attitude to imperialism.

They married in August 1912 and travelled in France, Spain, and Italy for their honeymoon. Returning to London, they abandoned Bloomsbury and moved to rather basic and bohemian rooms, without a servant, off Fleet Street, in order to save money. Virginia now pushed herself hard to complete *The Voyage Out*, which Leonard presented in manuscript to Gerald Duckworth (publisher of his own novel) in March 1913. By May, she was reading her proofs. But she found the process of reading her own work in print so excruciating that she fell seriously ill after completing it. In September, after taking a drug overdose, she nearly died. Publication was postponed until 1915. For two years, Virginia was under the care, on and off, of a variety of conflicting doctors, nurses, and Leonard, sometimes at home, sometimes with friends and relatives (including, surprisingly, George Duckworth), at other times in nursing homes offering 'rest cures', especially when she became violent during 1915. Her antagonism towards the medical profession, so pronounced a feature of *Mrs Dalloway*, dates from this long period of illness in 1913–15.

From watching Virginia's symptoms closely, Leonard had become convinced that her social life in Bloomsbury was too exciting for her mind and health. As she herself noted in her diary many years later:

> I believe these illnesses are in my case—how shall I express it?—partly mystical. Something happens in my mind. It refuses to go on registering impressions. It shuts itself up. It becomes chrysalis. I lie quite torpid, often with acute physical pain...Then suddenly something springs. Two nights ago, Vita [Sackville-West] was here; & when she went, I began to feel the quality of the evening—how it was spring coming: a silver light; mixing with the early lamps; the cabs all rushing through the streets; I had a tremendous sense of life beginning...& Vita's life so full & flush; & all the doors opening; & this is I believe the moth shaking its wings in me. I then begin to make up my story whatever it is; ideas rush in me; often though this is before I can control my mind or pen. It is no use trying to write at this stage.

Against her wishes, in 1914 Leonard moved them both out of central London to the suburbs at Richmond, some months before the outbreak of war. There, in 1915, they found and leased a substantial eighteenth-century building, Hogarth House, where they would live for the next nine years until they returned to life in post-war Bloomsbury in 1924, during the drafting of *Mrs Dalloway*. Hogarth House provided the name of the printing press and publishing firm, the Hogarth Press, which the Woolfs established in the house in 1917, partly as a therapeutic distraction for Virginia, who enjoyed typesetting, and partly so that they could publish the books and essays they liked, including all her writings, without any editorial interference or commercial publishing pressures.

The First World War, which is responsible for the shell shock that drives the volunteer soldier Septimus Smith mad in *Mrs Dalloway*, was a divisive issue for the Bloomsbury Group. Two of Virginia's distant cousins on her mother's side were killed, while Leonard lost one brother and another was injured. None of the Woolfs' closest friends fought, preferring instead to do 'alternative service' after the introduction of conscription in 1916. Virginia was an out-and-out pacifist, Leonard much less so, though he was opposed to the war (unlike in 1939–45). The worst thing about the air raids at Richmond, Virginia wrote to her sister in early 1918, was having to make conversation with the servants all night in the shelter.

Her lack of sympathy for and knowledge of the fighting weakens the impact of the war on Septimus Smith in *Mrs Dalloway*. A single, perfunctory, coldly detached, paragraph describes his friendship with his officer Evans,

like 'two dogs playing on a hearthrug', and the death of Evans in action in
Italy just before the 1918 armistice, leaving Smith unscathed. 'Septimus,
far from showing any emotion or recognizing that here was the end of a
friendship, congratulated himself upon feeling very little and very reasonably. The War had taught him. It was sublime.' Only after the war is
over, and he becomes engaged to an Italian woman, does he begin to
panic because he cannot feel. It is the first inkling of his gradually
deepening conviction that he is guilty of a great crime, for which the
only penalty is death. But since the reader is never given any opportunity
to understand the quality of his wartime friendship with Evans, his
subsequent mental decline, though powerfully detailed, is not as involving as it should be.

In *Jacob's Room*, the first novel Woolf wrote after the end of the war,
during 1920–22, the fighting is kept off-stage altogether. Only a handful of
references in the book, most of them discrete, speak of war, as Jacob
Flanders (a clearly symbolic name) passes from childhood by the sea in
Cornwall via Cambridge University to artistic life in London, travel in
Greece and, after an ellipsis, premature death. The final striking scene
takes place in Jacob's abandoned room in London with: 'Nothing arranged.
All his letters strewn about for anyone to read'—perhaps an image based
on a memory of Thoby Stephen's room at the Gordon Square house after
his sudden death in 1906. This book was Woolf's first attempt at an
experimental novel free from pre-war literary expectations, written at the
same time as T. S. Eliot's *The Waste Land* and James Joyce's *Ulysses*, both of
which she read during 1922 with mixed reactions. *Jacob's Room* was criticized
by Leonard for being populated by 'ghosts' and 'puppets, moved hither and
thither by fate', according to her diary. She herself felt its diffuseness while
planning her next novel; 'but I think Jacob was a necessary step, for me, in
working free'. Eliot nonetheless told her that the book was 'a remarkable
success', in which she had freed herself 'from any compromise between the
traditional novel and your original gift'.

Mrs Dalloway finally got underway in late 1922, after Woolf embarked in
the summer on several short stories around the figure of the MP's wife
Clarissa Dalloway, first seen on board ship in *The Voyage Out*. One of them,
'Mrs Dalloway in Bond Street', was completed. Then, according to Leonard
Woolf, who was immersed in standing (unsuccessfully) for election as an
MP during this year, 'for a short time [she] hesitated whether to expand it
into a full-length novel'.

On 6 October, at Hogarth House she wrote two pages of notes, including the following:

Thoughts upon beginning a book to be called, perhaps, At Home; or At the Party.

This is to be a short book consisting of six or seven chapters, each complete separately. In them must be some fusion. And all must converge upon the party at the end. My idea is to have some characters, like Mrs Dalloway, much in relief; then to have some interludes of thought or reflection, or moments of digression (which must be related, logically, to the next) all compact, yet not jerked.

The chapters might be

1. Mrs Dalloway in Bond Street
2. The Prime Minister
3. Ancestors
4. A dialogue
5. The old ladies
6. County house?
7. Cut flowers
8. The party

One, roughly to be done in a month; but this plan is to consist of some very short intervals, not whole chapters. There should be fun.

A few elements of the final book are already present, such as Mrs Dalloway's opening foray into Mayfair (to buy flowers) and the final party. But there is no hint of war, madness, or suicide, or indeed the character who became Septimus Smith. Yet only a week later, on 14 October, Woolf told her diary: 'Mrs Dalloway has branched into a book; & I adumbrate here a study of insanity & suicide: the world seen by the sane & the insane side by side—something like that. Septimus Smith—is that a good name?—& to be more close to the fact than Jacob.' What had brought about her abrupt change of direction?

On 8 October, Woolf had heard the news of Kitty Maxse's death four days earlier, aged only 55, as a result of falling down a flight of stairs in her house. Maxse was, as we know, the original model for Mrs Dalloway. Although she and Virginia had not spoken for almost 15 years, the news brought back uncomfortable memories and feelings all day. 'Not that I ever felt at my ease with her. But she was very charming—very humorous', Virginia noted. After the memorial service in London, attended by the socially prominent including George Duckworth but not Virginia Woolf, she again noted on 14 October: 'now Kitty is buried & mourned by half the grandees in London; & here I am thinking of my book. Kitty fell, very mysteriously, over some bannisters'. Woolf suspected suicide, despite the lack of any evidence. It was this suspicion, working on her rich memories of Maxse's life, which seems to have led directly to her new vision of her novel, now entitled 'The Hours'—in reference to the chiming of Big Ben as the story progresses. ('The leaden circles dissolved in the air.')

At least three other external circumstances had a bearing on the writing, too, during the two years between *Mrs Dalloway*'s inception and its completion in October 1924. Leonard Woolf's intense involvement in Labour Party and international politics undoubtedly sharpened his wife's depiction of the political world of the Dalloways. Second, in December 1922, Virginia met for the first time the aristocratic Vita Sackville-West, and began to feel stirred erotically by her, as suggested by the youthful flirtation in the novel between Clarissa Dalloway and Sally Seton, who eventually marries and becomes the prosperous, middle-aged Lady Rosseter.

Lastly, and most importantly, the move back from suburban Richmond to Bloomsbury in March 1924, energized Woolf's feeling for London. In May, she noted in her diary:

> London is enchanting. I step out upon a tawny coloured magic carpet, it seems, & get carried into beauty without raising a finger. The nights are amazing, with all the white porticoes & broad silent avenues. And people pop in & out, lightly, divertingly like rabbits; & I look down Southampton Row, wet as a seal's back or red and yellow with sunshine, & watch the omnibus going & coming, & hear the old crazy organs. One of these days I will write about London, & how it takes up the private life & carries it on, without any effort...But my mind is full of The Hours...It is becoming more analytical & human I think; less lyrical...[To] see human beings freely & quickly is an infinite gain to me. And I can dart in & out & refresh my stagnancy.

The 'analytical and human' qualities of *Mrs Dalloway* are solid strengths, which help to account for its special position and popularity among Woolf's novels. A fine example is the following passage about Peter Walsh killing time in a London street, immediately after the suicide of Septimus Smith (of whose life and death he is completely unaware):

> One of the triumphs of civilization, Peter Walsh thought. It is one of the triumphs of civilization, as the light high bell of the ambulance sounded. Swiftly, cleanly, the ambulance sped to the hospital, having picked up instantly, humanely, some poor devil; some one hit on the head, struck

down by disease, knocked over perhaps a minute or so ago at one of these crossings, as might happen to oneself. That was civilization. It struck him coming back from the East—the efficiency, the organization, the communal spirit of London. Every cart or carriage of its own accord drew aside to let the ambulance pass. Perhaps it was morbid; or was it not touching rather, the respect which they showed this ambulance with its victim inside—busy men hurrying home, yet instantly bethinking them as it passed of some wife; or presumably how easily it might have been them there, stretched on a shelf with a doctor and a nurse... Ah, but thinking became morbid, sentimental, directly one began conjuring up doctors, dead bodies; a little glow of pleasure, a sort of lust, too, over the visual impression warned one not to go on with that sort of thing any more—fatal to art, fatal to friendship. True. And yet, thought Peter Walsh, as the ambulance turned the corner, though the light high bell could be heard down the next street and still farther as it crossed the Tottenham Court Road, chiming constantly, it is the privilege of loneliness; in privacy one may do as one chooses. One might weep if no one saw. It had been his undoing—this susceptibility—in Anglo-Indian society; not weeping at the right time, or laughing either.

However, this originality of structure and psychological acuity cannot altogether disguise Woolf's disconnected attitude to her central character: a reflection, perhaps, of her real-life split attitude to Kitty Maxse when she died. Did Mrs Dalloway's creator, on the whole, feel admiration or distaste for her creation? Is Clarissa's mind meant to be profound or shallow? Is she mainly genuine or essentially snobbish in her desire to give a party? The novel gives ambivalent answers.

Lytton Strachey was the first to detect the disconnection, and with the frankness of a 'Bloomsberry', he told Virginia of his reservations. 'Lytton does not like Mrs Dalloway, &, what is odd, I like him all the better for saying so, & don't much mind', she noted in her diary. 'What he says is that there is a discordancy between the ornament (extremely beautiful) & what happens (rather ordinary—or unimportant). This is caused he thinks by some discrepancy in Clarissa herself; he thinks she is disagreeable & limited, but that I alternately laugh at her, & cover her, very remarkably, with myself.'

A further disconnection occurs with Septimus Smith. As with Mrs Dalloway, Woolf here draws upon long personal experience, of mental illness and its medical treatment. Smith's descent into madness, and his shocking suicide by jumping out of a window on to some sharp London railings so as to avoid the clutches of his doctors, is handled with outstanding authority and sympathy. Septimus, like Virginia herself, hears the sparrows in Regent's Park sing to him in Greek. And yet, in the end, his insanity fails to move us, because his character, before he suffers from shell shock, is sketched with the unappealing condescension and disdain that Virginia Stephen had once felt for her students at Morley College. In her words:

> [Septimus Smith] was, on the whole, a border case, neither one thing nor the other; might end with a house in Purley and a motor car, or continue renting apartments in back streets all his life; one of those half-educated, self-educated men whose education is all learnt from books borrowed from public libraries, read in the evening after the day's work, on the advice of well-known authors consulted by letter.

Thus the novel fails to connect satisfactorily the lives of Mrs Dalloway and Septimus Smith. When, at her party, Mrs Dalloway hears the bare bones of his terrible death from the conversation of Smith's 'obscurely evil' doctor Sir William Bradshaw, a late-arriving guest, she retreats to a window and reflects to herself: 'Somehow it was her disaster—her disgrace.' Yet since Clarissa Dalloway has never met Septimus Smith, and knows virtually nothing about him, this sentiment cannot but appear false to the reader. (In a good film adaptation of *Mrs Dalloway* made in 1997, Clarissa at least sets eyes on the shambling Septimus in the street, while buying flowers for her party.) There can be no convincing connection between the cosseted society hostess and the deranged former soldier.

Virginia Woolf, it is clear from many entries in her diary and remarks in her letters, was aware of this fatal flaw in the novel, as was Leonard. In August 1923, she even called the novel 'sheer weak dribble' and considered abandoning the manuscript. But at the same time she was rightly conscious of *Mrs Dalloway*'s innovative structure and style, its brilliant social comedy, and its many passages of fascinating beauty. It was the first of her novels, she proudly noted on completion, to be written without a breakdown. Its considerable success with the public launched her career as a novelist, and began to define the unique reputation her name now enjoys.

CHAPTER 14

HENRI CARTIER-BRESSON

The Decisive Moment

[In 1932] I had just discovered the Leica. It became the extension of my eye, and I have never been separated from it since I found it. I prowled the streets all day, feeling very strung-up and ready to pounce, determined to 'trap' life—to preserve life in the act of living. Above all, I craved to seize, in the confines of one single photograph, the whole essence of some situation that was in the process of unrolling itself before my eyes.

Henri Cartier-Bresson, introduction to *The Decisive Moment*, 1952

Photography, from its invention in France and Britain in the 1830s, had been hugely influential for a century before the appearance in 1952 of Henri Cartier-Bresson's first book, *Images à la Sauvette*—known in its simultaneous English edition as *The Decisive Moment*. But generally speaking, it was regarded more as a craft, or a science, than as an art. Cartier-Bresson's large-format volume of black-and-white images, with its wholly non-photographic colour cover design—a ravishing, semi-abstract, découpage by the artist Henri Matisse—proved to be a turning point in the history of photography. After *The Decisive Moment*, photographs were widely regarded as worthy of gallery display like paintings. Exhibitions of Cartier-Bresson's work were held in leading art institutions throughout the world over the following decades; he became the first living photographer to see his work hung at the Louvre. During the second half of the twentieth century, thanks to his photographs more than those of any other, photography was accepted as one of the fine arts. He himself was saluted, first and foremost by leading photographers, as the 'eye of the century', by the time of his death in 2004 at the age of almost 96.

Yet Cartier-Bresson, a famously paradoxical man, consistently asserted that he had never been interested in photography! His actions and behaviour over his lifetime bear out this astonishing claim. As he told me dismissively in an interview in 1998: ' "The great photographer"—what does it mean? I'm just an ordinary human being.'

Painting, not photography, was his passion as a child, and in the late 1920s he trained as a painter at an academy of fine art. He took up photography as his main pursuit only when he acquired a Leica camera in 1932. After three years of concentrated shooting, he turned away from photography towards film-making, and did not return to it full time until 1944, with a series of photo–portraits of French artists and writers, including Matisse. Not until 1947, with his breakthrough exhibition at the Museum of Modern Art in New York, and his co-founding of the agency Magnum Photos, did he regard himself as a professional photographer. Even then, he always left the printing of his negatives to others; the darkroom and developing techniques never appealed to him. After becoming probably the world's most celebrated photojournalist in the 1950s, he candidly told a French interviewer in 1962: 'Deep down ... I'd have as much fun without film in the camera. The great joy, for me, is to have my subject, and to press the shutter at the right moment ... It lasts a fraction of a second, and that's the moment of creation.' Finally, around 1970, now in his early sixties, he abandoned his photographic career at its zenith. In his remaining three decades, Cartier-Bresson, encouraged by friends such as Saul Steinberg and Jean Renoir, focused almost all of his creative drive on his first love: painting and drawing; in 1975, he held his first art exhibition, in New York. On the walls of his apartment in Paris, he hung no photographs, whether by himself or others, only paintings and drawings. To many people, especially professional photographers, his apparent volte-face looked like something of a betrayal of art photography by one of its founding figures.

Cartier-Bresson's work with a pencil and brush, his *violon d'Ingres*, never equalled his work with a camera, he was acutely aware. But his youthful formal education and lifelong immersion in drawing and painting would be crucial to his artistic success as a photographer. Although no one, including

Cartier-Bresson himself, has been able to articulate exactly how he created his unique images, they certainly sprang from his training in art. It taught him not only composition, but also the self-control vital for great creative achievement. To take a photo–portrait, for example, requires the constantly alert and agile photographer to pounce on a particular moment that will 'capture the inner silence of a willing victim', as Cartier-Bresson observed in his late eighties. 'With a pencil portrait, it is the draughtsman who must possess an inner silence.'

There was drawing ability in Cartier-Bresson's family, going back through his father to his grandfather and great-grandfather, who all filled sketchbooks; a favourite uncle, Louis Cartier-Bresson, was a professional painter, who won the Prix de Rome in 1910, two years after Henri was born. However, the predominant ethos of the Cartier-Bresson family was not artistic but rather commercial. The Cartier-Bressons were a long-established part of the wealthy *haute-bourgeoisie* of Paris. Their factory, a small empire on the Rue Cartier-Bresson in the town of Pantin (now a suburb of Paris), made thread for sewing, embroidery, darning, knitting, and lace-making. Cartier-Bresson thread was a leading brand in homes throughout France, with a logo consisting of the letters C and B in stylized script, set in an oval ribbon and separated by a cross: 'the coat-of-arms of the upper middle-classes', according to Cartier-Bresson's biographer Pierre Assouline.

From an early age, Henri rebelled against the family atmosphere, at the same time permitting it to shape certain of his attitudes—symbolized by his vacillation between the informal 'Cartier' and the more elitist 'Cartier-Bresson' in his printed credits as a photographer and film-maker in the 1930s. He had a tense relationship with his parents, especially his business-man father, as he grew up. In one of his rare published references to them, he remarked:

> My father was stern and quiet, and looked very much like an English gentle-man. He was always in his study writing—he gave me a distaste for business, except when he had samples of threads of different colours. Then I'd enjoy helping him judge one blue swatch against another blue swatch. Then we were chums! My mother was extraordinarily beautiful, right up to old age. She was highly sensitive, nervous, always wondering whether she was right or wrong, and she had a passion for psychology and philosophy, and for music.

One of her ancestors, of whom she was proud, was the assassin of Jean-Paul Marat, Charlotte Corday, who stabbed him in his bath and was guillotined in 1793.

Her eldest child Henri had a temper notorious in the family, which he was never able fully to control, even in old age. Formal schooling exacerbated it, since Henri had no interest in the syllabus or in sports, and resisted any restriction on his freedom and independence. 'Only interest at school was painting', Cartier-Bresson baldly noted in a chronology of his life published with his New York exhibition in 1947. His school days were a painful period in a privileged upbringing, relieved only by one senior teacher, who secretly sympathized with the boy's rebellion and allowed him to read compulsively in his office off-syllabus novels and poetry—by Marcel Proust, Fyodor Dostoyevsky, Stéphane Mallarmé, Arthur Rimbaud, Charles Baudelaire, even James Joyce, among other authors. He failed the baccalaureate thrice, the first time by three marks, the second by thirteen, and the third by 30 marks. Even his spelling, use of accents, and punctuation in French, were erratic. The traditional door to university education was therefore closed, which suited Henri well enough. In later years he joked while turning down yet another offer of an honorary doctorate from a university: 'What do you think I'm a professor of? The little finger?'

Apart from reading literature, Henri was passionate about watching films and making art, with a more casual interest in taking holiday snapshots with a Box Brownie camera. He was deeply impressed by recently released films such as D. W. Griffith's *Broken Blossoms*, Sergei Eisenstein's *Battleship Potemkin*, and Carl Dreyer's *Jeanne d'Arc*, and developed a more intense love of silent films than of the later talkies, which had some significance for his mature photography. 'It's difficult to look and listen at the same time', he remarked. 'I have lived in countries where I haven't spoken the language and so you have to use your eyes a lot more!'

Learning to paint and draw was a more disciplined process, as expected by his family. No doubt his painter uncle would have taken Henri in hand, had he lived. Henri first visited his uncle's studio when he was five on Christmas Eve, 1913, and smelt the paints—a memory that stayed with him for the rest of his life (as evocative smells often do). He became a frequent visitor. But in 1915, Uncle Louis was killed at the front in the Great War, and Henri lost the man he later regarded as his 'mythical father'. (In 1918, Uncle Pierre died, too, from war wounds.) An artist friend of Louis took over, and arranged for Henri to have painting and drawing lessons on Thursdays and Sundays, the days when schoolchildren did not have to attend school. A little later, another artist friend of the family, Jacques-Emile Blanche, who had been on intimate terms with Edouard Manet, encouraged Henri by inviting him to watch him in his studio, and in time introduced him to influential figures such as the dandy René Crevel.

But his chief artistic training came after leaving school and entering the Lhote Academy, where he spent two years in the period 1926–28. André Lhote, a self-taught artist who ardently admired Paul Cézanne, saw his own art as a bridge between the classicism of earlier French painting and the cubism of his own time, with an emphasis on the need for order, rules, and discipline. Lhote's main legacy, however, was as a teacher, theorist, and critic, the author of significant books on landscape and figure painting, who strongly advocated the study of nature and drawing based on models. In 1927, Lhote commented in an article: 'For me photography, far from having liberated painting from the concept of likeness, has actually fixed it and made a definitive criterion out of it ... All that is necessary now is to get the painter to create a "handmade photograph".'

Lhote was obsessed with geometry in art, and talked constantly of 'the golden section', 'divine proportions', 'the laws of composition', and 'universal harmony'. He introduced Cartier-Bresson to the celebrated words inscribed on the door of Plato's Academy: 'No one enters here but geometricians.' His student took them to heart, and later applied them to photography. But while Cartier-Bresson honoured Lhote for teaching him 'to read and write' as a photographer, as he put it, in the end he found Lhote's prescriptive purism annoying. More appealing was the surrealist movement centred on André Breton, which was then *au courant* among René Crevel and his circle, to which he was already being introduced.

In 1929, Cartier-Bresson spent eight months in England, at Cambridge with his cousin Louis Le Breton, who was a student at the university. Apart from attending some literature courses, he continued to paint. Two paintings from this year are among the few to survive from his early period: one depicts the couple who were his hosts in Cambridge, quite competently, and the other, less successful, a contorted female nude with a blanked-out face lying on a bed surrounded by ornamental symbols, including a mysterious seashell and a coloured cube. This painting appears to have been an attempt to synthesize Lhote's geometrical purism with the surrealist cult of excess. (Cartier-Bresson later joked that the cube contained Lhote.) A comparable synthesis, though far better integrated, would characterize many of his early photographs.

On return to Paris, Cartier-Bresson was obliged to submit himself for military service, and chose the air force. He was put into barracks at Le Bourget, not far from his family's factory in Pantin. Predictably, he soon clashed with the authorities and was frequently punished for insolence. But by a happy coincidence—something that would often befall Cartier-Bresson—the farcical situation also led to his meeting a rich and eccentric American expatriate, Harry Crosby, who lived near the air base and took flying lessons from its personnel. Crosby and his wife, who had founded the Black Sun Press in 1925 to publish writers they admired, then introduced the young 'Cartier', as they called him, to their wide circle of friends, among them the Americans Julien Levy and the couple Gretchen and Peter Powel.

According to Cartier-Bresson, it was the Powels who first encouraged his serious interest in photography, in 1930, while Levy was the first to appreciate his photographs. Levy was the son of a New York property tycoon, who had studied art history at Harvard University. Three years later, in 1933, the Julien Levy Gallery in New York would stage the inaugural exhibition of Cartier-Bresson photographs.

Crevel, Breton, and surrealist artists such as Salvador Dalí and Max Ernst, also came to parties at the Crosbys' house. Surrealism flourished from the mid-1920s as a response to the moral crisis in French society in the wake of the Great War. Its disgust with bourgeois institutions and its violent yearning for liberty chimed with Cartier-Bresson's feelings. He devoured surrealist writings, in particular Breton's poetic novel *Nadja* of 1928, and Louis Aragon's *Le Paysan de Paris* (Paris Peasant), published in 1926, which compares a poet's love for Paris with a peasant's love for his land. (In the 1990s, Cartier-Bresson returned to Aragon's book and created some lithographs for a limited edition.)

For a while, introduced to the surrealist gatherings around Breton by Crevel, he was a fascinated but uncommitted observer of the movement. 'I was once a diligent presence, sitting at one end of the table, at the surrealists' meetings at the café on Place Blanche, too shy and too young to say a word', Cartier-Bresson recalled in old age. Eventually he got to know Breton. 'He was as intimidating as the Sun King, but he was just as intimidated as I was; there was an onslaught of politeness and compliments, but you never knew if, without prior warning, he might become angry and excommunicate you.' Cartier-Bresson's photo–portrait of the Sun King, taken after much difficulty in 1961, shows a leonine Breton, seated at home beside some primitive but powerful carvings, with his eyes cast thoughtfully downwards. 'It's odd, there was nothing effeminate about him, with his lion's mane and his head always held high, but still there was something a bit feminine—maybe it was his wide buttocks', wrote

Cartier-Bresson. 'I recall that Dalí said of him, "I had a dream in which I slept with Breton", and Breton, tremendously dignified, shot back: "I wouldn't advise you to try it, my dear."' There were innumerable anecdotes about Breton, he noted (as there would be about Cartier-Bresson, too), 'but beyond the anecdotes, I owe an allegiance to surrealism, because it taught me to let the photographic lens look into the rubble of the unconscious and of chance'.

In 1929–31, Cartier-Bresson took a handful of photographs that were directly inspired by surrealist art, for example, the distorted face of a woman with a silk stocking over her head. After 1931, there were to be many echoes of surrealism in his photographs. Yet it was the surrealist attitude towards living—encountered at first hand in his contacts with Breton, Dalí, Ernst, Man Ray, and others—that really influenced Cartier-Bresson, not surrealist artworks. 'His allegiance was to its ethics rather than to its aesthetics', comments Assouline.

Writers, more than artists, prompted the next big step in Cartier-Bresson's life. Restless in Paris, and inspired by his boyhood reading of Rimbaud, he decided to travel to Africa. Rimbaud, rejecting bourgeois life in France, had settled in Abyssinia in the 1880s in his late twenties. More recently, André Gide had written a book about his travels in the Congo in 1925, accompanied by Marc Allégret, who published photographs of the trip seen by Cartier-Bresson. There was also a long tradition of French artists, beginning with Napoleon's expedition to Egypt, such as Eugène Delacroix and Matisse, who lived for spells in North Africa to stimulate their imaginations. Cartier-Bresson settled on going to West Africa. In October 1930, with the help of his grandfather, he got a berth on a wine tanker travelling from Rouen to Douala in Cameroon. From there, he went to the French colony of Ivory Coast, where he lived for almost a year.

He took various jobs, as a timber merchant and planter, and then met an Austrian hunter, who taught him how to hunt at night with a gun and an acetylene lamp fixed to his forehead so he could identify his prey by the colour of its eyes. Later he would compare hunting with a rifle to shooting with a camera, and conclude that in both cases it was the stalking he enjoyed more than the meat or the photograph. He also took some photographs, using a French-made Krauss camera. When eventually they were developed back in France, they suffered from double exposures and fern-like patterns due to mildew in the tropical climate. But the surviving images, showing riverboats, rowers, and naked children, show that Cartier-Bresson had already developed an eye for composition. None of the 1930–31 photographs, however, made the cut in *The Decisive Moment* (which means that black Africa is missing from Cartier-Bresson's published oeuvre, since he never went back there after 1931).

The adventure came to an inadvertent end when he contracted blackwater fever, a complication of malaria: a disease that turns the urine black and is generally fatal, even today. Expecting to die in Africa, Cartier-Bresson managed to write a postcard to his grandfather, asking for his body to be sent back to France and buried among the beech trees of a favourite forest, to the strains of a Debussy string quartet. An uncle replied bluntly: 'Your grandfather thinks that will be too expensive. It would be better if you came home.' Cartier-Bresson recovered thanks only to his Ivorian hunting companion and friend, Doua, who treated him with medicinal herbs.

His convalescence in France in 1931–32 marked the start of his serious commitment to photography. Some time after he returned from abroad, he destroyed all his canvases, except for the few that were rescued by his mother. At the same time, probably in early 1932, he came across a photograph of Africa published in the special 'Photographie 1931' issue of *Arts et Métiers Graphiques* (Graphic Arts and Design), which greatly excited him. Taken by the Hungarian photojournalist Martin Munkácsi, a former sports photographer, it showed three naked black boys seen from behind, running towards waves on the shoreline of Lake Tanganyika. According to Cartier-Bresson, the image was like a spark setting alight fireworks in his mind. Although he does not mention Munkácsi's photograph (or indeed any photograph) in his introduction to *The Decisive Moment*, when writing to Munkácsi's daughter in 1977 he was effervescent about its impact:

> I suddenly understood that photography can fix eternity in a moment. It is the only photo that influenced me. There is such intensity in this image, such spontaneity, such *joie de vivre*, such miraculousness, that even today it still bowls me over. The perfection of form, the sense of life, a thrill you can't match...I said to myself: Good Lord, one can do that with a camera...I felt it like a kick up the backside: go on, have a go!

Cartier-Bresson's purchase of his first Leica in Marseilles seems to have coincided more or less with Munkácsi's trigger to his ambition. (He does not record exactly when in 1932 he bought the camera.) Designed in 1913 by Oskar Barnack, launched in 1925 by the Leitz company—the name derives from '*Leitz camera*'—and constantly improved thereafter, the Leica was the first practical 35 mm camera, using the ordinary 35 mm film previously confined to the cinema and obviating the need for a cumbersome photographic plate. For photographers such as Cartier-Bresson, the camera's small size (fitting into a hand), its lightness, the precision of its framing through the viewfinder, the clarity of its image, its fast exposure time, its sensitivity to reduced light levels, and its ease of operation, came together as a revelation. With a Leica, Cartier-Bresson rapidly discovered that he could snap life as it happened with a combination of quickness and invisibility that became a legendary hallmark of his working method.

In 1932, however, when he broke the news of his possible choice of career to the family—taking along the much older Max Ernst for support—his father was unimpressed. He shared the general view that photography was a pastime, not fit to be called serious art. Most painters agreed, even if they dabbled in it. Pablo Picasso, for instance, told Brassaï, who had taken up photography: 'You are a born draughtsman! Why don't you continue? You have a gold mine and you are exploiting a salt mine!' Eugène Atget, the distinguished photographer of Paris, died in poverty in 1927.

Cartier-Bresson, by contrast, perceived both the sharply rising popularity of the hand camera in the late 1920s, as evidenced by the growth in illustrated magazines, and its artistic possibilities, which were already being explored by photographers such as André Kertész. From his knowledge of painting, he could see that hand cameras, such as the Leica, worked fast enough to emulate the nineteenth-century impressionist painters like Edgar Degas, 'who deliberately constructed their pictures of contemporary life as if they were momentary perceptions of a passing observer' (to quote Peter Galassi in Henri Cartier-Bresson: The Early Work). As for composition, his love of geometry and his knowledge of surrealism and cubism offered intriguing new opportunities for composing life on film.

Now, photography became the reason for his travelling, rather than the reverse as in Africa. In 1932–33, in the company of friends, Cartier-Bresson took photographs in Poland, Czechoslovakia, Austria, Germany, Italy, and Spain, as well as in France and Belgium. A few of these images form part of The Decisive Moment—all of which, bar one photograph, was shot with the Leica. They include classics such as a man jumping over a puddle behind a railway station in Paris; boys (one of them on crutches) playing in a ruined building in Seville; and an unemployed man with a haunted gaze holding a child in Madrid. These first established his artistic reputation in the form of exhibitions in New York and Madrid. Some of his photographs were also published in magazines, which drew attention to his name in France for the first time. 'It was indeed an emotional experience for me when I sold my first photograph (to the French magazine *Vu*)', writes Cartier-Bresson in his introduction to *The Decisive Moment*. This was in November 1933: it was a Spanish reportage on the occasion of the republic's parliamentary elections, published in the leading French picture magazine that became the model for *Life* and *Paris Match*. He had, however, forgotten his very first reportage: a story on Italian cemeteries published in *Voilà* in October 1932.

The next two years were spent in the New World, first in Mexico, then in New York. Cartier-Bresson's Mexican expedition began inauspiciously, with his being defrauded of all his money. But it ended with some formative experiences and resonant photographs, based on living at the edge of poverty in Mexico City, in small towns, and in the countryside—perhaps most famously his images of prostitutes squeezing their heads and busts out of open shutters in the red-light area of Mexico City. The Mexican photographs give free rein to surrealist impulses while at the same time showing Cartier-Bresson's rare ability to see through an exotic surface to the human condition beneath. Whether in Spain or in Mexico, his people feel equally individual. They made an indelible impression on the young Satyajit Ray in India, whose films (such as the Apu Trilogy) share a similar universal quality. 'The deep regard for people that is revealed... in his photographs of any people anywhere in the world invests them with a palpable humanism', Ray wrote in his 1980s foreword to *Henri Cartier-Bresson in India*. The year spent in Mexico culminated in a joint exhibition with the Mexican photographer Manuel Alvarez Bravo at the Palacio de Bellas Artes in Mexico City in March 1935.

Cartier-Bresson's first visit to the United States, later that year, was productive of friendships and useful contacts, rather than images. He renewed his relationship with the gallery owner Levy, who arranged a second exhibition of his friend's photographs, jointly with Alvarez Bravo and the American photographer Walker Evans, who was already a keen admirer of Cartier-Bresson. Staying in the Manhattan apartment of the composer Nicolas Nabokov (a cousin of the writer Nabokov), Cartier-Bresson spent much of his time during the day wandering the streets of Harlem with his camera, and at night visiting restaurants and nightclubs in the company of a black woman he was living with, along with other friends such as the writer Paul Bowles. Together they listened to a lot of jazz; his arresting portrait of Joe the trumpeter and his wife May dates from this time.

But, fond as he was of New York, if not so much of the United States—Cartier-Bresson would always photograph that country, especially its racial segregation, with ambivalence—he felt he was beginning to stagnate. Only one photograph in *The Decisive Moment* is credited to 'New York, 1935' (as opposed to eight from his second New York visit after the war). His ambitions now turned decisively away from photography towards filmmaking. Other French photographers—notably Marc Allégret, Maurice Cloche, Jean Dréville, and Robert Bresson—had gone into film-making. So had the New York photographer Paul Strand, who was at work on a documentary about fishermen in Mexico. Having learned something of shooting technique and editing from the radical, Russian-influenced Nykino group around Strand, Cartier-Bresson realized he was out of sympathy with Strand's liking for abstraction and Stalinism. Early in 1936, he got on a boat and returned to France.

Contrasting still photography with film-making in later life, Cartier-Bresson remarked: 'In photography...there is immediacy, and your subconscious and sensitivity grab the subject—it will never repeat itself. The eye takes its pleasure with the plastic rhythms, geometry of instant composition. Whereas in movies you give a shape, a montage. In film, as in music, time counts. Editing is the backbone, a musical rhythm just like a geometrical composition in photography and painting.'

Back in Paris, he offered his services as an assistant director to both Luis Buñuel and G. W. Pabst—without success. Then he prepared a selection of his European and Mexican photographs in an album and showed it to Jean Renoir, who immediately took him on and soon became a key influence on his life.

Between 1936 and 1939, with a gap in 1937–38 for his own documentary film-making, Cartier-Bresson assisted Renoir on three films: the propagandistic *La Vie est à Nous*, commissioned by the French Communist Party; the unfinished *Une Partie de Campagne*, based on a story by Guy de Maupassant; and the original screenplay *La Règle du Jeu*, often regarded as the greatest of all Renoir's films. It was a unique initiation into film-making, which Cartier-Bresson compared to an apprenticeship during the Renaissance. He did a bit of almost everything (except, oddly enough, cinematography): honing the dialogue before shooting, finding a chateau for filming, teaching the actors how to hunt with a rifle, acting before the camera as a young seminarian and as an English butler and, most importantly, maintaining the easily discouraged Renoir in a creative mood with good conversation and Beaujolais wine. Decades later, in an edition of Renoir's letters, Cartier-Bresson ended an appreciation of Renoir's genius with the perceptive comment: '[Jean] was not a specialist of anything except generosity, and life for him always came first. I owe him a great deal.'

Not least—the honest advice that he would never become a feature film director. Both Renoir and Cartier-Bresson knew that he lacked literary imagination; his understanding of time was inappropriate to storytelling in cinema. 'Because a great director must treat time as a novelist would, while the metier of a photojournalist is closer to a documentary film-maker', wrote Cartier-Bresson.

Even in his documentaries, the weakness lies in the structure, the strength in the compelling details of facial expressions, behaviour and personality, as in his photographs. Two of these documentaries were made in 1937–38 as propaganda for the Republican cause in the Spanish Civil War; the third, Le Retour, as a documentation of the massive return home of prisoners of war from Germany in 1944–45; while the remaining two were impressionistic sketches of life in California and the southern United States, made in 1969–70 for CBS News. All are now period pieces, though often fascinating and sometimes moving, especially Le Retour, which was inspired by his own wartime experience as a prisoner. But together they show why Cartier-Bresson was right not to pursue a career as a film-maker in the 1930s.

His lack of interest in still photography at this time is plain from the fact that he took not a single photograph on the sets of Une Partie de Campagne in 1936, and none of the Spanish Civil War while making his two documentaries in Spain in 1937–38, despite his heartfelt support for the Spaniards fighting Fascism. He soon regretted this lost opportunity—which brought fame to his friends Robert Capa and Chim (David Seymour) as war photographers; and this may partly have prompted a revival of his interest in photography, now as a form of journalism, rather than of art. Moreover, he needed income from selling photographs, having married Ratna Mohini, a Javanese dancer, in early 1937.

Two significant but very different illustrated publications were launched in Paris in 1937, both of which immediately used Cartier-Bresson's photographs. The first, Ce Soir, was an evening daily newspaper edited by Louis Aragon, the one-time surrealist who, after breaking with Breton, had become an ardent Communist. At Aragon's invitation, Cartier-Bresson became a staff photographer in 1937–38, working on daily news assignments, alongside Capa and Chim. Not all were worthy of his talents:

'I photographed *chiens écrasés* [run-over dogs] on a regular basis', he recalled— in other words, mundane news events. The second publication, *Verve*, was by contrast devoted to art, the avant-garde, and aimed to be the most beautiful magazine in the world. Its editor was Efstratios Eleftheriades, known as Tériade, a Francophile Greek from a business background, and a friend of Cartier-Bresson. In due course Tériade started Éditions Verve, a major art publisher in France, which conceived and published *Images à la Sauvette* (*The Decisive Moment*) in 1952.

However, the most memorable of Cartier-Bresson's reportages in the 1930s appeared in the left-of-centre weekly *Regards*. In May 1937, Cartier-Bresson covered the coronation of King George VI in London for *Regards*. But rather than showing the king and queen and the processions—the obvious thing to do—he photographed only the faces and actions of the London crowds. His best-known image, reproduced in *The Decisive Moment*, shows a mass of individuals, sitting and standing on a stone platform in Trafalgar Square, watching the unseen royal events, while down below them a man in a suit and scarf lies sleeping on the pavement in a sea of discarded newspapers. 'One wearier than the others had not yet wakened to see the ceremony for which he had kept such a late vigil', comments the caption at the back. The image is superb photojournalism, destined to be discussed and then discarded with yesterday's newspaper—yet it is also timeless in its subtle observation of human behaviour. Cartier-Bresson had the uncommon ability to achieve both aims in a single image, as he would go on to prove in the world after 1947.

With the outbreak of the Second World War in 1939, he was called up and eventually captured at the fall of France to the Nazis in June 1940. Not long before this, he had buried his Leica in a farmyard in the Vosges and sent his most important negatives to his parents for safe keeping. He took no photographs during his three-year captivity in Germany but managed to paint a little, while dreaming of becoming a painter after the war. It was a desperate period for him, which he seldom spoke of and then with visible emotion. Yet, he wryly reflected half a century on, given that photography involves considerable physical activity, and demands that the body and spirit be one, 'despite the inconvenience, it was useful for a young surrealizing bourgeois, during the three years of his captivity, to do some manual labour—pounding in railway cross-ties, working in cemeteries and auto-factories, washing grub in huge copper cauldrons, making hay. And all the time with one idea in mind: escape.'

Of the approximately 1,600,000 French prisoners transported to Germany in the war, some 70,000 escaped. Cartier-Bresson failed twice, but on the third attempt got free with a friend in February 1943. With forged papers and railway tickets obtained by an SS man from Alsace, they travelled to a farm in Indre-et-Loire, where they hid for three months along with ten others, including Resistance fighters and Jews. Soon after Cartier-Bresson left the hideout, it was betrayed to the Gestapo and its remaining occupants deported to Buchenwald, except for the farmer's wife.

The war changed his photography, Cartier-Bresson told a New York newspaper in 1946. 'I became increasingly less interested in what one might call an "abstract" approach to photography. Not only did I become more and more interested in human and plastic values, but I believe I can say that a new spirit arose among photographers in general; in their relationships not only to people, but to one another.'

Le Retour, the film he made about the return of prisoners during 1944–45, embodied this change. Even more so, the series of photo–portraits of French artists, writers, and thinkers he made for a publisher at this time, which the art historian E. H. Gombrich would compare with the 'sitters of Titian, Van Dyck, Rembrandt, or Velázquez'. Pierre Bonnard, Jean-Paul Sartre, and the Joliot-Curies, whom he photographed, all have extraordinary presence on the page.

Matisse, especially, has been forever fixed in our minds by Cartier-Bresson: whether he is drawing a white pigeon held in one hand, sitting at his easel in front of a buxom model, or gazing askance at a voluptuous vase by Picasso. Since Matisse was seriously ill and had no wish to be photographed, Cartier-Bresson succeeded only by very patiently and silently awaiting his moment, watching from a corner of the room for hours during regular visits, so that the artist forgot he was there. Having seen these classic photo–portraits, one can easily believe Matisse's crushing response when Cartier-Bresson summoned up the courage to show him one of his gouaches. Taking a box out of his pocket, Matisse held it to the top of Cartier-Bresson's painting, and remarked drily: 'My box of matches does not disturb me any more than what you have painted.'

In another anecdote reported by Cartier-Bresson, Bonnard, an even more reluctant subject who persistently tried to hide his face, broke the silence by asking the photographer: 'Why did you press the button at that precise moment?' Cartier-Bresson pointed at a detail in one of the painter's unfinished canvases leaning against a wall, and replied: 'Why did you put a little touch of yellow here?' Bonnard laughed, recognizing an ineffable truth about creativity.

Of course, Cartier-Bresson well knew that photography and painting actually proceed very differently. While the painter can make endless adjustments to his painting, the photographer must in the end choose and print a single image from his contact sheets—unless he is willing to crop or retouch, both of which were strictly taboo for Cartier-Bresson. Writing in 1991, he vividly described the experience of selecting photographs:

> The photographer's reading of the contact print, red pencil in hand, as it leaves the lab is for me like reading a seismograph, with highs and lows: calm, flattened by an uninteresting photo—but what was it that sparked me off? Move on. Ah! A slight jolt, yes, but it was badly composed. I was too far away or too close—go to the next one. Ugh, the subject has disappeared, the person's smile has vanished. One continues to read the 36 photos on the contact print, hoping to discover the image that brings everything together: form and emotion, and it's very rare…

At the end of the war in Europe in May 1945, word reached Cartier-Bresson via his photographer friend Chim that the Museum of Modern Art in New York had for some time been planning a 'posthumous' exhibition of his photographs, believing him to have died in captivity. After considerable negotiations via letter, and the completion of Le Retour, he travelled to New York in the summer of 1946 with some prints, purchased a scrapbook, pasted 346 images into it, and presented it to the curators of the exhibition, in order that a selection could be made.

Leafing through this scrapbook, which was reconstructed by the Fondation Henri Cartier-Bresson and posthumously published in 2006, one cannot help but be struck by how indecisive Cartier-Bresson was about his photographs in 1946—given his later towering reputation. Not only are there many mediocre images, by his standard, there are also a surprising number of excellent ones where he offers a patently inferior alternative or several inferior alternatives.

For example, there is absolutely no contest between the two portraits of Sartre on offer, showing the same expression on Sartre's face, the inferior of which is simply devoid of background and composition. And there is little contest among the 16 portraits of Matisse, at least half of which are mere repetitions. Perhaps most revealing of all, the scrapbook offers three photographs of the classic chance moment of exposure of a female Gestapo informer caught pretending to be a refugee in a displaced persons camp in

Germany in 1945. In *Le Retour*, the camera operator films this encounter in which another woman, a genuine refugee, suddenly recognizes the informer, and within seconds, overcome by rage, hits her full in the face. The film's director Cartier-Bresson, with his Leica and usual presence of mind, snapped the moment of recognition, too. It is one of his most powerful images—far more so than the act of violence almost casually depicted in the film. But instead of including this one image in the scrapbook, he offers two more that are much less well composed and without any of the pregnant confrontation of the first image: they show the dishevelled informer reeling under physical attack. ('Don't kill me, I will give their names', she cried out, according to Cartier-Bresson's note written on the back of one of the photos.) These two fractionally later images are of no more than documentary value. Perhaps Cartier-Bresson saw them as part of a picture story, a reportage, even so his inclusion of them surely suggests an unexpected indecision in 1946 about the initial, iconic, image—especially when it is viewed in the context of the many other inferior images in the scrapbook.

It was the success of the Museum of Modern Art exhibition in New York in February–April 1947 that gave Cartier-Bresson, by his own reckoning, the confidence to break through into full-time photography. Lincoln Kirstein, a leading New York arts critic, wrote an appreciation of his photographs in the MoMA catalogue, which perceptively noted: 'But the more he effaces himself, the more he ignores his particular Frenchness or contemporaneity, the more he becomes the crystal eye, the more his pictures sign themselves.' The New York exhibition with its catalogue is generally regarded as the 'decisive moment' of Cartier-Bresson's career; *The Decisive Moment* itself would essentially be a public revelation of all he had taught himself about photography between 1932 and 1946.

At the same time, Cartier-Bresson received some invaluable practical advice from his close friend Capa, with whom he founded the Magnum Photos cooperative in New York in May 1947, along with Chim, the Englishman George Rodger, and the American William Vandivert. As Cartier-Bresson explained in 1947 in a letter to the curator of photography at MoMA:

> Robert Capa warned me: 'Watch out for labels. They are reassuring. But people will attach one to you that you will not be able to remove. That of little Surrealist photographer' (since after all it was surrealism as a way of life that perhaps had the most influence on me, not surrealist painting). 'You will become precious and mannered. Continue in the way you are going,

but with the label of photojournalist, and keep the rest in your heart of hearts. This will place you directly in touch with what is happening in the world.'

Cartier-Bresson took Capa's advice. In 1947, he set off for Asia with his wife Ratna, and stayed away for three years. Working as a photojournalist for *Life* and many other magazines, he photographed the independence of India and Mahatma Gandhi a mere half an hour before Gandhi was assassinated, followed by his tumultuous funeral. He was present at the Chinese Revolution of 1949, where he captured the last days of the Kuomintang and the arrival of the Communists in Peking and Shanghai. He witnessed the birth of Indonesian independence in Djakarta. 'Contrary to the impression that Cartier-Bresson wandered the streets of the world discovering his photographs through a serendipitous conjunction of intuition and luck, the evidence at Magnum Photos shows he researched, planned, and positioned himself to take advantage of major events, and then worked hard to photograph them with great thoroughness', writes Claude Cookman, a professor of journalism whose research was assisted by Cartier-Bresson. At the same time, he captured the cultural, social, and religious traditions of India, China, Burma, Indonesia, Egypt, and other countries in photographs of astonishing beauty. All of these subjects found their way into *The Decisive Moment*, alongside his more experimental, less newsworthy, 1930s European and Mexican photographs, scenes of life in the United States in 1946–47, and 1940s portraits of famous individuals like Matisse, Sartre, and William Faulkner.

The book's brilliant introduction—Cartier-Bresson's sole sustained piece of writing about photography—was extracted from the reluctant photographer by his Paris publisher Tériade. The English title was chosen, also somewhat against his will, by the New York publisher Richard Simon. It comes from Cartier-Bresson's epigraph at the beginning of the book, taken from Cardinal Retz: 'There is nothing in this world without a decisive moment.' Near the end, Cartier-Bresson famously relates this idea to photography: 'To me, photography is the simultaneous recognition, in a fraction of a second, of the significance of an event as well as of the precise organization of forms which give that event its proper expression.' This was a valiant attempt to explain the inexplicable in words. The real proof of the statement's validity lies in *The Decisive Moment*'s miraculously enduring images.

CHAPTER 15

SATYAJIT RAY

Pather Panchali

The entire conventional approach (as exemplified by even the best American and British films) is wrong. Because the conventional approach tells you that the best way to tell a story is to leave out all except those elements which are directly related to your story, while the master's work clearly indicates that if your theme is strong and simple, then you can include a hundred little apparently irrelevant details which, instead of obscuring the theme, only help to intensify it by contrast, and in addition create the illusion of actuality better.

> Satyajit Ray, in a letter to his art director Bansi Chandragupta, 1950

When Satyajit Ray began the struggle to make his first film *Pather Panchali*, in 1950, cinema everywhere was dominated by film-makers from the West. The most popular successes were produced in Hollywood, directed either by Americans or by Europeans who had been attracted to Hollywood, such as Charles Chaplin, Alfred Hitchcock, Fritz Lang, Ernst Lubitsch, and Jean Renoir. Japanese films, although they already had a substantial record of artistic excellence, were still virtually unknown outside Japan. The Indian cinema, though prolific from the 1920s onwards, was invisible beyond the subcontinent, mainly because of its penchant for melodrama, mythology, and songs, its theatrical scripts, and its technical inadequacy.

Ray's Apu Trilogy—*Pather Panchali* (*Song of the Little Road*), *Aparajito* (*The Unvanquished*), and *Apur Sansar* (*The World of Apu*)—telling the story of the growth of Apu from child to man in the first half of the twentieth century, significantly reoriented this situation. Besides showing Indian civilization to the world for the first time on screen, the Trilogy offered a sophisticated alternative vision of cinema: one influenced by, but not imitative of, American and European films. It was a vision subsequently established by some 30 feature films made by Ray between the 1950s and 1991. Ray's admirers among his fellow directors ranged from Lindsay Anderson, James Ivory, and Martin Scorsese through Renoir and Michelangelo Antonioni to Akira Kurosawa. 'You cannot make films like this in a studio, nor for money', Anderson wrote of *Pather Panchali* from the Cannes Film Festival in 1956. 'Satyajit Ray has worked with humility and complete dedication; he has gone down on his knees in the dust. And his picture has the quality of intimate, unforgettable experience.' Kurosawa said in 1975: 'I can never forget the excitement in my mind after seeing it. I have had several more opportunities to see the film since then and each time I feel more overwhelmed. It is the kind of cinema that flows with the serenity and nobility of a big river.' In 1992, just before his death, Ray became the first Indian director to be awarded an Oscar by Hollywood—given for his lifetime achievement, in honour of his alternative vision, especially that of *Pather Panchali*.

Two further characteristics of Ray and his films are particularly remarkable, if not quite so unique. First, his versatility. Apart from film-making, he had a parallel career in Bengali as a best-selling story writer and illustrator, an editor of a children's magazine, and a composer of some highly popular film songs. Behind the camera, his versatility was almost unparalleled among film directors, as already noted in the preface. He wrote the scripts of his films; they were all solo efforts, and often original or near-original screenplays. As a trained illustrator and painter, he designed the sets and costumes (and even the publicity posters) down to the smallest details. He operated the camera throughout the shooting. He edited each frame of the film. He composed and recorded the music after scoring it in a mixture of Western and Indian notation (from 1962 onwards). He acted out the roles for the cast with consummate nuance, as his actors and actresses generally admitted. Short of acting in front of the camera like Chaplin (which he was invited to do by the Hollywood producer David O. Selznick), Ray was in direct charge of just about everything in his films: the very model of a film *auteur*. He liked to work in this way not because it helped to keep his budgets within manageable limits—although he had always to be keenly conscious of costs, given his comparatively small home audience in Bengal—but because then he could truly call his creations his own, in the same way as a novelist, a painter, or a composer can.

Second, he was completely self-taught, right from the beginning, like Renoir. Before starting *Pather Panchali*, he worked neither as an assistant director nor in any other capacity on films directed by others. The nearest he came to a film set was to watch a little shooting by Renoir, who happened to visit Bengal in 1949–50. 'I never imagined that I would become a film director, in command of situations, actually guiding people to do things this way or that', Ray said in the mid-1980s. 'No, I was very reticent and shy as a schoolboy and I think it persisted through college. Even the fact of having to accept a prize gave me goose-pimples. But from the time of *Pather Panchali* I realized that I had it in me to take control of situations and exert my personality over other people and so on—then it became a fairly quick process. Film after film, I got more and more confident.'

Ray was born, an only child, in Calcutta in 1921, into a distinguished though not wealthy family notable for its love of music, literature, art, and scholarship. His grandfather Upendrakisore Ray, who died in 1915, was a pioneer of half-tone printing, a musician, and composer of songs and hymns, and a writer and illustrator of classic children's literature. His father Sukumar was a writer and illustrator of nonsense literature, the equal of Lewis Carroll and Edward Lear. They regarded themselves as Brahmos, that is, Christian-influenced Hindus who rejected caste, idolatry, and the Hindu festivals, but not the teachings of the original Hindu scriptures. Although the adult Ray would regard the social reforming side of Brahmoism as generally admirable, he was not attracted to its theology (or to any other theology).

Of his grandfather Upendrakisore, one of whose stories Ray adapted to make a hit film, he wrote:

> My grandfather was a rare combination of East and West. He played the *pakhwaj* [drum] as well as the violin, wrote devotional songs while carrying out research on printing methods, viewed the stars through a telescope from his own roof, wrote old legends and folk-tales anew for children in his inimitably lucid and graceful style and illustrated them in oils, water-colours and pen-and-ink, using truly European techniques. His skill and versatility as an illustrator remain unmatched by any Indian.

Of his father Sukumar, who was the subject of a documentary film by Satyajit, he remarked: 'As far as my father's writing and drawing goes, nearly all his best work belongs to his last two and a half years'—that is, after his father contracted kala-azar ('black fever', a parasitic disease of the viscera), which eventually killed him in 1923 at the age of only 35.

Satyajit was less than two and a half years old then. He retained only one memory of his father. But he had many memories of the house in north Calcutta where he lived with his father's extended family until the age of five or six. It was designed and built by his grandfather as a house-cum-printing press. Here, apart from books written by the family, was printed *Sandesh* (a Bengali title meaning both 'news' and a kind of milk sweet famous in Bengal), the monthly children's magazine founded by Upendrakisore in 1913, edited by Sukumar after grandfather Ray's death, and revived, much later, in 1961, by Satyajit and other family members. 'Even today', wrote Ray in his memoir of his childhood published in *Sandesh* in 1981, 'if I catch a whiff of turpentine, a picture of U. Ray and Sons' block-making department floats before my eyes.'

In early 1927, however, the firm had to be liquidated, because there was no one in the family able to manage it competently. The joint family had no option but to leave the house and split up. Satyajit and his widowed mother were fortunate to be taken in by one of her brothers living in south Calcutta. When he was growing up he would never have much money. He did not miss it, though; and in adult life he would simply maintain the relatively spartan habits of his early years.

Although the move was a drastic change, Satyajit did not feel it as a wrench. Nevertheless, he was thrown back on his own resources. He had been taken from a world of writers, artists, and musicians, where West mixed freely and fruitfully with East, science with arts, into a typically middle-class milieu of barristers and insurance brokers, with the exception of his mother, an aunt about to become a famous singer of Rabindranath Tagore's songs and, a little later, a 'cousin' Bijoya, Ray's future wife, who was musical and interested in acting. There were no children of Satyajit's age in the new house. Yet in later life he did not think of his childhood as lonely: 'Loneliness and being alone—bereft of boys and girls of your own age as friends—is not the same thing. I wasn't envious of little boys with lots of sisters and brothers. I felt I was all right and I had a lot to do, I could keep myself busy doing various things, small things—reading, looking at books and looking at pictures, all sorts of things including sketching. I used to draw a lot as a child.'

Like the films he would make, the young Satyajit was very sensitive to sounds and lighting. Half a century later, he could remember various vanished street cries and the fact that in those days you could spot the make of a car, such as a Ford, Humber, Oldsmobile, Opal Citroen, or La Salle (with its 'boa horn'), from inside the house by the sound of its horn. Small holes in the fabric of the house taught Satyajit some basic principles of light. At noon in summer, rays of bright sunlight shone through a chink in the shutters of the bedroom. Satyajit would lie there alone watching the 'free bioscope' created on a wall by this pinhole camera: a large inverted image of the traffic outside. He could clearly make out cars, rickshaws, bicycles, pedestrians, and other passing things.

Stereoscopes and magic lanterns were popular toys in Bengali homes of the period. The magic lantern was a box with a tube at the front containing the lens, a chimney at the top, and a handle at the right-hand side. The film ran on two reels with a kerosene lamp for a light source. 'Who knows?' wrote Ray in his memoir. 'Perhaps this was the beginning of my addiction to film?'

Outings to the cinema began while he was still at his grandfather's house and continued at his uncle's house. Until he was about 15, when Satyajit took control, they were comparatively infrequent and each film would be followed by 'weeks of musing on its wonders'. Although his uncles enjoyed going, they did not altogether approve of the cinema and for many years restricted the boy to certain foreign films, ruling out Bengali productions as being excessively passionate for the young mind. This suited him well enough, as he had disliked the only Bengali film he happened to see.

In Calcutta cinema halls, these were the days of Silents, Partial Talkies, and One Hundred Per Cent Talkies. Chaplin, Buster Keaton, and Harold Lloyd made a tremendous and lasting impression on Satyajit. So did *The Thief of Baghdad* and *Uncle Tom's Cabin*. Other memories of Hollywood films seen at this time included:

> Lillian Gish, in *Way Down East*, stepping precariously from one floating chunk of ice to another while fiendish bloodhounds nosed along her trail; John Gilbert, as the Count of Monte Cristo, delirious at the sight of gold in a treasure chest; Lon Chaney, as the Hunchback, clutching with dead hands the bell ropes of Notre Dame, and—perhaps the most exciting memory of all—the chariot race in *Ben Hur*, undimmed by a later and more resplendent version, for the simple reason that the new Messala is no match for the old and dearly hated one of Francis X. Bushman.

One kind of film permissible to him that did *not* appeal, either to Satyajit or to his family, was the British film. Technical superiority notwithstanding, it was marred by the same faults that Ray would later ridicule in the typical Bengali film: stagey settings, theatrical dialogue, affected situations, and acting.

As the 1930s wore on, Ray saw films more and more frequently, including some Bengali ones. He began to keep a notebook with his own star ratings, and learnt to distinguish the finish of the different Hollywood studios. But at no point did he consider that he might direct films himself. This idea did not strike him until his late twenties, well after he had left college.

He also read a lot in these early years, but as with films he was mainly interested in books in English, not in Bengali, apart from the ancient stories and folk tales that as a young child he enjoyed hearing told in the Bengali versions of his grandfather and one or two other writers. His favourite reading was the *Book of Knowledge*, ten copiously illustrated, self-confidently imperial volumes, and later, the *Romance of Famous Lives*, which his mother bought him; there he first encountered Beethoven, and developed an adolescent taste for Western painting from the Renaissance up to the beginning of Impressionism. He also liked comics and detective stories, the *Boy's Own Paper*, Sherlock Holmes stories, and P. G. Wodehouse. Throughout his youth, and to a great extent in later life too, Ray's taste in English fiction was light, rather than classic.

And in his teens he developed yet another interest in the arts, one distinctly unusual for a Bengali: Western classical music. He already owned a hand-cranked Pigmyphone, given to him when he was about five. The song 'Tipperary' (which appears incongruously in *Pather Panchali*) and 'The Blue Danube' were two of the earliest pieces of music he played on it. Now he began listening to some other records, mainly by Beethoven, which happened to be in the house. His response, perhaps partly because he had been primed by his earlier reading, was one of immense excitement. Here was music that was completely new, totally unlike his grandfather's hymns, Tagore's songs that surrounded him, and the improvized Indian instrumental music he also listened to, if without much enthusiasm. With what little money he had, he started hunting for bargains in Calcutta's music shops and attending concerts of the Calcutta Symphony Orchestra, and he joined a gramophone club whose members were almost all Europeans and Parsees. Much later, in Bombay, he discovered a source of miniature scores and began buying them and reading them in bed. He taught himself Western musical notation partly by comparing the score with his phenomenal musical memory, which could retain a symphony once he had heard it three times or so. At this time, inevitably, all the music was on 78 rpm records and he discovered that 'although the top line [of the score] could be heard clearly enough, a great many details which one could *see* on the page were virtually inaudible in the recording'.

Ray was fascinated by the parallels between cinema and Western classical music—Sergei Eisenstein's films reminded him of Bach, Vsevolod Pudovkin's of Beethoven, for example—and he was certain that his love of Western music was of profound importance in structuring his own films. For example, Mozart's operas were a strong influence on the ensemble playing in his 1964 masterpiece *Charulata*. But he insisted: 'It is not as if I am thinking of music when I am writing the screenplay. It's a musical habit, which you find in many directors. I think Austrian and German directors show this tendency most—Lang and Lubitsch, for instance, and Billy Wilder.'

School, which he attended from the age of 9 to 15, meant comparatively little to Satyajit, though he was never unhappy or unpopular there. And the same was true of his college education at the best institution in Calcutta, Presidency College, studying first science and then economics, both with reluctance. As Ray admitted in his only major lecture, given in his early sixties: 'Erudition is something which I singularly lack. As a student, I was only a little better than average, and in all honesty, I cannot say that what I learnt in school and college has stood me in good stead in the years that followed...My best and keenest memories of college consist largely of the quirks and idiosyncrasies of certain professors.' Which is exactly how Ray portrays Apu's college days in Calcutta in his second film *Aparajito*.

It was his time at Shantiniketan—Tagore's university in a poor rural district of Bengal about a hundred miles from Calcutta, where Ray was a student of Indian and far Eastern fine art from 1940 to 1942—that was the part of his formal education that would have a genuine influence on the future course of his life. Shantiniketan reoriented him from the West towards the East. As he fascinatingly explained in his Calcutta lecture, 40 years later:

> My relationship with Shantiniketan was an ambivalent one. As one born and bred in Calcutta, I loved to mingle with the crowd in Chowringhee [the city's most famous thoroughfare], to hunt for bargains in the teeming profusion of second-hand books on the pavements of College Street, to explore the grimy depths of the Chor Bazaar for symphonies at throwaway prices, to relax in the coolness of a cinema, and lose myself in the

make-believe world of Hollywood. All this I missed in Shantiniketan, which was a world apart. It was a world of vast open spaces, vaulted over with a dustless sky, that on a clear night showed the constellations as no city sky could ever do. The same sky, on a clear day, could summon up in moments an awesome invasion of billowing darkness that seemed to engulf the entire universe. And there was the Khoyai [a ravine], rimmed with the serried ranks of tal trees, and the [river] Kopai, snaking its way through its rough-hewn undulations. If Shantiniketan did nothing else, it induced contemplation, and a sense of wonder, in the most prosaic and earthbound of minds.

In the two-and-a-half years, I had time to think, and time to realize that, almost without my being aware of it, the place had opened windows for me. More than anything else, it had brought me an awareness of our tradition, which I knew would serve as a foundation for any branch of art that I wished to pursue.

Ray's training as a painter at Shantiniketan—along with his first-hand, awed confrontation with the wonders of Indian art on a tour of the famous sites by third-class train in 1941–42—convinced him that he did not have it in him to be a painter. Like Henri Cartier-Bresson, whose 1930s photographs had already impressed him with their fusion of head and heart, Ray abandoned his training in fine art in his early twenties. He left Shantiniketan without completing the five-year course, and a few months later, in 1943, took a job as a commercial artist in Calcutta, with a British-owned advertising agency.

He started as a junior visualizer, and rapidly progressed to art director. His contribution to advertising imagery in India over the next decade or so was distinctive, if hard to define. Like all the best graphic designers, Ray combined visual flair with a feel for the meaning of words and their nuances. He brought to his work a fascination with typography, both Bengali and English, shared with his father and grandfather, which would regularly surface in his film credit sequences and film posters. He also introduced more calligraphy into advertising (and created the fully callig-raphic wedding invitation), as well as genuinely Indian elements: everyday details and motifs from past and present, emphatically not the limp, prettified borrowings from Hindu mythology he strongly disliked in what was then considered to be Oriental Art. But despite the fact that his work was widely appreciated, he detested dealing with philistine clients and soon yearned to break free of advertising and work only for himself.

In 1944, he began illustrating books and designing jackets, too. His very first illustrations were some woodcuts of simple vitality for an abridgement of *Pather Panchali*, a novel by Bibhutibhusan Banerjee, first published in the late 1920s and already regarded as a classic. Some of the scenes that appealed to him as an illustrator, such as the children Apu and Durga huddling together during a monsoon storm, found their way on to celluloid a decade later. Book design and illustration allowed him to experiment with a wide range of styles and techniques of drawing, painting, and typography, and gave him a growing familiarity with fiction in Bengali to offset his teenage predilection for English. Through illustrating he gradually acquired a clear sense of the strengths and weaknesses of Bengali literature from a cinematic point of view. He soon perceived that *Pather Panchali* could make a fine film.

Around 1946, Ray began writing film scripts as a hobby. He had acquired a copy of René Clair's published script *The Ghost Goes West* and also the 1943 anthology *Twenty Best Film Plays*, compiled by John Gassner and Dudley Nichols. When plans for a Bengali film were announced he would write a scenario for it, in fact often two scenarios—'his' way and 'their' way. In all, he wrote ten or twelve such scenarios. But as yet he had no thought of turning any of them into a film himself.

The analysis involved led to his first published film criticism, 'What is wrong with Indian films?', which appeared in a Calcutta newspaper in 1948. Anticipating the French polemics of *Cahiers du Cinéma* in the 1950s, Ray dissected the failure of Indian directors to grasp the nature of the medium, and concluded with a resounding manifesto: 'The raw material of cinema is life itself. It is incredible that a country that has inspired so much painting and music and poetry should fail to move the film-maker. He has only to keep his eyes open, and his ears. Let him do so.'

The Calcutta Film Society, founded by Ray with a small group of film fans in late 1947, at the time of Indian independence, started a bulletin, which he designed. They screened mainly Russian and European films. Actors, directors, and other film people visiting Calcutta, such as Pudovkin and Renoir, were invited to speak. In 1948, one of the group, intending to become a Hollywood-style director, bought the film rights to Tagore's novel *The Home and the World*, and embarked with Ray on an attempt to film it. Ray wrote a script and, along with Bansi Chandragupta as art director, they began looking for locations and properties, an actress to play Tagore's heroine, and a producer. But after some months the project collapsed, because Ray refused to make the changes to his script required by a potential producer. He felt 'like a pricked balloon' at the time, yet when he reread the screenplay in the mid-1960s, he decided it was 'the greatest good fortune the film was never made'. He could see 'how pitifully superficial and Hollywoodish' his tyro screenplay was.

The following year, Ray was able to be of considerable assistance to Renoir, who had come from his Hollywood 'exile' in search of locations and actors for his Indian film, *The River*. Ray described their meetings in an article for the British film magazine *Sequence*, published in early 1950. The encounter changed his life. It was not that Ray and Renoir were similar as personalities, rather that Ray recognized in Renoir a real film artist—the first he had come to know personally—and drew strength from the knowledge that such a person existed. 'Undoubtedly, it was Renoir who planted the idea of making a film in my mind', Ray recalled in 1991. 'He actually asked me if I were interested in becoming a film-maker. I found myself saying "yes".' They discussed the story of *Pather Panchali*, and Renoir warmly encouraged Ray to film it, simultaneously requesting him not to borrow from Hollywood films: 'If you could only shake Hollywood out of your system and evolve your own style, you would be making great films here.' While receiving the French Legion of Honour in Calcutta in 1989, Ray told the president of France that he had always considered Renoir to be his 'principal mentor'.

The shooting of *The River* began in late 1949 and continued through the first half of 1950. Bansi Chandragupta assisted Renoir's art director Eugene Lourié; Subrata Mitra, soon to be Ray's lighting cameraman, took stills. Ray himself was present as an observer on two or three weekends, but was unable to get further involved. His advertising job took up his weekdays, moreover his agency had made him a seductive offer of a period of training in London.

Of the roughly 100 films Ray saw during his four months in London in 1950, the revelation was Vittorio de Sica's neo-realist story of post-war poverty, *Ladri di Biciclette (Bicycle Thieves)*, made in Rome in 1948, which won an Oscar in 1949. 'It just gored me', Ray remembered. He came out of the theatre with his mind fully resolved on film-making. As soon he got home to Calcutta, he would go all out to find a sponsor for *Pather Panchali*, make the film, and give up his safe job in advertising. Hollywood be damned, 'I would make my film exactly as De Sica had made his: working with non-professional actors, using modest resources, and shooting on actual locations. The village which Bibhutibhusan [Banerjee] had so lovingly described would be a living backdrop to the film, just as the outskirts of Rome were for De Sica's film.' In a review of *Bicycle Thieves* written for the Calcutta Film Society's bulletin in 1951, in which he largely dismissed the other Italian films he had seen in London, Ray seemed virtually to describe his own future film *Pather Panchali*. 'Simplicity of plot allows for intensive treatment, while a whole series of interesting and believable situations and characters sustain interest.' He concluded that:

> *Bicycle Thieves* is a triumphant rediscovery of the fundamentals of cinema, and De Sica has openly acknowledged his debt to Chaplin. The simple universality of its theme, the effectiveness of its treatment, and the low cost of its production make it the ideal film for the Indian film-maker to study. The present blind worship of technique emphasizes the poverty of genuine inspiration among our directors. For a popular medium, the best kind of inspiration should derive from life and have its roots in it. No amount of technical polish can make up for artificiality of theme and dishonesty of treatment. The Indian film-maker must turn to life, to reality. De Sica, and *not* DeMille, should be his ideal.

Seeing *Bicycle Thieves* in London was an epiphany for Ray—a breakthrough moment that gave him the confidence to create his personal vision of cinema. This would turn out very differently from De Sica's vision, but from the first it shared the same conviction that a strong and simple theme about actual human behaviour, continually intensified by telling and contrasting details, was far more powerful on screen than the twists and turns of a slick plot about artificial behaviour, favoured by Hollywood. The seeds of his own film were sown by the Italian film in the soil of a mind prepared by years of exposure to Western and Indian literature, art, and music. Over five long years, mainly because of lack of funds rather than experience, they germinated; grew through a combination of conscious and chance nurture; and flowered as *Pather Panchali* in 1955.

The original novel by Banerjee has a plethora of characters. But the main ones, as in the film, are the growing boy Apu, his elder sister Durga, their mother Sarbajaya and father Harihar Ray, who is a priest, and his elderly distant relative Indir Thakrun. The sad history of Indir, who is about 75 when the main story begins, is described. She is very soon dead, treated with callousness by Sarbajaya, who cannot bear to share with her what meagre food she can scrape together for herself and her children; Durga's affection for the old woman cannot save her. The bulk of the novel is about the small family's struggle to survive in their ancestral home in the village. Durga dies of a fever, and the house decays beyond repair. Harihar goes away to earn money. Eventually, penury forces him to pull up his roots and leave the village. He, his wife, and Apu depart for Benares where their life continues; in fact, nearly a fifth of the novel takes place in the city. Ray incorporated this section into *Pather Panchali*'s sequel, *Aparajito*.

His adaptation involved drastic compression, elision, and omission of scenes in the novel, as well as occasional additions. Out of a seemingly random sequence of significant and trivial episodes, Ray had to extract a simple theme, while preserving the loitering impression created by the original. 'The script had to retain some of the rambling quality of the novel', commented Ray, 'because that in itself contained a clue to the feel of authenticity: life in a poor Bengali village does ramble.' Much of the power of the film lies in this calculated enriching of an elemental situation by contrasts: as Durga delights her old 'auntie' with a stolen fruit, her mother Sarbajaya ticks her off for taking it; as Indir Thakrun wanders off to die in the forest, Apu and Durga bubble with life; and as Harihar returns to the village, terribly overdue but happy because he is bearing gifts for his wife and children, Sarbajaya can think only of their child Durga, who has gone forever during her husband's absence.

Ray's principal challenge in filming his adaptation was, ironically enough—given the praise lavished on the film for its evocation of village life—to dispel his personal ignorance of village life. Unlike Tagore, and many other Bengali writers, Ray had been born and brought up almost entirely in the metropolis and had very little first-hand knowledge of rural life, apart from what he had seen in the villages around Shantiniketan as an art student. He had to invent ways to convey on screen the all-important atmosphere of Banerjee's novel. He beautifully depicted the problem in 1982, as follows:

> You had to find out for yourself how to catch the hushed stillness of dusk in a Bengali village, when the wind drops and turns the ponds into sheets of glass, dappled by the leaves of *saluk* and *sapla*, and the smoke from ovens settles in wispy trails over the landscape, and the plaintive blows on conch shells from homes far and near are joined by the chorus of crickets, which rises as the light falls, until all one sees are the stars in the sky, and the stars that blink and swirl in the thickets.

Most of his solutions arose from spending as much time as possible in the village near Calcutta chosen for the shooting, talking to the villagers (some of whom appear in wonderful cameos in *Pather Panchali*), sharing their tea and homemade sweets, sympathetically observing them and their environment and attentively listening to natural and man-made sounds. This last accounts for the adroit and utterly convincing soundtrack of the film: the way that a tall bamboo grove eerily creaks as the children discover their dying 'auntie', for example, or the way that the passing of a distant railway train through the night subliminally suggests to an alert Apu (who has never seen a train) the existence of a wider world, beyond their village. Some of Ray's best ideas occurred while waiting in the village for days, either for funds to arrive from the producer or for the weather to change in the film's favour.

Partly as a consequence, *Pather Panchali* never had a proper script. Unlike every other Ray film, there is no red cloth-bound shooting notebook for it, full of scribbled sketches of shot sequences. Instead, Ray had a treatment that he had started on board ship sailing from London to India in 1950 and, from early 1952, a sheaf of sketches of the most important shots in black ink that he eventually deposited at the Cinémathèque in Paris. Most of the film's dialogue, three-quarters of which came from the novel, he kept in his head. By showing producers these sketches, and telling them the story, he hoped to raise interest in a film with him as its (first-time) director.

Pather Panchali's financial problems are well known, even legendary, but they need not concern us here. In the end, desperate for some pilot footage to show to producers, Ray began shooting one weekend in October 1952 with his own money. He felt that the scene in which Apu chases Durga through a field of tall white *kash*—similar to pampas grass—and sees a steam train for the first time, would make a fine come-on for a producer. (It is now probably the most famous scene in the film.) But he did not appreciate just how tough a target he had set himself as a director. Some of the lessons it taught him concerned the correct use of camera and lenses, but one involved the direction of Apu. The boy, who had no experience of acting, was expected merely to walk in a halting way through the *kash* as if on the lookout for his lost sister Durga. 'Little did I know then that it was twice as hard to achieve impeccability in a shot like that than in a shot of, say, charging cavalry.' The first take was completely lifeless. So Ray decided to lay twigs in the boy's path at irregular intervals for him to step across, and instructed various assistants hiding in the *kash* on either side to call the boy at prearranged moments. Second take around, the boy turned his head each time he was called, walked irresolutely forward stepping on the twigs, and looked just right. 'It was perfect and I could shout "Eureka" for the discovery I had made about handling a child who was emphatically not a born actor.' Ray's perception of the way that De Sica handled the father in *Bicycle Thieves* (rather than the boy) helped, also, in giving him the confidence to direct his child actor as a puppet.

The entire shooting of *Pather Panchali* was a mixture of the premeditated and the improvized. Filmed in sequence, the second half is much more technically assured than the first half. It is abundantly clear from Ray's initial 1952 sheaf of sketches how much he improved his scenario by his more than two years of exposure to the locations during 1952–54. All the elements in the opening sequence of the film—Durga picking up fallen fruit and skipping home to Indir Thakrun, Sarbajaya drawing water wearily from the well, her suspicious neighbour watching her and then ticking off Durga for stealing the fruit—are there in the initial sketches; but in the film the inter-relationships are made more graphic because the neighbour actually *sees* Durga take a fruit and Sarbajaya is forced to overhear her caustic comments on the soundtrack.

One of the premeditated sequences was the passing away of Indir Thakrun. Her solitary dying, followed by the children discovering her body, was entirely Ray's invention; as Durga playfully shakes Indir's squatting form, it keels over and her head hits the ground with a sickening thud. This is the only scene at which the 80-year-old actress Chunibala Devi demurred—not because of the potential injury to her but because she felt Indir's death at the village shrine, as it is in the novel, would be more appropriate. Ray persuaded Chunibala both to do the scene his way and not to worry about hurting herself. He would always remember the mixture of elation and exhaustion on her face after taking this shot.

For Indir's funeral, which is not described in the novel, Ray again decided to be unconventional by avoiding the usual Hindu chant; in his experience there were always some people in an Indian audience who would feel obliged to join in. His aim was to invest the scene with beauty as well as sadness, rather than just making it grim. So he decided to have Indir Thakrun's body carried out on a bier at sunrise down a village path, to the accompaniment of her own familiar mournful song.

At five in the morning they were standing ready to shoot. When Chunibala arrived by taxi Ray plucked up his courage and broke the news to the old actress: 'Today we will carry you out on a bier.' She was not in the least put out. So they spread a mat on a bamboo bier, covered her with the new shawl that in the story she begs from a neighbour, and fastened everything securely with rope. There was a rehearsal and the funeral procession began. The shot complete, the bier was put down and the ropes untied. But Chunibala Devi did not stir. The team looked at each other. What could have happened? They were in a cold sweat. Suddenly they heard

Chunibala's voice—'Is the shot over? Why didn't anyone tell me? I'm still laying here dead!'

Another scene involving death was handled with less certainty by Ray. This is the return of Harihar to find his house ruined and his daughter dead, followed by Sarbajaya's breakdown. Her grief-stricken wail is expressed not by her own voice but by the four-stringed *tarshehnai* playing a passage of high-pitched notes in raga *Patdeep* (one of the many haunting and vivifying pieces of music selected for *Pather Panchali* by composer Ravi Shankar); the effect is to intensify Sarbajaya's grief and to transform it into something nobler and universal.

This substitution was not in Ray's mind at the time of shooting. The day before, he had written a note about the situation for the actress playing Sarbajaya, and on the day itself she recalled that he told her: 'Don't be afraid to distort your face. If it gets distorted, don't worry, just be normal, as it comes.' But in the editing room he came to feel that the scene required a 'special, heightened quality' not accessible to the naked voice. After adding the music he considered keeping the actress's crying sound too, but then decided it was ineffective in combination. He did not tell her, though; when she first saw the film, she jerked forward in surprise at that point. Yet although it disappointed her then, she soon felt that Ray's notion was a wonderful one. It is surely among the most searing scenes of agony in the cinema.

A tiny detail from the same sequence gives a good idea of how definite Ray's intentions in his first film normally were. When Sarbajaya first hears the returning Harihar calling out for his children, she is vacantly squatting, with her arm and a white bangle pressed against her cheek. Involuntarily, she reacts to her husband's voice and moves her arm; the bangle slips down slightly. The indifference of her gesture suggests just how indifferent to the world she has become. It took Ray seven takes to get the bangle to move exactly as he wanted it to.

He was also determined to get a typical village dog to trot along behind Durga and Apu as they follow an itinerant sweet seller. The dog he chose was fine in rehearsal but wholly uninterested under the camera's gaze. This time it took twelve takes, about a thousand feet of film, and a tempting sweet *sandesh* invisibly held out behind Durga's back, to make the dog perform properly.

Of the scenes that were wholly improvised, three are outstanding. First, there are the water skaters and dragonflies exploring the twigs and plants in the pond like Apu exploring his village; along with Ravi Shankar's expectant sitar playing on the soundtrack, they herald the coming of the monsoon. This intensely lyrical combination of image and music occurred to Ray only after the music had been composed.

Second, there is the train rumbling away from Apu and Durga into the distance leaving a swathe of black smoke against the white *kash* flowers. Five trains were used in shooting the scene. After the last had departed, Ray noticed the unusual spectacle produced by the smoke: 'Within seconds, the camera was set up and the shot taken in fast-fading sunlight. But I think that this last-minute improvization added a lot of beauty to the sequence.'

Lastly, there is Apu's accidental discovery near the end of the film of a necklace, which he instantly recognizes as the necklace stolen by his now-deceased sister from a neighbour long ago. Acting on the spur of the moment, Apu conceals the incriminating evidence by hurling it into the pond near the family house; the pond scum slightly opens and then slowly closes over the place where the necklace falls, like an eye, hiding Durga's shameful secret forever. The image is a delicate visual rendering of the same event described in the novel, where Apu hurls the necklace into a bamboo grove. This touch, along with the sight of a snake slithering into the recently deserted house—which is not in the novel at all—were Ray's two masterly solutions to the problem of how to hold his audience's interest once they know that Harihar and his family are about to abandon their ancestral village.

Ray had long been pondering how to handle the scene with the necklace, which he knew would not make sufficient impact if taken literally from the novel. The idea of using the pond scum struck him one day at the location when he, his art director, and his lighting cameraman were compelled to 'picnic' during a patch of wrong weather. While chatting, he was idly throwing pebbles into the pond without being aware of their impact on the surface scum. 'Suddenly I noticed this phenomenon happening.' Instead of a pebble, why not the necklace? He almost jumped up, tingling with excitement at the dramatic idea.

Lucky coincidence or creative association of ideas? It is not easy to decide. Certainly, Ray's mind was well prepared to associate the natural phenomenon with its expressive potential on screen—and he was also lucky. The moment is a perfect illustration of his view of creativity quoted in the preface: 'This whole business of creation, of the ideas that come in a flash, cannot be explained by science. It cannot. I don't know what can explain it but I know that the best ideas come at moments when you're not even thinking of it. It's a very private thing really.'

A perceptive reviewer of *The World of Apu*, the third part of the Apu Trilogy, wrote at the time of its New York release in 1960: 'The connoisseur must feel a kind of glow of surprised enthusiasm at the endless rightness of Ray's effects. If they seem in the beginning merely happy, the endless aptness soon makes clear that chance could have little place in the making of a work so beautifully controlled. Yet it is not entirely adequate to speak of control, rather a sort of constancy of inspiration.' Whatever the spark was for the scene with the necklace at the end of *Pather Panchali*, there is no doubt that the magic of Ray's first film derives from hundreds of such ideas carefully woven by its director around a strong and simple theme to create one of the century's great works of cinematic art.

PART III

PATTERNS OF GENIUS

CHAPTER 16

FAMILY MATTERS

Human genius has always been a problem for both environmentalists and hereditarians to understand. There have been families of genius, of course, the Bernoullis and the Bachs, the Darwins and the Huxleys, the musical Marsalis family. But it is the solitary genius, rising like a great oak in a forest of scrub and bramble, who challenges our understanding. Carl Friedrich Gauss, ranked with Archimedes and Newton as one of the 'Princes of Mathematics', had uneducated parents, his mother was illiterate, yet the boy had taught himself to read and do simple arithmetic by the time he was three years old.

David Lykken, 'The genetics of genius', in *Genius and the Mind: Studies of Creativity and Temperament*, 1998

A genius, as we know, has yet to beget another genius—despite the title of Francis Galton's founding study, *Hereditary Genius*. Great names like Shakespeare, Bernini, Newton, Beethoven, Faraday, Byron, Gauss, Tolstoy, and Cézanne, occur but once in the roll-call of genius; and even among the several distinguished individuals bearing the names Bach, Bernoulli, Darwin, or Tagore, there is only one generally accepted genius: Johann Sebastian Bach, Daniel Bernoulli, Charles Darwin, and Rabindranath Tagore. No geniuses are to be found in the ancestors or descendants of any of the ten exceptionally creative individuals in Part II.

By contrast, a distinguished creative family may beget a genius. The families that gave birth to these ten individuals cover a spectrum of distinction—from the most eminent, the Darwin/Wedgwood family, to the totally obscure, the ancestors of Champollion. In between, in diminishing order of relevance to the individual's particular genius, come the families of Ray, Woolf, Mozart, Curie, Cartier-Bresson, Wren, Einstein, and

Leonardo da Vinci, the last two of which offer no premonition of future genius whatsoever. As Einstein frankly observed in old age: 'Exploration of my ancestors...leads nowhere.'

Thus, Darwin was the grandson of two men distinguished in eighteenth-century science, the physician Erasmus Darwin and the potter Josiah Wedgwood, the first of whom was an important theorist of evolution; and the son of a well-known physician. Ray's grandfather Upendrakisore Ray and father Sukumar Ray were both celebrated artists and writers, who also ran a pioneering printing and publishing business in Calcutta, while several other members of the Ray family were talented in scholarship, literature, art, and music. Virginia Woolf came from a line of scholars and writers on her paternal side, the Stephens, most notably her father Leslie Stephen, and a maternal great-aunt was the photographer Julia Margaret Cameron. Mozart's father Leopold was a considerable musician, composer, and teacher, and there was also musical achievement on the maternal side of his family. Curie's grandfather was a professor of physics and chemistry, and her father and mother were noted educationists with a commitment to science. On the other hand, Cartier-Bresson's family ran a leading manufac-turing company and had no professional involvement with the arts apart from one of Cartier-Bresson's uncles, Louis, who was a prize-winning, if now forgotten, painter. Wren's father and uncle, leading churchmen, were not distinguished in mathematics and science, though they were versed in intellectual matters and scholarship, including science in the case of Wren's father. Einstein's family consisted of merchants and businessmen, admit-tedly with some practical interest in science and technology, but not at the forefront; his father's electrical supply company fell victim to more ad-vanced competitors. Da Vinci's paternal family were prosperous, if unim-portant, lawyers and landowners without any recorded interest in science or the arts, and his mother was an illiterate farmer's daughter. Champollion's father was an erstwhile itinerant pedlar, turned bookseller, whose wife was illiterate. Overall, one might say that about half of the ten individuals—Darwin, Ray, Woolf, Mozart, and Curie—had immediate predecessors who showed talents directly relevant to their genius, whereas the other half—Cartier-Bresson, Wren, Einstein, Da Vinci, and Champollion—did not.

A correlation between heredity and exceptional creativity is therefore problematic, although clearly some relationship between them does exist. What about an environmental influence, a role for parental upbringing? Here, too, we should expect to find some connection with genius.

One of the most interesting patterns among geniuses concerns the effect of the early loss of a parent. A remarkably high fraction of our ten individuals—nine out of ten—suffered the early loss of a parent. The illegitimate Leonardo, though his parents did not die young, was brought up by his grandparents from a very early age, as a result of the marriages of his father and then of his mother, soon after Leonardo's birth. Ray's father died when he was only two years old. Darwin lost his mother at the age of eight, Curie her mother when she was ten. Virginia Woolf's mother died when she was thirteen, Champollion's mother when he was 17, and Wren seems to have lost his mother in his teens (there is no reliable record). Mozart's mother, Woolf's father, and Einstein's father died when their children were in their early twenties. Only Cartier-Bresson in this group did not suffer premature parental bereavement.

This is no chance result. A survey of 699 famous historical personages conducted by the psychologist J. M. Eisenstadt in 1978, revealed that 25 per cent of them had lost at least one parent before the age of ten, 34.5 per cent before the age of 15, 45 per cent before the age of 20, and 52 per cent—more than half—before the age of 26. Famous instances include J. S. Bach, Robert Boyle, Coleridge, Dante, Antoine Lavoisier, Michelangelo, Newton, Peter Paul Rubens, Leo Tolstoy, and Richard Wagner, who each lost one or both parents in their first decade; and Hans Christian Andersen, Beethoven, Humphry Davy, Edgar Degas, Fyodor Dostoevsky, Handel, Hooke, Victor Hugo, Tagore, and Mark Twain, who each lost one or both parents in their second decade. Certainly, these mortality figures tell us nothing definite about orphanhood and genius without access to the mortality figures for the general population during the same period; and such estimates of life expectancy are tricky to make until we reach quite recent times. But they are supported by figures from the early twentieth century, such as a survey of eminent American scientists by Anne Roe in 1953, which tend to show that the death of a mother or both parents by the age of 15 is around three times more frequent (26 per cent) among the eminent than among the general population (8 per cent). That is about the same relative frequency of early parental mortality as for those who become delinquents or suicidal depressives, compared to the general population.

This naturally raises the issue of why some children become stronger through the loss of a parent, while others are weakened and even destroyed. In the words of Winston Churchill (whose father Randolph died tragically in 1895, when his son was 21): 'Solitary trees, if they grow at all grow strong; and a boy deprived of a father's care often develops, if he escapes the perils of youth, an independence and vigour of thought which may restore in after life the heavy loss of early days.' Virginia Stephen suffered her first nervous breakdown as a result of her mother's early death in 1895, followed by a period of excruciating tension with her widower father that eventually precipitated her next breakdown after his death in 1904. What was it in her that permitted her to recover, at least for a while, and make a career as a writer, rather than withdraw into despair and creative sterility, or worse, in her formative years?

The reasons are no doubt complicated, and different for different individuals, according to their development and circumstances at the time of their bereavement. Ray had only a single, if sharply etched, memory of his father; Darwin noted in old age that as a child he was barely aware of his mother's death; Champollion appears to have been indifferent to his mother's dying; Curie sank into a profound depression after her mother died; Einstein was dazed with desolation and guilt by his father's death, and later called it the deepest shock he had ever experienced; Mozart was so overwhelmed by his mother's death that he wanted to die beside her in Paris. The response to the early death of a parent must inevitably involve a mixture of conflicting emotions and motives, ranging from anxiety to anger, from an urge for self-preservation and security to a desire for self-advertisement and love. But why should creativity sometimes emerge from this experience of youthful trauma?

Various explanations have been proposed by psychologists. One suggestion is that creative achievement, delinquency, and suicide should all be viewed as dissatisfied responses to the society that took away the life of the parent. By criticizing or attacking existing social beliefs and practices, creative achievement enables an individual to develop in an independent, nonconformist way, rejecting society's rules and regulations. Another suggestion is that creative production offers an outlet for coping with feelings of isolation, sadness, guilt, and unworthiness arising from abandonment by the deceased parent, which would otherwise prove self-destructive. A third possibility is that the admiration, prestige, and power that can derive from creative achievement may allow achievers to manipulate and dominate those around them, so that they feel in control of their destiny and can protect themselves from receiving further shocks. The psychiatrist and psychoanalyst Karen Horney proposed that the possible reactions to early bereavement have three basic goals. In 'turning towards people', the individual solicits their love, approval, admiration, and protection—quite like

Darwin; in 'turning away from people', he or she withdraws and seeks
independence and self-sufficiency, perfection, and unassailability—rather
like Einstein; lastly, in 'turning against people', he or she seeks power,
prestige, and domination, or exploits them—definitely like Newton and
perhaps also Leonardo. Creative achievement is capable of bringing all
these goals within reach of individuals. Those in Part II exhibit Horney's
three reactions in varying proportions. As the psychologist Mihaly Csikszentmihalyi sums up, in his study of creativity based on interviews in the
1990s with nearly 100 creative individuals (12 of them Nobel laureates):

> While creative adults often overcome the blow of being orphaned, Jean-
> Paul Sartre's aphorism that the greatest gift a father can give his son is to die
> early is an exaggeration. There are just too many examples of a warm and
> stimulating family context to conclude that hardship or conflict is necessary
> to unleash the creative urge. In fact, creative individuals seem to have had
> either exceptionally supportive childhoods or very deprived and challen-
> ging ones. What appears to be missing is the vast middle ground.

Other surveys nevertheless suggest a preponderance of deprived over
supportive childhoods among the highly creative. A study of 400 eminent
historical figures, *Cradles of Eminence*, published in 1962 by the psychologists
Victor and Mildred Goertzel, found that 75 per cent of the eminent had
suffered broken homes and rejection by their parents. More than one in
four had a physical handicap. A later study of 300 eminent figures from the
twentieth century (mentioned in the introduction), also by the Goertzels,
found an even higher incidence, 85 per cent, of very troubled home
backgrounds—highest (89 per cent) among novelists and playwrights, lowest (56 per cent) among scientists. It is also the case that literary Nobel
laureates come more often from poor backgrounds than scientific laureates,
and suffer more physical disabilities than them. 'From the evidence, one may
indeed go so far as to suggest that creators typically suffered some deprivation and distress in childhood', writes R. Ochse. 'Some were bereaved of
parents, some were rejected, some were sternly disciplined. Some were
exposed to emotional tensions, financial insecurities, or physical hardships.
Some were overprotected, lonely, or insecure, and some were ugly, deformed,
or physically disabled. Many suffered several of these hardships in
combination.'
    Anecdotal evidence from novelists tends to confirm this picture, even
after making due allowance for the embellishment of childhood memories
by a sensitive adult writer. Charles Dickens's childhood misery is legion.

Woolf's home was highly troubled after the death of her mother, as already described. Joseph Conrad recalled his childhood between the ages of eight and twelve—that is, between the deaths of his mother and his father from tuberculosis—as follows: 'I don't know what would have become of me if I had not been a reading boy. My prep finished, I would have nothing to do but sit and watch the awful stillness of the sickroom flow through the closed door and coldly enfold my scared heart. I suppose that in a futile childish way I would have gone crazy. Often, not always, I cried myself into a good sound sleep.' Anton Chekhov, who was the son of a struggling grocer who had been born a serf, had painful, though creatively productive, memories of childhood. 'Despotism and lies so disfigured our childhood that it makes me sick and horrified to think of it', he wrote. 'I remember father began to teach me, or to put it more plainly, whip me, when I was only five years old. He whipped me, boxed my ears, hit me over the head, and the first question I asked myself on awakening every morning was "Will I be whipped today?" I was forbidden to play games or romp.'

The idea that genius is nurtured by such extreme childhood circumstances—whether of adversity and conflict or support and love—is a tempting one. It is easy to believe that exceptional creativity must be the product of exceptional emotions. However, the home environments of the ten individuals in Part II only partially confirm the validity of this simple picture, while at the same time complicating it.

At one extreme, Leonardo unquestionably suffered from extreme parental neglect, since he was abandoned by his father and mother in infancy, except for his father's valuable introduction of the teenager to Andrea del Verrocchio and his studio. At the other extreme, Mozart was cosseted by his father, mother, and sister, during his every waking minute from infancy until his early twenties. Through his father's full-time tuition and promotion, Mozart's music-making was given every available encouragement to flourish. Einstein, however, occupies the middle ground, mentioned by Csikszentmihalyi, so far as his immediate family were concerned: neither much neglected nor much encouraged. At no point did Einstein's parents or close relatives discourage his teenaged interest in mathematics and theoretical physics, but neither did they greet it with enthusiasm (there are no letters to his father about physics, for example)—that was left to others, outside the Einstein family circle. Darwin also occupies the middle ground. Though certainly not discouraged by his physician father from indulging his childhood interest in collecting natural objects, Darwin was at first nudged towards a career in medicine, and when this foundered at Edinburgh, a career in the church. Only later, after leaving Cambridge, was he generously supported by his father as a naturalist on the *Beagle*. And the same was true of Cartier-Bresson. When he failed to shine academically at school, and showed no inclination whatsoever towards a business career in the family firm, his parents, without great enthusiasm, agreed to help him train as an artist, which soon became a key element in his success as a photographer, despite parental disapproval.

Rather than allotting the ten either a 'deprived' or a 'supportive' childhood, it is truer to say there was a tension or conflict between deprivation and support for each of the developing individuals, which seems to have proved creative for their work.

To oversimplify, the young Leonardo lacked parental love and direction, but enjoyed unusual freedom to explore, both literally in Vinci and Florence, and also figuratively in art and science. The Wren family's involvement with King Charles I and the royalist cause deprived Wren of a normal childhood during the English Civil War and its turbulent aftermath, but made possible his later architectural career as the royal architect and builder of St Paul's. Mozart's fanatical supervision by his father hampered his development as an autonomous individual, but allowed him to blossom as a musician and performer; only when he broke with his father in his mid-twenties could he realize himself fully as a composer. Champollion's dearth of support from his parents developed the independence of mind, fostered by his elder brother, which allowed him to challenge received opinion on ancient Egypt. Darwin's youthful differences with his father about his choice of career had the same effect, giving conviction and breadth of vision to his work as a naturalist. Curie (somewhat like Wren) was deprived of important educational opportunities by her family's opposition to the Russian occupation of Poland, but this adversity, and her father's devoted support, made her more resourceful and determined to succeed as a scientist. Woolf's intimate struggle with her father's domineering personality, and her home-based education (unlike that of her brothers), gave her the material and the self-discipline required for her later writing. Einstein's lack of intimacy with his parents, and his rebellion against their choice of school and their conventional social values, helped to prepare the ground for his revolutionary transformation of physics. The same was true of Cartier-Bresson and his innovations in photography, although Cartier-Bresson received more parental support than Einstein. Ray, too, despite lacking the encouragement of his artistic father (who died when he was very young), eventually rebelled against the conventional expectations of his mother and her family, in choosing to leave art school and become a commercial artist and then a film-maker, but he nonetheless enjoyed the lifelong support of his mother.

Support is a social act, which raises a further general aspect of family and genius: the question of sociability versus solitude in exceptional creativity. The historian Edward Gibbon wrote in his memoirs that: 'conversation enriches the mind, but solitude is the school of genius'—and it is clear that most geniuses have agreed with this. However useful others may have been in stimulating the mind, their best ideas came to them when alone. The statue of Newton in the chapel of Trinity College Cambridge is, according to Wordsworth's *Prelude*, 'the marble index of a mind forever Voyaging through strange seas of Thought, alone'. Edison, although acutely conscious of the importance of societal demand and marketability in inventing, said: 'the best thinking has been done in solitude'. Pierre Curie wrote in his youthful diary (as reported by Marie Curie): 'Whenever, rotating slowly upon myself, I attempt to speed up, the merest nothing—a word, a story, a newspaper, a visit—stops me, prevents my becoming a gyroscope or top, and can postpone or forever delay the instant when, equipped with sufficient speed, I might be able to concentrate within myself in spite of what is around me.' Wagner noted that: 'isolation and complete loneliness are my only consolation and my salvation'. Byron stated: 'society is harmful to any achievement of the mind'; and his friend Coleridge blamed 'a person on business from Porlock' for stymying the dream-induced composition of his poem 'Kubla Khan'. Naipaul believed: 'Writing comes from the most secret recesses of the person, and the writer himself does not know those recesses. So it's a kind of magic.' Tagore captured the general desire of great creators to be alone when creating in a letter written from his solitary houseboat on the Ganges to his favourite niece in Calcutta. 'Where the outside world with its flow of incident is not constantly employed in checking on my daily activities, moments become hours and hours moments, as in a dream', he wrote. 'And then it seems to me that the subdivisions of time and space are figments of my mind. Each atom is immeasurable and each moment infinite.'

Our ten individuals and their creative breakthroughs add further support to this picture of solitary genius. Leonardo worked alone on *The Last Supper*, as we know from a contemporary account of his standing on the scaffolding before the painting, lost in thought for hours and even days. Wren, as an architect, naturally held regular discussions with his craftsmen, but, being his own engineer, he kept his design for the dome of St Paul's almost entirely to himself. Mozart was often exuberantly sociable, but when composing a major work like *The Marriage of Figaro*, he shared little with his librettist Lorenzo da Ponte, shut himself away at home, and became abstracted from his surroundings, according to his wife. Champollion worked almost entirely alone on the decipherment of Egyptian hieroglyphic writing, and only after his breakthrough revealed his results to his beloved brother before collapsing with exhaustion. Darwin kept his theory of natural selection secret, even from his wife, for more than five years after he first noted it down. Einstein formulated special relativity after intense discussion with friends, but his crucial thinking and calculating were done in isolation. Woolf, more than most writers, spent long periods alone with her thoughts while writing novels such as *Mrs Dalloway*, showing her work to her husband Leonard only on completion of a draft. Cartier-Bresson virtually always worked alone while shooting, and ruthlessly edited his contact sheets before permitting others to exhibit or publish his photographs in books such as *The Decisive Moment*. Ray, as a film-maker, obviously collaborated with his technical team and actors, but always wrote his own scripts unaided and kept almost all the major creative decisions on his films, including *Pather Panchali*, in the privacy of his shooting notebooks or in his head. Only Curie may be said to have collaborated as a matter of course, with her husband Pierre. However, the original discovery of a new radioactive element, polonium, was made by her alone (and named in honour of her native Poland); only after this discovery occurred was she joined by Pierre in a joint effort to isolate radium.

So much for solitary geniuses in adulthood. Are they solitary in childhood, too? According to Ochse, they tend to be. 'Another recurrent theme in the literature on the childhood of creative achievers is social isolation and loneliness', he writes. 'Many creative achievers were isolated from other children because of restrictions placed upon them by parents; illness; constant movement of the family from one community to another; lack of siblings; or natural shyness. For whatever reason, it seems that creators typically engaged in solitary activities in childhood.' Conrad, for example, was an only child, forced to leave his native Poland at the age of four with his mother when his patriot father was exiled to the harsh climate of northern Russia, and then orphaned by the deaths of both parents.

By and large, this picture is borne out by our ten individuals, if with some notable exceptions. During their early years, Cartier-Bresson, Champollion, Curie, Darwin, Einstein, Ray, and Woolf, though they at times enjoyed company, liked to spend long periods alone. Mozart, on the other hand, seems to have been naturally sociable, when not practising his instruments. Little is recorded of Wren's youth, but he was apparently sometimes sociable, judging from his participation, aged about 15, in the weekly meetings of men interested in science. About Leonardo, so little is known of his childhood and early youth that it is impossible to make a reliable assessment; perhaps suggestive of a solitary disposition is that he never mentions his master Verrocchio in his notebooks.

To give some detail, Cartier-Bresson's youthful passions were for solitary activities: painting, reading, and watching silent films. He had very little interest in competitive sport, and when he took up scouting, he was nicknamed 'Slippery Eel', because he was always trying to run away. Champollion taught himself to read and very early on focused his attention on books, from which he began to learn ancient languages with the help of his elder brother and a few specialist scholars—so dedicatedly that he damaged his eyesight while trying to read secretly at night in his boarding school dormitory. Curie, though an active member of her substantial family and a star pupil at school, reserved her main energies for solo reading and study as a girl. Young Darwin, while part of a large family and with many school friends, had a solitary streak, evident in his strong taste for long hours spent in angling by the river and walking alone in the countryside. Einstein's love of 'private study' recurs throughout his early life, and enabled him to calculate even when he was surrounded by noisy company. From early on, he had an aversion for taking part in any kind of formal group activity. Ray, who had no siblings of his own age, filled his childhood with drawing, reading, looking at pictures, listening to music, and observing the passing scene, including the somewhat childish behaviour of his mother's family. Although as an adult he accepted that he was undoubtedly a solitary child, he did not feel that he had been lonely. Woolf was of course a voracious reader as a child, and spent long periods of her youth alone restlessly comparing the disconnected social and intellectual worlds, downstairs and upstairs, in her parents' London house. Even Mozart, for all his childhood love of performing, could be solitary as a child. In one telling incident on tour in 1765 when he was nine, his bedridden sister Nannerl lay close to death from a fever, watched over by her anxious parents, while 'little Wolfgang in the next room was amusing himself with his music', as noted by Leopold.

Thus, collaboration and teamwork tend not to be a feature of the lives of the exceptionally creative—inconvenient though this fact may be for advocates of 'brainstorming' and 'group creativity' in commercial companies and other institutions. Genius does not sit well on committees. It perhaps goes without saying that the greatest poetry, novels, paintings, music, and even films, are almost always the vision of one person—hence the fact that the Nobel Prize for literature has almost always been awarded to a single individual. Plainly this is not true of science and scientific Nobel Prizes. Science is by its very nature collaborative, particularly in recent decades; and there have been some celebrated scientific partnerships, such as Marie Curie with her husband Pierre Curie, William Bragg with his son Lawrence Bragg (X-ray crystallography), Francis Crick with James Watson (the molecular structure of DNA), and Michael Ventris with John Chadwick (the decipherment of Linear B). Yet, it is still the case that the most revered scientists—Galileo, Newton, Faraday, Darwin, Einstein, and some others—have published their most important work alone.

The roles of partners and offspring provide the final pattern in considering family and genius. Whatever their real talents may have been, the wives, husbands, and children of geniuses have typically seemed insubstantial or totally forgotten figures in the eyes of posterity. In encyclopaedias and reference books, they are often relegated to a mere sentence or phrase, if that, even in the case of Darwin, some of whose sons distinguished themselves in science. Perhaps this is inevitable, especially when they try to achieve in the same domain as their eminent partner or parent, as Leonard Woolf did in fiction and Mozart's second son, also called Wolfgang Amadeus, did in musical performance. (Einstein's first son Hans Albert deliberately avoided theoretical physics, and became a hydraulic engineer.) Such partners and children will always be compared and found wanting. Our ten geniuses mainly, yet not wholly, conform to this picture.

Leonardo, of course, had no wife or child; he appears to have lived with a younger man who had no part in his work. The wives of Wren (who married again after the premature death of his first wife), and Champollion, played no role at all in their achievements. However, Wren's son Christopher assisted in the later stages of building St Paul's and compiled the important memoir of the Wren family, *Parentalia*. Champollion's only child, a daughter, was undistinguished. The wives of Cartier-Bresson, Darwin,

Einstein, Mozart, and Ray, all had at least some creative input into their work, despite two of their marriages—Cartier-Bresson's and Einstein's—ending in divorce. Cartier-Bresson's first wife Ratna Mohini, a Javanese dancer, opened doors into Eastern cultures for him during his visit to India and the Far East in 1947–50, which led to some classic photographs in *The Decisive Moment*. Darwin's loyal wife, Emma Wedgwood, 'the patient ghost behind his never-ending struggle for perfection' (Janet Browne's words), acted as a significant and necessary editor of his often tangled prose, including *On the Origin of Species*, and discussed many of his ideas with him, challenging though they were to her religious beliefs. Einstein's first wife, his former classmate in physics Mileva Marić, helped him with some calculations in the early stages of special relativity. Mozart's wife, Constanze Weber, a trained and gifted singer who sang a solo in a Mozart mass, though not herself a composer, was intimately involved in his composing and performing; she also organized the publication of his manuscripts after his death. Ray's wife, Bijoya Das, also musical, assisted him with costumes and make-up, and read every screenplay in draft, often suggesting significant changes, which Ray generally incorporated. In addition, his son Sandip Ray ably assisted with camera operation, and in due course became a film-maker himself.

This leaves two obvious exceptions: Curie and Woolf. Both of them married important creative figures, each of whom played a wholly atypical role as partners of genius. Collaboration with Pierre Curie brought out the best in Marie Curie—a fact openly recognized by her and the Swedish Academy in its award of the Nobel Prize for their joint discovery of radium. Leonard Woolf was, if anything, even more crucial to Virginia Woolf. A sensitive and honest critic and editor of her work (judging from her comments on him in her diary), Leonard saved her from suicide when she was writing her first novel, *The Voyage Out*. In her much-quoted last letter, before she drowned herself in the river in 1941, Virginia told him:

> What I want to say is that I owe all the happiness of my life to you. You have been entirely patient with me and incredibly good. I want to say that—everybody knows it. If anybody could have saved me it would have been you. Everything has gone from me but the certainty of your goodness. I cant go on spoiling your life any longer. I dont think two people could have been happier than we have been. V.

CHAPTER 17

PROFESSOR OF THE LITTLE FINGER

It is quite strange how little effect school—even high school—seems to have had on the lives of creative people. Often one senses that, if anything, school threatened to extinguish the interest and curiosity that the child had discovered outside its walls. How much did schools contribute to the accomplishments of Einstein, or Picasso, or T. S. Eliot? The record is rather grim, especially considering how much effort, how many resources, and how many hopes go into our formal educational system.

Mihaly Csikszentmihalyi,
Creativity: Flow and the Psychology of Discovery and Invention, 1996

E xceptional creativity and breakthroughs have long had an uneasy co-existence with formal education. Some exceptional creators enjoyed their school days, but the majority did not. Only a small minority went on to become highly educated by taking doctoral degrees. Some important breakthroughs have emerged from colleges and universities, notably in the sciences, but on the whole they have not. None of the ten breakthroughs discussed in this book came from someone working in an established university; and only three of them, those by Champollion, Curie, and Wren, had any connection with academia—formal or informal. Mark Twain's quip remains pertinent: 'I have never let my schooling interfere with my education.' So does Cartier-Bresson's, mentioned earlier, when refusing an honorary doctorate: 'What do you think I'm a professor of? The little finger?' Thomas Young stated, more prosaically, after studying at three leading universities (Edinburgh, Göttingen, and Cambridge): 'Masters and mistresses are very necessary to compensate for want of inclination and exertion: but whoever would arrive at excellence must be self-taught.' Darwin, Einstein, and many other geniuses, firmly agreed.

In 2000–02, the BBC broadcaster and arts administrator John Tusa interviewed on radio about a dozen figures well known in the arts about their creative process, and later published the conversations in full in his collection *On Creativity*. They were: the architect Nicholas Grimshaw; the artists Frank Auerbach, Anthony Caro, Howard Hodgkin, and Paula Rego; the photographer Eve Arnold and the film-maker Milos Forman; the composers Harrison Birtwhistle, Elliott Carter, and Gyorgy Ligeti; the writers Tony Harrison and Muriel Spark; and the art critic and curator David Sylvester. Their formal education varied greatly, from ordinary schooling in the case of Arnold and Sylvester to Carter's doctoral training in music and subsequent academic appointments. There was nothing in what they said of their careers to indicate that a basic education, let alone a university degree, is a requirement in order to be a creative person, Tusa concluded.

A much larger sample of the exceptionally creative—nearly 100 individuals—were interviewed, as remarked in the previous chapter, by the psychologist Mihaly Csikszentmihalyi, who is based at the University of Chicago. Unlike Tusa's subjects, Csikszentmihalyi's interviewees included, as well as those eminent in the arts, many scientists, mostly working in universities, some of whom were Nobel laureates. Their school days were rarely mentioned by any of them as a source of inspiration. In some cases, extracurricular school activities were remembered, for example, the literary prizes won by the writer Robertson Davies or the mathematical prize won in a competition by the physicist John Bardeen. Some inspiring individual teachers were also recalled, though chiefly by the scientists. But overall, Csikszentmihalyi was surprised by how many of the interviewees had no memory of a special relationship with a teacher at school.

This picture of schooling is strongly confirmed by the ten exceptionally creative individuals in Part II. None of them can be said to have embraced school education. One has to look hard in their records and recollections for any sign of their time at school as a creative spark for their later achievements.

Leonardo and Wren, it is true, offer meagre evidence of their early education. We do not even know whether or not Leonardo was sent to school in Vinci. He must have had some rudimentary tuition, other than from his relatives. Absence of evidence is not evidence of absence, but it would seem odd that Leonardo should make no mention of school in his voluminous writings, if it really was a stimulating experience. Wren was sent as a boarder to Westminster School in London for less than five years, between the ages of about nine and thirteen—the very years of the English Civil War—after which he was removed by his father, because in 1646 the capital had become too dangerous for the son of a well-known royalist. The school's headmaster, Richard Busby, was a staunch royalist and stern disciplinarian, who thrashed boys at the least provocation, especially if they showed any inclination towards the parliamentary cause. Only one letter by Wren survives from this period, written to his father in what appears to be a Latin exercise on his tenth birthday, and it reveals nothing at all of his attitude to his school. In adult life, Wren never spoke of his school days. Again, we are surely justified in assuming that they were not an enlightening experience.

Mozart, as everyone knows, never went to school; he was educated entirely at home under his musician father's direction. Although he is often cited as an example of the benefits of home education, along with such child prodigies as Blaise Pascal and John Stuart Mill, there are counterexamples. The composer Hector Berlioz, home educated by his cultured physician father as a result of the disruption of the Napoleonic wars, was discouraged from learning music (his father wanted him to study medicine), and had to teach himself. Virginia Woolf, educated by her father Leslie Stephen and by her own efforts, had ambivalent feelings about her home education, which undoubtedly shaped her entire body of fiction and non-fiction. One cannot avoid the feeling that a university education—like that of her two unremarkable brothers—would have diluted or even destroyed her uniqueness as a writer. 'No proper study has been reported which would assign home environment a proper place and weight in the histories of geniuses', notes Hans Eysenck in his *Genius: The Natural History of Creativity*. Much must clearly depend on the individuals in question.

Champollion is a particularly instructive example of the effects of both self-education and school on exceptional creativity. In the small town of his birth, Figeac, he was home educated, mostly by self-teaching, but partly by his elder brother, hardly at all by his parents, until the age of eight. Then the local primary school reopened in 1798, in the aftermath of the French Revolution. He was sent there for a short period, until it became clear that the mechanical teaching did not suit him. Some subjects were too easy for him, while others, especially mathematics, went over his head—as with many a gifted child. His brother had him taken away from the school and put in charge of a private tutor, a former Benedictine monk, for two years. One-to-one, he made good progress in Latin and Greek, and displayed his gift for languages and linguistics, along with the mood swings that would characterize his adult life. 'There are days when he appears to want to learn everything, others when he would do nothing', his tutor told his brother, as mentioned before. Then, aged eleven, in 1801 he was transferred to the city of Grenoble and became a boarder at the government *lycée*, even though his brother could barely afford the expense. (Champollion therefore lacked for shoes, clothes, and books.) This institution he hated and wanted to run away from—and yet, he became its star pupil. Neither the curriculum nor the teachers held much appeal to him. 'Even when he was enthusiastic', write Lesley and Roy Adkins in *The Keys of Egypt*, 'his independent mind and obvious abilities made enemies of some teachers who merely categorized him as lazy, insolent, and rebellious' (the very same labels applied to Einstein by some of his school and college teachers). Moreover, official regulations meant that Champollion was forbidden to study subjects outside the curriculum during his leisure hours, so he was compelled to work on Hebrew, Arabic, Coptic, and other Oriental languages, secretly at night from books discreetly given to him by his brother. Nevertheless, he did extremely well in the official examinations. Probably, Champollion was fortunate that his private interests were *not* part of the curriculum. Had he been forced to study Oriental languages or ancient Egypt by official methods, he might well have lost his passion for them. Undoubtedly, his formal schooling in Grenoble did little or nothing to set him on the path to his later fame, though it was necessary in order for him to obtain a place to study Oriental languages in Paris.

With Darwin, too, 'It is possible that had science been taught at school, it would have become associated in [his] mind with the compulsory and competitive elements of school work that he disliked. His interest in natural history might then have been extinguished at an early stage', thinks the psychologist Michael Howe. This is certainly what happened at Edinburgh University to Darwin's interest in medicine, which he studied only at his father's insistence. Instead of science, at Shrewsbury School he was fed on a diet of the classics, which made little impression. Science had its place only at home, mainly in collaboration with his elder brother, who built a chemistry laboratory in a toolhouse in the garden, but also on walks in the countryside, as he began a natural history collection. When he did carry out a few chemical experiments at school with a blowpipe and a gaslight in his bedroom, he was nicknamed 'Gas' by his fellow pupils, and banned from continuing with a public rebuke from the headmaster, Samuel Butler.

Pulling Darwin's ear, he called the boy a 'poco curante', an eighteenth-century word meaning a careless trifler, but, 'as I did not understand what he meant, it seemed to me a fearful reproach', Darwin wrote in his auto-biography. Soon after, his father took him away early from the school, realizing that it was doing him no good. All those concerned, including Darwin himself, regarded him as an indifferent pupil at school, and had no inkling of his future genius.

Curie's experience of school is reminiscent of Champollion's, rather than Darwin's: dislike, accompanied by brilliant academic success. Like Champollion, she was top of the class, and received a gold medal when she graduated. But hers is a special case, as she was being educated in a school system ruled by foreigners, which had harshly dismissed her schoolteacher father from his post. Her dislike was to a great extent a reaction to the Russian dominance of Polish education, which aimed to suppress all signs of Polish nationalism. Looking back four decades later, after Poland had become free of Russian rule, she wrote that the teachers 'treated their pupils as enemies', the curriculum was 'of questionable value', and 'the moral atmosphere was altogether unbearable', so that children 'lost all joy of life, and precocious feelings of distrust and indignation weighed upon their childhood'. Yet at the time, during the summer of her thirteenth year, 1881, she wrote to her closest friend at the school: 'I like school. Perhaps you will make fun of me, but nevertheless I must tell you that I like it, and even that I love it. I can realize that now. Don't go imagining that I miss it! Oh no; not at all. But the two years I have left to spend there don't seem as dreadful, as painful and long as they once did.' The sadness of Curie's later years, after the accidental death of her husband, seems to have coloured her adult recollections of school.

Einstein's case is more complicated. Notwithstanding legends that he was a failure at his schools, he was neither an indifferent student like Darwin, nor an excellent one like Champollion and Curie, but rather well above average. At his more authoritarian high school in Munich, which he left early after a disagreement with his class teacher who informed him 'he would never get anywhere in life', his record was patchy—consistently highest in mathematics and science, though even in Latin and Greek he managed a mark only one below the top mark. At his more liberal school in Aarau in Switzerland, where he studied for a year in preparation for the Swiss Polytechnic in Zurich, he did well, and received the top mark both in physics and in mathematics (and in history). In both institutions, he grew fond of some individual teachers, but he disliked the regimentation in the Munich school, and indeed in formal education as a whole. However, no school could have been entirely to his taste, because there were 'powerful reasons within Einstein himself which prevented harmonious integration', remarks the biographer Albrecht Fölsing. Young Einstein preferred, by far, private study over class study. It began as a child and became a habit as a teenager; as an adult, he came to believe that the school matriculation exam should be abolished. Without the slightest doubt, although he was not a poor student, Einstein's originality had nothing to do with his school training, and everything to do with his youthful auto-didacticism.

Cartier-Bresson certainly was a poor student: he failed the baccalaureate three times, and did not matriculate. 'He was mediocre at his studies, not because he lacked the intellectual capacity but because he simply wasn't suited to the discipline of a Catholic education', writes his biographer Assouline. 'The traditional form photographs show a youth who is partly aloof, looking anywhere but at the camera, and partly rebellious, his arms defiantly folded.' His lack of sympathy for organized religion, and the expectations of his conventional, *haut bourgeois*, Parisian family, added fuel to the fire. The only redeeming feature of the school was one teacher, the chief supervisor, a layman in a Catholic institution, who admonished him for secretly reading poetry by Arthur Rimbaud in class but privately encouraged him to read off-curriculum poetry and novels in his office. Ironically, this chance incident fostered his lifelong love of reading, which fed the curiosity that later drove his career as a photographer.

Finally, Ray, though almost as unimpressed by his Calcutta schooling as Cartier-Bresson, had a school record similar to Einstein's: above average, this time in the arts, especially drawing, but far from excellent or scholas-tically oriented. Ray, too, derived all his inspiration from private study—of books, paintings, and music. He also disliked regimentation, and group activities, but did not rebel against the school authorities openly like Einstein. Instead, he incorporated his uninspiring school experiences in his films, stories, and caricatures, notably the Apu Trilogy, in which the numbing effect of most Indian formal education is unflatteringly portrayed, both at school and college. In his memoir of his childhood, school gets a section separate from the rest of his life, suggesting its irrelevance to his work. Here Ray gives character sketches of many of his school teachers. He found not a single one of them really inspiring, but on the whole they were not too bad tempered or sardonic a bunch; and their speech, foibles, and apparel were the stuff of light-hearted mockery. One of his headmasters had trousers that were notably baggy. Their appearance happily coincided with the reading of 'Rip Van Winkle' in Ray's class, who soon alighted on the wide hose known as galligaskins as the correct term for the head's trousers.

Leaving school and moving on to higher education and professional training, one finds the pattern of reactions less clear cut. Some exceptionally creative achievers receive no further formal education after school, but this has become relatively unusual in recent decades, with the worldwide expansion in higher education. Of the ten in this book, six of them—Cartier-Bresson, Leonardo, Mozart, Ray, Woolf, and Wren—did not receive institutional training in their field (though we might regard Verrocchio's studio as the equivalent of a modern art school for Leonardo). However, Champollion, Curie, Darwin, Einstein, Ray, and Wren took university degrees; Curie and Einstein gained doctorates; and Champollion, Curie, Einstein, and Wren became full-time university professors (although Champollion did not retain his appointment for very long). Cartier-Bresson and Ray attended art schools, but did not complete their courses. By way of comparison, among Tusa's sample of twentieth-century creators (which excludes scientists), three of them—Arnold, Spark, and Sylvester—received no institutional training in their field, and indeed had no further formal education. Only three of them—Carter, Caro, and Harrison—took university degrees; Carter alone went on to do a doctorate. Auerbach, Grimshaw, Hodgkin, and Rego went to art schools. Birtwhistle and Ligeti trained at academies of music. Forman went to film school.

The saga of Einstein's physics doctorate is revealing about training and creativity. In the summer of 1900, Einstein graduated from the Swiss Polytechnic, but was not offered an assistant's post in the physics department, because of his spotty attendance record at lectures and his critical attitude to the professors, leaving him in an uncomfortable situation of financial and professional uncertainty. During 1901, unable to interest professors at other institutions in employing an unknown, he decided that he needed a doctorate to make an academic career, and submitted a thesis to the University of Zurich. To his dismay, it was rejected. Then, in the summer of 1902, he at long last landed his first full-time job, at the Swiss Patent Office in Bern. The idea of a doctorate was put aside. In early 1903, Einstein told his friend Michele Besso that he had abandoned the plan, 'as [it] doesn't help me much and the whole comedy has begun to bore me'. But in the summer of 1905, his 'miraculous year', after completing his theory of special relativity, he revived the doctorate plan for the same reason as before: he needed a doctoral degree to get out of the Patent Office and into a university.

Second time around, he submitted his paper on special relativity to the University of Zurich—and it too was rejected! At least this is what happened according to his sister Maja, who was close to her brother: she wrote that relativity 'seemed a little uncanny to the decision-making professors'. There is no proof, although both Einstein's choice of this paper and the professors' sceptical reaction to it seem plausible, since special relativity was clearly important enough for a thesis but had not yet been vetted and published by the scientific establishment (and it would remain intensely controversial after publication). For whatever reason, in the end Einstein selected some less challenging, though still significant, work he had completed in April 1905 just before special relativity—a paper on how to determine the true size of molecules in liquids, respectably based on experimental viscosity data rather than relying on purely theoretical arguments like relativity—and resubmitted the thesis. According to him, perhaps speaking half in jest, the professors informed him that the manuscript was too short, so Einstein added one sentence. Within days, this more orthodox paper was accepted, and by the end of July 1905 he could finally call himself 'Herr Doktor Einstein'. Only later was a small but important mistake discovered in the thesis, which Einstein duly corrected in print in 1906, and further refined in 1910, as better experimental data became available.

The point is, of course, that academia has an inherent tendency to ignore or reject highly original work that does not fit the existing paradigm. Einstein was self-evidently just as original and creative in 1905 without a PhD as with a PhD. To get one, he seems to have been encouraged to show less, rather than more, originality. Might it be that too much training and education can be a handicap for the truly creative? In 1984, Dean Keith Simonton studied the education level of more than 300 exceptionally creative individuals born in the period 1450–1850, that is, before the introduction of the recognizably modern university system—post-Darwin, but pre-Einstein, so to speak. Simonton discovered that the top creators—including Beethoven, Galileo, Leonardo da Vinci, Mozart, and Rembrandt van Rijn—had attained an educational level equivalent to approximately halfway through a modern undergraduate programme. Those with more (or less) education than this had a lower level of creative accomplishment, generally speaking.

Not too much weight should be put on Simonton's discovery, given the difficulty of estimating the educational level of some highly creative historical individuals, and of comparing levels of education in different societies at different periods. However, the finding is supported by the regularity with which highly creative individuals lose interest in academic work during their undergraduate degree course and choose to focus instead on what fascinates them. Some even drop out of university to pursue their hunches, such as the computer scientist Bill Gates at Harvard University in the 1970s. This is what happened to Ray, too. Having taken a bachelor's degree from Presidency College, Calcutta in 1936–39, he then, aged only 18, decided to look for a job as a commercial artist. But his mother eventually persuaded him to begin a five-year fine art training at Tagore's rural art school at Shantiniketan. Yet, Ray gave it up halfway through, in 1942, essentially because he did not feel that he could become a great painter, and the lure of films in the big city was too strong. 'I never ceased to regret that while I had stood in the scorching summer sun in the wilds of Shantiniketan sketching *simul* and *palash* in full bloom, *Citizen Kane* had come and gone, playing for just three days in the newest and biggest cinema in Calcutta', Ray recalled of his student days, in his mid-fifties. Thus, at roughly the level of education mentioned by Simonton for his peak creators, Ray abandoned formal education in favour of pursuing his perceived creative vocation.

Simonton's finding may also provide a clue as to why, in higher education, the post-war increase in the number of PhDs has not led to more exceptionally creative research—if Simonton is correct that the optimum education for exceptional creativity does not require a PhD. In the sciences, the twentieth-century expansion of higher education at doctoral level produced a proliferation of new research specialisms and new journals catering to these specialisms. 'Since 1945, the number of scientific papers and journals in highly industrialized societies—particularly in the United States—has risen almost exponentially, while the proportion of the workforce in research and development and the percentage of gross national product devoted to it have grown more modestly', the sociologist of science J. Rogers Hollingsworth wrote in *Nature* in 2008, after spending several decades studying innovation in different societies. 'Yet the rate at which truly creative work emerges has remained relatively constant. In terms of the scale of research efforts to make major scientific breakthroughs, there are diminishing returns.'

A more likely explanation of this fact, however, is that in contemporary society exceptionally creative scientists and artists differ in the periods of training they require, because of the changed nature of the scientific enterprise, as compared to that of the late nineteenth century and before. Exceptionally creative artists do not require doctoral training now any more than they did in earlier times—but this is not true of their equivalents in science, who must master a greater breadth of knowledge and techniques before they can reach the frontier of their discipline and make a new discovery.

Scientists also need to be much better students than artists, in terms of their performance in school and university examinations. Simonton notes that: 'the contrast in academic performance between scientists and artists appears to reflect the comparative degree of constraint that must be imposed on the creative process in the sciences versus the arts'. Whether this fact has the tendency to squeeze out of the system potential Darwins and Einsteins in favour of the merely productive academic scientist is an endlessly discussed subject, to which no one has yet given a satisfactory answer. What is generally accepted, though, is that the huge growth in size and competitiveness of higher education in the second half of the twentieth century and after did not increase the number of exceptionally creative scientists. According to one American physics Nobel laureate interested in education, Carl Wiemann, who helped to create the first Bose–Einstein condensate in 1995, physics education needs a radical overhaul, somewhat reminiscent of Einstein's emphasis on 'private study' and informal debate in teaching and learning. At school, Wiemann did well but was never top of his class, and at the Massachusetts Institute of Technology, he spent more time in solitary reading and experimental tinkering along with others in the laboratory than on the recommended lectures and class material. As for physics teaching, Wiemann wants to discourage the typical writing of equation after tedious equation on the board, which tests mainly the memory and patience of students. 'If your teaching requires them to reason through ideas and argue their points of view, then you will get a different result', he told Physics World in 2007.

The decipherment of Linear B by Michael Ventris in 1952, mentioned in the preface—a breakthrough that cut across art and science—illustrates well much of what we have been discussing in this chapter. Ventris's breakthrough required both training and exceptional creativity, but no undergraduate degree or PhD. Let us take a closer look at what happened.

Although the challenge of reading the ancient Minoan script excavated at Knossos in 1900 by Sir Arthur Evans had attracted the attentions of dozens of scholars during the first half of the twentieth century, the key figures in the decipherment were Emmett Bennett Jr, Alice Kober, Sir John Myres, John Chadwick, and Ventris. Bennett was an epigraphist, with wartime experience of cryptography, who had written a doctorate on Linear B under the archaeologist Carl Blegen at the University of Cincinnati in the late 1940s; soon after this, he moved to Yale University. Kober was a classicist with a PhD in Greek literature from Columbia University, who had developed a consuming interest in Linear B in the mid-1930s. The ageing Myres was professor of ancient history at Oxford University until 1939 and was widely considered a leading authority on the ancient Greeks; in addition, he had become the custodian and editor of the Linear B tablets after the death of his friend Evans in 1941. Chadwick had an undergraduate degree in classics from Cambridge University but no PhD; after wartime service as a cryptographer and work in Oxford on the staff of the *Oxford Latin Dictionary*, he became a lecturer in classics at Cambridge in 1952, the year he began collaborating with Ventris. Unlike the other four, Ventris never went to university and had no professional training in classics, other than at school, where his passion for deciphering Linear B began as a fourteen year old. Instead, he underwent training as an architect at the Architectural Association School in London in the 1940s—interrupted by war service—before beginning to practise architecture professionally.

Bennett, Kober, Myres, and Chadwick were all older than Ventris; were better trained than him in classical studies; and had more opportunity than him to concentrate on the problem of 'cracking' Linear B. Yet they all failed, where he succeeded. One is compelled to ask why.

There are many reasons, which I discuss in my book about Ventris, *The Man Who Deciphered Linear B*. But the most important ones are: first, the fact that Ventris was knowledgeable in three very different domains (classics, modern languages, and architecture); and second, that he did not have the same investment as the professional scholars in orthodox thinking about Linear B. Myres, for instance, was hamstrung by the incorrect theories of the extremely influential Evans. Kober, though brilliantly logical, was temperamentally unwilling to hazard guesses. She wrote of Linear B in 1948:

'When we have the facts, certain conclusions will be almost inevitable. Until we have them, no conclusions are possible.' Bennett, though highly intelligent, suffered too from scholarly over-restraint: he greeted the decipherment in public with a 'fine set of cautious, non-committal phrases' (as he privately admitted to Ventris). In a sense, Ventris succeeded because he did not have a degree or a doctorate in classics. He had enough training in the subject, but not too much to stifle his curiosity and originality. As his collaborator Chadwick nicely says in his book, *The Decipherment of Linear B*:

> The architect's eye sees in a building not a mere façade, a jumble of ornamental and structural features; it looks beneath the appearance and distinguishes the significant parts of the building. So too Ventris was able to discern among the bewildering variety of the mysterious signs, patterns and regularities which betrayed the underlying structure. It is this quality, the power of seeing order in apparent confusion, that has marked the work of all great men.

In addition, Ventris conforms to the general attitude of geniuses to their school days. He was above average at Stowe School, but not excellent; in fact he left before finishing his course. He derived little inspiration from the teaching, though he did have fond memories of one teacher, Patrick Hunter, who taught him classics and accidentally introduced him to Linear B on a school expedition to a London exhibition on the Minoan world. And he was not interested in group activities, such as team sports, preferring to remain detached. Like his great predecessor Champollion, he even worked secretly at night—under the bedclothes by the light of a torch after official 'lights-out', as one of his fellow boarders amusingly recalled.

Can formal education ever instil this kind of exceptional creativity? Not on the evidence of past geniuses. In Professor Eysenck's parting shot at the academic system at the end of his study *Genius*, he writes: 'The best service we can do to creativity is to let it bloom unhindered, to remove all impediments, and cherish it whenever and wherever we encounter it. We probably cannot train it, but we can prevent it from being suffocated by rules, regulations, and envious mediocrity.' Unfortunately, very few educational institutions or national governments, for all their insistent claims to foster excellence and innovation, manage to take this lesson to heart and put it into practice in schools and universities.

CHAPTER 18

CREATIVE SCIENCE VERSUS ARTISTIC CREATION

One feature that is shared by the creative processes in art and science is that the progress one makes is not linear with time. For any given amount of time spent, you often get nothing in return. And then, all of a sudden, the breakthrough comes, the flash of inspiration, and the problem is solved in a relatively short time.... [However], science is knowing nature. This implies that there exists a fixed set of facts that everyone wants to know.... In fact, if two competing scientists generate different results and reach different conclusions, the field does not rest until this discrepancy has been resolved and it is understood why these different answers have been obtained. In contrast, I suspect that artists are not striving for commonality, but rather, that the content as well as the form of their work is unique.

Thomas Cech, Nobel laureate in chemistry, in *The Origins of Creativity*, 2001

Of the many projects that have aimed to bring together science and art, the Festival Pattern Group was one of the most productive and curiously fascinating. In the 1951 Festival of Britain, manufacturers exhibited futuristic designs in silk, lace, wool, cotton, paper, plastics, glass, and other materials closely based on cutting-edge X-ray diffraction images of molecules ranging from zinc hydroxide to haemoglobin. The designs are now kept at the Victoria and Albert Museum in London and were put on display once more in 2008 in a Wellcome Trust exhibition entitled *From Atoms to Patterns*. Three of the X-ray crystallographers—Dorothy Hodgkin, John Kendrew, and Max Perutz—won Nobel Prizes for their science in the 1960s.

With one exception, the crystallographers were not personally involved with the creation of the designs; indeed their names were not credited, in order to protect their scientific reputations. But when they saw the results, their responses were overwhelmingly positive. In 1951, the pioneering crystallographer Lawrence Bragg, director of the Cavendish Laboratory in Cambridge—where the structure of DNA was about to be investigated by Francis Crick and James Watson—informed Mark Hartland Thomas, a professional architect who was chief industrial officer of the Council of Industrial Design: 'When in 1922 I worked out the first crystal of any complexity that had been analysed, aragonite, I remember well how excited my wife was with the pattern I showed her as a motif for a piece of embroidery.' Bragg continued: 'Ever since then I have been urging industrial friends to use these patterns as a source of inspiration, and I was delighted when Miss Megaw...told me two years ago that she had aroused your interest. The patterns she showed me yesterday are the practical realization of what we have long wished to see.'

Helen Megaw, the one exception, was a crystallographer at the Cavendish Laboratory, and the scientific authority behind the 1951 exhibition, while Hartland Thomas was its organizer. The artistically sensitive Megaw had first suggested the idea in 1946, but it was not until Hartland Thomas became interested in 1949, after seeing a lecture containing some of Megaw's crystal structure diagrams, that it took off. He responded to the diagrams as designs of a new and unfamiliar kind: 'they were essentially modern because the technique that constructed them was quite recent, and yet, like all successful decoration of the past, they derived from nature'.

Some of the designs were ugly, and very few eventually went into production after the close of the festival, yet a significant number of the fabrics were, and still are, strikingly appealing. In the hands of a leading textile designer, Marianne Straub, Megaw's crystal structure of the mineral afwilite inspired a furnishing fabric called 'Surrey', a lovely Jacquard-woven warp tapestry made from wool, cotton, and continuous filament rayon. Afwilite is a naturally occurring calcium hydroxide nesosilicate, which also forms artificially when cement sets to concrete. Afwilite's electron density map has 'peaks' with six or seven contours for calcium atoms, five for silicon, and fewer still for hydroxyl groups and water. Straub made some creative adjustments to the numbers of contours and their relative positions, but essentially her design—overseen by Megaw—is faithful to the scientific image. 'Surrey' was used to create a dark green (for the background) and gold (for the contours) colourway of curtains for the Festival of Britain's Regatta Restaurant on London's South Bank. But since it was prohibitively expensive to produce, it was never manufactured commercially.

All the crystallographers had waived rights in their structure diagrams. Only Megaw's friend Hodgkin refused to sign the permission form to use her structure of insulin. Instead, she gave permission in a letter to Megaw and added disarmingly: 'I feel rather doubtful whether I own any copyright of a pattern perpetrated by nature. But I suspect that if I do, I shouldn't sell it for £5. But I think it's a nice idea!'

Most art–science projects are less fruitful than the Festival Pattern Group. It is a rare artist who can illuminate scientific concepts, the process of scientific discovery, and the working life of scientists. The greatest painters and sculptors have neglected these subjects. The same is true of great film-makers: they leave science to lesser talents, who make movies such as *Madame Curie*, *A Beautiful Mind* (about the mathematician John Nash), and *Flash of Genius* (the story of the inventor of the intermittent windscreen wiper, Robert Kearns), which, though often enjoyable and well acted, invariably concentrate on personalities at the expense of science. Stage productions about science that rely on argument about ideas and ethics have a better chance of artistic success, for example, the play *Copenhagen* (on the wartime meeting of Niels Bohr and Werner Heisenberg), as opposed to those that resort to exciting stage effects and intrusive music to distract the audience from the paucity of real science, such as *A Disappearing Number* (about the mathematician Srinivasa Ramanujan), and operas like *Doctor Atomic* (on Robert Oppenheimer and the Manhattan Project) and *Einstein on the Beach*. Perhaps the best results are obtained on the page, by fiction writers who began their careers with a scientific training, such as Arthur C. Clarke and Fred Hoyle, rather than novelists who in later life pick up science from their own research, like Martin Amis and Ian McEwan. Even so, the depiction of science in fiction is yet to reach the heights of great literature.

Part of the reason has to be that leading artists are typically not very interested in science—certainly much less interested than leading scientists are in the arts. The notorious division of society into 'two cultures'—the humanistic and the scientific—which do not communicate, first mentioned in 1959 by the scientifically trained novelist C. P. Snow, is still alive, if not as clear cut as it was. The arrogance once common on both sides may have diminished, but it has not given way to widespread enthusiasm for bridging the gap. By way of a small but significant instance, among the 800 or so eminent individuals commemorated on the buildings of London with an official 'blue plaque', 194 plaques are for literary figures (there are more plaques for other kinds of artist, such as painters, composers, and so on), while a mere 134 plaques cover all of science, including medicine, engineering, and industry and invention. Furthermore, among the dozen or so artists interviewed by John Tusa for the BBC in 2000–02 (listed in the previous chapter), science barely makes an appearance: only two of the interviewees mention science in passing, and one of them is an architect who is constantly immersed in questions of engineering. Tusa, it is necessary to say, asks no questions about science, yet this cannot entirely explain the silence of the interviewees. None of them makes even a casual reference to Darwin, Einstein, or Freud, let alone any psychologist, in over 250 pages of published interviews. Judging from Tusa's *On Creativity*, artists and scientists appear to inhabit separate worlds.

The ten exceptionally creative individuals in Part II present a somewhat more open-minded picture. However, the artists overall are definitely less interested in science than the scientists are in the arts.

To take the artists first, Leonardo da Vinci is a shining exception. Not only was he fascinated by anatomy, he was also immersed in engineering and invention. Some of his most famous drawings show the workings of the human body, designs for flying machines and military devices such as a 'tank', and the movement of water. His great skill as an artist fed his ability to visualize mechanical and optical concepts.

Mozart seems to have taken little notice of science, judging from his letters and his compositions. Indeed, standard reference books on Mozart are silent on this subject. His only friendship with a scientist was with the controversial physician, Franz Anton Mesmer, inventor of hypnotism, which was originally known as 'mesmerism' or 'animal magnetism', and involved the use of magnets for inducing therapeutic trances. For some years, mesmerism enjoyed a cult status, until 1784, when it was discredited by a French royal commission including the scientists Antoine Lavoisier and Benjamin Franklin, and Mesmer was forced into retirement. Mozart and his librettist Da Ponte's spoof on mesmerism in their 1789 opera *Così fan tutte* suggests that Mozart accepted the scientific evidence against it. This attitude is also found in his membership of the Freemasons, where he associated not with the mystical Rosicrucians or the Asiatic Brethren but with the rationalist and illuminist lodges; his closest Masonic brothers were anti-clerical and believers in natural law. 'He nowhere expressed even veiled sympathy for occult or pseudo-scientific currents', notes the biographer Maynard Solomon.

Virginia Woolf may be said to epitomize one half of the 'two cultures' that Snow deplored in 1959. She appears to have had almost no relationship with either science or scientists during her lifetime, though she did admire the futuristic novels of Olaf Stapledon and not only read Freud (who had been published by the Woolfs' Hogarth Press) during the Second World War, but also actually met him. 'Not for nothing did Freud, on the only occasion they met, in 1939, give her a narcissus', writes Hermione Lee in her biography of Woolf. As any reader of Woolf soon discovers, like Freud she was extremely interested in conscious and unconscious thinking. In her essay, 'Modern fiction'—published in 1925, the same year as *Mrs Dalloway*—she observed her mental processes as follows:

> The mind receives a myriad of impressions. From all sides they come, an incessant shower of innumerable atoms; and as they fall, they shape themselves into the life of Monday or Tuesday...Let us [the modern novelist] record the atoms as they fall upon the mind in the order in which they fall, let us trace the pattern, however disconnected and incoherent in appearance, which each sight or incident scores upon the consciousness.

Although Woolf's introspections are well worth reading, they are very far from being scientific, since they concern only herself and her novels. She felt no attraction to materialist theories of the brain. She was neither a philosopher nor a neuroscientist, regardless of the attempt to claim her as one by Jonah Lehrer in a chapter on Woolf in his *Proust Was a Neuroscientist*. Experimental science, for Woolf, was a closed book.

Cartier-Bresson and Ray, despite being friends and fellow admirers, differed in their attitude to science. Cartier-Bresson had Woolf's indifference, tinged with hostility to technology, whereas Ray was sympathetic to Leonardo's Renaissance vision, without his commitment to the practical investigation of nature.

Cartier-Bresson's attitude to science is suggested by a letter he sent me about one of my books on writing and ancient scripts, handwritten with his usual fountain pen. 'I am ignorant of graphology but it gives such a pleasure by the link between the eye the mind and the fingers handling a little tool. Instead of the dehumanization in communication through electronic systems.' As a photographer dependent on technology, throughout his life he nevertheless pooh-poohed photography's technical aspect and stressed the mind and eye behind the shutter. The simplicity of operation of his small Leica camera was compelling for him, so that he could pass unobtrusively and swiftly to the heart of the matter without being distracted by technology. Most of his photographs of machines and technology stress the human aspect. Thus, he shows a few white-shirted American space engineers relaxing in front of banks of blank computer monitors in an otherwise empty Kennedy Space Center at Cape Canaveral; a couple of engineers in south India wheeling a rocket cone balanced on the saddle of a sturdy bicycle; a sad-faced monkey in California hooked up to electronic test instruments in a psychology laboratory. In his book *America in Passing*, there are only two or three shots that make technology look at all glamorous. Even Cartier-Bresson's minuscule number of photo–portraits of scientists—for example, Irène and Frédéric Joliot-Curie, and Oppenheimer—portray their subjects as severe and burdened figures.

Ray, on the other hand, was the son and grandson of artists with scientific training, obtained through managing a pioneering printing press and also via higher education in the case of his father. He himself had friends who were scientists, though not particularly close to him; he wrote a fair amount of non-fiction on science for children; and he created and illustrated bestselling novellas around a Bengali detective duo based on Arthur Conan Doyle's Holmes and Watson, and, less successfully, a series of stories about an Indian scientist–inventor similar to Conan Doyle's Professor Challenger. His films were also frequently concerned with science, which is presented as a rational alternative to orthodox Hinduism in the Apu Trilogy and forms the central theme of his adaptation of Henrik Ibsen's play *An Enemy of the People*, in which Ray is firmly on the side of the persecuted medical doctor who decides to fight against obscurantism and prejudice. In 1983, he said: 'I think someday the human mind will explore all the mysteries of life and creation the way the mysteries of the atom have been explored.' Yet, as we know from the preface, he did not believe science could explain creativity. In the final analysis, Ray was more of a humanist than a scientist, like his predecessor Tagore—'the two great stalwarts of the Indian Cultural Scene of the twentieth century', as the astrophysicist Subrahmanyan Chandrasekhar, a Nobel laureate with a strong interest in the arts, dubbed Ray and Tagore in 1995.

Turning now to the scientists in Part II, there is a revealing paragraph in Darwin's autobiography, recalling his school days. 'I used to sit for hours reading the historical plays of Shakespeare, generally in an old window in the thick walls of the school', he writes. 'I read also other poetry, such as Thomson's *Seasons*, and the recently published poems of Byron and Scott. I mention this because in later life I wholly lost, to my great regret, all pleasure from poetry of any kind, including Shakespeare.' Instead, in order to relax from reading heavy scientific works, some written in German, Darwin developed a keen taste for novels, which he liked to have read to him by his wife and family. 'Walter Scott, Miss Austen, and Mrs Gaskell were read and re-read till they could be read no more', his son Francis recalled. But most of Darwin's novel reading was of light romances borrowed from Mudie's Circulating Library: a 'seamless web of deserted sweethearts, secret weddings, wicked cousins, mistaken identities, and the age-old quests for love and passion', writes Darwin biographer Janet Browne. With these novels, he enjoyed suspending the critical faculties that he honed for his scientific work. 'If he was given a scientific thought to analyse, his mind was alert, clear, and concise. But given a character in a novel, his responses were entirely predictable', says Browne. As for painting, his taste was for accurate representation. He could not appreciate the landscapes of his near-contemporary J. M. W. Turner shown to him by John Ruskin, for example, and claimed to prefer photographic over painted portraits. In music, he loved bits of Bach, Beethoven, and Handel, but had no ear: he was unable to recognize a tune when he heard it again.

Curie's taste in the arts was principally for literature, especially poetry, which developed as a child from hearing her father recite to her in Polish, and sometimes in a running translation from another language, as with Charles Dickens's *David Copperfield*. 'I willingly learned by heart long passages from our great poets, the favourite ones being Mickiewecz, Krasinski, and Slowacki', her autobiography records. 'This taste was even more developed when I became acquainted with foreign literatures; my early studies included the knowledge of French, German, and Russian, and I soon became familiar with the fine works written in these languages. Later I felt the need of knowing English and succeeded in acquiring the knowledge of that language and its literature.' Rudyard Kipling's *The Jungle Book* and *Kim*, and Colette's *Naissance du Jour* and *Sido*, were favourites Marie shared with her grown-up daughter Eve, who became a concert pianist and writer. But it seems from Eve Curie's biography *Madame Curie* that, like Darwin, Marie Curie's taste for serious literature faded with age, the tragedy of losing her literature-minded husband Pierre when she was only 39 years old, and the drive to continue her scientific research alone in her own laboratory. It played no evident role in her research. When Einstein went on an Alpine holiday with the Curies in 1913, he was privately critical of her as rather grim and insensitive. 'Madame Curie never heard the birds sing!' he said later. To his cousin Elsa—soon to become his second wife—Einstein remarked at the time that Curie was 'very intelligent but has the soul of a herring, which means that she is poor when it comes to the art of joy and pain'. Perhaps he was exaggerating to impress Elsa with his faithfulness to her. Yet much later, after Curie's death in 1934, when Einstein publicly extolled her 'strength of character and devotion', he could not refrain from adding that she had 'a curious severity unrelieved by any artistic strain'.

Einstein's own chief artistic interest was of course music. He showed little interest in painting—notwithstanding recent scholarly attempts to recruit him as one of the inspirations for the contemporary cubist movement (neither Einstein nor Picasso showed any recorded interest in cubism or relativity, respectively)—and he was not inclined towards poetry or fiction, though he was keenly interested in philosophy. From an early age, he learnt to play the violin and the piano, focusing on Mozart's sonatas, and gave some public performances on the violin as an adult, before abandoning the instrument in his final years in favour of casual piano playing. At home, playing music helped him relax from doing physics. 'Music does not influence research work', he remarked in 1928, 'but both are nourished by the same sort of longing, and they complement each other in the release they offer.' The composers he consistently revered were J. S. Bach and Mozart. After them came Schubert, and he also admired aspects of the music of Beethoven, Brahms, Handel, Mendelssohn, and Richard Strauss— no modernist composers. Wagner's musical personality he found so indescribably offensive that 'for the most part I can listen to him only with disgust', he remarked in 1939, admittedly during the period of Nazi worship of Wagner.

As for Champollion and Wren, it is difficult to divine a meaningful separation between the artistic and scientific threads in their life and work because of the intrinsic nature of linguistics and architecture. Champollion, in his passion for ancient Egypt and its writings, immersed himself in all aspects of its culture: natural history, history, languages and literature, painting and sculpture, religion, mathematics, and 'science'. Wren, besides his intimate understanding of the mathematical and engineering aspects of architecture as a scientist, was a superb draughtsman steeped in the aesthetics of building and decorative styles, from ancient Greece and Rome up to the work of contemporary architects like Bernini. For Wren, neither science nor art on its own was enough to satisfy his needs.

Architecture 'absorbed all his capacities', to repeat John Summerson's remark, and was 'the complete answer'.

If we set aside the tiny handful of geniuses such as Leonardo and Wren, who were almost equally versed in science and art, it is fair to say that there is virtually no artist who deserves an entry in the scientific reference books, and scarcely any scientist who has made a major contribution to the arts. Perhaps Johann Wolfgang von Goethe might qualify in the first category for his 1810 theory of colours, and Freud in the second category for his 1899 theory of dreams and the unconscious, although both theories remain controversial. Arthur C. Clarke might also be a contender for his publication of the concept of the communications satellite in the magazine *Wireless World* in 1945, before he became a science fiction writer. And there is also the captivating example of Tom Lehrer, a Harvard University mathematics lecturer who became one of the most quoted satirical songwriters of the twentieth century, although it must be admitted that he does not qualify as a major mathematician.

Lehrer certainly saw a connection between his mathematical training and his musical composition. 'To begin a song is not hard, it's where you are going to end that's hard. You gotta have the joke at the end', he said in an interview in 2000. 'The logical mind, the precision, is the same that's involved in math as in lyrics. And I guess in music too...It's like a puzzle, to write a song. The idea of fitting all the pieces so it exactly comes right, the right word at the end of the sentence, and the rhyme goes there and not there.'

Mathematicians, unlike natural scientists, are enthralled by elegance, Lehrer stressed. 'That's the word you hear in mathematics all the time. "This proof is elegant!" It doesn't really matter what it proves. "Look at this—isn't that amazing!" And it comes out at the end. It's neat. It's not just that it's proof, because there are plenty of proofs that are just boring proofs. But every now and then there's a really elegant proof.' Lehrer gave an example from his own songwriting, after citing a comment on rhyme from the autobiography of the famous mathematician Stanislaw Ulam (who helped to build the atomic bomb) that rhyming 'forces novel associations...and becomes a sort of automatic mechanism of originality'. In Lehrer's song 'Wernher von Braun', about the amoral German rocket engineer who first built the V2 rocket for the Nazis and then the Saturn V rockets for the US Apollo programme, there are the rhymed lines: '"Once the rocket goes up who cares where it comes down?/ That's not my department", says Wernher von Braun.' According to Lehrer: 'If "Von Braun" didn't happen to rhyme with "down" (and a few other words), the most quoted couplet in the song would not exist, and in all probability the song itself would not have been written.'

Lehrer's argument seems to imply that there is more in common between mathematical discovery and artistic creation than meets the eye. Numbers follow rules—of addition, multiplication, commutation, and so on—which generate mathematics; and so do words, if they are to make meaningful prose and poetry. But of course there is a crucial difference between mathematical and linguistic rules: mathematical rules are natural and eternally valid, while the rules of grammar, syntax, and pronunciation for any spoken language are invented and change over time. Mathematical truth exists independently of humankind, so we think, while linguistic meaning has no existence beyond that of human beings. 'Our natural point of view in regard to the existence of truth apart from humanity cannot be explained or proved, but it is a belief which nobody can lack—not even primitive beings', Einstein told Tagore (who disagreed) in a conversation in 1930. 'We attribute to truth a superhuman objectivity. It is indispensable for us—this reality which is independent of our existence and our experience and our mind—though we cannot say what it means.'

This is why we generally speak of 'discovering' a mathematical or a scientific truth, yet 'creating' a work of art. The principle of natural selection was discovered by Darwin in the 1830s, but it had existed in nature since the beginning of life on earth and could have been discovered by someone else; in fact it was independently discovered by Alfred Russel Wallace in 1858, which forced Darwin to publish his theory or lose his priority. The theory of special relativity was almost discovered by Henri Poincaré, not Einstein. The structure of DNA was nearly discovered by Linus Pauling, and also Rosalind Franklin, rather than by Crick and Watson. 'In science, what X misses today Y will surely hit upon tomorrow (or maybe the day after tomorrow). Much of a scientist's pride and sense of accomplishment turns therefore upon being the *first* to do something', wrote the Nobel laureate Peter Medawar in 1964, encapsulating a widely shared view. 'Artists are not troubled by matters of priority, but Wagner would certainly not have spent 20 years on *The Ring* if he had thought it at all possible for someone else to nip in ahead of him with *Götterdämmerung*.' Leonardo's *The Last Supper* was created in the 1490s from his particular mind and imagination, and surely could not have been painted by any other individual. No one but Ray could have made *Pather Panchali* in 1950–55.

This distinction between science and art sounds straightforward. However, it tends to disappear on closer examination, at least to some extent. Scientific breakthroughs are not simply waiting to happen; they occur in a historical context. Artistic breakthroughs do not arise out of nowhere; they have antecedents in other work. Both scientific discoveries and artistic creations require a combination of individual and consensual thinking. Earlier thinkers on evolution influenced Darwin; the same is true in physics of Einstein's work on relativity and quantum theory; previous Renaissance paintings of 'The Last Supper' influenced Leonardo's painting; contemporary Italian operas influenced Mozart's *The Marriage of Figaro*; and so on. This has led some thinkers to see artistic and scientific creativity as being located on a theoretical continuum, rather than in separate compartments. The psychologist Robert Weisberg, for instance, visualizes at the left-hand extreme of the continuum God's creation of something out of nothing and at the right-hand extreme a person's discovery of a dollar bill in the street. Artistic creativity then occupies the left-hand side and centre of the continuum, where it overlaps with scientific creativity, which occupies the centre and right-hand side of the continuum. 'From this perspective', writes Weisberg, 'it is not absurd to say that Watson and Crick created the double helix, although it seems less acceptable to say that Picasso discovered *Guernica*.'

The point has been forcefully argued by the molecular biologist and philosopher of science, Gunther Stent, over many years, beginning with the publication of Watson's memoir *The Double Helix* in 1968, a book that took essentially the same line on scientific discovery as Medawar. In Stent's article, 'Meaning in art and science', published in 2001, he argues that:

> the structure of the DNA molecule was not what it was before Watson and Crick defined it, because there was and there still is no such thing as the DNA molecule in the natural world. The DNA molecule is an abstraction created by century-long efforts of a succession of biochemists, all of whom selected for their attention certain ensembles of natural phenomena. The DNA double helix is as much a creation as it is a discovery; the realm of existence of the double-helical DNA molecule is the mind of scientists and the literature of science, but not the natural world (except insofar as that world also includes minds and books). Hence, as applied to art and science, the antinomy of discovery versus creation has little philosophical merit.

Stent makes a good point. DNA is often said—even by commentators who should know better—to have been 'discovered' by Watson and Crick. In fact, it was discovered in 1869; its role in genetic inheritance was discovered in 1943; and its double-helix structure was discovered in 1953. Thus, the scientific conception of DNA changed radically in this time period, even though DNA's function in nature remained precisely the same.

But Stent, and Weisberg, are on less convincing ground in arguing for the similarity between the 'creation' of DNA's structure and the creation of a work of art. Weisberg compares the discovery of the structure in 1953 with the painting of *Guernica* by Picasso in 1937, for which Picasso kept detailed and dated sketches. From both these and *The Double Helix*, it is plain that Picasso, and Crick and Watson, were systematic in their approaches, and that the artist and the two scientists were influenced by pre-existing works. But in the DNA case, the influences, such as Pauling's and Franklin's work, are easily identified and their working is clearly understood, whereas Picasso never names his influences, forcing Weisberg to speculate.

He chooses, reasonably enough, a 1935 etching by Picasso, *Minotauromachy*, which shares elements with *Guernica*—most evidently the bull and the raised head of a horse—plus an etching from Francisco de Goya's *Disasters of War*, which Picasso definitely admired. In this etching, Weisberg identifies, for example, a mother figure by Goya with a posture (somewhat) similar to that of Picasso's woman with her dead child, and also claims that Picasso changed a falling man with outstretched hands in Goya's etching into a falling woman in *Guernica*, because 'Her profile is similar to that of Goya's man, and her outstretched hands with exaggeratedly splayed fingers echo those of the Goya figure.' Maybe, maybe not: Picasso does not tell us. For Weisberg, such resemblances show there to be 'layers of antecedents to *Guernica'*—as with the structure of DNA. Of this there is no doubt, but was Picasso thinking of such antecedents while painting *Guernica*? Even if they were in his conscious mind, it is not the borrowed elements that make a work of art, but, rather obviously, the way that they are transformed by the artist to make a whole. Surely Goya did influence Picasso, but if Picasso really is of Goya's stature, his borrowings from Goya in *Guernica* will have been subtler and more complex than Weisberg's suggested connections. If Weisberg's literal-minded analysis were true of Picasso, it would actually reduce, not enhance, the quality of his painting.

For the same reason, the X-ray crystallographic diagrams turned into fabric designs by the Festival Pattern Group in 1951 are not works of art, because the designers were not permitted by the scientists to transform the scientific originals sufficiently. Creative science and artistic creation, at the highest level, are more separate, than similar, activities.

CHAPTER 19

IS THERE A CREATIVE
PERSONALITY?

Probably the personalities of creative people are not as diverse as are
creative people themselves—that is, there probably is not a unique personality configuration for each creative person. However, there is reason to
believe that there are at the very least numerous creative personalities, and it
is probably true that even people working within the same subfield of the
arts or the sciences can approach their work from very different perspec-
tives, meaning that their personalities would probably be different. Therefore, looking for simple relationships between personality characteristics
and creative achievement may be a fruitless task.

> Robert Weisberg, *Creativity: Understanding Innovation in Problem Solving,*
> *Science, Invention, and the Arts,* 2006

When I consider some of the most interesting of the highly
creative artists and scientists from various domains whom I
have personally encountered—Lindsay Anderson, Philip W.
Anderson, Henri Cartier-Bresson, Subrahmanyan Chandrasekhar, Arthur C.
Clarke, V. S. Naipaul, R. K. Narayan, and Satyajit Ray—no single personality
trait stands out as common to all of them. The two film-makers, Lindsay
Anderson and Ray, though friends from before the making of *Pather Pan-*
chali, were antithetical personalities: the English Anderson physically short,
abrasive, and theatrical, the Bengali Ray towering, restrained, and reticent.
Even the two novelists, Narayan and Naipaul, who are often regarded as the
greatest fiction writers to emerge from India during the twentieth century,
were as disparate in personality as, say, Graham Greene was from his
English contemporary Evelyn Waugh. Narayan was as well known for his
mild manneredness as Naipaul is for his acerbity. Perhaps the only common
factor among these eight individuals is their self-confidence in regard to

their work. Whether in physics or photography, literature or film-making, all of them struck me as decidedly aware of their own creative worth.

The scientific study of personality was for many decades a poor relation in psychology. Freud launched it with his concepts of id, ego, and psycho-analysis, a century or so ago. Yet Freud openly stated that psychoanalysis was not a science. He said of himself: 'I am not a man of science, not an observer, not an experimenter, not a thinker. I am by temperament nothing but a conquistador—an adventurer, if you want it translated—with all the curiosity, daring, and tenacity characteristic of a man of this sort.' The terms extraversion and introversion, basic to today's studies of personality, were introduced by Carl Jung as long ago as 1921. But during the twentieth century, no particular measure of personality enjoyed anything like the agreement attaching to the measurement of intelligence by IQ (controversial as IQ is).

Instead, there were as many theories and measures of personality as there were psychologists studying the subject. According to one of them, Daniel Nettle, writing in his 2007 book *Personality*, during this confused period 'one psychologist might give you a score for Reward Dependence and Harm Avoidance, whilst another might classify you as a Thinking, Feeling, Sens-ing, or Intuiting type. This led to a frustrating profusion of different studies measuring different constructs without seeming to relate to each other in any systematic way.' If personality psychology was to become a discipline, rather than operating at a level similar to the entertaining personality questionnaires published in general-interest magazines, then its practi-tioners had to establish that for individuals there truly was such a thing as an enduring personality, which remained the same in the flux of everyday life and social encounters, and was stable from year to year, decade to decade. Yet this claim was by no means self-evident. If it were really so, what dimensions should be used to measure and define it? How should psychologists check whether or not it endured? And how should they find out which of these dimensions were relevant to creativity?

Recently, however, there has been some progress in answering these questions, at least for the personality of ordinary people, if not very much for that of exceptional creators. As a result, there is now more of a consensus in personality research.

The first reason for progress is that the so-called five-factor model of personality seems to fit the evidence from studies of individuals and groups. Personality is now widely tested and factored along five dimen-sions, which are the following character traits: extraversion, neuroticism, conscientiousness, agreeableness, and openness. (These are Nettle's choice of categories, but other psychologists use broadly similar ones.) High scorers on extraversion are, says Nettle, 'outgoing, enthusiastic', whereas low scorers are 'aloof, quiet'. High scorers on neuroticism are 'prone to stress and worry', low scorers 'emotionally stable'. High scorers on conscientiousness are 'organized, self-directed', low scorers 'spontaneous, careless'. High scorers on agreeableness are 'trusting, empathetic', low scorers 'uncooperative, hostile'. Finally—and supposedly most relevant to creativity—high scorers on openness are 'creative, imaginative, eccentric', low scorers 'practical, conventional'. These five-factor scores for ordinary individuals are found to be as constant when measured over a decade as when measured over a week.

Other reasons for consensus come from neuroscience, genetics, and evolutionary psychology. Brain imaging scans, which began in the 1990s, suggest that individual differences in brain structure and functioning may be mappable onto the dimensions of the five-factor model. In other words, a statement like 'X is high in extraversion' should have a biological correlate in the brain, perhaps in the mid-brain dopamine reward systems, though this has yet to be satisfactorily located. Then there is the evidence from the sequencing of the human genome, completed in 2001. Personality appears to be partly determined by an individual's genetic variants. For example, a study of New Zealand adults over time showed that those with the greatest tendency to depression—that is, high scorers on neuroticism—had two copies of short forms of the serotonin transporter genes, as opposed to either one copy of the short form and one of a long form or two copies of the long form, inherited from the subjects' parents. Lastly, there is the infusion into psychology of evolutionary thinking, from the 1980s on- wards. Why should natural selection have produced human personality traits? The evolutionary explanation for the existence of a high level of neuroticism is that it originally gave highly neurotic individuals the advan- tage of being better able to anticipate danger (such as being attacked by a large predator) than those with low neuroticism, despite the disadvantage to them of increased anxiety and risk of depression. Those who scored high for openness were presumably good at adaptation, at finding new and creative solutions to unfamiliar problems, while at the same time being prone to bizarre beliefs and psychosis (like the paranoid schizophrenic mathematician John Nash in *A Beautiful Mind*).

Unfortunately for the understanding of any putative 'creative personality', openness is the least well analysed of the five-factor traits. Nettle calls his fifth trait 'mysterious and difficult to pin down', and admits that other psychologists define it somewhat differently: 'It is the dimension called variously "Culture", "Intellect", or, the label I prefer, "Openness to experience".' Weisberg, as quoted above, is very cautious in drawing firm conclusions about any relationship between personality and creativity; he uses 'probably' four times in one short paragraph. He points out that the convincing method to determine whether there are causal links between personality characteristics and creative performance would be to begin with a group of young people before they show any eminence and study their personality and their creativity over the course of their lives, as Lewis Terman did with the intelligence of his gifted children from the 1920s onwards. But so far there have been almost no such longitudinal studies of creative personality.

If this last limitation is true of the moderately creative, it applies a fortiori to the exceptionally creative. According to Freud, 'before creativity, the psychoanalyst must lay down his arms', and 'the nature of artistic attainment is psychoanalytically inaccessible to us'. At present, personality psychology has nothing very useful to say about genius. The only empirical study of the personality traits of creative, compared with exceptionally creative, people is the historical survey of genius carried out by Terman's student Catharine Cox in the 1920s, discussed in Chapter 2—and we already know how flawed her study was. It also predates the present-day five-factor model. To compile a personality profile for a long dead genius like Mozart or Darwin is likely to be an ad hoc procedure of little scientific value. Of Cox's roughly 300 geniuses, only 100 of them could be rated for personality traits, for lack of sufficient evidence.

The chief difficulty is not lack of evidence, though. In my view, it is the near-certainty that exceptionally creative people do not actually have the kind of enduring personality on which the five-factor model is predicated. My guess—based on the lives of the exceptionally creative figures in this book—is that the more creative a person is, the more multifarious is his or her personality. There is therefore no point in looking for a single personality in an exceptionally creative individual, because it does not exist. To be exceptionally creative means to have a chameleon personality. Exceptionally creative individuals modify their personalities to suit their context.

An insightful comment by one genius on another illustrates this chameleon tendency well. In 1991, the bicentenary of Mozart's death, Satyajit Ray, who adored Mozart's music and acknowledged his debt to it as a film-maker, recorded a Calcutta radio tribute, What Mozart Means to Me.

It included the following response by Ray to Milos Forman's controversial film about Mozart based on Peter Shaffer's play *Amadeus*:

> The music in Milos Forman's *Amadeus* is well handled and used with imagination. But I have the strongest reservations about the portrayal of Mozart in the film. It is true that Mozart was a bundle of contradictions. In spite of being prodigiously gifted, he had a flippant side to him. He wrote letters which contained jokes in poor taste and in fact occasionally bordered on the obscene. But the fact remains that he must have applied himself very seriously to the task of composing his masterpieces, and at these moments he must have undergone a complete change of personality. This is not there in the film.

Anyone who has seen *Amadeus* must agree that Ray is correct. The Mozart of the movie is a mainly social, rather frivolous creature, into whose head profound music comes unbidden, under semi-divine dictation. Ray, as a musically gifted person himself (unlike the film's director Forman, by his own admission to John Tusa), and a film and song composer of note, was confident that the film's portrayal of immortal musical creativity was spurious. It is worth repeating here Constanze Mozart's fascinating recollection of her husband's contrasting behaviours during the process of composing: 'When some grand conception was working in his brain he was purely abstracted, walked about the apartment and knew not what was passing around, but when once arranged in his mind, he needed no Piano Forte but would take music paper and whilst he wrote would say ... "Now, my dear wife, have the goodness to repeat what has been talked of", and [my] conversation never interrupted him'.

To reinforce Ray's point about genius—at any rate, Mozart's genius—being a 'bundle of contradictions', and the existence of a 'complete change of personality' in genius when hard at work, here is an extended eyewitness account of the changeable personality of a great scientist. Einstein, throughout his adult life, never shied away from vigorous debate with friends (for example, the 'Olympia Academy', pre-relativity) and with fellow scientists (arguments with Niels Bohr and Max Born concerning quantum theory), from incisive and witty press interviews, and from personal celebrity; such extraverted behaviour was among the reasons for Einstein's unique fame in his lifetime. But his most creative science was done in privacy and relative isolation. The account is a vivid personal reminiscence of Einstein's interaction with two physicist collaborators, Banesh Hoffmann and Leopold Infeld, in the late 1930s. Hoffmann recalled:

Whenever we came to an impasse the three of us had heated discussions—in English for my benefit, because my German was not too fluent—but when the argument became really intricate Einstein, without realizing it, would lapse into German. He thought more readily in his native tongue. Infeld would join him in that tongue, while I struggled so hard to follow what was being said that I rarely had time to interject a remark till the excitement died down.

When it became clear, as it often did, that even resorting to German did not solve the problem, we would all pause, and then Einstein would stand up quietly and say, in his quaint English, 'I vill a little t'ink'. So saying he would pace up and down or walk around in circles, all the time twirling a lock of his long, greying hair around his forefinger. At these moments of high drama Infeld and I would remain completely still, not daring to move or make a sound, lest we interrupt his train of thought. A minute would pass in this way and another, and Infeld and I would eye each other silently while Einstein continued pacing and all the time twirling his hair. There was a dreamy, far-away, and yet sort of inward look on his face. There was no appearance at all of intense concentration. Another minute would pass and another, and then all of a sudden Einstein would visibly relax and a smile would light up his face. No longer did he pace and twirl his hair. He seemed to come back to his surroundings and to notice us once more, and then he would tell us the solution to the problem and almost always the solution worked.

So here we were, with the magic performed triumphantly and the solution sometimes was so simple we could have kicked ourselves for not having been able to think of it by ourselves. But that magic was performed invisibly in the recesses of Einstein's mind, by a process that we could not fathom. From this point of view the whole thing was completely frustrating. But, from the more immediately practical point of view, it was just the opposite, since it opened a way to further progress and without it we should never have been able to bring the research to a successful conclusion.

A third revealing example of a change in personality is that of Ray himself. On meeting him for the first time, in London in 1982, I was very struck—like many others before me—by the contrast between his personal reserve and aura of privacy, and the outgoing demands of film-making and celebrity. Asked if he had to make a tremendous mental adjustment just before he started to shoot a film, he replied: 'I'm equally at home in both situations. I can sit and not talk for hours on end and keep working, sometimes for 17 or 18 hours at a stretch. Then on the set, working with 20 or 25 other people, I think I'm a very different person. I can be both. My shooting is extremely energetic work because we work very fast and everybody is on their toes.' He further explained:

It's not as if you must work quickly, otherwise it will cost more money. It's
not like that. It's just that it gives you a certain energy to be doing something
which excites you, a certain extra energy. If you can get the work done
quickly, it means that everyone is helping and doing their best. It's hard to
describe it. And it infects the others... the actors become part of the team in
no time at all. Nobody's dawdling and everybody's using their time in the
best possible way.

On another occasion, he claimed with a laugh (since he was subverting the
archetypal image of a film director as a dictator): 'When I'm working I'm a
complete democrat. It's when I'm sitting at home alone and doing nothing
that it seems aristocratic. Film-making is a democratic undertaking, I think.'

The personalities of Mozart and Einstein, and also Ray, in these vignettes
do not lend themselves to easy classification according to the five-factor
model. Consider extraversion. Mozart would score high for extraversion
('outgoing, enthusiastic') when giving a concert performance in front of an
audience or personally conducting one of his operas such as *The Marriage of
Figaro*, yet low ('aloof, quiet') when composing at home. And the same would
be the case for Einstein on one of his world tours in the 1920s, as compared
with Einstein at home alone working on his theory of special relativity; or for
Ray directing *Pather Panchali* with his technical team, actors, and a crowd of
locals in a village on the outskirts of Calcutta, as compared with Ray sitting at
home for days mostly alone while writing a film script. In fact, 'aloof'—and
even 'arrogant'—were adjectives that often cropped up in acquaintances'
descriptions of Ray, undoubtedly with justification, while Einstein was
often said, not least by himself, to seem 'apart' from the world. 'I am truly a
"lone traveller" and have never belonged to my country, my home, my
friends, or even my immediate family, with my whole heart', Einstein stated
in 'The world as I see it', a sort of credo published when he was about 50, as
noted earlier. Thus, Mozart, Einstein, and Ray could be extraverts—and also
introverts. Any attempt to measure their degree of extraversion would be
bound to suggest not a fixed personality but rather something mercurial.

As for the other four traits in the five-factor model, they might well vary
considerably across these three individuals, thereby implying that there is
no such thing as 'a creative personality'. For conscientiousness ('organized,
self-directed', as opposed to 'spontaneous, careless') and openness to
experience ('creative, imaginative, eccentric', rather than 'practical, conventional'), Mozart, Einstein, and Ray would tend to score high under most
circumstances. However, it is worth observing that Mozart had a penchant

for spontaneous improvization during performances; and that his father Leopold frequently berated him for his lack of organization. And while Einstein seems to have enjoyed being a celebrated tourist when he travelled, open to a wide variety of unexpected experiences, Ray had relatively little interest in tourism (or in celebrity) and stuck mostly to work-related activity while travelling. Also, Einstein was the only one of the three who might commonly be described as eccentric.

For neuroticism, all three would probably score low ('emotionally stable'). None of them suffered from depression or fits of temper, and none was by nature a worrier, otherwise he would not have survived as an independent creative figure, especially in the case of Mozart, who lacked the security of being a court composer. All had overwhelming confidence in their talents, which enabled them to take on creative challenges that would have daunted a less confident person. Nevertheless, Ray's anxiety while shooting led him to chew handkerchiefs to bits, and Einstein, as we know, noted of his work on general relativity: 'The years of anxious searching in the dark, with their intense longing, their alternations of confidence and exhaustion and the final emergence into the light—only those who have experienced it can understand that.'

For agreeability, the picture is more mixed. Mozart would score relatively high ('trusting, empathetic')—certainly in the jaundiced opinion of his misanthropic father Leopold—except in his uncompromising and bitter dealings with his Salzburg employer Archbishop Colloredo, who unceremoniously sacked him. Einstein and Ray, by contrast, would probably score nearer the low end of the scale ('uncooperative, hostile'). Although both were generally courteous men, there was a streak of self-absorption in their personal dealings that could lead to their rejection of people formerly close to them. In Einstein's case, it caused the breakdown of his first marriage to Mileva Marić, a strained relationship with his two sons, and the near-failure of his second marriage. 'Nothing tragic really gets to him, he is in the happy position of being able to shuffle it off. That is also why he can work so well', Einstein's second wife Elsa confided to a woman friend soon after the trauma of losing her elder daughter from her first marriage to disease. In Ray's case, his self-absorption led to breaks with several of his most talented collaborators and actors, notably his long-time art director Bansi Chandragupta and his lighting cameraman Subrata Mitra (both of whom made important contributions to *Pather Panchali*), and to his having hardly any close friends, especially later in life. Low agreeableness is quite common in exceptionally creative people. 'You have to be ruthless and put yourself and your progress first if you want to get on', is Nettle's summary of the situation on agreeableness for great creators. He adds Oscar Wilde's comment in De Profundis: 'Nothing really at any period of my life was ever of the smallest importance to me compared to Art.'

Einstein would surely have agreed in regard to Science. His steely motivation to do physics never dimmed: he was still making mathematical calculations in hospital on the day before he died, in his decades-long quest for a unified field theory of gravity and electromagnetism. Indeed, all ten of the exceptionally creative individuals in Part II would likely have sympathized with Wilde's view, at least in private. Champollion drove himself into an early grave through his passion for ancient Egypt. Curie continued to work unprotected with strongly radioactive elements up to her death, despite being acutely aware of how they had already damaged her eyes and skin—she was known to rub her thumb regularly against the ends of her fingers, which had been desensitized by exposure to radiation decades earlier. Darwin said of his scientific work that it was his 'sole pleasure in life', and that he was 'never happy except when at work', despite the anxiety and ill health it seems to have caused. Mozart went on composing his Requiem (K626) on his deathbed as long as he physically could. Ray wrote a screenplay for his next film, when he was dying, knowing that he would probably be too ill to direct it. (His son directed it, after his father's death.) Woolf took her own life, when she realized that the return of her dreaded mental illness would prevent her from reading and writing. Leonardo da Vinci, Wren, and Cartier-Bresson went on working as long as they were able—into their eighties and nineties in the case of the last two.

Darwin's life shows, yet again, how changeable is the personality of exceptionally creative people, and how greatly personality varies from genius to genius. It is quite difficult to believe that the person who experienced and described the romantic adventures of the Voyage of the Beagle in the 1830s is the same person who settled at Down House in the 1840s and published the distinctly unromantic treatise On the Origin of Species in 1859.

Consider this, fairly representative, entry from Darwin's Voyage dated May 1835, which describes the author's South American journey through the Andes by horse and mule:

> In the evening, Captain FitzRoy and myself were dining with Mr Edwards, an English resident well known for his hospitality by all who have visited

Coquimbo, when a sharp earthquake happened. I heard the forecoming rumble, but from the screams of the ladies, the running of servants, and the rush of several of the gentlemen to the doorway, I could not distinguish the motion. Some of the women afterwards were crying with terror, and one person said he should not be able to sleep all night, or if he did, it would only be to dream of falling houses. The father of this gentleman had lately lost all his property at Talcuhano, and he himself had only just escaped a falling roof at Valparaiso, in 1822. He mentioned a curious coincidence which then happened: he was playing at cards, when a German, one of the party, got up, and said he would never sit in a room in these countries with the door shut, since, owing to his having done so, he had nearly lost his life at Copiapó. Accordingly he opened the door, and no sooner had he done this, than he cried out, 'Here it comes again!' and the famous shock commenced. The whole party escaped. The danger in an earthquake is not from the time lost in opening a door, but from the chance of its becoming jammed by the movement of the walls.

Less than ten years later, at Down House, such a tumultuous evening had become unthinkable for Darwin. In his thirties, he developed a clockwork routine revolving around long hours of solitary work in his study—which was banned to the rest of his family—and in his garden, interrupted by meals, light reading, a long and unaccompanied walk, and periodic visitors, with occasional trips to London and other places in the United Kingdom, such as the house of his birth at Shrewsbury and the Wedgwood house at Maer. Admittedly, this routine was partly to keep control of his chronic ill health, which started around 1840, but it was also a deliberate change in his way of life, so as to reserve as much time as available for his research. On the *Beagle* voyage, Darwin had deliberately laid himself open to as many new encounters and experiences—scientific, anthropological, and simply human—as chanced to come his way. At Down House, in contrast, his creativity flourished in an atmosphere of *lack* of openness to experience. In due course, he became something of a hermit. Of course Darwin remained open to the research and opinions of other scientists through his wide reading and vast network of correspondence, but he intentionally avoided the variety of accidental encounters and associations typical of his university and globetrotting days.

In addition, there was a change in his neuroticism. The youthful Darwin of his autobiography and *Voyage* strikes one as rather phlegmatic, with few worries or outbursts of emotion. (Hence, probably, his father's mortifying accusation, already quoted: 'You care for nothing but shooting, dogs, and rat-catching, and you will be a disgrace to yourself and all your family.') In mid-life, however, Darwin became extremely anxious, even about something as mundane as catching a train. The illness of his children, two of whom died prematurely, was one easily understandable cause. So was money—less understandably, given his handsome private income. His overriding anxiety, though, concerned his evolutionary theory and its potentially scandalous public reception, a neurosis that apparently brought on his own desperate and untreatable illness. That is why he wrote the theory down in 1844 and gave the essay to his wife Emma with instructions for its publication in the event of his early death. Thereafter, until 1859, it was his neuroticism that drove his dogged research programme to bolster the scientific evidence for the controversial theory.

Virginia Woolf, born in the very year of Darwin's death, at the height of the Victorian age, like him combined a high level of neuroticism with openness to experience mixed with a strong love of privacy. Her curiosity about others vied with her solipsism. Like her character Clarissa Dalloway, Woolf needed parties and social life, but felt both agitated by and detached from other people. At least two contradictory personalities seem to have coexisted in her mind, stimulating her creativity: the neurotic individual constantly trembling on the brink of a mental breakdown, and the confident, ruthless, sometimes snobbish observer poised to record her experiences in her diary and fiction.

Perhaps her character was influenced by that of her writer father Leslie Stephen, whose private, domestic persona differed markedly from his public and literary personae. He too was highly neurotic, which took the form of a violent temper at home, beginning as a child. 'This temper that he could not control...considering his worship of reason, his hatred of gush, of exaggeration, of all superlatives, seems inconsistent. It was due, I suppose, to the fact that he was spoilt as a child', his daughter writes in her 'Sketch of the past'.

> But it was also, I guess, the convention, supported by the great men of the time, Carlyle, Tennyson, that men of genius were naturally uncontrolled. And genius when my father was a young man was in full flower...Those who had genius in the Victorian sense were like the prophets; different, another breed. They dressed differently; wore long hair, great black hats, capes, and cloaks. They were invariably 'ill to live with'. But it never struck my father, I believe, that there was any harm in being ill to live with. I think he said unconsciously as he worked himself up into one of these violent

outbursts: 'This is a sign of my genius', and he called in Carlyle to confirm him, and let himself fly. It was part of the convention that after these outbursts, the man of genius became 'touchingly apologetic'; but he took it for granted that his wife or sister would accept his apology, that he was exempt, because of his genius, from the laws of good society.

Leslie Stephen was by no means a genius like Tennyson, as he despondently knew and once openly admitted to his daughter. His neuroticism did not have a connection to exceptional creativity, unlike his daughter's. In fact, a high level of neuroticism characterizes less than half of the ten individuals in Part II: Darwin and Woolf, and Cartier-Bresson and Champollion, both of whom easily lost their tempers and suffered mood swings. Curie, Einstein, Mozart, Ray, and Wren were even tempered, and this appears to be true, too, of Leonardo, from the limited surviving evidence. Nevertheless, as we know from Chapter 3, depression, and therefore neuroticism, is remarkably common among writers, poets, and artists. As Nettle remarks, 'there are an extraordinary number of very high achievers who have suffered [mood disorder], so at least some people high in neuroticism must be doing well by it'.

Overall, it is plain that there is no specific configuration of traits, or specific proportions of traits—no 'creative personality', in other words—that underlie exceptional creativity. All geniuses share a personality that is highly motivated to work and determined to succeed in their field. But the source of this motivation and determination cannot be analysed according to any simple model. Some degree of extraversion, neuroticism, conscientiousness, agreeableness, and openness is required for genius, along with other factors, like intellectual ability. But it is the unique way in which all these factors interact in an individual in a particular context that produces genius.

CHAPTER 20

REPUTATION, FAME, AND GENIUS

If you contemplate the wide span from Homer to Samuel Beckett, what leaps out at you is how minimal the changes have been in the qualities that sustain the identity of genius...Every era exalts works that, in a few generations, prove to be period pieces. A pragmatic definition of a genius of language is that she or he is not a producer of period pieces. With only a double or triple handful of exceptions, everything we now freshly acclaim is a potential antique, and antiques made out of language wind up in dustbins, and not in auction houses or museums.

Harold Bloom, *Genius: A Mosaic of One Hundred Exemplary Creative Minds*, 2002

Anyone older than a teenager knows that fashion is fickle, fame is transitory, and reputations rise and fall. Although this is particularly true of the arts, it also applies to a considerable extent in the sciences. During the early nineteenth century, the chemist Sir Humphry Davy—discoverer of nitrous oxide (laughing gas) and of many chemical elements such as sodium and potassium, inventor of the miner's safety lamp, a sought after and effervescent lecturer, a friend of the powerful, and president of the Royal Society from 1820–27—was Britain's most famous living scientist, whose Royal Institution assistant was the humble young Michael Faraday. Today, Davy, unlike Faraday, is not much remembered and his scientific work, though undoubtedly significant in its time, is a period piece studied only by historians of science—in contrast to that of his predecessor Newton, his successor Darwin, and even his far less fashionable immediate contemporary, Thomas Young.

In the visual arts, the ephemerality of reputation is especially evident, compared to, say, literature and music. Some of the old masters, for instance Titian, have waxed and waned in reputation with extraordinary rapidity. In a discourse in 1771, and after, the painter Joshua Reynolds, president of the Royal Academy of Arts, dismissed Italian painters such as Titian, Veronese, and Tintoretto as 'mere decorators, obsessed with colour at the expense of form': propaganda that had the effect of debasing the market for the sixteenth-century Venetian school of painting well into the nineteenth century, and raising the price of works by the seventeenth-century Italian masters owned by Reynolds's patrons, as he had intended.

Among the modern masters, Pablo Picasso's reputation is extremely high, but there is sound reason to question if this will last. Picasso himself expressed doubts about the value of much of his oeuvre, hinting that he had created it only to satisfy the demands of art dealers and the public. Even during his lifetime, high prices were paid only for his more realistic works, with the highest prices reserved for those painted in his twenties—a trend that has become more pronounced since the artist's death in his nineties in 1973, as the economist David Galenson has analysed in his *Old Masters and Young Geniuses*. With Paul Cézanne, the opposite is true. 'The auction market clearly values Cézanne's late work most highly ... the estimated peak of his age-price profile is at age 67; a painting done in that year is worth approximately 15 times that of a work the same size he painted at age 26', writes Galenson. 'In contrast, Picasso's age-price profile reaches a peak at age 26—in 1907, the year he painted *Les Demoiselles d'Avignon*. A painting he did in that year would be worth more than four times as much as one the same size he produced when he was 67.' Hence the title of Galenson's book: he dubs Cézanne an 'old master' who matured late, Picasso a 'young genius' who did his best work early on. This fact may not bode well for Picasso's reputation in the longer term. The critic David Sylvester, despite his deep interest in twentieth-century art, judged that none of its leading artists—he named Picasso, Matisse, and Piet Mondrian, in particular—was 'the equal of the great old masters'; Sylvester regarded Cézanne as 'the last of the pantheon'. The psychologist Colin Martindale, in his treatise attempting to find artistic 'laws' in creative trends over the centuries, *The Clockwork Muse: The Predictability of Artistic Change*, suggests that if the past is any guide, Picasso's paintings may, 'at some point in the future ... be seen as so ugly, and their value will be so low, that no one will want them'. While this deliberately provocative view is too extreme to be credible, a future aesthetic downgrading of Picasso from his present Olympian dominance appears more than probable during the century after his death.

It is sobering to realize that less than half of the modern and contemporary artists listed a quarter of a century ago in the contemporary art catalogues of the auction houses Sotheby's and Christie's are still offered at any major auction. Not many people now know the name of the Czech-German painter Jiri George Dokoupil, for example, who in 1988 was ranked at 30 on the *Kunstkompass* (Art Compass) scale of top international artists, which is calculated from data such as exhibitions at major institutions and reviews in art magazines. At the Royal Academy's annual summer exhibition in London, started in the mid-eighteenth century, every year it is impossible to avoid the sensation that the majority of the most reputed artists of the day will fade away within a decade or two, once they have ceased to produce new work, or have died.

Some artists' reputations rise, fall, and rise again. Titian is an obvious example, as is Rembrandt, who enjoyed three short waves of great popularity prior to his present high estimation: in England during the Napoleonic wars, in Germany and America in the 1870s–80s, and universally in the first 30 years of the twentieth century. An intriguing example is the rise, fall, and rise of the Dutch-born Lawrence Alma-Tadema—possibly the most successful painter of the Victorian era. Settling in London in 1870, Alma-Tadema became a friend of the pre-Raphaelite artists, and created a house-cum-studio that was a sumptuous temple of the arts, much talked about, 'a home which more than any other in London illustrates the artistic beauty of domiciles such as Horace and Cicero knew', according to the *Strand Magazine* critic after a visit there in 1899. Alma-Tadema specialized in lush history painting of the ancient world, and was a stickler for accuracy based on his detailed archaeological and architectural research. He was soon elected a Royal Academician, and in due course was not only knighted but also created a member of the exclusive Order of Merit, established by King Edward VII in 1902—despite his having been derided by the critic John Ruskin as the worst painter of the nineteenth century. The year after his death in 1912, there was a tremendous memorial exhibition of all of Alma-Tadema's paintings at the Royal Academy.

In 1888, Alma-Tadema began one of his most celebrated works, *The Roses of Heliogabalus*, depicting an episode from the scandalous life of the Roman emperor Heliogabalus in which the emperor arranged to smother a party of his unsuspecting guests to death with rose petals released from false ceiling panels. For four months in 1888, roses were sent daily from the French

Riviera to Alma-Tadema's studio during a London winter, in order to ensure the correctness of each petal in the painting. The work was commissioned for the exorbitant sum of £4000 (at 1888 prices). A second famous Alma-Tadema painting, this time on a biblical theme, *The Finding of Moses*, was commissioned for £5250 in 1904. Yet, at a Christie's auction in 1960, *The Roses of Heliogabalus* fetched a mere £105, and *The Finding of Moses* commanded a price of just £252. By mid-century, half a century after his death, Alma-Tadema—unlike the pre-Raphaelites—did not rate a mention in general histories of painting, such as Gombrich's *The Story of Art*. Nor is he once referred to in a current history of the Royal Academy, *School of Genius* by James Fenton.

These financial figures come from the third and final volume of Gerald Reitlinger's monumental history of the fluctuating price of art, *The Economics of Taste*, published in 1970. But even then, signs of an Alma-Tadema revival in the saleroom were visible. 'It would be premature to suggest that there are the beginnings of a cult for this most fallen of all fallen idols', commented a dismayed Reitlinger. 'The rise in Alma-Tadema can hardly be because these crowds of artists' models in togas and chitons, posed in stage photographs under the same top-light, have been equated with the *Zeitgeist* of the age'—that is, the spirit of the late 1960s. Yet, a cult is what subsequently transpired. A quarter of a century later, in 1995, *The Finding of Moses* set a new auction record of $2.8 million at Christie's in New York. The main reason seems to have been that Alma-Tadema's meticulous, gorgeous, if lacklustre recreations of scenes from antiquity, caught the attention of Hollywood film-makers during the century, as they had the eye of moneyed Victorians. D. W. Griffith's early epic films about the ancient world, *Intolerance*, *Ben Hur*, and *Cleopatra*, were influenced by Alma-Tadema's paintings. So was the 1956 remake of *The Ten Commandments* by Cecil B. DeMille, who used prints of Alma-Tadema paintings to instruct his set designers. Later, in 2000, they were a key source of inspiration for *Gladiator*, Ridley Scott's Oscar-winning Roman epic. Much as many of us may like to mock Alma-Tadema—as Ruskin first did—his sentimental, sometimes mildly pornographic, tableaux of Victorians dressed as ancient Greeks and Romans cannot be entirely ignored. Indeed, this fêted nineteenth-century painter of classical scenes enjoys a kind of kitsch celebrity in the early twenty-first century.

Past fashion, fame, and reputation, including expert acceptance and rejection, therefore foreshadow and influence current fashion, fame, and reputation in both straightforward and unforeseeable ways. What about 'genius'? Is genius, too, subject to the vagaries of time and taste?

In 1997, just as the World Wide Web he had imagined in the 1960s film *2001: A Space Odyssey* began to spread everywhere, Arthur C. Clarke mused on the future of genius in a thought-provoking interview with me, as follows:

> It's the fractal future. Although everybody is ultimately connected to everybody else, the branches of the fractal universe are so many orders of magnitude away from each other, that really nobody knows anyone else. We will have no common universe of discourse. You and I can talk together because we know when I mention poets and so on who they are. But in another generation this sort of conversation may be impossible because everyone will have an enormously wide but shallow background of experience that overlaps only a few per cent. As time goes on, all the great classics —who will even know what they are? Who will even know who Shakespeare is in a thousand years' time? It's a terrible tragedy, isn't it? I don't know the answer.

Regardless of whether or not Clarke is correct to doubt Shakespeare's future fame a millennium from now (who can know?), and whether the internet is uniting or dividing individuals, as of now, his main point is valid. Without a community of experts, sharing a 'common universe of discourse', there can be no meaning to terms like 'exceptional creativity' or 'genius'. Shakespeare, or Leonardo, or Newton, or Bach, were not geniuses until they were recognized as such by others sufficiently knowledgeable in literature, or art, or mathematics, or music, to understand the originality of their achievements. In a sense, Mozart was a genius because his rival Viennese contemporary Antonio Salieri was seen to be his foil.

The point may seem obvious, yet it contradicts our cherished belief about how creativity and genius may be present in individuals, even perhaps in ourselves—but go unrecognized. The psychologist Csikszentmihalyi pinpoints this contradiction clearly:

> The usual way to think about this issue is that someone like Van Gogh was a great creative genius, but his contemporaries did not recognize this. Fortunately, now we have discovered what a great painter he was after all, so his creativity has been vindicated. What we are saying is that we know what great art is so much better than Van Gogh's contemporaries did—those bourgeois philistines. What—besides unconscious conceit—warrants this belief? A more objective description of Van Gogh's contribution is that his creativity came into being when a sufficient

number of experts felt that his paintings had something important to contribute to the domain of art. Without such a response, Van Gogh would have remained what he was, a disturbed man who painted strange canvases.

In Csikszentmihalyi's domain/field/person model of creativity, creativity is not inherent in a person but emerges from the interaction of a person's work in a domain with a field of experts. Rather than asking the question, What is creativity?, we should instead ask, Where is creativity?, suggests Csikszentmihalyi. Moreover, according to his model, a person cannot be creative in a domain if he or she has not been exposed to the domain— either by formal training or self-education. Furthermore, creativity can manifest itself only in domains that already exist.

This model has some merits, not least in acting as a corrective to the common debasement of the word creativity to mean any imaginative expression by an individual, however, it is too rigid to encompass exceptional creativity. How can the model account for, say, Faraday's seminal contributions to physics with only a little knowledge of mathematics, or the poet Tagore's becoming India's leading modernist painter without any training in art, or the architect Ventris's brilliant decipherment of Linear B —in which there existed neither a domain of 'decipherment' nor one of 'Linear B studies'? (There are still no university departments of decipherment.) Anyone who crosses disciplinary boundaries, manages to make a breakthrough, and forges a new domain—as Darwin did in drawing upon biology, palaeontology, geology, and economics to create his theory of natural selection—is apparently disqualified from being considered creative by Csikszentmihalyi's model.

A more valuable aspect of the model is its prediction that the appellation genius should come and go with the fluctuating opinions of experts. In other words, geniuses can be made and unmade over long periods; all attributions of genius are provisional. This chimes with the evidence from studies of reputation. In Chapter 1, we saw that J. S. Bach has generally ranked first among musical geniuses in recent decades, though somewhat lower in the first half of the twentieth century, when Beethoven was widely considered the greatest composer. But this was far from being true during the eighteenth century, when Bach's music was neglected after his death in 1750, except by a few composers, notably Mozart, Haydn, and Beethoven. The change in Bach's reputation began after 1800 and took off in 1829, the centenary of Bach's St Matthew Passion, thanks to the 20-year-old composer

Felix Mendelssohn's conducting the first performance of the great choral work since Bach's death, at a concert in Berlin. The Bach revival that followed during the nineteenth and twentieth centuries was the first prominent example of the deliberate exhumation of old music, accompanied by biographical and critical studies; and it has subsequently inspired scholarly revivals of other composers.

Two centuries after the birth of Mendelssohn in 1809, something similar is happening to him and his music. Where Bach was once considered old-fashioned and churchy, Mendelssohn has tended to be considered a facile Romantic. He had a middling rank in twentieth-century surveys of composers. 'It is only recently that Mendelssohn has made the transition from being an "easy" composer to being a "composer with problems"', writes the veteran conductor and musicologist Christopher Hogwood in a 2008 foreword to a volume of essays by eleven different scholars entitled *Mendelssohn in Performance*. Hogwood compares Mendelssohn with Mozart, and explains:

> In his lifetime he, like Mozart, outlived his reputation as a wunderkind. However, whereas Mozart then proceeded to a career in which the public decided that his performing was a spectacle worth applauding, but his later compositions were simply too difficult, Mendelssohn (we were led to believe) inherited a lifestyle that was easy and untroubled, his upbringing elegant and catholic, his musical tours a fluent litany of *jeu perlé* performances, and his compositions effortless outpourings; even his watercolors were dismissed as evidence of 'too much talent'.

Other published scholarship on Mendelssohn since the 1990s involves the greater availability of his correspondence, several biographical studies, and critically scrutinized editions of many major works. 'Although it would be nice if the Mendelssohn-piano returned with as much prestige as the Mozart-piano currently enjoys, this is not exclusively a matter for period instruments; other types of curiosity and initiative would also be rewarding', thinks Hogwood. He suggests that: 'The independent-minded violinist (with either ancient or modern equipment) who dared to program "solo" Bach with Mendelssohn's intriguing piano accompaniments would discover that it no longer spells professional death.' In his view, 'To deal successfully with a composer who was a genius by both nature and nurture requires all the assistance we can muster.' The long-term results of all this labour by experts in the domain of Mendelssohn studies are still unclear. Conceivably, Mendelssohn's reputation will eventually rise to a level of genius close to that of Bach, Mozart, and Beethoven, where Hogwood believes it properly belongs.

Of the ten individuals in Part II, only a couple of them can be said to have enjoyed the double distinction of being seen as geniuses when alive and ever since their deaths: Leonardo and Einstein. Few Italian artists and patrons seriously questioned Leonardo's unique stature by the time of his death in 1519, despite his failure to complete many of his works—as is abundantly clear from Vasari's effulgent account of Leonardo in his mid sixteenth-century *Lives*. Einstein's theory of relativity was compared by Max Planck to the Copernican revolution within a few years of its publication, though it required two or three decades to be universally accepted by physicists (who nevertheless rejected the work of Einstein's last three decades). By contrast, the reputations for genius of Champollion, Curie, Darwin, Mozart, and Wren, which now seem beyond dispute, took decades to become established, and underwent substantial dips on the way to their present eminence. In the case of Cartier-Bresson, Ray, and Woolf, there is still some establishing to do. This is partly because photography and film-making have yet to acquire the respectability of literature, music, painting, and science, and partly also because Cartier-Bresson, Ray, and Woolf did their best work comparatively recently, within the past two or three generations, whereas the breakthroughs of Einstein (1905), Curie (1898), Darwin (1859), Mozart (1780s), Wren (late seventeenth century), and Leonardo (circa 1500), occurred a century and more ago.

The trajectory of each individual's reputation is, not surprisingly, different. Yet in all cases, two factors extraneous to their breakthroughs came into play in the general public's crowning of them as geniuses.

In the first place, personal accidents and idiosyncrasies have often contributed to a reputation for genius, as already mentioned in the introduction—whether they be Mozart's early death at the height of his musical powers, Curie's devoted but tragic coupling of science and marriage, or Woolf's drowning herself to avoid succumbing to mental illness. All three of these familiar facts cater to deep-rooted, if ill-founded, beliefs: those whom the gods love die young (Mozart's death); true scientists cannot be romantics (Curie's marriage); great artists must be somewhat mad (Woolf's suicide).

Second, historical accidents can be important. Mozart fortuitously came to maturity as a composer at the very moment, 1781, when his key patron Emperor Joseph II—who adored Italian opera buffa—acquired a position of sole authority in Vienna, after the death of his mother (who distrusted the Mozarts). Darwin's theory of natural selection happened to be published in 1859 in a period of intense questioning of orthodox Christianity. The validation of general relativity by solar eclipse observations in 1919 chanced to come at a time of global exhaustion after the slaughter of the First World War, and thus answered a yearning for transcendent cosmic truths, intensified by the coincidence that the theory was the work of a pacifist German (Einstein), while the astronomical observations were carried out by a pacifist Englishman (Arthur Eddington). This post-war *Zeitgeist* does not altogether explain the furore created by relativity, however. 'I never understood why the theory of relativity with its concepts and problems so far removed from practical life should for so long have met with a lively, or indeed passionate, resonance among broad circles of the public', Einstein commented in 1942 in a preface to a biography of himself. 'I have never yet heard a truly convincing answer to this question.' As one of his biographers put it some years after Einstein's death: 'The speed with which his fame spread across the world, down through the intellectual layers to the man in the street, the mixture of semi-religious awe and near hysteria which his figure aroused, created a startling phenomenon which has never been fully explained.'

The role of experts in the making of genius is also naturally crucial, as Csikszentmihalyi's model of creativity predicts. But the effects of their judgement are not necessarily predictable. Sometimes the experts greet original work with unanimous acclaim, as with Leonardo's *The Last Supper* and Curie's discovery of radium, but more often they are divided. Frequently, their criticism, even their hostility, has the long-term effect of enhancing the reputations of artists and scientists who make breakthroughs. The stronger the initial opposition from some experts, the more original the breakthrough is likely to be.

All of the other eight breakthroughs in Part II were to some extent controversial; those of Champollion, Darwin, Einstein, Ray, and Woolf, highly so. The authorities at St Paul's Cathedral quarrelled with Wren and decorated his completed edifice against his expressed wishes, causing him to wash his hands of the project in the 1710s. Mozart's opera *The Marriage of Figaro* divided audiences in Vienna in 1786, was neglected in Italy, and bowdlerized in England for many years. Cartier-Bresson's lauded New York exhibition of 1947 provoked his closest professional colleague, war photographer Robert Capa, to warn him against becoming a pretentious surrealist. Champollion's hieroglyphic decipherment of 1823 continued to be attacked and defended by scholars for many decades, until the second half of the nineteenth century, long after his death in 1832. His most vigorous detractors tended to be scholars from his own country France. Woolf's novels, generally speaking, continue to attract both lavish praise and dismissive criticism from both novelists and literary scholars —coloured by the growth in her status as a feminist writer. 'Woolf's reputation in this country [Britain] has always been extremely mixed', her biographer Hermione Lee admitted in 2002.

   With Darwin's reputation, there was a unique complication to add to the intense controversy over his ideas. As we know, the scientific newcomer Alfred Russel Wallace came up with his own theory of natural selection independently of Darwin, and both theories were published jointly in the same journal in 1858, at the behest of Darwin's expert friends Joseph Hooker and Charles Lyell. The idea might fairly have become known to posterity as the Darwin–Wallace theory of natural selection, but the joint name never caught on with scientists. Wallace did nothing to fight for it, because he enormously admired Darwin and *On the Origin of Species*, comparing the book to Newton's *Principia* in importance. He even penned an exposition of natural selection entitled *Darwinism*. Darwin, for his part, was content to leave the issue for others to decide. But he made an honest admission in a letter to Wallace soon after publication: 'you speak far too modestly of yourself;—you would, if you had had my leisure, [have] done the work just as well, perhaps better, than I have done it'. Presumably, Darwin knew that his already large scientific reputation, his higher social position than Wallace's, and the active support of his friends in the scientific establishment, would come down in his favour as the official sole author of the theory. During his long lifetime, Wallace eventually became established, too; he was a member of the Order of Merit on his death in 1913. Yet today, the reputation of Darwin is unassailable among both scientists and the general public, whilst that of Wallace, despite recent attempts to rescue him from obscurity during Darwin's bicentenary in 2009, is limited mainly to naturalists and historians of evolution.

   Ray and his controversial first film *Pather Panchali* offer a particularly fine example of the complexity of reputation, especially the role of experts versus the public. When *Pather Panchali* had its Indian premiere at a special screening of the Advertising Club of Calcutta in 1955, Ray recalled a disastrous response. None of the well-heeled Bengalis in the audience praised it, only the English who were present. There was little support from the

Calcutta literati. Soon, however, the film caught on with ordinary Bengali cinema-goers, and became a surprise hit. Nonetheless, there was sustained opposition to the film within the West Bengal Government (despite its being the film's producer) and in the Government of India in New Delhi; both governments opposed the idea of sending *Pather Panchali* to represent India at the Cannes Film Festival in 1956, on the grounds that it depicted poverty and therefore projected the wrong image of Independent India to foreigners. Prime Minister Jawaharlal Nehru personally overruled his officials.

At Cannes, the unknown film by an unknown director almost died a death. By a quirk of fate, its screening clashed with a party given by the Japanese delegation for a film by Akira Kurosawa. Those who did see *Pather Panchali* or knew of its merits independently—who included the major film critics Lindsay Anderson (from Britain), André Bazin (from France), and Gene Moskowitz (from the United States)—were incensed. A rescreening was arranged and the British member of the festival jury, James Quinn of the British Film Institute, put forward Ray's film as worthy of a prize. 'The initial reaction was one of shock if not of horror by most of those present', Quinn recalled in 1985, 'especially the French scriptwriter Henri Jaenson who referred to *Pather Panchali* as "cette ordure"—as I vividly remember'—a disdain for Ray's films also found in French directors of the New Wave such as François Truffaut and Jean-Luc Godard (though not, it should be said, Jean Renoir). But *Pather Panchali* was too good for French hubris to kill it off; it was awarded a special prize at Cannes, for 'Best Human Document'.

When it reached New York in 1958, there was yet another split in critical opinion. Ray himself attended the first screening at the Fifth Avenue Playhouse. In 1982, he described the scene:

> I watched the audience surge out of the theatre blear-eyed and visibly shaken. An hour or so later, in the small hours, came the morning edition of *The New York Times*. It carried Bosley Crowther's review of my film. Crowther was the doyen of New York critics, with the power to make or mar a film's prospects as a saleable commodity. Crowther was unmoved by *Pather Panchali*. In fact, he said the film was so amateurish that 'it would barely pass for a rough cut in Hollywood.'

About a week later, Crowther was compelled to recant in a follow-up *New York Times* review, at least to some extent, such was the public's response to the film. In addition, almost every other major American film critic, including the critic of *The New Yorker*, disagreed with Crowther. *Pather Panchali* ran for an extraordinary eight months at the New York theatre.

Half a century on, many of these attitudes and divisions of opinion persist. Ray's long-term reputation is not yet settled. When he was awarded an Oscar for lifetime achievement by the Academy of Motion Picture Arts and Sciences in 1992, it was given more for the celebrated *Pather Panchali* than for his body of 30 or so feature films. Yet a veteran British film critic and long-time admirer of Ray's films, Derek Malcolm of *The Guardian*, suspected, almost certainly accurately, that 'half of the Academicians probably think *Pather Panchali* is a curry'.

Virtually alone in the arts in the twentieth century, Ray drew with authority on the cultures of the East and the West in equal measure. His reputation therefore suffered, and will continue to suffer, from the dearth of experts and audiences who are comparably bicultural. Whether the avowedly more multicultural world of the twenty-first century will narrow this historic gap in cultural understanding remains to be seen. At the time of writing, the inanities of Bollywood movies, rather than the intelligence, depth, and subtlety of Ray's films, have come to represent Indian cinema to both Indians and to the world. Maybe in time this fashion will pass. However, Ray himself was doubtful. 'But why should the West care?' he asked. 'The cultural gap between East and West is too wide for a handful of films to reduce it. It can happen only when critics back it up with study on other levels as well. But where is the time, with so many films from other countries to contend with? And where is the compulsion?'

There is of course no compulsion—except, perhaps, with works of genius. It may be that it is the compelling quality of a scientific theory or work of art, which demands the attention of each new generation, that defines what we mean by 'genius'. The theories of evolution by natural selection and of relativity are still required reading by every working biologist and physicist. They continue to generate fresh thinking and experiments around the world. The melodies and harmonies of Mozart and the photographs of Cartier-Bresson have the power to make people listen and look closely, even when they do not know the identity of the composer or photographer. Individual geniuses may come and go, but the idea of genius will not let go of us. Genius is the name we give to a quality of work that transcends fashion, fame, and reputation: the opposite of a period piece. Somehow, genius abolishes both the time and the place of its origin.

CHAPTER 21

THE TEN-YEAR RULE

Before the gates of Excellence the high gods have placed sweat.

An unnamed ancient Greek poet who predated Plato

T his book began with the age-old question of where creative ideas come from. In part one, we considered some of the ingredients of creativity, such as intelligence, unconscious processing, and mental illness, from the point of view of psychologists. Part II looked at how these ingredients interacted within the minds of ten exceptionally creative individuals to produce breakthroughs in the arts and sciences. The final part of the book has tried to find some patterns in their particular genius and that of other geniuses, for instance, in parental upbringing, formal education, and personality. In the last chapter, we return to the original question, to consider what generalizations and theories about exceptional creativity as a whole, if any, are reasonable.

The first one is that creative breakthroughs may appear to be examples of 'sudden genius', but in reality are always the outcome of a gradual accumulation of knowledge and experience. As seen in Part II, this was true of all ten individuals and their breakthroughs, from Leonardo and *The Last Supper*—completed around 1498—which had its origins as far back as works made by Leonardo in 1481, through Einstein and the theory of special relativity—created in 1905—which began with Einstein's thought experiment involving a light ray in 1895–96, to Ray and *Pather Panchali*—completed in 1955—which originated in illustrations for an edition of the original novel made by Ray in 1944. In none of these ten cases was the breakthrough the result of an accident; each emerged from a long period of preparation.

Second, many, albeit not all, breakthroughs involve a eureka experience, that is, a pivotal revelatory episode. Good examples are the overnight creation of special relativity by Einstein in his flat in Bern after a long talk with his friend Besso, and the screening of the Italian film *Bicycle Thieves* in London during which Ray first visualized the essentials of his Indian film. Champollion in September 1822, Curie in February 1898, Darwin in September-October 1838, Einstein in May 1905, and Ray in May 1950, all passed through epiphanic periods of inspiration leading to their breakthroughs, as described earlier. So, less emphatically, did Cartier-Bresson probably in early 1932, when he took up photography with a Leica, and Woolf in October 1922, during the initial planning of *Mrs Dalloway*. A case could also be made for a eureka experience by Mozart, in the six weeks of late 1785 during which he is said (by his librettist Da Ponte) to have composed the entire first draft of the score for *The Marriage of Figaro*. With Leonardo and Wren, there is no evidence, for or against, of an epiphany.

A third major generalization concerns the dogged work that leads to creative breakthroughs. In Edison's classic words, dating from around 1903, 'Genius is one per cent inspiration, ninety-nine per cent perspiration.' Another version of this idea, attributed to George Bernard Shaw, alters the proportions to 'ninety per cent perspiration, ten per cent inspiration'. A recent editorial in the *New Scientist* magazine even misattributed Edison's remark to Einstein—such is its ring of truth.

Late in life, Darwin made the same basic point less pithily but with profound insight in a letter to his son Horace, as follows:

> I have been speculating last night what makes a man a discoverer of undiscovered things, and a most perplexing problem it is.—Many men who are very clever,—much cleverer than the discoverers—never originate anything. As far as I can conjecture, the art consists in habitually searching for causes or meaning of everything which occurs. This implies sharp observation and requires as much knowledge as possible of the subject investigated.

There can be no doubting that geniuses work habitually and continually. Edison was the owner of 1093 patents, lodging an average of one patent every two weeks of his adult life; Bach on average composed 20 pages of finished music per day—sufficient to keep a copyist occupied for a lifetime of standard working hours in writing out the parts by hand; Picasso created more than 20,000 works; Poincaré published 500 papers and 30 books; Einstein produced 240 publications; Freud had 330. 'These figures lead one to realize a very important fact—these people must have spent the major part of their waking hours and their energy on their work', remarks R. Ochse in *Before the Gates of Excellence: The Determinants of Creative Genius*.

Our ten individuals confirm this picture without exception. All were prolific, compared with their contemporaries, and all continued working up to their dying days, though of course their breakthroughs occurred earlier in their lives with the obvious exceptions of Mozart and Champollion, who died young. I am reminded of the indefatigable Thomas Young, Champollion's rival, who worked on the proofs of his *Rudiments of an Egyptian Dictionary* when he lay dying in 1829 in his mid-fifties, able to manage only a pencil instead of his customary pen. As a professional physician, Young had a better idea of his medical condition than most patients have. But when a close friend remonstrated with him that the writing would exhaust him, Young answered: 'that it was a work which if he should live it would be a satisfaction to him to have finished, but that if it were otherwise, which seemed most probable, as he had never witnessed a complaint which appeared to make more rapid progress, it would still be a great satisfaction to him never to have spent an idle day in his life'.

Further convincing generalizations about exceptional creativity are trickier to arrive at. There is little consensus among creators as to whether inspiration is separate from perspiration or not. Inspiration evidently emerges, 'unbidden and incomprehensible to its very begetter' (writes psychologist Chris McManus), from both concentrated work on a problem and from apparently unrelated work. Most likely, inspiration and perspiration are inseparable twins. 'If there is inspiration, it's not something that comes at the beginning of the piece. It comes in the course of writing it', the composer Elliott Carter remarked. 'The more I get into the piece the more the inspiration—well, I don't know exactly what inspiration means—but I would see more clearly and with more excitement and more interest new things, and would not be in the process of discarding a great many things I don't want to do.' On the other hand, a second composer, Aaron Copland, said: 'You can't pick the moment when you are going to have ideas. It picks you and then you might be completely absorbed in another piece of work...I think composers will tell you that they get ideas when they can't possibly work on them. They put them down where they can find them when they need to look for ideas and they don't come easily.'

As for where an idea comes from, the possibilities seem to be as diverse as the individual creators. The sculptor Anthony Caro said of himself:

> There are so many ways in which it comes. It comes from thinking about art. It comes from looking at art. It comes from a conversation you had.

It comes from the last work you did. It comes from what the architects are doing. It comes from paintings you saw. It comes from seeing two bits of steel on the ground together or it comes from coming across something and saying, 'That's a start, now wait a minute, what else does it need?'

Several psychologists, such as Arthur Koestler, David Perkins, and Dean Keith Simonton, have attempted to design theories of creativity. None of these has been truly explanatory, which is why this book has neglected them thus far, except for Wallas's preparation/incubation/illumination/ verification model (Chapter 3) and Csikszentmihalyi's domain/field/person model (Chapter 20). One of the more useful is Simonton's theory that creativity arises as 'a joint product of logic, chance, genius, and Zeitgeist— with chance *primus inter pares*', which Simonton sets out in his *Creativity in Science*. The first three elements—logic, chance, and genius—are straight-forward enough to grasp and self-evidently important; *Zeitgeist* is a bit more complicated to understand and uncertain in its validity. It is worth having a look at Simonton's evidence for the role of the *Zeitgeist*, because his discus-sion clearly demonstrates the difficulty of separating the constituent elem-ents of exceptional creativity.

Zeitgeist can be translated from the German as 'the spirit of the times', meaning the trend of thought and feeling in a period. It is a product of the sociocultural system, and therefore the antithesis of the notion that history is made by the ideas and actions of great individuals—geniuses—standing outside their society and culture. Good examples of the *Zeitgeist* are the Romanticism of the nineteenth century and the anti-imperialism of the second half of the twentieth century. Applied to the history of science, the term suggests that a discovery or invention, such as the structure of DNA or the World Wide Web, is determined not by individual scientists but by developments internal to a particular science or by emerging social needs. In other words, discoveries and inventions become virtually inev-itable when the level of human knowledge has reached a certain point and sufficient numbers of scientists are focused on solving a problem. It is the *Zeitgeist* that is said to bring about the phenomenon of more or less simultaneous discovery or invention by two or more independent investigators.

Famous instances of multiple discovery, with approximate dates, include: the discovery of sunspots by Galileo in 1610, and by three other individuals independently in 1611; the discovery of the calculus by Newton in 1671, and by Leibniz in 1676; the invention of photography by Louis Daguerre, and by

William Henry Fox Talbot, in 1839; the discovery of ether anaesthesia in surgery by Crawford Long in 1842, and by William Morton in 1846; the discovery of the conservation of energy by Julius Robert Mayer in 1843, by Hermann Helmholtz in 1847, and by James Joule in 1847; the discovery of evolution by natural selection by Darwin in 1838, and by Wallace in 1858; the discovery of the periodic table of the chemical elements by Béguyer de Chancourtois in 1862, by John Newlands in 1864, by Julius Lothar Meyer in 1864, and by Dmitri Mendeleev in 1869; the invention of the telephone by Alexander Graham Bell, and by Elisha Gray, in 1876; and the invention of the incandescent carbon-filament lamp by Edison, and by Joseph Swan, in 1878. Multiple discoveries and inventions became much rarer in the twentieth century, as scientific communication became faster. As soon as the structure of DNA was announced by Watson and Crick in the journal *Nature* in 1953, for example, other investigators working on the problem, such as Linus Pauling, abandoned their efforts. In 1979, Simonton investigated and analysed multiple discoveries in detail. He found the overwhelming majority of cases to be doublets, that is, two claimants to be the discoverer. There were 449 doublets, 104 triplets, 18 quadruplets, 7 quintuplets, and 1 octuplet.

On the face of it, such a list is good evidence for the importance of the *Zeitgeist* in discovery and invention. It suggests that great ideas were 'in the air', ready to be perceived by any mind that was sufficiently receptive. However, the evidence becomes weaker when carefully examined, as Simonton himself readily concedes.

For a start, over three quarters of the multiple discoveries are doublets: 449 out of 579. If sociocultural trends are indeed an important determining factor in exceptional creativity, we should expect a higher proportion of triplets, quadruplets, and higher-grade multiples than is actually observed. Wafted by the *Zeitgeist*, a great idea should have occurred to more than two individuals fairly frequently.

Second, many of the multiples are not strictly simultaneous, despite being independent. Only about a fifth of them took place within a one-year interval. The wider the spread in the dates of the independent discoveries, the less convincing they are as examples of the *Zeitgeist* at work. Five years elapsed between Newton's and Leibniz's discovery of the calculus (which led Newton to accuse Leibniz of plagiarism). There was a gap of some 20 years, almost a generation, between Darwin's first conception of natural selection and Wallace's very similar discovery. And there was an even longer gap, 35 years, between Gregor Mendel's discovery of genetic laws in 1865 (of which Darwin was totally unaware before his death in 1882) and their co-discovery in 1900 by Hugo de Vries, Carl Correns, and Erich von Tschermak, each of whom worked independently. Was Mendel 'ahead of his time'? Such a concept is meaningless if it is the 'spirit of the times' that determines the date of a discovery. 'If the discovery of genetic laws was absolutely inevitable in 1865, then why did they have to be rediscovered in 1900?' asks Simonton.

Third, some scientists participate in more than one multiple discovery. The more productive a scientist is in general, the larger the number of multiples in which he participates. High individual productivity is a feature of genius, as we know, and has nothing to do with the *Zeitgeist*. Hence, genius must have a significant role in multiples.

Lastly, what appears to be a multiple may in fact not be a case of true identity, thereby casting doubt on the whole claim that frequent multiple discoveries occur. In a doublet, the 'same' discoveries may have only one or two elements in common out of many elements; moreover, the two processes of arriving at the same discovery may be quite different. Patent applications bring out this fact prominently, because lawyers are compelled to consider if the specifications of a new patent application may infringe upon those of an existing patent. 'Typically, the overlap involves merely one feature out of over a hundred that may be specified in the application', writes Simonton. 'It is extremely rare for two features to be involved, and genuine duplication practically never occurs.' In a comparable way, Nobel Prizes for a single discovery in science are very often shared between three scientists, each of whom has looked at the same problem from a different perspective and contributed differently to the discovery—as happened with the structure of DNA, where the Nobel Prize was shared between Crick, Watson, and Maurice Wilkins in 1962. When nuclear magnetic resonance was discovered in 1946 by two groups of American scientists working independently of each other, one at Harvard University and the other at Stanford University, to begin with one group was literally unable to under-stand what the other group was talking about, because their two approaches to the physical phenomenon they had discovered differed so radically. Highly unusual is the close identity that occurred between Darwin's and Wallace's writings, as described by Darwin in a despairing letter to Lyell written at the time: 'I never saw a more striking coincidence; if Wallace had my MS. sketch written out in 1842, he could not have made a better short abstract! Even his terms now stand as heads of my chapters...So all my originality, whatever it may amount to, will be smashed.'

In sum, the idea that the *Zeitgeist* contributes to creative breakthroughs is too flawed to be taken very seriously—fascinating as the phenomenon of multiple discoveries may be. Like all existing attempts to devise a model of creativity, the *Zeitgeist* idea founders on the sheer diversity of what it tries to model.

The only widely respected 'law' of creativity is really the so-called ten-year rule, discussed briefly in the introduction. The psychologist John Hayes was the earliest to argue for the ten-year rule, in the 1980s, on the evidence of the time taken by composers to produce their first great work —almost always ten years or more. Howard Gardner endorsed the rule in the 1990s in his *Creating Minds*, which explicitly claimed to show that the breakthroughs of seven major figures of the modern era—Freud, Einstein, Picasso, Igor Stravinsky, T. S. Eliot, Martha Graham, and Mahatma Gandhi —obeyed the ten-year rule. Gardner commented that: 'Even Mozart, arguably the exception that proves the rule, had been composing for at least a decade before he could regularly produce works that are considered worthy of inclusion in the repertory.' More recently, Robert Weisberg stated that: 'the ten-year rule is relevant to outstanding creative achievement in many domains, including composition of classical music, painting, and poetry'. And the psychologist Keith Sawyer, a student and collaborator of Csikszentmihalyi, remarked: 'One of the most solid findings in creativity research is the ten-year rule: It takes a minimum of ten years of hard work and practice before attaining the high level of performance that results in great creativity.'

Not every psychologist is as enthusiastic to apply the rule to exceptional creativity, yet all of them treat it seriously. Nonetheless, before considering the evidence for its validity, it is wise to bear in mind a general warning of Daniel Nettle: 'Psychology is not like physics...The best that any kind of psychology can hope for is *some* predictive power at the statistical level across a group of people. We will never be at the stage of making exact predictions about what individuals will do and when.'

In my own view, the ten-year rule is best considered in three versions: weak, medium, and strong. (Even physicists sometimes use such weak/strong distinctions.) The *weak* version is similar to the one stated by Sawyer above: a breakthrough requires a minimum of ten years of hard work and practice in a relevant domain—and it may take much longer. The *medium* version is more restrictive: a breakthrough requires a minimum of ten years of hard work and practice focused on the particular problem solved by the breakthrough. The *strong* version is more restrictive still: a breakthrough requires about ten years—no less and no more—of hard work and practice focused on the particular problem solved by the breakthrough. To introduce three versions of the rule may seem slightly pedantic, but it serves to highlight the strengths and weaknesses of the rule's operation in practice.

If we apply the rule to the ten individuals in Part II, the results are interesting and significant. All ten geniuses obey the weak version of the rule. Eight of them—Cartier-Bresson, Champollion, Darwin, Einstein, Mozart, Ray, Woolf, and Wren—obey the medium version. Five of these— Cartier-Bresson, Darwin, Einstein, Ray, and Wren—obey the strong version, too, with Woolf as a plausible sixth contender. Let us look at the details of each breakthrough to see how this analysis has been arrived at.

Boyhood snaps with a Box Brownie camera aside, Cartier-Bresson began taking photographs casually in 1929–30, and acquired his Leica camera in 1932. He then worked professionally as a photographer (with a significant break as a film-maker) from 1933 until 1940, when he was captured by the Germans—after burying the Leica for the duration of his captivity—and again as a professional from 1944–46, which led to his breakthrough exhibition at New York's Museum of Modern Art in early 1947, and the subsequent publication of *The Decisive Moment*. Thus, Cartier-Bresson committed about ten years to photography, before making his breakthrough.

Champollion's first exposure to ancient Egypt appears to have been in 1802, at the age of eleven, two decades before he announced his preliminary decipherment of the hieroglyphs in 1822 and published the full version in 1824. But he did not begin studying the subject seriously until he arrived in Paris as a student in 1807. There he first examined the problem of deciphering the Rosetta Stone in 1808, made no progress with it, and set it aside for a while to concentrate on his study of other aspects of Egypt, including the Coptic language, although it is clear from his own statements during this period that he constantly thought about the Rosetta Stone. He did not take up the problem in earnest until 1814, when he received some assistance from Thomas Young. Thereafter he worked at it persistently, except for a period of almost two years in 1816–18, when his difficult personal circumstances intervened. If we allow for this break in concentration, Champollion worked on the problem of the Rosetta Stone and the hieroglyphs for twelve or thirteen years before his breakthrough.

Discounting school science, Curie began to study physics and chemistry seriously around 1886, when she was a governess in Poland, eleven or twelve years before her breakthrough in Paris in 1898, when she discovered polonium and radium. In 1890–91, she had access to a physics and chemistry laboratory in Warsaw, where she conducted some simple experiments. However, her main scientific training did not begin until 1891, at the Sorbonne, and she did not focus on radioactivity until 1896–97. Her extraordinarily rapid progress may appear to suggest a contravention of the ten-year rule. However, she had the inestimable advantage of collaborating closely from 1895 onwards with a highly experienced scientist, Pierre Curie, who built the piezoelectric quartz balance crucial for his wife's experiment. Under these unique circumstances, the rule cannot be expected to apply, except in its weak version.

Darwin and Einstein are clear-cut exemplars of the strong version of the rule. Darwin began to study the natural world as a child through his interest in collecting. The hobby developed at Edinburgh University via his activities in the Plinian Society in 1826–27. It became serious at Cambridge University in 1828, through his association with John Stevens Henslow and other scientists. From then until 1838, about ten years later, when he made his breakthrough, Darwin focused on natural history and the problem of species. Einstein studied some physics at school in Germany, but did not begin to address the subject seriously until he dropped out of school in 1894 and spent many months at home in Milan in 1895, when he probably made his thought experiment with a light ray. From then on, he devoted most of his time and energy to reading, thinking, and talking about mathematics and physics. His breakthrough with special relativity came ten years later, in 1905.

Leonardo, as usual, is more difficult to analyse, because so few of the events of his early life are dated. It appears that he showed early artistic talent, judging from the story of the horrific shield he made for his father. He was apprenticed to Verrocchio's workshop some time between 1469 and 1472 and worked there for some years, probably until 1477–78. His first major work, *The Adoration of the Magi*, dates from 1481, some ten years after he began working for Verrocchio. In the same year, he seems to have begun thinking about a version of 'The Last Supper', judging from a pen-and-ink sketch and from some of the faces in *The Adoration*. But he did not begin to paint *The Last Supper* in Milan for well over ten years: started in about 1494, it was completed in 1498. Thus, Leonardo certainly obeys the weak version of the ten-year rule, and maybe also the medium version, depending on how one assesses the relevance of the 1481 work as the germ of *The Last Supper*.

Mozart is said by his father to have begun composing at the age of four, but his published career dates from 1764, when he was eight. Yet, despite his precociousness, it was not until twelve years later, in January 1777, around the time he turned 21, that Mozart composed what is widely regarded as his first masterwork, the piano concerto No. 9, K271, known as the 'Jeune-homme' Concerto: 'a landmark in Mozart's piano concerto oeuvre', according to *The Cambridge Mozart Encyclopedia*—a view supported by many other respected music critics. This subjective opinion is substantiated by objective research by Hayes that defines a 'masterwork' as a work for which five different recordings are available in a leading music guide. 'By this definition, Mozart's first masterwork [K271] was written in the twelfth year of his career', writes Hayes. As for opera composing, Mozart again required some twelve years to move from his first opera, *La Finta Semplice*, composed in 1768, to his first operatic masterwork, *Idomeneo*, composed in 1780–81; and yet another five or six years before he composed *The Marriage of Figaro*. 'It is strange to say of a composer who started writing at six, and lived only 36 years, that he developed late, but that is the truth', wrote the *New York Times* music critic Harold Schonberg in 1970. 'Few of Mozart's early works, elegant as they are, have the personality, concentration, and richness that entered his music after 1781.'

Ray offers another clear case of the rule in its strong version. Like many children he enjoyed visiting the cinema, but his interest in film as an artistic medium did not become serious until his time as an art student in the early 1940s. When, as an illustrator, he was asked to make woodcuts for an abridged edition of the novel *Pather Panchali* in 1944, it soon occurred to him that it would make a fine film. During the second half of the 1940s, he wrote screenplays (none of which was filmed), started a film society, and assisted Jean Renoir with his search for film locations in Bengal. His film, *Pather Panchali*, started in 1950, was finally completed in 1955, about ten years after he first became interested in adapting the novel for the screen.

Woolf, by contrast, took much longer than ten years to make her breakthrough with *Mrs Dalloway*, published in 1925. By then, she had been publishing her writing for some two decades. Her first articles had appeared in print soon after her father's death in 1904. In 1907, she began her first novel, but did not complete it until 1913. Published in 1915 as *The Voyage Out*, it sketched out the characters of Mr and Mrs Dalloway, whom she would later expand. Arguably, therefore, Woolf obeys the strong version of the ten-year rule, since about ten years elapsed between her introduction of Mrs Dalloway into her fiction around 1913 and her creation of a central role for the character, completed in 1923–24.

Finally, there is Wren. He seems to have had some interest in architecture while at Oxford in the 1650s, but the evidence is slight. In 1663, however, his interest blossomed. In this year he designed a chapel for Pembroke College, Cambridge, at the behest of his uncle, and, more significantly, presented his plans for the Sheldonian Theatre in Oxford, completed by him in 1669. Meanwhile, he was asked to advise on the rebuilding of St Paul's Cathedral. By the end of the 1660s—when he was officially appointed the royal architect—architecture had become the focus of almost all his attention. His Great Model for St Paul's was made in 1673–74, and, despite major changes to it during the construction of the cathedral, the model dominated his thinking ever after. So we may reasonably conclude that Wren, also, obeys the strong version of the ten-year rule.

The clear relevance of the ten-year rule to our ten individuals is surely suggestive. As noted in the introduction, a variety of other exceptionally creative individuals and their breakthroughs obey the rule in its strong version, ranging from scientists like Faraday and Kekulé to artists like Hemingway and Picasso. Of course, there are also many exceptions to the strong version. However, exceptions to the weak version of the rule—in which a scientist or artist makes a breakthrough after *less* than ten years of hard work and practice in a domain—are extremely rare. Neither Einstein nor Mozart fits this bill, despite our natural expectations of such prodigies.

Hayes, using his above-mentioned criterion to define a 'masterwork', discovered only three exceptions among classical composers, none of whom is in the top rank: Erik Satie composed a masterwork in year eight of his career, while Niccolò Paganini and Dmitry Shostakovich composed one masterwork each in year nine of their careers. In the visual arts, Van Gogh painted some of his classic works in 1888 only eight years after beginning to paint; but he had earlier spent six or seven years working for an art dealer in London and Paris where he was in daily contact with master-pieces that had trained his eye and aroused his sensibility, so Van Gogh certainly did not start painting from square one in 1880. In the sciences, the theoretical physicist Werner Heisenberg, one of the pioneers of quantum theory, created matrix mechanics in 1925, aged 23, only about five years after beginning his university study of physics; but Heisenberg had two leading physicists, Max Born and Niels Bohr, as very close mentors during this period. Paul Dirac, another great theoretical physicist, may provide another exception: in 1928, he formulated the relativistic theory of the electron from which he predicted the existence of the positron, aged 25, about six years after beginning his university training in applied mathematics; but Dirac had previously taken a three-year degree in electrical engineering. Perhaps only Newton fairly and squarely beats the ten-year rule in science: his *annus mirabilis*, 1665–66, occurred after less than five years of study at Cambridge, at the age of only 22–23.

The predominance of theoretical physics among the handful of exceptions may be a small clue to the explanation of the ten-year rule in exceptional creativity. In theoretical physics, years of laboratory grind are not required, nor is any of the corpus of facts about nature that has to be memorized and assimilated in other sciences, such as engineering, chemistry, geology, and biology. So the theoretical physicist needs to expend less time in perspiration than other scientists before he or she can reach the frontier of the subject and perhaps make a breakthrough. Indeed, the ten-year rule seems to me to be an empirical truth about perspiration and inspiration equivalent to that of Edison's personal guess—not only in its underlying rationale but also approximately in its ratio. Instead of Edison's ninety-nine per cent versus one per cent estimate, for every ten years (120 months) of hard work, an individual may be granted, so to speak, a month or two's worth (one per cent) of 'sudden genius'. Discouraging as this may be in one sense, it also means that hardly any genius in history—not even Darwin, Einstein, Leonardo, and Mozart—has been permitted to short-cut the long and gradual path to creative breakthroughs.

POSTSCRIPT

Genius and Us

I n the early twenty-first century, talent appears to be on the increase, genius on the decrease. More scientists, writers, composers, and artists than ever earn a living from their creative output. During the twentieth century, performance standards and records continually improved in all fields—from music and singing to chess and sports. But where is the Darwin or the Einstein, the Mozart or the Beethoven, the Chekhov or the Shaw, the Cézanne or the Picasso or the Cartier-Bresson of today? In the cinema, the youngest of the arts, there is a growing feeling that the giants—directors such as Chaplin, Kurosawa, Ray, Renoir, and Welles—have departed the scene, leaving behind the merely talented. Even in popular music, genius of the quality of Louis Armstrong, The Beatles, or Jimi Hendrix, seems to be a thing of the past. Of course, it may be that the geniuses of our time have yet to be recognized—a process that can take many decades after their deaths, as we know—but sadly this seems unlikely, at least to me, for the following reasons.

First and foremost is surely the ever-increasing professionalization and specialization of domains, especially in the sciences. The breadth that feeds genius is harder to achieve today than in the eighteenth and nineteenth centuries, if not downright impossible. Had Darwin been required to do a PhD in the biology of barnacles, and then joined a university life sciences department, it is difficult to imagine his having the varied experiences and exposure to different disciplines that led to his breakthrough. If Ray had gone straight to film school from college, skipping his years as an art student, commercial artist, and book illustrator, would we have *Pather Panchali*? A second reason appears to be the ever-increasing commercialization of the arts. True originality takes time—at least ten years—to come to fruition; and the results of a breakthrough may well take further time to find their audience and market. Few beginning artists, or scientists, will be fortunate enough to enjoy financial support over such an extended period. It is much less challenging, and more remunerative, to make a career by producing imitative, sensational, and repetitious work, like Andy Warhol (or Alma-Tadema). Third, if less obviously, our expectations of a modern genius have become more sophisticated and discriminating since the time of the nineteenth-century Romantic Movement, partly as a result of twentieth-century advances in psychology and psychiatry. The 'long hair, great black hats, capes, and cloaks' of the bona fide Victorian hero, ironically mentioned by Virginia Woolf, are now period pieces, concealing complexes more than genius.

There is also the anti-elitist *Zeitgeist* to consider. Genius is an idea that invites attack by scientific sceptics and cultural levellers. In 1986, the psychologist Robert Weisberg published a short and readable book with the title *Creativity: Beyond the Myth of Genius: What You, Mozart, Einstein, and Picasso Have in Common.* Perhaps the second subtitle was chosen by the hopeful publisher (who reprinted the book in 1993), rather than the author. At any rate, it encapsulates a widespread desire to cut genius down to normal size.

As this book has shown, I trust, genius is not a myth. Very few of us, regrettably, will have a lot in common with the ten individuals in Part II. However, 'sudden genius' is a myth. The ten breakthroughs did not involve magic or miracles. They were the work of human grit, not the product of superhuman grace. From this truth we can surely derive both strength and stimulus for our own life and work. Knowing Ray, Cartier-Bresson, Arthur C. Clarke, and other exceptional creators personally, changed my life. For this, I shall always be grateful.

REFERENCES

Preface

xi   'Dr Pauling' Quoted in Hager: 529

xiii 'Not to have seen the cinema of Ray' Quoted in Robinson, *Satyajit Ray: The Inner Eye*: 96

xiii 'The whole business of creation' Quoted in Robinson, *Satyajit Ray: A Vision of Cinema*: 358 (interview with author)

xiii 'Young probably had' Quoted in Robinson, *The Last Man Who Knew Everything*: ix

Introduction

xvii 'Having drunk a pint of beer' Housman: 49

xviii 'I suddenly understood that photography' Quoted in Assouline: 61 (also in Cartier-Bresson, *Scrapbook*: 45)

xviii 'It just gored me' Interview with Folke Isaksson, *Sight and Sound*, summer 1970: 116

xviii 'My morale skyrocketed' Watson: 152

xviii 'Where observation is concerned' Address by Pasteur on the inauguration of the Faculty of Science, University of Lille, 7 Dec. 1854, quoted in *The Oxford Dictionary of Quotations*

xix 'reverie' Quoted in Weisberg, *Creativity*: 76

xix 'During my residence in Ghent' Quoted in Rocke: 355–6

xxi 'fully formed' Quoted in Rocke: 367

xxi 'an inexhaustible treasure-trove' Quoted in Rocke: 370

xxi 'Contrary to most accounts' Rocke: 377

xxiii 'though because the script' George: xvi

xxiii 'The Web resulted' Berners-Lee: 2

xxiii 'the application of the fractal concept' Benoit Mandelbrot, 'The fractal universe', in Pfenninger and Shubik (eds): 205

xxiii 'Journalists have always asked me' Berners-Lee: 3

xxiii 'The moment when we generated' Benoit Mandelbrot, 'The fractal universe', in Pfenninger and Shubik (eds): 204–5

xxiv 'epiphany' Lederman and Teresi: 7

xxv 'Just as the creative world' Fletcher: 24

xxvi 'Our clear concepts' Quoted in Whyte: 99

xxvi 'in a certain sense a continuous flight' Albert Einstein, 'Autobiographical notes', in Robinson, *Einstein*: 29

xxvii 'Wednesdays are always blue' Tammet: 1
xxviii 'most of the canon' Nettle, *Strong Imagination*: 147
xxviii 'Now, darkness is a familiar friend' Quoted in Tusa: 165
xxx 'Mozart's music is so pure' Quoted in Robinson, *Einstein*: 232
xxxi 'It is my great regret' Interview with Andrew Robinson, *The Times*, 7 Aug. 2002
xxxiii 'It is a sobering thought' Introduction to the song 'Alma' on Tom Lehrer's album *That Was The Year That Was*, recorded in July 1965

1: Genius and Talent: Reality or Myth?

3 'The word "genius" is often used' Simonton: 18
4 'Utterly unassuming' Hoddeson and Daitch: 6
5 'I propose to show' Galton: 11
5 'yet we feel it to be' Ibid: 18
6 'The general result is, that exactly' Ibid: 293
7 'Galton in his book dealt with' Eysenck: 14
8 'Taste is lawful' Quoted in Eysenck: 29
8 'It does seem that we must accept' Eysenck: 34
8 'It's not about recognizing talent' Quoted in Coyle: 159
9 'How can anyone know' Françoise Gilot, 'A painter's perspective', in Pfenninger and Shubik (eds): 163
9 'If I skip practice' Quoted in Coyle: 88
9 'no talent is a free gift' Ochse: 177
10 'I suggest the explanation' Andrew Steptoe, 'Mozart: resilience under stress', in Steptoe (ed.): 144
11 'This suggests that practice' Levitin: 196
12 'We instinctively think of each' Quoted in Coyle: 104
13 'Certainly white matter is key' Fields: 49
14 '(1) It originates in genetically transmitted' Howe, Davidson, and Sloboda: 399–400
14 'individual differences in some special abilities' Ibid: 407
14 'there may be little or no basis' Ibid: 405

2: Intelligence is Not Enough

16 '[Lewis] Terman devised a method' Shurkin: 296
17 'merely respectable' Gleick: 30
17 'What is the speed of sound?' Quoted in Paul Collins, '163 ways to lose your job', *New Scientist*, 9 Aug. 2008: 46–7
18 'Dr Cox's meticulous attention' Robert R. Sears, 'Catharine Cox Miles 1890–1984', *American Journal of Psychology*, 99 (1986): 431
18 'a half century old it remains' Quoted in Ochse: 40
18 'the only proper study' Eysenck: 53
18 'a primary curiosity' Gould: 213–14
18 'one of the silliest experiments' Shurkin: 68
18 'fossil IQs' Gould: 213
19 'My dear Adèle' Pearson: 66

20 'with considerable assurance' L. M. Terman, 'Psychological approaches to the biography of genius', in Vernon (ed.): 27–8

21 'There is no question that the Cox study' Eysenck: 57

21 'the more data is available' Ibid: 56

21 'Two basic results of Cox's study' Gould: 215

22 'faithfulness' Quoted in Cox: 91

22 'It appears that all of the IQ ratings' Cox: 81

22 'The net result was' Robert R. Sears, 'Catharine Cox Miles 1890–1984', *American Journal of Psychology*, 99 (1986): 431

24 'The important thing is' Introduction to the song 'New Math' on Tom Lehrer's album *That Was the Year That Was*, recorded in July 1965

24 'devastating for the enterprise' Gardner: 20

25 'Intelligence and its measurement' All quotations from this symposium are from Robert J. Sternberg's entry on 'Intelligence' in Gregory (ed.): 375–6

25 'Innumerable tests' Ibid: 375

26 'Much time was wasted' Flynn: 56–7

27 'Either the children of today' Ibid: 3

27 'The ability to improve working memory' Klingberg: 151

27 'During the twentieth century, people invested' Flynn: 176

3: Strangers to Ourselves

28 'There are theologians' Eysenck: 180

29 'the idea of unconscious mental processes' Whyte: 63

29 'It is plain to me' Quoted in Whyte: 94

29 'One would think, there was nothing' Quoted in Whyte: 98

30 'the link with instinct' Whyte: 104–5

30 'one of the most original minds' Quoted in Galison: 300

31 'Other mathematicians have recorded' Fitzgerald and James: 123

31 'It was often observed' Quoted in Fitzgerald and James: 121

31 'For fifteen days...without difficulty.' Quoted in Koestler: 115–16

32 'Most striking at first' Quoted in Fitzgerald and James: 50

35 'The results from laboratory studies' Weisberg: 426

35 'For instance, how exactly' Brook (ed.): x

35 'The content of dreams may be' 'The Act of Creation', in Medawar: 254 (review of Arthur Koestler's *The Act of Creation*)

36 'The current neuroscientific evidence' Mark Solms, 'The interpretation of dreams and the neurosciences', in Wellcome Trust (ed.): 144

36 'a psychological curiosity' Quoted in Richard Holmes: 82

36 'In the summer of the year 1797' Coleridge: 102

37 'it is difficult to accept' Richard Holmes: 82–3

37 'I walked with him' Quoted in Jamison: 109–10

38 'I don't dream. I dream all day' Quoted in Tusa: 159

38 'for providing the first evidence' Kandel: 91–2

38 'The night before Easter Sunday' Quoted in Koestler: 205
39 'The story of this discovery shows' Ibid: 206

4: Blue Remembered Wednesdays

40 'For scientists, savant talents' Foreword to Hermelin: 10
42 'To the question why' Hermelin: 151–2
42 'precocious...a rage to master' Winner: 3
42 'Gifted children, especially the extreme ones' Ibid: 313
43 'areas of excellence' Frith: 146
43 'estimates from surveys of parents and carers' Happé and Vital: 1369
43 'one or two in 200' Hermelin: 17
44 'The painter has led us' Frith: 78
44 'On the cover of your book' Quoted in Frith: 78–9
45 'In this sense they are mind-blind' Ibid: 79
45 'They treated people as if they were things' Quoted in Hermelin: 23
45 'First, it might be argued...intellectually disabled groups.' Happé and Vital: 1370
47 'In the social world there is' Baron-Cohen: 189
47 'It is characteristic of the savant memory' Sacks: 190–91
48 'This time the children' Hermelin: 171
49 'skill in mathematical calculation' Quoted in Fitzgerald and James: 18
49 'Auditory calculators' Fitzgerald and James: 16
50 'cry and be distressed' Colburn: 179
50 'Such first-person explanations' Foreword to Tammet: xi
50 'I was born on 31 January' Tammet: 1
50 '[If] we assume they are independent' Foreword to Tammet: xiv
50 'When someone gives me a number...which is round' Interview with Daniel Tammet, 'Peek inside a singular mind', New Scientist, 3 Jan. 2009: 40
51 'When I multiply two numbers' Quoted in Fitzgerald and James: 19
51 'the question "Are you a synaesthete?" ' Van Campen: 126
51 'As I'm talking, I see' Quoted in Van Campen: 86–7
51 'Woodwind and brass' Quoted in Van Campen: 21
52 'The confessions of a synaesthete' Quoted in Van Campen: 93

5: The Lunatic, the Lover, and the Poet

53 '[Shakespeare] had Theseus' Nettle, Strong Imagination: 10
53 'Why is it that all men' Quoted in Jamison: 51
54 'mild...marked...severe' Post: 25
55 'The book allows us to enquire' Andrew Steptoe, 'Artistic temperament in the Italian Renaissance: a study of Giorgio Vasari's Lives', in Steptoe (ed.): 255
56 'just as likely to be tarred' Ibid: 264–5
56 'High ability...jealous of others.' Ibid: 261
57 'There is little here to endorse' Ibid: 262
57 'If this was the case' Ibid: 268

58 'It can be seen that a strikingly high rate' Jamison: 62
58 'At various times described himself' Ibid: 67
58 'Recurrent, often agitated, melancholia' Ibid: 69
58 'We gaze on the powerful' Quoted in Jamison: 179
59 'The fates and character' Quoted in Jamison: 72
61 'two apparently conflicting' Andreasen: 96
61 'It's something that they manage' Quoted in Evans and Deehan: 105
62 'They are part of me' Quoted in Jamison: 241
62 'I believe these illnesses are' Woolf, *Diary*, 3: 287
62 'Poetry is not a turning loose' Quoted in Jamison: 122–3
62 'How could you believe' Quoted in Nasar: 11
62 'The years of anxious searching' 'Notes on the origin of the general theory of relativity', in Einstein, *Ideas and Opinions*: 289–90
62 'my poetry has lost' Quoted in Sacks: 261
63 'Only two of my eight books' Gwyneth Lewis, 'Dark gifts', in Berlin (ed.): 19
63 'Periods of remarkable creativity' Jamison: 204
64 'If Schumann's periods of mania' Weisberg: 364
65 'It seems that the age-old notion' Ochse: 116

6: Leonardo da Vinci

69 'One who was drinking' Leonardo, *Notebooks*: 171–2
70 'For centuries our grasp' Barcilon and Marani: 328
70 'incapable of achieving' Vasari: 289
71 'Even in its ruined state' Gombrich: 300
71 'all we know for certain' Bramly: 88
72 'emerging from a dark' Vasari: 288
72 'for the head that of a mastiff' Quoted in Kemp, *Marvellous Works*: 146
72 'immediately shaken' Vasari: 288
72 'very good friend' Ibid: 285
73 'The painters after the Romans' Quoted in Kemp, *Marvellous Works*: 2
74 'day of Saint Mary' 'Chronology' in Leonardo, *Notebooks*: xl
74 'There is a kind of genial' Clark: 51
74 'Driven by an ardent desire' Quoted in Bramly: 86
75 'would never touch colours' Vasari: 287
75 'is implicit in a large section' Clark: 107
76 'He was not...a religious-minded man' Ibid: 137
76 'has generally been regarded: Kemp, *Marvellous Works*: 338
77 'argumentative *Last Supper*' Ibid: 46
77 'he began many projects' Vasari: 287
77 'Alas, this man' Quoted in Vasari: 297
77 'You who made a model' Quoted in Bramly: 345
78 'To have carried the *Adoration*' Clark: 80–81
78 'the life that Leonardo leads' Quoted in 'Introduction' to Leonardo, *Notebooks*: xxvi
78 'di mi se mai' Quoted in Clark: 237

78 'Like a kingdom divided' Quoted in Bramly: 401
79 'I can carry out sculpture' Quoted in Bramly: 175
79 'family architect' 'Chronology' in Leonardo, *Notebooks*: xlviii
79 'he was regarded as an ornament' Kemp: 73
80 'O anatomical painter' Quoted in Clark: 191
81 'clearly of capital importance' Barcilon and Marani: 14
82 'the young count' Quoted in Barcilon and Marani: 18
82 'of several people of very high stature' Ibid
82 'Painted figures must' Quoted in 'Introduction' to Leonardo, *Notebooks*: xxiii
82 'with his hands spread' Leonardo, *Notebooks*: 171–2
83 'There is so much order' Gombrich: 298
83 '[The] movement is frozen' Clark: 153
83 'more akin to egg tempera' Kemp, *Marvellous Works*: 180
84 'He sometimes stayed there' Quoted in Bramly: 281
84 'There is only the head of Judas' Quoted in Bramly: 295

7: Christopher Wren

86 'An Architect ought to be' Quoted in Wren: 237
87 'St Paul's embodies' Summerson: 128
89 'well-informed and widely read' Bennett: 14–15
89 'physick, anatomy' Quoted in Tinniswood: 23
89 'one of the long-standing mysteries about his later career' Jardine: 86
90 'foremost geometers' Newton (Cohen and Whitman, eds): 424
90 'Wren's science has been neglected' Bennett: 2
90 'Although the evidence of his writings' Soo: 196
91 'His way...was briefly this' Quoted in Wren: 63
92 'prepar'd his Nose' Thomas Sprat on Jonathan Goddard, quoted in Wren: 96
92 'the mathematical Wits' Quoted in Wren: 25
92 'the apparent Absurdity' Ibid: 30
93 'certainly Nature' Quoted in Wren: 57
94 'To many scientific minds' Summerson: 23
94 '[Architecture] absorbed' Ibid: 60–61
95 'the archetypal Renaissance' Downes [1982]: 20
96 'Bernini's Design' Quoted in Wren: 106
96 'He learned from Bernini' Tinniswood: 130
96 'I cannot propose a better Remedy' Quoted in Wren: 129
97 'after much contest' Quoted in Jardine: 228
98 'The Romanists' Quoted in Wren: 195–6
98 'What are we to do next' Quoted in Wren: 132–3
99 'With nothing remaining' Wren: 153
100 'The layout of the pillars' Campbell: 32
101 'from the old Gothick Form' Wren: 137
101 'The idea of congregational assembly' Summerson: 102
101 'in private Conversation' Wren: 139

102 'not enough of a Cathedral-fashion' Ibid
102 'resolved to make no more Models' Ibid
104 'The real elegance' Keene, Burns and Saint (eds): 215

8: Wolfgang Amadeus Mozart

106 'I don't know, but it seems' Mozart, Mozart's Letters, Mozart's Life: 289 (trans. slightly modified by author)
108 'It brought a new dramatic' Basil Deane, 'A musical commentary', in Mozart, The Marriage of Figaro: 18
109 'The beautifully "curled" lion's head' Quoted in Solomon: 28
110 'My son, to find' Mozart, A Life in Letters: 218
110 'in many respects' Landon: 129–30
110 'true to the deep-rooted outlook' Solomon: 10
110 'The king gave him' Mozart, A Life in Letters: 38
111 'The lively finales' Holden, The New Penguin Opera Guide: 598
112 'The writing and performance' Glover: 204
112 'better shaped' Michael F. Robinson, 'Mozart and the opera buffa tradition', in Carter: 22
113 'I have an inexpressible desire' Mozart, Mozart's Letters, Mozart's Life: 69
113 'Don't forget my wish' Mozart, A Life in Letters: 240
113 'Salzburg is no place' Ibid: 340
114 'I advise you when composing' Quoted in Solomon: 235
114 'With brilliant control' Glover: 215
115 'kick up the arse' Mozart, A Life in Letters: 423
115 'It is the heart' Mozart, Mozart's Letters, Mozart's Life: 269
115 'Nobility, wealth, rank' Beaumarchais: 192
115 'I hope I don't need to say' Mozart, A Life in Letters: 470
116 'There is really not the slightest evidence' Letter to New York Times, 16 July 1989
117 'Mozart had been fêted' Steptoe: 22
117 'Despite Mozart's immense productivity' Solomon: 310
117 'Poor Italy!' Quoted in Holden, The Man Who Wrote Mozart: 59
118 'Well, the Italian opera buffa has started again' Quoted in Carter: 6
118 'worthy, in its freshness and charm' Quoted in Carter: 8
119 'Mozart put his foot' Carter: 8
119 'In this opera there are two fascinating' Landon: 134
119 'I set to work accordingly' Da Ponte: 150
120 'what was probably the most spectacular' John Wells, 'A society marriage', in Mozart, The Marriage of Figaro: 13
120 'since this piece contains much' Quoted in Deutsch: 235
120 'omitted or cut anything' Da Ponte: 151
120 'extract' Quoted in Deutsch: 273–4
121 'In the second quatrain' Carter: 83
121 'When some grand conception' Quoted in Glover: 355–6
121 'both a triumph and a disappointment' Solomon: 304
121 'those in the orchestra' Quoted in Deutsch: 533

122 'doubts, reserves, headshakings' Da Ponte: 162
122 'at 7 o'clock' Quoted in Deutsch: 274
122 'disappointed that the opera' Steptoe: 184
122 'Here they talk of nothing but "Figaro"' Mozart, *Mozart's Letters, Mozart's Life*: 384–5

9: Jean-François Champollion

123 'Hieroglyphic writing is a complex system' Champollion, *Précis* (1824): 327
124 'Je tiens l'affaire!' Quoted in Faure: 429
124 'without having any knowledge' Champollion, *Précis* (1824): 17
125 'for employing some poor Italian' Quoted in Peacock: 451
125 'I am Egypt's captive' Champollion, *Egyptian Diaries*: 120
125 'violent mood swings' Adkins: 4
126 'There are days when' Quoted in Adkins: 47
127 'not built up from syllables' Quoted in Boas: 101
128 'puerile' Young: 267
129 '[W]hen they wish to indicate' Boas: 63
129 'sometimes called the last' *Encyclopaedia Britannica*, 15th edn: entry for 'Kircher, Athanasius'
129 'the last man who knew' Subtitle of the book by Findlen
129 'The protection of Osiris' Quoted in Pope: 31–2
130 'notae phoneticae' Pope: 58
131 'This decree shall be inscribed' Quoted in Andrews: 28
132 '[They] proceeded upon' Young: 270
134 'is no more than a simple modification' Quoted in Solé and Valbelle: 76
134 'striking resemblance' Young: 54
134 'I am not surpised that' Ibid: 53
134 'imitations of the hieroglyphics' Ibid: 54
134 'it seemed natural to suppose' Ibid: 133
135 'straight away' Quoted in Adkins: 157
135 'Once one embraces' Koestler: 134
136 'something like a hieroglyphic alphabet' Young: 182
137 'as I had not leisure' Ibid: 296
138 'I hope it is not too rash' Champollion, *Lettre*: 1; Champollion, *Précis* (1828): 41
141 'So poor doctor Young' Champollion, *Egyptian Diaries*: 184

10: Charles Darwin

142 'Thus, from the war of nature' Darwin, *Origin of Species*: 459–60
143 'In October 1838' Darwin, *The Autobiography* (Francis Darwin, ed.): 42–3
144 'I am studying my "Zoonomia" ' Quoted in Gruber and Barrett: 68
144 'Would it be too bold' Quoted in Stott: 7
144 'much ingenuity' Quoted in Robinson, *The Last Man Who Knew Everything*: 43
144 'much disappointed' Darwin, *The Autobiography* (Francis Darwin, ed.): 13
145 'I consider that all I have learnt' Quoted in Browne, 2: 399

338   REFERENCES

145 'The school as a means of education' Darwin, *The Autobiography* (Francis Darwin, ed.): 9
145 'I believe I was considered' Ibid: 9
145 'which leads a man' Ibid: 6
146 'I had strong and diversified tastes' Ibid: 9
146 'very bad' Ibid: 12
146 'You care for nothing but' Quoted in Darwin, *The Autobiography* (Francis Darwin, ed.): 9
146 'mind as far as one individual's sense' Quoted in Gruber and Barrett: 39
147 'very properly vehement' Darwin, *The Autobiography* (Francis Darwin, ed.): 17
147 'Species have a real existence' Quoted in Eldredge: 164
147 'During the three years' Darwin, *The Autobiography* (Francis Darwin, ed.): 18
147 'I can remember the exact appearance' Ibid: 22
148 'Bug-hunting' Introduction to Darwin, *Origin of Species*: 19
148 'The voyage of the *Beagle* has been' Darwin, *The Autobiography* (Francis Darwin, ed.): 28
149 'It is hardly possible' Darwin, *Origin of Species*: 293–4
149 'on no account to accept' Quoted in Browne, 1: 187
150 'With this additional instance' Darwin, *Voyage of the Beagle*: 238
150 'The elevation of the land' Ibid: 239
150 'deeply interesting' Ibid: 235
151 'I am convinced that all our ancient formations' Darwin, *Origin of Species*: 300
151 'palaeontology's trade secret' Quoted in Eldredge: 176
151 'It is impossible to reflect' Darwin, *Voyage of the Beagle*: 164
152 'I was much struck' Darwin, *Origin of Species*: 104
152 'When I recollect' Quoted in Browne, 1: 339
153 'Why, the shape of his head' Quoted in Darwin, *The Autobiography* (Francis Darwin, ed.): 30
153 'to fill up the wide gaps' Darwin, *Voyage of the Beagle*: 377
153 'I worked on true Baconian principles' Darwin, *The Autobiography* (Francis Darwin, ed.): 42
154 'not in a golden moment of insight' Gruber and Barrett: xiv
154 'The pandemonium' Ibid: 122
154 'Was witty in a dream' Quoted in Gruber and Barrett: 293
155 'It is difficult to believe' Quoted in Eldredge: 132
155 'One invisible animalcule' Quoted in Gruber and Barrett: 161
155 'One may say there is a force' Quoted in Gruber and Barrett: 456
156 'Three principles will account for all' Quoted in Gruber and Barrett: 459
156 'As many more individuals of each species' Darwin, *Origin of Species*: 68
158 '[F]or I have not the love of work' Quoted in Darwin, *The Autobiography* (Francis Darwin, ed.): 201
158 'I would as soon have died' Quoted in Browne, 2: 125
158 'the law of higgledy-piggledy' Quoted in Darwin, *The Autobiography* (Francis Darwin, ed.): 232
158 'He has opened a path of inquiry' Quoted in Browne, 2: 186

11: Marie Curie

159 'A great discovery' Marie Curie, *Pierre Curie*: 144

159 'Marie Curie is, of all celebrated beings' Quoted in Eve Curie: xvii

161 'enemies...their families' Marie Curie, *Autobiographical Notes*: 159

162 'a profound depression' Ibid: 157

162 'When she left' Quoted in Quinn: 42

162 'Thanks to her father' Eve Curie: 49

162 'With all her intellectuality' Marie Curie, *Autobiographical Notes*: 157

163 'This method could not be' Ibid: 166

163 'It seems to me that I am coming' Quoted in Eve Curie: 80

163 'For one thing' Quinn: 81

164 'The room I lived in' Marie Curie, *Autobiographical Notes*: 170–71

164 'It isn't necessary to lead' Quoted in Eve Curie: 357

165 'Upon entering the room' Marie Curie, *Autobiographical Notes*: 173

165 'We are obliged to eat' Quoted in Eve Curie: 126

166 'What was he dreaming of' Quoted in Eve Curie: 246

166 'time to look' Quoted in Quinn: 109

167 'Such a renunciation' Marie Curie, *Autobiographical Notes*: 179

167 'an exchange of energy' Quoted in Quinn: 130

168 'the silhouettes appeared' Quoted in Romer: 11

168 'Whether this represents simple thrift' Romer: 9

169 'invisible phosphorescence' Quoted in Romer: 21

170 'Impossible!' Quoted in Goldsmith: 73

171 'In this way the amount of electricity' R. F. Mould, 'The discovery of radium in 1898 by Maria Sklodowska-Curie (1867–1934) and Pierre Curie (1859–1906) with commentary on their life and times', *British Journal of Radiology*, 71 (1998): 1241

172 'Two minerals of uranium' Marie Sklodowska Curie, 'Rays emitted by compounds of uranium and of thorium', *Comptes Rendus*, 126 (1898): 1101–3 at http://web.lemoyne.edu/~giunta/curie98.html

172 'To interpret the spontaneous radiation' Ibid

172 'This observation astonished me greatly' Mme Sklodowska Curie, 'Radium and radioactivity', *Century Magazine*, Jan. 1904: 461–6 at http://www.aip.org/history/curie/article.htm

172 'restrained, ardent voice' Quoted in Eve Curie: 157

173 'If the existence of this new metal' Pierre Curie and Marie Sklodowska Curie, 'On a new radioactive substance contained in pitchblende', *Comptes Rendus*, 127 (1898): 175–8 at http://web.lemoyne.edu/~giunta/curiespo.html

174 'The intensity of this line increases' P. Curie, Mme P. Curie, and G. Bémont, 'On a new, strongly radioactive substance contained in pitchblende', *Comptes Rendus*, 127 (1898): 1215–17 at http://web.lemoyne.edu/~giunta/curiesra.html

174 'Irène can walk' Quoted in Eve Curie: 164

174 'a stable or potato cellar' Quoted in Goldsmith: 91

174 'it must be dreadful' Quoted in Goldsmith: 91
174 'Yet it was this miserable old shed' Marie Curie, *Autobiographical Notes*: 186–7
175 'It was really a lovely sight' Ibid: 187
175 'It is not an exaggeration' Quoted in Quinn: 172
176 'It is not absurd to suppose' Pierre Curie, 'Radioactive substances, especially radium' (Nobel lecture, 6 June 1905): 76–7 at http://nobelprize.org/nobel_prizes/physics/laureates/1903/pierre-curie-lecture.html

12: Albert Einstein

177 'An hour sitting with a pretty girl' Quoted in Sayen: 230
177 'But it would hardly be correct' Letter to Carl Seelig quoted in Holton: 192
178 'Something deeply hidden' Einstein, 'Autobiographical Notes': 9
178 'For me it is not dubious' Ibid: 9
178 'exploration of my ancestors' Quoted in Seelig: 56
178 'entirely irreligious' Einstein, 'Autobiographical Notes': 3
179 'I am truly a "lone traveller" ' 'The world as I see it' in Einstein, *Ideas and Opinions*: 9
179 'Let us return to Nature' Quoted in Moszkowski: 66
180 'lie down on the sofa' Einstein, *Collected Papers*, 1: lxiv
180 'Einstein expressed' Born and Einstein: 105
180 'Einstein was more of an artist' Whitrow: 52
180 'a second wonder' Einstein, 'Autobiographical Notes': 9
180 'earth-measuring' 'Geometry and experience' in Einstein, *Ideas and Opinions*: 234
181 'suspicion against every kind of authority' Einstein, 'Autobiographical Notes': 5
181 'he would never get anywhere' Einstein, *Collected Papers*, 1: lxiii
181 'impudence' Einstein and Marić: 67
181 'To punish me' Quoted in Hoffmann: 24
182 'a personal gift' Quoted in Hoffmann: 28
182 'creating a new theory' Einstein and Infeld: 159
183 'Shut yourself up' Quoted in Guilini: 12–13
184 'How does the state of motion' 'The mechanics of Newton and their influence on the development of theoretical physics' in Einstein, *Ideas and Opinions*: 255
184 'Every body perseveres' Newton (Cohen and Whitman, eds): 416–17
185 'To any action there is always' Ibid: 416–17
185 'Absolute, true, and mathematical time' Ibid: 408
186 'God informed' Gleick: 152
186 'It may be, that there is no' Newton (Motte, ed.): 8
186 'eminently fruitful' 'The fundaments of theoretical physics' in Einstein, *Ideas and Opinions*: 325
186 'He was justified in sticking' Ibid: 326
187 'absolutely stationary' Kaku: 11
188 'Before Maxwell' 'Maxwell's influence on the evolution of the idea of physical reality' in Einstein, *Ideas and Opinions*: 269
189 'I'm convinced more and more' Einstein and Marić: 10
190 'impudence' Ibid: 67

190 'I will soon have graced' Ibid: 42
191 'three intellectual musketeers' Highfield and Carter: 96
191 'So that was caviar' Quoted in Highfield and Carter: 98
191 'laughed so much' Quoted in Highfield and Carter: 102
192 'Dear Habicht!' Quoted in Einstein, *The Persistent Illusion of Transience*: 66
192 '[The first] deals with radiation' Quoted in Fölsing: 120
193 'He was sitting in his study' Quoted in Highfield and Carter: 130
193 'was intrigued rather than dismayed' Rigden: 8
194 '[Einstein] would carefully study' Introduction to Einstein and Marić: xxii
194 'far less childish' Quoted in Highfield and Carter: 97
194 'Thank you. I've completely solved' Quoted in Fölsing: 155
195 'steadfastness' Quoted in Fölsing: 195
195 'started from the postulate' Quoted in Robinson, *Einstein*: 42
195 'misdeed' Einstein, *Relativity*, 10
195 'The stone traverses' Ibid: 11
197 'If I pursue a beam of light' Einstein, 'Autobiographical Notes': 53
197 'We should catch them' Einstein and Infeld: 177
197 'unjustifiable hypotheses' Einstein, *Relativity*: 32
197 '[relativity] required abandoning' Quoted in Robinson, *Einstein*: 44
198 'Not only do we have' Quoted in Fölsing: 175
199 'We are accustomed' 'Physics and reality' in Einstein, *Ideas and Opinions*: 299
199 'A new scientific truth' Planck: 33–4
199 'modification' Quoted in Fölsing: 120
199 'In boldness' Quoted in Fölsing: 271
200 'not compatible with' Quoted in Bernstein: 82
200 'in my opinion, these [other] theories' Quoted in Pais: 159

13: Virginia Woolf

202 'I am now galloping' Virginia Woolf, *Diary*, 2: 323
203 'Virginia Woolf's story' Lee: 769
204 'who sat like a frog' Virginia Woolf, *Diary*, 1: 221
205 'Living alone, I sometimes' James Stephen: 61–2
205 'irritable and nervous temperament' Quoted in Lee: 60
206 'it was as though' Virginia Woolf, *Moments of Being*: 11
206 'she was impetuous' Ibid: 10–11
207 'Downstairs there was pure convention' Ibid: 158
207 'There were so many different worlds' Ibid: 159–60
208 'takes in a great deal' Quoted in Lee: 57
208 'I was a snob' Virginia Woolf, *Moments of Being*: 119
208 'I don't get anyone to argue with' Virginia Woolf, *Letters*, 1: 77
208 'Arguably' Lee: 148
209 'Suppose I, at fifteen' Virginia Woolf, *Moments of Being*: 123
209 'His life would have entirely ended mine' Virginia Woolf, *Diary*, 3: 208
209 'If you ask me would I' Virginia Woolf, *Moments of Being*: 65

209 'There were originals' Virginia Woolf, *Letters*, 3: 195
210 'Talk—even the talk' Virginia Woolf, *Moments of Being*: 48
210 'degenerate poet' Virginia Woolf, *Letters*, 1: 321
210 'shy, and stammering' Virginia Woolf, *Mrs Dalloway*: 110
211 'on or about December 1910' Virginia Woolf, *Essays*, 3: 421
211 '[The Edwardian novelists] have laid' Ibid: 432
211 'had invented a plough' Virginia Woolf, *Mrs Dalloway*: 63
212 'penniless Jew' Virginia Woolf, *Letters*, 1: 500
212 'a respectable Anglo-Indian family' Virginia Woolf, *Mrs Dalloway*: 71
213 'I believe these illnesses are' Virginia Woolf, *Diary*, 3: 287
214 'two dogs playing' Virginia Woolf, *Mrs Dalloway*: 112–13
214 'Nothing arranged' Virginia Woolf, *Jacob's Room*: 246
214 'ghosts' Virginia Woolf, *Diary*, 2: 186
214 'but I think Jacob' Ibid: 208
214 'a remarkable success' Quoted in Bell, 2: 88
214 'for a short time [she] hesitated' Leonard Woolf: 61
215 'Thoughts upon beginning' Quoted by Claire Tomalin in her introduction to Virginia Woolf, *Mrs Dalloway*: xvii–xviii
215 'Mrs Dalloway has branched into a book' Virginia Woolf, *Diary*, 2: 207–8
215 'Not that I ever felt' Ibid: 206
215 'now Kitty is buried' Ibid: 207
216 'The leaden circles' Virginia Woolf, *Mrs Dalloway*: 62
216 'London is enchanting' Virginia Woolf, *Diary*, 2: 301–2
216 'One of the triumphs of civilization' Virginia Woolf, *Mrs Dalloway*: 197–8
217 'Lytton does not like' Virginia Woolf, *Diary*, 3: 32
218 '[Septimus Smith] was, on the whole' Virginia Woolf, *Mrs Dalloway*: 109
218 'obscurely evil' Ibid: 242
218 'Somehow it was her disaster' Ibid: 243
218 'sheer weak dribble' Virginia Woolf, *Diary*, 2: 260

14: Henri Cartier-Bresson

219 'I had just discovered' 'The decisive moment' in Cartier-Bresson, *The Mind's Eye*: 22
220 '"The great photographer"' Quoted in Robinson, 'Blurred image, sharp vision', *Times Higher Education Supplement*, 16 May 2003: 25
220 'Deep down' Interview with Jean Bardin and Bernard Hubrenne in the documentary film *Henri Cartier-Bresson: L'Aventure Moderne*, directed by Roger Kahane, made for ORTF in 1962 (available as a DVD, *Henri Cartier-Bresson*, published by the Fondation Cartier-Bresson/mk2 in 2006)
221 'capture the inner silence' Quoted in Chéroux: 78
221 'the coat-of-arms' Assouline: 15
221 'My father was stern' Quoted in Hofstadter (pt 1): 72
222 'Only interest at school' Cartier-Bresson, *The Photographs of Henri Cartier-Bresson*: 15
222 'What do you think I'm a professor of?' Quoted in Assouline: 253

222 'It's difficult to look and listen' Quoted in Montier: 9
222 'mythical father' Quoted in Assouline: 18
223 'For me photography, far from' Quoted in Chéroux: 16
223 'to read and write' Quoted in Chéroux: 17
224 'I was once a diligent presence' 'André Breton: Sun King' in Cartier-Bresson, *The Mind's Eye*: 97–8
225 'His allegiance was to its ethics' Assouline: 38
226 'Your grandfather thinks' Quoted in Assouline: 46
226 'I suddenly understood that photography' Quoted in Assouline: 61 (also in Cartier-Bresson, *Scrapbook*: 45)
227 'You are a born draughtsman' Quoted in Montier: 68
227 'who deliberately constructed' Galassi: 28
228 'It was indeed an emotional experience' 'The decisive moment' in Cartier-Bresson, *The Mind's Eye*: 40
228 'The deep regard for people' Foreword to Cartier-Bresson, *Henri Cartier-Bresson in India*: 6
229 'In photography...there is immediacy' Quoted in Halberstadt: 59
230 '[Jean] was not a specialist' 'A memoir by Henri Cartier-Bresson' in Renoir: 559
230 'Because a great director' 'Jean Renoir' in Cartier-Bresson, *The Mind's Eye*: 90
231 'I photographed *chiens écrasés*' Quoted in Galassi: 24
231 'despite the inconvenience' 'Sarah Moon' in Cartier-Bresson, *The Mind's Eye*: 87
232 'I became increasingly less interested' Interview with Dorothy Norman in *New York Post*, 26 Aug. 1946, in Cartier-Bresson, *Scrapbook*: 15
232 'sitters of Titian' E. H. Gombrich, 'The mysterious achievement of likeness', introduction to Cartier-Bresson, *Tête à Tête* (unpaginated)
232 'My box of matches' Quoted in Assouline: 125
232 'Why did you press the button' Quoted in Assouline: 126
233 'The photographer's reading' Quoted in Chéroux: 107
234 'Don't kill me' Cartier-Bresson, *Scrapbook*: 229
234 'But the more he effaces himself' Lincoln Kirstein, 'Henri Cartier-Bresson: documentary humanist', introduction to Cartier-Bresson, *The Photographs of Henri Cartier-Bresson*: 10
234 'Robert Capa warned me' Quoted in Montier: 84
235 'Contrary to the impression' Claude Cookman, 'Henri Cartier-Bresson: master of photographic reportage', in Cartier-Bresson, *The Man, the Image and the World*: 395
235 'To me, photography is the simultaneous recognition' 'The decisive moment' in Cartier-Bresson, *The Mind's Eye*: 42

15: Satyajit Ray

236 'The entire conventional approach' Quoted in Seton: 165
237 'You cannot make films like this' *Observer*, 13 May 1956
237 'I can never forget the excitement' Translation of remarks made in Moscow in 1975, authenticated by Kurosawa in a letter to the author in 1988, quoted in Robinson, *Satyajit Ray: The Inner Eye*: 91

238 'I never imagined' Quoted in Robinson, *Satyajit Ray: A Vision of Cinema*: 25 (interview with author)

238 'My grandfather' Introduction to Sukumar Ray, *The Select Nonsense of Sukumar Ray*, (Sukanta Chaudhuri, trans.), Calcutta: Oxford University Press, 1987 (unpaginated)

239 'As far as my father's writing' Ibid

239 'Even today' Quoted in Robinson, *Satyajit Ray: The Inner Eye*: 29

239 'Loneliness and being alone' Quoted in Robinson, *Satyajit Ray: The Inner Eye*: 35 (interview with author)

240 'free bioscope' Quoted in Robinson, *Satyajit Ray: The Inner Eye*: 35

240 'Who knows?' Ibid: 36

240 'weeks of musing' 'My life, my work' in Satyajit Ray, *Telegraph*, Calcutta, 27 Sept. 1982

240 'Lillian Gish' 'Hollywood then and now' in Satyajit Ray, *Our Films Their Films*: 129

242 'although the top line' Quoted in Robinson, *Satyajit Ray: A Vision of Cinema*: 41

242 'It is not as if I am thinking of music' Quoted in Robinson, *Satyajit Ray: A Vision of Cinema*: 305 (interview with author)

242 'Erudition is something' 'My life, my work' in Satyajit Ray, *Telegraph*, Calcutta, 27 Sept. 1982

242 'My relationship with Shantiniketan' 'My life, my work' in Satyajit Ray, *Telegraph*, Calcutta, 28 Sept. 1982

244 'The raw material of cinema' 'What is wrong with Indian films?' in Satyajit Ray, *Our Films Their Films*: 24

244 'like a pricked balloon' 'My life, my work' in Satyajit Ray, *Telegraph*, Calcutta, 29 Sept. 1982

245 'Undoubtedly, it was Renoir' Satyajit Ray, *My Years with Apu*: 17

245 'If you could only shake Hollywood' 'Renoir in Calcutta' in Satyajit Ray, *Our Films Their Films*: 119

245 'principal mentor' Speech accepting the Legion of Honour from President François Mitterrand, 2 Feb. 1989

245 'It just gored me' Interview with Folke Isaksson, *Sight and Sound*, summer 1970: 116

245 'I would make my film exactly as De Sica' 'My life, my work' in Satyajit Ray, *Telegraph*, Calcutta, 29 Sept. 1982

246 'Simplicity of plot' 'Some Italian films I have seen' in Satyajit Ray, *Our Films Their Films*: 126–7

247 'The script had to retain' 'A long time on the little road' in Satyajit Ray, *Our Films Their Films*: 33

247 'You had to find out for yourself' 'My life, my work' in Satyajit Ray, *Telegraph*, Calcutta, 30 Sept. 1982

248 'Little did I know' 'Film making' in Satyajit Ray, *Our Films Their Films*: 51

248 'It was perfect' Satyajit Ray, *My Years with Apu*: 41

249 'Today we will carry you out' Quoted in Robinson, *Satyajit Ray: The Inner Eye*: 85

250 'Don't be afraid to distort your face' Karuna Banerjee, quoted in Robinson, *Satyajit Ray: The Inner Eye*: 86 (interview with author)

250 'special, heightened quality' Quoted in Robinson, *Satyajit Ray: The Inner Eye*: 86 (interview with author)

251 'Within seconds' Quoted in Firoze Rangoonwalla, *Satyajit Ray's Art*, New Delhi: Clarion, 1980: 125

251 'Suddenly I noticed this phenomenon' Quoted in Robinson, *Satyajit Ray: The Inner Eye*: 87 (interview with author)

252 'The connoisseur must feel' Paul Beckley, *New York Herald Tribune*, 5 Oct. 1960

16: Family Matters

255 'Human genius has always been' David Lykken, 'The genetics of genius', in Steptoe (ed.): 30

256 'Exploration of my ancestors' Quoted in Seelig: 56

257 'Solitary trees' Quoted in Ochse: 78

258 'turning towards people' Quoted in Ochse: 77

259 'While creative adults often overcome' Csikszentmihalyi: 171

259 'From the evidence, one may indeed' Ochse: 81–2

260 'I don't know what would have become' Quoted in Illingworth and Illingworth: 31

260 'Despotism and lies' Quoted in Illingworth and Illingworth: 18

262 'conversation enriches the mind' Quoted in Ochse: 169

262 'the best thinking has been' Edison: 56

262 'Whenever, rotating slowly on myself' Quoted in Eve Curie: 126

262 'isolation and complete loneliness' Quoted in Ochse: 169

262 'society is harmful' Quoted in Ochse: 169

262 'Writing comes from' Television interview with V. S. Naipaul, in *Arena: The Strange Luck of V. S. Naipaul*, broadcast on BBC 4, 11 April 2008

262 'Where the outside world' Tagore: 39

263 'Another recurrent theme' Ochse: 77–8

265 'little Wolfgang in the next room' Quoted in Solomon: 54

266 'the patient ghost' Browne, 2: 90

266 'What I want to say is that' Quoted in Lee: 756–7

17: Professor of the Little Finger

267 'It is quite strange' Cszikszentmihalyi: 173

267 'What do you think I am a professor of?' Quoted in Assouline: 253

267 'Masters and mistresses' Quoted in Robinson, *The Last Man Who Knew Everything*: 15

269 'No proper study' Eysenck: 133

270 'There are days when' Quoted in Adkins: 47

270 'Even when he was enthusiastic' Adkins: 54

270 'It is possible that had science' Michael J. A. Howe, 'Prodigies and non-prodigies', in Steptoe (ed.): 103

271 'poco curante' Darwin, *The Autobiography* (Francis Darwin, ed.): 11

271 'treated their pupils as enemies' Marie Curie, *Autobiographical Notes*: 159

271 'I like school' Quoted in Eve Curie: 36

271 'he would never get anywhere' Einstein, *Collected Papers*, 1: lxiii

272 'powerful reasons within Einstein himself' Fölsing: 19

272 'He was mediocre at his studies' Assouline: 20–21

274 'as [it] doesn't help me much' Quoted in Fölsing: 123

274 'seemed a little uncanny' Quoted in Fölsing: 123

275 'I never ceased to regret' Ray, *Our Films Their Films*: 5

275 'Since 1945, the number' Hollingsworth et al: 412

276 'the contrast in academic performance' Simonton, *Creativity in Science*: 127–8

276 'If your teaching requires them' Profile of Carl Wiemann, in Edwin Cartlidge, 'New formula for science education', *Physics World*, Jan. 2007: 11

278 'When we have the facts' Quoted in Robinson, *The Man Who Deciphered Linear B*: 72

278 'fine set of cautious, non-committal phrases' Quoted in Robinson, *The Man Who Deciphered Linear B*: 116

278 'The architect's eye' Chadwick: 4

278 'The best service we can do' Eysenck: 288

18: Creative Science versus Artistic Creation

279 'One feature that is shared' Thomas R. Cech, 'Overturning the dogma: catalytic RNA', in Pfenninger and Shubik (eds): 14–15

280 'When in 1922' Quoted in Jackson: 26–7

280 'they were essentially modern' Quoted in Jackson: 9

281 'I feel rather doubtful' Quoted in Jackson: 119

282 'He nowhere expressed' Solomon: 327

283 'Not for nothing did Freud' Lee: 5

283 'The mind receives a myriad' Quoted in Lehrer: 175

283 'I am ignorant of graphology' Letter from Cartier-Bresson to author, 23 Oct. 1995

284 'I think someday the human mind' Quoted in Robinson, *Satyajit Ray: The Inner Eye*: 300

284 'the two great stalwarts' Letter from Subrahmanyan Chandrasekhar to author, 10 April 1995

284 'I used to sit for hours' Darwin, *The Autobiography* (Francis Darwin, ed.): 9–10

285 'Walter Scott, Miss Austen, and Mrs Gaskell' Darwin, *The Autobiography* (Francis Darwin, ed.): 82

285 'seamless web of deserted sweethearts' Browne, 2: 69–70

285 'I willingly learned by heart' Marie Curie, *Autobiographical Notes*: 160

285 'Madame Curie never heard . . . any artistic strain.' Quoted in Robinson, *Einstein*: 143

286 'Music does not influence' Einstein, *The New Quotable Einstein*: 148

286 'for the most part I can listen to him' Ibid: 147

287 'absorbed all his capacities' Summerson: 60–1

287 'To begin a song . . . a really elegant proof.' Profile of Tom Lehrer, in Jack Boulware, 'That was the wit that was', *San Francisco Weekly*, 19 April 2000

287 'forces novel associations' Ulam: 181

288 'If "Von Braun" didn't happen to rhyme' E-mail from Tom Lehrer to author, 30 Jan. 2008

288 'Our natural point of view in regard to' Quoted in Tagore: 531–2

288 'In science, what X misses today' Medawar: 253

289 'From this perspective, it is not absurd to say' Weisberg: 57

289 'the structure of the DNA molecule was not' Gunther Stent, 'Meaning in art and science', in Pfenninger and Shubik (eds): 37

290 'Her profile is similar' Weisberg: 51
290 'layers of antecedents' Ibid: 51

19: **Is there a Creative Personality?**

292 'Probably the personalities' Weisberg: 505–6
293 'I am not a man of science' Quoted in Hughes: 52
293 'one psychologist might give you' Nettle, *Personality*: 9
294 'outgoing, enthusiastic' Ibid: 29
295 'mysterious and difficult to pin down' Ibid: 183
295 'before creativity, the psychoanalyst' Quoted in Gardner: 24
296 'The music in Milos Forman's *Amadeus*' Quoted in Robinson, *Satyajit Ray: A Vision of Cinema*: 15–16
296 'When some grand conception' Quoted in Glover: 355–6
297 'Whenever we came to an impasse' Quoted in Robinson, *Einstein*: 228–9
297 'I'm equally at home' Andrew Robinson, 'A conversation with Satyajit Ray', *Films & Filming*, Aug. 1982: 22
298 'When I'm working I'm a *complete* democrat' Quoted in Robinson, *Satyajit Ray: The Inner Eye*: 7
298 'I am truly a "lone traveller" ' Quoted in Robinson, *Einstein*: 140–1
299 'The years of anxious searching' Quoted in Robinson, *Einstein*: 66
299 'Nothing tragic' Quoted in Robinson, *Einstein*: 141
300 'You have to be ruthless' Nettle, *Personality*: 178
300 'sole pleasure' Quoted in Desmond and Moore: 620
300 'never happy except when at work' Quoted in Desmond and Moore: 650
300 'In the evening, Captain FitzRoy' Darwin, *The Voyage of the Beagle*: 260–1
301 'You care for nothing' Darwin, *The Autobiography* (Francis Darwin, ed.): 9
302 'This temper that he could not control' Virginia Woolf, *Moments of Being*: 117–18
303 'there are an extraordinary number' Nettle, *Personality*: 125

20: **Reputation, Fame, and Genius**

304 'If you contemplate' Bloom: 813
305 'mere decorators' Reitlinger, 1: 4
305 'The auction market clearly values' Galenson: 22
305 'the equal of the great old masters' Quoted in Tusa: 247
305 'at some point in the future' Martindale: 36
306 'a home which more than any other' Quoted in Cole (ed.): 488
307 'It would be premature' Reitlinger, 3: 31
308 'It's the fractal future' Profile of Arthur C. Clarke, in Andrew Robinson, 'The cosmic godfather', *Times Higher Education Supplement*, 10 Oct. 1997: 20
308 'The usual way to think' Csikszentmihalyi: 30–1
310 'It is only recently that Mendelssohn . . . we can muster.' Foreword to Reichwald (ed.): vii–ix
312 'I never understood why the theory of relativity' Quoted in Robinson, *Einstein*: 140

312 'The speed with which' Quoted in Robinson, *Einstein*: 141
313 'Woolf's reputation in this country' Introduction to Virginia Woolf, *Moments of Being*: viii
313 'you speak far too modestly' Quoted in Browne, 2: 139
314 'The initial reaction was' Quoted in Robinson, *Satyajit Ray: The Inner Eye*: 104
314 'I watched the audience surge' Satyajit Ray, 'Under western eyes', *Sight and Sound*, autumn 1982: 271
315 'half of the Academicians' Quoted in Robinson, *Satyajit Ray: The Inner Eye*: 361
315 'But why should the West care?' Quoted in Robinson, *Satyajit Ray: The Inner Eye*: 322

21: The Ten-year Rule

316 'Before the Gates of Excellence' Quoted in Edith Hamilton, 'The lessons of the past', in Thruelsen and Kobler (eds): 76
317 'ninety per cent perspiration' Quoted in Koestler: 120
317 'I have been speculating' Darwin, *The Autobiography* (Nora Barlow, ed.): 163
317 'These figures lead one to realize' Ochse: 100
318 'that it was a work which' Quoted in Robinson, *The Last Man Who Knew Everything*: 235
318 'unbidden and incomprehensible' Chris McManus, 'Nine ladies bare?', *British Medical Journal*, 301 (27 Oct. 1990): 999 (review of R. Ochse's *Before the Gates of Excellence*)
318 'If there is inspiration' Quoted in Tusa: 97
318 'You can't pick the moment' Quoted in Evans and Deehan: 96
318 'There are so many ways' Quoted in Tusa: 76–7
319 'a joint product of logic' Simonton, *Creativity in Science*: 13
321 'If the discovery of genetic laws' Ibid: 33
321 'Typically, the overlap' Ibid: 37
321 'I never saw a more striking coincidence' Darwin, *The Autobiography* (Francis Darwin, ed.): 196
322 'Even Mozart, arguably the exception' Gardner: 32
322 'the ten-year rule is relevant' Weisberg: 212
322 'One of the most solid findings' Sawyer: 124
322 'Psychology is not like physics' Nettle, *Personality*: 44
325 'a landmark in Mozart's piano concerto oeuvre' Eisen (ed.): 113
325 'By this definition, Mozart's first masterwork' J. R. Hayes, 'Three problems in teaching problem solving skills', in S. Chipman, J. W. Segal, and R. Glaser (eds), *Thinking and Learning Skills*, Vol. 2, Hillsdale (NJ): Erlbaum, 1985: 394
325 'It is strange to say of a composer' Quoted in J. R. Hayes, 'Three problems in teaching problem solving skills', in S. Chipman, J. W. Segal, and R. Glaser (eds), *Thinking and Learning Skills*, Vol. 2, Hillsdale (NJ): Erlbaum, 1985: 392–3

Postscript

329 'long hair, great black hats' Virginia Woolf, *Moments of Being*: 117–18

BIBLIOGRAPHY

Adkins, Lesley and Roy, *The Keys of Egypt: The Race to Read the Hieroglyphs*, London: HarperCollins, 2000

Andreasen, Nancy C., *The Creating Brain: The Neuroscience of Genius*, New York: Dana Press, 2005

Andrews, Carol, *The Rosetta Stone*, London: British Museum Publications, 1981

Assouline, Pierre, *Henri Cartier-Bresson: A Biography*, London: Thames & Hudson, 2005

Barcilon, Pinin Brambilla and Pietro C. Marani, *Leonardo: The Last Supper*, Chicago (IL): University of Chicago Press, 2001

Baron-Cohen, 'Is Asperger syndrome necessarily viewed as a disability?', *Focus on Autism and Other Developmental Disabilities*, 17 (2002): 186–91

Beaumarchais, Pierre-Augustin Caron de, *The Figaro Trilogy*, (David Coward, trans.), Oxford: Oxford University Press, 2003

Bell, E. T., *Men of Mathematics*, London: Victor Gollancz, 1937

Bell, Quentin, *Virginia Woolf: A Biography*, 2 vols, London: Hogarth Press, 1972

Bennett, J. A., *The Mathematical Science of Christopher Wren*, Cambridge: Cambridge University Press, 1982

Berlin, Richard M., ed., *Poets on Prozac: Mental Illness, Treatment and the Creative Process*, Baltimore: Johns Hopkins University Press, 2008

Bernstein, Jeremy, *Einstein*, 2nd edn, London: Fontana, 1991

Bloom, Harold, *Genius: A Mosaic of One Hundred Exemplary Creative Minds*, London: Fourth Estate, 2002

Boas, George, *The Hieroglyphics of Horapollo*, Princeton (NJ): Princeton University Press, 1993

Born, Max and Albert Einstein, *The Born-Einstein Letters*, 2nd edn, London: Macmillan, 2005

Bramly, Serge, *Leonardo: The Artist and the Man*, London: Michael Joseph, 1992

Brook, Stephen, ed., *The Oxford Book of Dreams*, Oxford: Oxford University Press, 1983

Browne, Janet:
—— *Charles Darwin: Voyaging*, Vol. 1, London: Pimlico, 2003
—— *Charles Darwin: The Power of Place*, Vol. 2, London: Pimlico, 2003

Campbell, James W. P., *Building St Paul's*, London: Thames & Hudson, 2007

Carr, Edward, 'The last days of the polymath', *Intelligent Life*, autumn 2009: 109–14

Carter, Tim, *Le Nozze di Figaro*, Cambridge: Cambridge University Press, 1987

Cartier-Bresson, Henri:
—— *The Photographs of Henri Cartier-Bresson*, New York: Museum of Modern Art, 1947
—— *The Decisive Moment*, New York: Simon and Schuster, 1952
—— *Photoportraits*, London: Thames & Hudson, 1985
—— *Henri Cartier-Bresson in India*, London: Thames & Hudson, 1987
—— *Line by Line: The Drawings of Henri Cartier-Bresson*, London: Thames & Hudson, 1989
—— *Mexican Notebooks*, London: Thames & Hudson, 1995
—— *Tête à Tête: Portraits*, London: Thames & Hudson, 1998
—— *The Mind's Eye: Writings on Photography and Photographers*, New York: Aperture, 1999
—— *The Man, the Image and the World: A Retrospective*, London: Thames & Hudson, 2003
—— *Les Choix d'Henri Cartier-Bresson*, Paris: Fondation Cartier-Bresson, 2003
—— *Scrapbook: Photographs 1932–1946*, London: Thames & Hudson, 2006
—— *Henri Cartier-Bresson*, Paris: Fondation Cartier-Bresson/mk2, 2006 (DVD including all films made by Cartier-Bresson and some films about him, with booklet)
Chadwick, John, *The Decipherment of Linear B*, rev. edn, Cambridge: Cambridge University Press, 1960
Champollion, Jean-François:
—— *Lettre à M. Dacier, relative à l'alphabet des hiéroglyphes phonétiques*, Paris: Firmin-Didot, 1822
—— *Précis du système hiéroglyphique des anciens Égyptiens*, Paris: Treuttel & Würtz, 1824
—— *Précis du système hiéroglyphique des anciens Égyptiens*, 2nd edn, Paris: Imprimerie royale, 1828
—— *Egyptian Diaries: How One Man Solved the Mysteries of the Nile*, (Martin Rynja, trans.), London: Gibson Square Books, 2001
Chéroux, Clément, *Henri Cartier-Bresson*, London: Thames & Hudson, 2008
Clark, Kenneth, *Leonardo da Vinci*, rev. edn, London: Penguin, 1989
Colburn, Zerah, *A Memoir of Zerah Colburn*, Springfield (MA): G. and C. Merriam, 1833
Cole, Emily, ed., *Lived in London: Blue Plaques and the Stories Behind Them*, London: Yale University Press, 2009
Coleridge, Samuel Taylor, *The Major Works*, (H. J. Jackson, ed.), Oxford: Oxford University Press, 2000
Colvin, Geoff, *Talent is Overrated*, London: Nicholas Brearley, 2008
Cox, Catharine M., *The Early Mental Traits of Three Hundred Geniuses*, (Vol. 2 of L. M. Terman, ed., *Genetic Studies of Genius*), Stanford (CA): Stanford University Press, 1926
Coyle, Daniel, *The Talent Code*, London: Random House, 2009
Csikszentmihalyi, Mihaly, *Creativity: Flow and the Psychology of Discovery and Invention*, New York: HarperCollins, 1996
Curie, Eve, *Madame Curie: A Biography*, New York: Da Capo Press, 2001 (first pubd 1937)
Curie, Marie [Sklodowska]:
—— 'Rays emitted by compounds of uranium and of thorium', *Comptes Rendus*, 126 (1898): 1101–3
—— 'Radium and radioactivity', *Century Magazine*, Jan. 1904: 461–6
—— *Pierre Curie. With Autobiographical Notes*, New York: Macmillan, 1923
Curie, Pierre, 'Radioactive substances, especially radium' (Nobel lecture, 6 June 1905): 73–8 at http://nobelprize.org/nobel_prizes/physics/laureates/1903/pierre-curie-lecture.html

——and Marie Sklodowska Curie, 'On a new radioactive substance contained in pitchblende', *Comptes Rendus*, 127 (1898): 175–8

——Mme P. Curie and G. Bémont, 'On a new, strongly radioactive substance contained in pitchblende', *Comptes Rendus*, 127 (1898): 1215–17

Cytowic, Richard E., *The Man Who Tasted Shapes*, Cambridge (MA): MIT Press, 2003

Da Ponte, Lorenzo, *Memoirs*, (Arthur Livingston, ed.; Elisabeth Abbott, trans.,), New York: J. B. Lippincott, 1929

Darwin, Charles:

——*The Voyage of the Beagle*, (Janet Browne and Michael Neve, eds), London: Penguin, 1989 (first pubd 1839)

——*The Origin of Species*, (J. W. Burrow, ed), London: Penguin, 1968 (first pubd 1859)

——*The Autobiography of Charles Darwin and Selected Letters*, (Francis Darwin, ed.), New York: Dover, 1958 (first pubd 1892)

——*The Autobiography of Charles Darwin, 1809–1882: with Original Omissions Restored*, (Nora Barlow, ed.,) London: Collins, 1958

Desmond, Adrian and James Moore, *Darwin*, London: Michael Joseph, 1991

Deutsch, Otto Erich, *Mozart: A Documentary Biography*, (Eric Blom, Peter Branscombe, and Jeremy Noble, trans), London: A & C Black, 1965

Downes, Kerry:

——*Sir Christopher Wren*, London: Whitechapel Art Gallery, 1982

——*Sir Christopher Wren: The Design of St Paul's Cathedral*, London: Trefoil Publications, 1988

Edison, Thomas Alva, *The Diary and Sundry Observations of Thomas Alva Edison*, (D. D. Runes, ed.), New York: Greenwood Press, 1968

Einstein, Albert:

——*Relativity: The Special and the General Theory*, London: Routledge, 2001 (first pubd 1917)

——'Autobiographical Notes', in Paul Arthur Schilpp, ed., *Albert Einstein: Philosopher-Scientist*, Evanston (IL): The Library of living Philosophers, 1949

——*Ideas and Opinions*, (Carl Seelig, ed.), New York: Three Rivers Press, 1982

——*The Collected Papers of Albert Einstein*, Vols 1–12, (various editors), Princeton (NJ): Princeton University Press, 1987

——*The New Quotable Einstein*, (Alice Calaprice, ed.), Princeton (NJ): Princeton University Press: 2005

——*The Persistent Illusion of Transience*, (Albert Einstein Archives, Ze'ev Rosenkranz, and Barbara Wolff, eds), Jerusalem: The Hebrew University Magnes Press, 2007

——and Leopold Infeld, *The Evolution of Physics: The Growth of Ideas from the Early Concepts to Relativity and Quanta*, Cambridge: Cambridge University Press, 1938

——and Mileva Marić, *Albert Einstein/Mileva Marić: The Love Letters*, (Jürgen Renn and Robert Schulmann, eds), Princeton (NJ): Princeton University Press, 1992

Eisen, Cliff and Simon P. Keefe, eds, *The Cambridge Mozart Encyclopedia*, Cambridge: Cambridge University Press, 2006

El Daly, Okasha, *Egyptology: The Missing Millennium: Ancient Egypt in Medieval Arabic Writings*, London: UCL Press, 2005

Eldredge, Niles, *Darwin: Discovering the Tree of Life*, New York: W. W. Norton, 2005

Evans, Peter and Geoff Deehan, *The Keys to Creativity*, London: Grafton, 1990

Eysenck, H. J., *Genius: The Natural History of Creativity*, Cambridge: Cambridge University Press, 1995

Faure, Alain, *Champollion: le savant déchiffré*, Paris: Fayard, 2004

Fields, R. Douglas, 'White matter matters', *Scientific American*, March 2008: 42–9

Findlen, Paula, ed., *Athanasius Kircher: The Last Man Who Knew Everything*, London: Routledge, 2004

Fitzgerald, Michael and Ioan James, *The Mind of the Mathematician*, Baltimore (MD): John Hopkins University Press, 2007

Flynn, James R., *What is Intelligence?: Beyond the Flynn Effect*, Cambridge: Cambridge University Press, 2007

Fölsing, Albrecht, *Albert Einstein: A Biography*, London: Viking, 1997

Frith, Uta, *Autism: Explaining the Enigma*, 2nd edn, Oxford: Blackwell, 2003

Galassi, Peter, *Henri Cartier-Bresson: The Early Work*, New York: Museum of Modern Art, 1987

Galenson, David W., *Old Masters and Young Geniuses: The Two Life Cycles of Artistic Creativity*, Princeton (NJ): Princeton University Press, 2006

Galison, Peter, *Einstein's Clocks, Poincaré's Maps: Empires of Time*, London: Hodder and Stoughton, 2003

Galton, Francis, *Hereditary Genius: An Inquiry into Its Laws and Consequences*, Amherst (NY): Prometheus, 2006 (first pubd 1869)

Gardner, Howard, *Creating Minds: An Anatomy of Creativity Seen Through the Lives of Freud, Einstein, Picasso, Stravinsky, Eliot, Graham, and Gandhi*, New York: Basic Books, 1993

George, Andrew, *The Epic of Gilgamesh*, (Andrew George, trans.), London: Allen Lane, 1999

Giulini, Domenico, *Special Relativity: A First Encounter*, Oxford: Oxford University Press, 2005

Gleick, James:
—— *Genius: Richard Feynman and Modern Physics*, London: Little, Brown, 1992
—— *Isaac Newton*, London: Fourth Estate, 2003

Glover, Jane, *Mozart's Women: His Family, His Friends, His Music*, London: Macmillan, 2005

Goertzel, Victor and Mildred Goertzel, *Cradles of Eminence*, London: Constable, 1962

Goldsmith, Barbara, *Obsessive Genius: The Inner World of Marie Curie*, London: Phoenix, 2005

Gombrich, E. H., *The Story of Art*, 15th edn, London: Phaidon, 1989

Gould, Stephen Jay, *The Mismeasure of Man*, rev. edn, New York: Norton, 1996

Gregory, Richard L., ed., *The Oxford Companion to the Mind*, Oxford: Oxford University Press, 1987

Gruber, Howard E., *Darwin on Man: A Psychological Study of Scientific Creativity*, London: Wildwood House, 1974

Hager, Thomas, *Force of Nature: The Life of Linus Pauling*, New York: Simon & Schuster, 1995

Halberstadt, Ilona, ed., *Pix 2*, London: British Film Institute, 1997: 5–72 (on Henri Cartier-Bresson)

Happé, Francesca and Pedro Vital, 'What aspects of autism predispose to talent?',
    Philosophical Transactions of the Royal Society B, 364 (2009): 1369–75
Hart, Vaughan, *St Paul's Cathedral*, London: Phaidon, 1995
Hermelin, Beate, *Bright Splinters of the Mind: A Personal Story of Research with Autistic Savants*, London: Jessica Kingsley, 2001
Highfield, Roger and Paul Carter, *The Private Lives of Albert Einstein*, London: Faber and Faber, 1993
Hoddeson, Lillian and Vicki Daitch, *True Genius: The Life and Science of John Bardeen*, Washington DC: Joseph Henry Press, 2002
Hoffmann, Banesh, *Albert Einstein: Creator and Rebel*, New York: Viking, 1972
Hofstadter, Dan, 'Stealing a march on the world' (profile of Henri Cartier-Bresson), *New Yorker*, 23 Oct. 1989: 59–93 (pt I), and 30 Oct. 1989: 49–73 (pt II)
Holden, Amanda, ed., *The New Penguin Opera Guide*, London: Penguin, 2001
Holden, Anthony, *The Man Who Wrote Mozart: The Extraordinary Life of Lorenzo da Ponte*, London: Weidenfeld & Nicolson, 2006
Hollingsworth, J. Rogers, Karl H. Müller, and Ellen Jane Hollingsworth, 'The end of the science superpowers', *Nature*, 454 (2008): 412–13
Holmes, Frederic Lawrence, *Investigative Pathways: Patterns and Stages in the Careers of Experimental Scientists*, New Haven (CT): Yale University Press, 2004
Holmes, Richard, *Coleridge*, Oxford: Oxford University Press, 1982
Holton, Gerald, *Thematic Origins of Scientific Thought: Kepler to Einstein*, 2nd edn, Cambridge: Harvard University Press, 1988
Horney, Karen, *Neurotic Personality of Our Times*, New York: Norton, 1937
Housman, A. E., *The Name and Nature of Poetry*, Cambridge: Cambridge University Press, 1933
Howard, Jonathan, *Darwin*, Oxford: Oxford University Press, 1982
Howe, M. J. A., J. W. Davidson, and J. A. Sloboda, 'Innate talents: reality or myth?', *Behavioral and Brain Sciences*, 21 (1998): 399–442
Hughes, James, *Altered States: Creativity under the Influence*, New York: Watson-Guptill Publications, 1999
Illingworth, R. S. and C. M. Illingworth, *Lessons from Childhood: Some Aspects of Early Life of Unusual Men and Women*, Edinburgh: Livingstone, 1969
Isaacson, Walter, *Einstein: His Life and Universe*, New York: Simon and Schuster, 2007
Jackson, Lesley, *From Atoms to Patterns: Crystal Structure Designs from the 1951 Festival of Britain*, Shepton Beauchamp (UK): Richard Dennis Publications, 2008
Jamison, Kay Redfield, *Touched with Fire: Manic-Depressive Illness and the Artistic Temperament*, New York: Free Press, 1994
Jardine, Lisa, *On a Grander Scale: The Outstanding Life and Tumultuous Times of Sir Christopher Wren*, New York: Perennial, 2004
Kaku, Michio, *Einstein's Cosmos: How Albert Einstein's Vision Transformed Our Understanding of Space and Time*, London: Weidenfeld & Nicolson, 2004
Kandel, Eric R., *In Search of Memory: The Emergence of a New Science of Mind*, New York: Norton, 2006

Keene, Derek, Arthur Burns and Andrew Saint, eds, *St Paul's: The Cathedral Church of London, 604–2004*, London: Yale University Press, 2004

Kemp, Martin:

—— *Leonardo da Vinci: Experience, Experiment and Design*, London: V&A Publications, 2006

—— *Leonardo da Vinci: The Marvellous Works of Nature and Man*, Oxford: Oxford University Press, 2006

Klingberg, Torkel, *The Overflowing Brain: Information Overload and the Limits of Working Memory*, New York: Oxford University Press, 2009

Koestler, Arthur, *The Act of Creation*, London: Hutchinson, 1964

Landon, H. C. Robbins, *Mozart: The Golden Years*, London: Thames & Hudson, 2006

Lederman, Leon and Dick Teresi, *The God Particle: If the Universe is the Answer, What is the Question?*, New York: Houghton Mifflin, 1993

Lee, Hermione, *Virginia Woolf*, London: Chatto & Windus, 1996

Lehmann, Andreas C., John A. Sloboda and Robert H. Woody, *Psychology for Musicians: Understanding and Acquiring the Skills*, Oxford: Oxford University Press, 2007

Lehrer, Jonah, *Proust Was a Neuroscientist*, New York: Houghton Mifflin, 2007

Leonardo da Vinci, *Notebooks* (Selected by Irma A. Richter; Thereza Wells, ed.), Oxford: Oxford University Press, 2008

Levitin, Daniel J., *This is Your Brain on Music: The Science of a Human Obsession*, New York: Dutton, 2006

Lyell, Charles, *Principles of Geology*, (James A. Secord, ed.), London: Penguin, 1997 (first pubd 1830–33)

McManus, Chris, *Right Hand, Left Hand: The Origins of Asymmetry in Brains, Bodies, Atoms and Cultures*, London: Weidenfeld & Nicolson, 2002

Martindale, Colin, *The Clockwork Muse: The Predictability of Artistic Change*, New York: Basic Books, 1990

Medawar, Peter, *Pluto's Republic*, Oxford: Oxford University Press, 1982

Montier, Jean-Pierre, *Henri Cartier-Bresson and the Artless Art*, London: Thames & Hudson, 1996

Moszkowski, Alexander, *Conversations with Einstein*, London: Sidgwick and Jackson, 1972 (first pubd 1921)

Mould, R. F., 'The discovery of radium in 1898 by Maria Sklodowska-Curie (1867–1934) and Pierre Curie (1859–1906) with commentary on their life and times', *British Journal of Radiology*, 71 (1998): 1229–54

Mozart, Wolfgang Amadeus:

—— *The Marriage of Figaro*, London: John Calder, in association with English National Opera and the Royal Opera, 1983

—— *Mozart's Letters, Mozart's Life: Selected Letters*, (Robert Spaethling, trans.), London: Faber and Faber, 2000

—— *A Life in Letters* (Cliff Eisen, ed.; Stewart Spencer, trans.), London: Penguin, 2006

Murdoch, Stephen, *IQ: The Brilliant Idea That Failed*, London: Duckworth, 2007

Nasar, Sylvia, *A Beautiful Mind: A Biography of John Forbes Nash, Jr.*, London: Faber and Faber, 1998

Nettle, Daniel:
—— *Strong Imagination: Madness, Creativity and Human Nature*, Oxford: Oxford University Press, 2001
—— *Personality: What Makes You the Way You Are*, Oxford: Oxford University Press, 2007
Newton, Isaac:
—— *Sir Isaac Newton's Mathematical Principles of Natural Philosophy and His System of the World*, (Andrew Motte, trans. [1729], revised by Florian Cajori), Berkeley: University of California Press, 1947
—— *The Principia: Mathematical Principles of Natural Philosophy*, (I. Bernard Cohen and Anne Whitman, trans), Berkeley (CA): University of California Press, 1999
Ochse, R., *Before the Gates of Excellence: The Determinants of Creative Genius*, Cambridge: Cambridge University Press, 1990
Olby, Robert, *Francis Crick: Hunter of Life's Secrets*, Cold Spring Harbor: Cold Spring Harbor Laboratory Press, 2009
Pais, Abraham, *'Subtle is the Lord': The Science and Life of Albert Einstein*, New York: Oxford University Press, 1983
Parkinson, Richard:
—— *Cracking Codes: The Rosetta Stone and Decipherment*, London: British Museum Press, 1999
—— *The Rosetta Stone*, London: British Museum Press, 2005
Peacock, George, *Life of Thomas Young, M.D., F.R.S.*, London: John Murray, 1855 (facsimile reprint edn, Bristol: Thoemmes Press, 2003)
Pearson, Karl, *The Life, Letters and Labours of Francis Galton*, Vol. 1, Cambridge: Cambridge University Press, 1914
Perkins, David, *The Eureka Effect: The Art and Logic of Breakthrough Thinking*, New York: Norton, 2000
Pfenninger, Karl H. and Valerie R. Shubik, eds, *The Origins of Creativity*, New York: Oxford University Press, 2001
Planck, Max, *Scientific Autobiography, and Other Papers*, London: Williams and Norgate, 1950
Pope, Maurice, *The Story of Decipherment: From Egyptian Hieroglyphs to Maya Script*, rev. edn, London: Thames & Hudson, 1999
Post, Felix, 'Creativity and psychopathology: a study of 291 world-famous men', *British Journal of Psychiatry*, 165 (1994): 22–34
Quinn, Susan, *Marie Curie: A Life*, London: Heinemann, 1995
Ramachandran, V. S., *A Brief Tour of Human Consciousness*, New York: Pi Press, 2004
Ray, John, *The Rosetta Stone and the Rebirth of Ancient Egypt*, London: Profile, 2007
Ray, Satyajit:
—— *Our Films Their Films*, New Delhi: Orient Longman, 1976
—— 'My life, my work', *Telegraph*, Calcutta, 27 Sept.–1 Oct. 1982 (republished in Tarapada Banerjee, *Satyajit Ray: A Portrait in Black and White*, New Delhi: Penguin, 1993: 15–28)
—— *The Apu Trilogy*, (Shampa Banerjee, ed.), Calcutta: Seagull Books, 1985 (translation of screenplay)
—— *My Years with Apu*, London: Faber and Faber, 1997
Reichwald, Siegwart, ed., *Mendelssohn in Performance*, Bloomington: Indiana University Press, 2008

Reitlinger, Gerald, *The Economics of Taste*, Vols 1–3, London: Barrie and Rockliff, Marrie and Jenkins, 1961–70

Renoir, Jean, *Letters*, (David Thompson and Lorraine LoBianco, eds), London: Faber and Faber, 1994

Richards, Robert J., *The Tragic Sense of Life: Ernst Haeckel and the Struggle over Evolutionary Thought*, Chicago (IL): University of Chicago Press, 2008

Rigden, John S., *Einstein 1905: The Standard of Greatness*, Cambridge (MA): Harvard University Press, 2005

Robinson, Andrew:

—— *The Man Who Deciphered Linear B: The Story of Michael Ventris*, London: Thames & Hudson, 2002

—— *Satyajit Ray: The Inner Eye*, 2nd edn, London: I. B. Tauris, 2004

—— *Satyajit Ray: A Vision of Cinema*, London: I. B. Tauris, 2005 (with photographs by Nemai Ghosh)

—— *The Last Who Knew Everything: Thomas Young*, Oxford: Oneworld, 2006

—— *Einstein: A Hundred Years of Relativity*, rev. edn, Bath (UK): Palazzo, 2010

—— *The Apu Trilogy: Satyajit Ray and the Making of an Epic*, London: I. B. Tauris, 2010

Rocke, Alan J., 'Hypothesis and experiment in the early development of Kekulé's benzene theory', *Annals of Science*, 42 (1985): 355–81

Romer, Alfred, ed., *The Discovery of Radioactivity and Transmutation*, New York: Dover, 1964

Ruelle, David, *The Mathematician's Brain: A Personal Tour through the Essentials of Mathematics and some of the Great Minds behind them*, Princeton (NJ): Princeton University Press, 2007

Sacks, Oliver, *An Anthropologist on Mars: Seven Paradoxical Tales*, London: Picador, 1995

Sawyer, Keith, *Group Genius: The Creative Power of Collaboration*, New York: Basic Books, 2007

Sayen, Jamie, *Einstein in America: The Scientist's Conscience in the Age of Hitler and Hiroshima*, New York: Crown, 1985

Seabrook, John, *Flash of Genius: And Other True Stories of Invention*, New York: St Martin's Press, 2008

Seelig, Carl, ed., *Helle Zeit, Dunkle Zeit: In Memoriam Albert Einstein*, Zurich: Europa Verlag, 1956

Seton, Marie, *Satyajit Ray: Portrait of a Director*, 2nd edn, London: Dennis Dobson, 1978

Shurkin, Joel:

—— *Terman's Kids: The Groundbreaking Study of How the Gifted Grow Up*, New York: Little, Brown, 1992

—— *Broken Genius: The Rise and Fall of William Shockley, Creator of the Electronic Age*, London: Macmillan, 2006

Simonton, Dean Keith:

—— *Genius, Creativity and Leadership: Historiometric Inquiries*, Cambridge (MA): Harvard University Press, 1984

—— *Creativity in Science: Chance, Logic, Genius, and Zeitgeist*, Cambridge: Cambridge University Press, 2004

Smith, C. U. M. and Robert Arnott, eds, *The Genius of Erasmus Darwin*, Aldershot: Ashgate, 2005

Solé, Robert and Dominique Valbelle, *The Rosetta Stone: The Story of the Decoding of Hieroglyphics*, London: Profile, 2001

Solomon, Maynard, *Mozart: A Life*, New York: HarperCollins, 1995

Soo, Lydia M., *Wren's 'Tracts' on Architecture and Other Writings*, Cambridge: Cambridge University Press, 1998

Stephen, Sir James, *Letters with Biographical Notes*, (Caroline Emelia Stephen, ed.), [London: privately circulated], 1906

Steptoe, Andrew, *The Mozart-Da Ponte Operas: The Cultural and Musical Background to Le Nozze di Figaro, Don Giovanni, and Così Fan Tutte*, Oxford: Clarendon Press, 1988

—— ed., *Genius and the Mind: Studies of Creativity and Temperament*, Oxford: Oxford University Press, 1998

Sternberg, Robert J. and Janet E. Davidson, eds, *The Nature of Insight*, Cambridge (MA), MIT Press, 1995

Stott, Rebecca, *Darwin and the Barnacle: The Story of One Tiny Creature and History's Most Spectacular Scientific Breakthrough*, London: Faber and Faber, 2004

Summerson, John, *Sir Christopher Wren*, London: Collins, 1953

Tagore, Rabindranath, *Selected Letters of Rabindranath Tagore*, (Krishna Dutta and Andrew Robinson, eds), Cambridge: Cambridge University Press, 1997

Tallis, Raymond, *The Kingdom of Infinite Space: A Fantastical Journey around Your Head*, London: Atlantic, 2008

Tammet, Daniel, *Born on a Blue Day: A Memoir of Asperger's and an Extraordinary Mind*, London: Hodder & Stoughton, 2006

Thruelsen, Richard and John Kobler, eds, *Adventures of the Mind*, London: Victor Gollancz, 1960

Tinniswood, Adrian, *His Invention So Fertile: A Life of Christopher Wren*, London: Pimlico, 2002

Treffert, Darold A., *Extraordinary People: Understanding Savant Syndrome*, New York: Bantam, 1989

Tusa, John, *On Creativity: Interviews Exploring the Process*, London: Methuen, 2003

Ulam, Stanislaw, *Adventures of a Mathematician*, New York: Scribner's, 1983

Usick, Patricia, *Adventures in Egypt and Nubia: The Travels of William John Bankes (1786–1855)*, London: British Museum Press, 2002

Van Campen, Cretien, *The Hidden Sense: Synaesthesia in Art and Science*, Cambridge (MA): MIT Press, 2008

Vasari, Giorgio, *The Lives of the Artists*, (Julia Conaway Bondanella and Peter Bondanella, eds), Oxford: Oxford University Press, 1991 (first pubd 1568)

Vernon, P. E., ed., *Creativity: Selected Readings*, London: Penguin, 1970

Watson, James D., *The Double Helix: A Personal Account of the Discovery of the Structure of DNA*, London: Weidenfeld & Nicolson, 1997

Weisberg, Robert W., *Creativity: Understanding Innovation in Problem Solving, Science, Invention, and the Arts*, Hoboken (NJ): John Wiley, 2006

Wellcome Trust, ed., *Sleeping and Dreaming*, London: Black Dog Publishing, 2007

Whinney, Margaret, *Wren*, London: Thames & Hudson, 1971

Whitrow, G. J., ed., *Einstein: The Man and His Achievement*, New York: Dover, 1967

Whyte, Lancelot Law, *The Unconscious before Freud*, London: Tavistock Publications, 1962

Winner, Ellen, *Gifted Children: Myths and Realities*, New York: Basic Books, 1996

Woolf, Leonard, *Downhill All the Way: An Autobiography of the Years 1919–1939*, London: Hogarth Press, 1967

Woolf, Virginia:

——*Jacob's Room*, (Kate Flint, ed.), Oxford: Oxford University Press, 1992 (first pubd 1922)

——*Mrs Dalloway*, (Claire Tomalin, ed.), Oxford: Oxford University Press, 1992 (first pubd 1925)

——*The Letters of Virginia Woolf*, Vols 1–6, (Nigel Nicolson and Joanne Trautmann, eds), London: Hogarth Press, 1975–80

——*The Diary of Virginia Woolf*, Vols 1–5, (Anne Olivier Bell and Andrew McNeillie, eds), London: Hogarth Press, 1977–84

——*The Essays of Virginia Woolf*, Vol. 3, (Andrew McNeillie, ed.), London: Hogarth Press, 1988

——*Moments of Being: Autobiographical Writings*, (Jeanne Schulkind, ed., rev. by Hermione Lee), London: Pimlico, 2002

Wren, Christopher, *Life and Works of Sir Christopher Wren. From the Parentalia or Memoirs by His Son*, (E. J. Enthoven, ed.,), London: Edward Arnold, 1903 (extracted from *Parentalia, or Memoirs of the Family of the Wrens*, pubd 1750)

Young, Thomas, *Miscellaneous Works*, Vol. 3, (John Leitch, ed.), London: John Murray, 1855 (facsimile reprint edn, Bristol: Thoemmes Press, 2003)

INDEX